Imperial Germany
1867–1918

Imperial Germany
1867–1918

Politics, Culture, and Society in an Authoritarian State

Wolfgang J Mommsen

Professor of History, Heinrich Heine University,
Düsseldorf, Germany

Translated by Richard Deveson

ARNOLD

A member of the Hodder Headline Group
LONDON • NEW YORK • SYDNEY • AUCKLAND

First published in Great Britain 1995 by
Arnold, a member of the Hodder Headline Group
338 Euston Road, London NW1 3BH

Fourth impression 1998

Co-published in the United States of America by
Oxford University Press Inc.,
198 Madison Avenue, New York NY 10016

Published in German as *Der autoritäre Nationalstaat*

British Library Cataloguing in Publication Data
A catalogue record for this book is available from the British Library

Library of Congress Cataloging-in-Publication Data
Mommsen, Wolfgang J., 1930–
[Autoritäre Nationalstaat. English]
Imperial Germany 1867–1918 : politics, culture, and society in
an authoritarian state / Wolfgang J. Mommsen : translated by
Richard Deveson.
    p.   cm.
Includes bibliographical references and index.
ISBN 0–340–59360–1 (pbk). —ISBN 0–340–64534–2
    1. Germany—Politics and government—1866–1871
2. Germany—Politics and government—1871–1918. 3. Political
culture Germany. 4. Germany Cultural policy. I. Title
DD220. M5613   1995
943.08—dc20   95–31744
                                                           CIP

ISBN 0 340 59360 1

Typeset in 10/12 Sabon by Anneset, Weston-super-Mare, Somerset
Printed and bound in Great Britain by J W Arrowsmith Ltd, Bristol

Contents

Preface

The German Empire remains, even today, a fixed point in the German people's sense of its national identity. Despite the fact that the Empire owed its existence to a 'revolution from above', rather than to a voluntary act on the part of the people, in the course of time its citizens came to perceive it as the embodiment of the German nation state. Although the German educated class, in particular, had initially continued to feel closely attached to the idea of the German nation as a cultural entity, embracing Germans beyond the borders of the Empire, the power of the Prusso-German authoritarian state – with its outward splendour and military pageantry, and with the prestige that it began to enjoy within the system of European states – gradually came to outweigh the traditions of cultural identity and emancipation that had characterized the German people's conception of nationhood during the first half of the nineteenth century.

At no stage of its existence did the German Empire cast aside the traces of its authoritarian origins in the masterful power politics of Bismarck. It is true that the founding of the Empire, and the shaping of the Imperial constitution in particular, were the result of a compromise between the forces of conservatism represented by Bismarck – notably in Prussia, which continued to be a bastion of authoritarianism under the new dispensation – and the liberal tradition. But the hopes of the liberal middle class that the Empire could gradually be brought to evolve along progressive lines remained unfulfilled. Indeed, some of the authoritarian features of the German nation state even outlasted the fall of the Hohenzollern dynasty at the end of the First World War. The survival of these features meant that the new democratic order that emerged after the revolution of 1918-19 was not fully capable of dealing with the adverse political and economic conditions that confronted it. To this extent, the great crises of Germany's more recent past cannot be understood unless we go back to the history of the German Reich.

The Imperial period also saw the formation of all of the principal institutional structures that have continued to govern life in Germany until the present day. A legal system based on liberal principles was established; an institutional and legal framework permitting the emergence of a market-orientated form of industrial capitalism was created; a highly effective educational system was built up. The foundations of Germany's present-day cultural life were also laid during the Imperial era: the origins of modernism and the avant-garde in the arts, with their extreme emphasis on individualism, go back to the turn of the century. Nevertheless, the German Empire never really broke free from the shackles of its origins. Compared with the other nations of Europe, it remained a state distorted by authoritarianism. The grandiose 'new German' nationalist sentiment that gradually came to the fore from the early 1890s onwards, increasingly becoming the trademark of the middle classes, was in many ways a substitute for genuine self-government. Thanks in part to the specific structure of the Imperial constitution, and in part to political and social circumstances, Germans were prevented from practising truly democratic politics until the Empire had come to an end.

The tension between authoritarian government and the parliamentary exercise of free opinion made itself felt in all areas of life under the German Empire: in domestic politics, in party politics, in the economy, in the arts, literature and scholarship, and in foreign policy. After 1897, under pressure from public opinion, the Reich adopted an aggressive 'Weltpolitik', or 'world policy', on the international stage, not so much in pursuit of specific imperialist objectives as in the hope that successes in foreign policy would ensure stability at home. The keenest advocates of such a 'Weltpolitik' were the rising middle classes, who yearned to belong to a large and powerful state and thus have a share, if only at one remove, in the great processes of political decision-making that the semi-democratic nature of the con-stitutional system debarred them from influencing directly. However, as constitutional reform failed to materialize, so the gulf between the political system and society grew ever wider, until ultimately the very governability of the Empire came into question. Bismarck's successors became steadily less able to achieve a balance between the interests and goals of the governing elites and those of the general public. In these circumstances, large sections of the middle classes fell prey to radical nationalistic aspirations that became ever more divorced from political realities. The government, however, found itself unable to assert control, since it was afraid that by trying to do so it would actually jeopardize its own authority and undermine the existing semi-authoritarian state order. It was under such conditions that the German Empire entered the First World War in 1914, a war that ended with the collapse of the Hohenzollern monarchy and the revolution of 1918-20.

The essays collected in the present volume examine this cluster of questions from a variety of points of view. They are the harvest of more than twenty years of intensive study of the history of the German Empire.

Although written at different times and for varying purposes, they nevertheless have an underlying unity. The first three essays attempt to give a precise characterization of the constitution of the Empire and of the relationship, still a matter for dispute today, between the Prussian conception of the state and the German idea of empire. The paper 'Society and state in Europe in the age of liberalism, 1870-1890' analyses the overall European context within which the so-called 'liberal' era after 1867 needs to be viewed. The essay on 'The causes and objectives of German imperialism before 1914' provides a broad outline of the Empire's imperialist endeavours. The next two essays deal with two central aspects of Imperial history: the economic and social structures of the Reich, and the question of the relationship between culture and politics, which has largely been neglected by earlier scholars. The following three essays, on Wilhelmine Germany, seek first and foremost to identify the domestic political reasons that led the Empire step by step down the slippery slope of an unbalanced foreign policy to the desperate gamble of the First World War. Two further essays deal with political, ideological and socio-economic developments during the First World War and their long-term effects on Germany's political culture. The final study offers an interpretation of the German revolution of 1918-20 that attempts to go beyond the conventional accounts, which all mirror the standpoints of the political parties of the time. The revolution of November and December 1918 was directed solely against the surviving remnants of the Empire's power elites, notably the military, but did not seriously call the prevailing social system into question; from the beginning of 1919, however, it turned into a broad groundswell of social protest that caught all sections of the political labour movement by surprise by failing to accord with the parties' doctrinal preconceptions.

Most of the essays gathered here have already been published elsewhere. They have been further checked and revised, but no attempt has been made to incorporate references to literature that has appeared since their original publication. They would seem, however, to have withstood time's ravages reasonably well, and they certainly address questions that remain at the forefront of contemporary research.

Wolfgang J. Mommsen
Düsseldorf, August 1990

Acknowledgements

The chapters in this book first appeared in the following forms.

1 'Das deutsche Kaiserreich als System umgangener Entscheidungen', in Helmut Berding et al (eds.), Vom Staat des Ancien Régime zum modernen Parteienstaat. Festschrift für Theodor Schieder (Munich, 1978), pp. 239-65.

2 'Die Verfassung des Deutschen Reiches von 1871 als dilatorischer Herrschaftskompromiß', in *Innenpolitische Probleme des Bismarck-Reiches*, edited by Otto Pflanze in collaboration with Elisabeth Müller-Luckner (Munich/Vienna, 1983), pp. 195-216.

3 'Preußisches Staatsbewußtsein und deutsche Reichsidee: Preußen und das Deutsche Reich in der jüngeren deutschen Geschichte', in *Geschichte in Wissenschaft und Unterricht* 35 (1984), pp. 685-705.

4 'Gesellschaft und Staat im liberalen Zeitalter. Europa 1870-1890' (German version first published in *Der autoritäre Nationalstaat*). An Italian version has been published under the title 'Società e politica nell'età liberale, Europa 1870-1890', in *La transformatione politica nell'Europa liberale 1870-1890* (Bologna, 1986).

5 'Triebkräfte und Zielsetzungen des deutschen Imperialismus vor 1914', revised version of an essay with the same title in Klaus Bohnen and Conny Bauer (eds.), *Text und Kontext*, Sonderreihe, vol. 11, *Kultur und Gesellschaft in Deutschland von der Reformation bis zur Gegenwart* (Copenhagen/Munich, 1981), pp. 98-129 and of the English translation, 'A Functionalist Interpretation of German Imperialism before 1914', in S. Bertelli (ed.), *Per Federigo Chabod (1801-1960)*, vol. 2, *Equilibrio Europea ed espansione coloniale (1870-1914)* (Milan, 1981).

6 'Wirtschaft, Gesellschaft und Staat im deutschen Kaiserreich 1870-1918' (German version first published in *Der autoritäre Nationalstaat*).

7 'Kultur und Politik im deutschen Kaiserreich' (German version first published in *Der autoritäre Nationalstaat*).

8 'Die latente Krise des Wilhelminischen Reiches: Staat und Gesellschaft in Deutschland 1890-1914', in *Militärgeschichtliche Mitteilungen* 15 (1974), pp. 7-28.

9 'Innenpolitische Bestimmungsfaktoren der deutschen Außenpolitik vor 1914' (German version, translated by Peter Theiner, first published in *Der autoritäre Nationalstaat*); originally published in English as 'Domestic Factors in German Foreign Policy before 1914', in *Central*

European History VI (1973), pp. 3-43; reprinted in James J. Sheehan (ed.), *Imperial Germany* (New York/London, 1976), pp. 223-268.

10 'Außenpolitik und öffentliche Meinung im Wilhelminischen Deutschland 1897-1914' (German version, translated by Hans-Günther Holl, first published in *Der autoritäre Nationalstaat*); originally published in English as 'Public Opinion and Foreign Policy in Wilhelmine Germany, 1897-1914', in John C. Font (ed.), *Politics, Parties and the Authoritarian State: Imperial Germany, 1871-1918*, Festschrift for Otto Pflanze, vol. 2 (St Paul, Minnesota, 1991).

11 'Der Geist von 1914: Das Programm eines politischen »Sonderwegs« der Deutschen', in Wolfgang J. Mommsen, *Nation und Geschichte. Über die Deutschen und die deutsche Frage* (Munich, 1990), pp. 87-105.

12 'Die sozialen Auswirkungen des Ersten Weltkrieges auf die deutsche Gesellschaft' (German version, translated by Petra Krauß, first published in *Der autoritäre Nationalstaat*); originally published in English as 'The Social Consequences of World War I: The Case of Germany', in Arthur Marwick (ed.), *Total War and Social Change* (Basingstoke, 1988), pp. 25-44.

13 'Die deutsche Revolution 1918-1920: Politische Revolution und soziale Protestbewegung', in *Geschichte und Gesellschaft* 4 (1978), pp. 362-91; an earlier English translation, by Jane Williams, has been published under the title 'The German Revolution 1918-1920: Political Revolution and Social Protest Movement' in R. Bessel and E.J. Feuchtwanger (eds.), *Social Change and Political Development in Weimar Germany* (London, 1981).

Preface to the English edition

I am grateful that this collection of essays on Imperial Germany has now been made available to English readers. For many years the study of German Imperial history has been conducted on an international plane, and the contribution of British and American scholarship to the reinterpretation of Bismarckian and Wilhelmine politics has been substantial, particularly with regard to the role of the middle classes in the Wilhelmine era. One might mention, for example, the work by Geoff Eley and David Blackbourn challenging the new orthodoxy of a 'deutscher Sonderweg', or 'special German path' towards modernity, and the work on the Bismarckian era by Gordon Craig, Otto Pflanze, James H. Sheehan and Peggy Anderson. I hope that the English publication of the present collection of essays, which attempt to present a coherent interpretation of this crucial period of German history, will further stimulate international research.

A number of essays from the original German version of the book have been omitted from this edition, largely for reasons of space. Two of those essays, however, are already available in English versions: 'Bismarck, the Concert of Europe and the Future of West Africa, 1883–1885' in Stig Förster, Wolfgang J. Mommsen and Ronald Robinson (eds), *Bismarck, Europe and Africa: The Berlin Africa Conference 1884–1885 and the Onset of Partition* (Oxford, 1988) and 'The Topos of Inevitable War in Germany in the Decade before 1914' in Volker R. Berghahn and Martin Kitchen (eds), *Germany in the Age of Total War: Essays in Honour of Francis L. Carsten* (London, 1981).

I should like to express my thanks to Richard Deveson for translating these texts, and for helping to eliminate some minor errors. The responsibility for the present edition is, of course, entirely mine.

June 30th, 1995
Wolfgang J Mommsen
The Woodrow Wilson Center
Washington, D.C.

Translator's note

Three of the essays in this volume – 9, 10 and 12 – were originally published in English and then translated into German for the book *Der autoritäre Nationalstaat* on which the present collection is based. For the sake of stylistic consistency, I have prepared fresh translations of these essays on the basis of the German versions (which in any case incorporate a number of amendments to the English originals). Naturally, however, I have carefully consulted the earlier English versions and have followed them at many points. The original English titles of the three essays have been retained.

Essays 5 and 13, originally published in German, have appeared in subsequent English translations but have also been freshly translated here.

I am most grateful yet again to Clare Deveson and Dick Bessel for helping me with a string of queries.

Richard Deveson

1

The German Empire as a system of skirted decisions

Modern studies of Bismarck, irrespective of their differences in political and social outlook, are in broad agreement that the founding of the Reich was a 'revolution from above' which, unlike the rapidly faltering bourgeois revolution of 1848-49, enabled a philosophy of social conservatism to hold sway for half a century. Certainly, there have been differences of nuance among scholars: Bußmann, for example, saw the fundamental thrust of Bismarck's policies as the 'fight against revolution in all its forms';[1] Rein argued that the mobilization of Prussian *raison d'état* was, itself, a revolutionary principle directed against the doctrine of democratic revolution; Rothfels and, in subtler form, Theodor Schieder have emphasized the thwarting of the liberal movement and the neutralization of the explosive potential of the forces of both social and nationalist revolution.[2] This overall approach, however, has continued to prevail in more recent research. It is almost universally agreed that Bismarck's policies were an attempt, in defiance of the trends of the age, to protect the existing social order against the stirrings of democracy, at whatever cost, and to crush all democratic political aspirations at birth.

There can certainly be no dispute that the Bismarckian system was dedicated to the pursuit of social-conservative goals. Hans-Ulrich Wehler is essentially right to assert that the political achievement of Bismarck, the 'white revolutionary', was a 'Flucht nach vorn', a resolute – if enforced – attempt to stabilize the prevailing political and social system by making limited concessions to progressive forces, and thus to preserve the pre-eminence of the traditional elites despite the changes that were taking place in German society. Bismarck's policies, in other words, were a defensive social strategy conducted on behalf of the ruling strata.[3] Studies from the German Democratic Republic have been couched in even more uncompromising terms. Ernst Engelbert and Horst Bartel, for example, describe the establishment of the Reich between 1866 and 1871 as 'greater-Prussian and militarist', and assert that its aim was to secure the supremacy of the ruling class for the foreseeable future, although, as heirs of Karl

Marx, they do not contest the notion that the creation of a 'little German' nation state was also a progressive step in the historical scheme of things.[4]

And yet if we try to ascertain, from all these studies, what were the specific political and social entities that made possible this 'revolution from above', we find, oddly enough, that the parties and social groups concerned are referred to only in highly generalized terms and that it is always the figure of Bismarck himself, and Bismarck's policies – admirable or satanic, as the case may be – that occupy centre stage. The sections of society that actually supported these policies remain in the background and rarely receive any precise definition. This is no accident, for on closer analysis Bismarck's policies cannot be unambiguously associated, at least before 1879, with any of the political and social groups of the period. The result is that historians have generally, if reluctantly, found themselves reverting to talking about the figure of Bismarck himself, even when their intention has been to write social history.

For earlier scholars, whose view of the Empire was primarily, though not exclusively, shaped by the assumption of the 'primacy of foreign policy', this dilemma was not such a significant one. For them, the creation of the Empire was essentially the result of Bismarck's personal diplomacy – as inspired as it was irreducible to any single political element. External factors determined not only the size and borders of the new 'little German' state but, to a great extent, its internal structure as well, particularly as far as constitutional questions were concerned. With Bismarck's achievements in foreign policy a central feature of these older Bismarckian studies, an emphasis on the statesman as an individual was only to be expected. Such studies focused on Bismarck's personal motives and on the strength of imagination that enabled him to reconcile conflicting or competing political forces and appease the anxieties of the other great powers as they watched the emergence of a new state in the centre of Europe. Even liberal and left-wing critics of Bismarck, such as Erich Eyck, felt compelled to recognize Bismarck's achievements as a statesman, particularly since it was on the question of external policy that the liberals had sought to prise him from power during the *Konfliktzeit*. Radical and liberal critics of Bismarck, from Max Weber to Eyck, have persistently, and shame-facedly, been fascinated by the phenomenon of Bismarck's personality while simultaneously detesting his domestic policies.

Later scholars, influenced by the principle of the 'primacy of domestic policy', have tried hard to interpret the emergence of the political system of 1871 in the light of domestic political and economic factors. They have placed particular emphasis on the shortcomings of the process that led to the establishment of the Reich, culminating with the formal enactment of the Imperial constitution in March 1871. Theodor Schieder refers to the 'internal fault lines' of the system set up in 1871 and describes the founding of the Reich as 'unfinished'.[5] Lambi and Böhme speak of a 'second founding of the Empire',[6] beginning with the domestic political about-turn that took place in 1879, and argues that it was not until then that Bismarck's Empire actually achieved stability; his thesis has been extended and popularized by Helmut Böhme.[7]

By the time of Wolfgang Sauer's essay on 'The Problem of the German Nation State',[8] if not earlier, a new approach had also begun to gain ground. On this view, the Bismarckian system was first and foremost the embodiment of a manipulative policy on the part of the ruling elites, designed to keep them in power at any price during a period of accelerating social change brought about by long-term processes of modernization and industrialization. It is noteworthy, however, that even this sort of analysis has been unable to throw off the preoccupation with Bismarck as an individual. Wehler and Stürmer, albeit reluctantly, both portray Bismarck as the evil genius who held Germany's destiny in the palm of his hand.[9] Bismarck, it is claimed, by using manipulative strategies of so-called 'secondary integration', including, in particular, the raising of the spectre of factitious 'enemies within', and by pursuing a policy of 'social imperialism', sought to immunize the prevailing pseudo-constitutional system against any contamination by the forces of progress.[10] The explanatory theoretical model commonly invoked to deal with the wide range of problems that arise here is that of 'Bonapartism', originally propounded by Karl Marx. In the often-quoted words of Hans-Ulrich Wehler (the most recent and certainly the most radical of such scholars), Bismarckian rule was a 'Bonapartist dictatorship: that is, an unstable, traditional framework of authority, threatened by powerful forces of social and political change, which [was protected by] the diversion of concern from the constitution on to the economy, from emancipation at home on to successes abroad, as well as by undisguised repression, tempered with limited concessions, on the domestic front'.

Both on empirical grounds (as a comparison of Bismarck's policies with those of Napoleon III shows) and as an analysis of Bismarck's personal motives, such an interpretation has much to be said for it.[11] It is, incidentally, a view as old as Bismarckian research itself: indeed, it can be shown that Bismarck's contemporaries themselves inclined towards a similar position. Modern scholars who invoke the Bonapartist model merely reverse, however, the polarities of the interpretative frameworks of the late nineteenth century: they do not open up a truly satisfying socio-historical perspective.[12] Even though the objective factors that placed constraints on Bismarck's domestic policies have been much more closely examined than before, in the final analysis Bismarck the individual is still seen as the driving force applying the manipulative strategies. Bismarck is no longer a national hero, but he has become a Bonapartist of genius.

As an explanatory model, this is not adequate. It takes Bismarckian studies into a cul-de-sac in which scholars can do no more than produce increasingly contrived accounts of Bismarck's Bonapartist strategies. Stürmer, for example, has magnified the Chancellor's thoughts about mounting a coup – thoughts that always existed, but were never actually put into practice – into the cornerstone of a thesis placing heavy stress on the socially repressive character of the political system after 1871. Against such views (which, as said, are largely an unintended feature of recent research on Bismarck) it is, I think, appropriate to quote the words of Bismarck himself:[13]

> I, at least, am not so presumptuous as to believe that history can be made by the likes of us. It is my task to observe history's currents and to steer my ship within them. I cannot guide the currents themselves, let alone create them.

More formally put, the point is that to be adequate to the requirements of modern historical analysis, an interpretation of the Bismarckian system should focus principally on general social processes, rather than on the techniques whereby authority was exercised or on the motives that lay behind these techniques. Bismarck's policies – which, after all, were consistently and strikingly capable of adaptation and were ideologically far less rigid than the members of the Chancellor's own conservative class would have liked – should be seen as the resultant of these social processes themselves and not, or not primarily, as a brilliant Bonapartist's answer to a crisis in politics and society.

Recent scholarship, in fact, from a justifiable desire to document the repressive character of government under Bismarck, has gone altogether too far in emphasizing the manipulative strategies of Bismarck and his colleagues, while portraying the role of social groups in the political process, and of the parties and organizations representing them, as more or less entirely reactive in character. In the work of Stürmer, in particular, the anti-parliamentary objectives of Bismarck's overall policies are so overdrawn as to imply the exact opposite of the conclusion intended. The excessive emphasis on the Bonapartist or manipulative aspect of Bismarck's method of exerting power actually ends up making Bismarck a heroic figure on the old model, albeit one with negative rather than positive connotations. The very fact that writers such as Stürmer and Wehler do not intend such a result indicates that this entire vein of analysis has reached the limits of its usefulness. Even if we regard Bismarck's domestic policies, in particular, as unmitigatedly Bonapartist in character, it remains the case that they were practicable only within a specific political and social context. This context was the state of relative paralysis that affected the rival social and political camps which confronted one another within the complicated pluralist division of power that had been partly created, and partly entrenched, by the Imperial constitution of 1871.

Thus it is quite misleading to speak, without further qualification, of the powerlessness of the Reichstag and the political parties within the German Empire, even though the parties were certainly not permitted to exert direct influence on the make-up of the executive. The impressive number of far-reaching changes that the Reichstag made to legislation during Bismarck's years in power, ranging from measures affecting the constitution itself to the social insurance laws, is powerful evidence against one-dimensional interpretations of this sort. Even the label 'negative politics', applied to the Reichstag, is inaccurate inasmuch as it does not recognize that the Chancellor and his colleagues were repeatedly driven to make compromises when trying to enact legislation. If it was Bismarck's express aim to do everything he could to restrain the growing power of the Reichstag and the parties – though in fact he pursued this aim with varying degrees of commitment – then by the beginning of the 1880s he had already failed completely. The argument that there was a 'second founding of the Empire' based upon an alliance of agrarian and heavy industry overlooks the fact that Bismarck's later 'Sammlungspolitik' was unsuccessful, at any rate to the extent that that policy was meant to 'gather together' the political interests that would provide a secure base for authoritarian conservatism.[14]

It does not, then, seem appropriate to describe the German Empire of the Bismarck era as a 'Bonapartist dictatorial regime' (Wehler)[15] or as an authoritarian system governed with the aid of extra-constitutional threats of a coup (Stürmer).[16] Rather, it was a *semi-constitutional system with supplementary party-political features*, which was incapable of undergoing evolutionary change both because of the conflicts of political principle that were present within it and because of social tensions between the lower classes and the propertied classes (indeed, within the ruling strata themselves) that were becoming markedly more pronounced with the onset of industrialization. The hostile interplay between, on the one hand, the executive (euphemistically called the 'Confederated Governments'), which was not directly dependent on a 'governing party' but nevertheless needed parliamentary majorities in order to implement its legislative programme, and, on the other hand, a series of shifting party coalitions was the source of the characteristic pattern displayed by events within the new Empire, namely, a process of continuous technocratic reform unaccompanied by any corresponding adjustment in the political base. We can best call this process *modernization without democratization*: that is, modernization without real participation by those directly affected. To the extent that the parties were prepared to put their own long-term political aspirations on hold, Bismarck was prepared to offer them (the particular combinations of parties varying according to circumstances) the opportunity to exert substantive influence in legal, economic and social questions; they could even be assigned the electorally rewarding role of an informal 'governing party' in the old constitutional sense. Conversely, since the 'Confederated Governments' were not strong enough to put up sustained head-on resistance to any well-rooted demands for modernization, the only way in which the executive could obtain redress for the political consequences of social reform, or at least seek to reduce these consequences to a minimum, was by securing prerogatives for itself or for the Crown (for example, in the form of articles of *lèse-majesté*)[17] or by gaining compensation for those social groups that were the main victims of social change, notably the great landed aristocracy.

The lack of progress towards democracy cannot be attributed simply to a failure of will on the part of the middle-class parties: that is, to a reluctance to carry through substantive constitutional reforms that would have opened up the possibility of step-by-step change in the political system in tandem with the rapid changes that were taking place in the economy and in society. It is true that after 1867 the Progressive party did little to reassert the aspirations of the radical democratic groups from the period before and after 1848. But there was, in fact, no shortage of searching criticism of the Bismarckian system: what was lacking was a sufficient number of citizens prepared to back such idealism with their votes. The potential for democratization was absent not so much on the party-political plane as in society itself, which had become politicized only to a limited degree.[18] This was certainly the case as far as the National Liberal party was concerned, which in the initial stages of the establishment of the Empire was far from being the engine of unswerving allegiance to Bismarck that was subsequently to enter the history books.[19]

The notion that the National Liberals capitulated to Bismarck on the domestic political front as a result of moral failure, or on grounds of economic self-interest, simply cannot be sustained. It may be the case that the liberal middle class gradually retreated into the embrace of the pseudo-constitutional Prusso-German authoritarian state, in response to the rise of the working class, but this is by no means the whole story, for the 1860s and 1870s at any rate. Indeed, the specific policies of the National Liberals were closely comparable to the basic strategy of the constitutional liberals of the *Vormärz* and the 1848 revolution, who had stood for a strategy of 'agreement' with governments long before there was any question of a sizeable social threat from the nascent proletariat. The view recently put forward by Michael Gugel (following Lothar Gall), that German liberalism – or the liberal right wing at least – surrendered its old ideal of a 'classless civic society', first in 1848 and then, conclusively, in 1867, succumbing to the selfish pursuit of its overt socio-economic class interests, does not square with the facts. The first effect of industrialization was actually a considerable increase in the number of people enjoying a middle-range standard of living; it was not until the mid-1880s that there was a dramatic rise in the size of the proletariat at the expense of middle-class groups.[20] It is certainly true, as Theodor Schieder has shown, that fear of revolution was a potent ingredient of middle-class political consciousness throughout the nineteenth century,[21] but we cannot speak of a concrete, quantitatively measurable threat to the middle classes emanating from the proletariat during the 1860s and 1870s. Indeed, it was the relative backwardness of social relations that induced a basically conservative outlook, especially among those sections of the population that were still largely passive in political terms.

There is a need, then, for some modification of the widely held view that the progressive forces within German society were, on the one hand, outmanoeuvred by Bismarck, with his pre-eminent skill in exercising authority, and, on the other, undone by their own failure of nerve or by blinkered class attitudes. Such an account is also questionable because the two liberal parties made considerable efforts, in the period between 1867 and 1878, to achieve progressive reforms of the political system, or at least to keep open the possibility of such reforms in the future. This was the case from the time of the initial arguments over the drafting of the Imperial constitution. The political system that was created in 1867 and extended in 1871 was undoubtedly the product of a 'revolution from above', but many of the features that had at first been envisaged for it were either averted or altered by the liberal parties, particularly the National Liberals, exploiting their pivotal parliamentary position within the North German Constituent Reichstag. Even though the constitution failed in many respects to meet the original demands of the National Liberals, let alone committed progressive liberals, nevertheless a legal and political framework was created that gave the parties a substantial measure of real influence, albeit at the cost of the postponement, temporary or otherwise, of far-reaching constitutional reform.

There is no denying that economic considerations played a significant role in these decisions as far as the National Liberals were concerned. Middle-class demands for the establishment of an integrated economic area, and the release of economic energies from the restraints of traditional economic regulations, were undoubtedly a crucial motive force behind the middle class's desire for a German nation state, although, as Zorn has shown,[22] that was far from being the whole story. In the eyes of the non-Prussian leaders of the Nationalverein (National Association), particularly Bennigsen, the prospect of implementing the economic aspects, at least, of the liberal programme was an important reason for making compromises with Bismarck. At the same time, however, there was an expectation that the pursuit of liberal economic policies within the Empire would create the conditions in which, in the long run, the political demands of liberalism could also be achieved.

With hindsight, of course, we have to ask whether it was not the National Liberals who were outwitted, by helping Bismarck bring into being the semi-democratic constitutional system of the German Empire, in the face of resistance from forces on the left as well as on the right. Was not this system a cleverly constructed apparatus whose primary purpose was actually to divert the political energies of the German liberal movement into safe channels – satisfying the liberals' nationalist and economic demands, but withholding from them any real responsibility for, or participation in, major political decisions?

Such a thesis is tempting *ex post facto*, but it assumes too much rational calculation on Bismarck's part. For one thing, it does not accord with the complex process whereby the Imperial constitution actually came into existence. Even granting the force of Otto Becker's well-known views,[23] there is no escaping the fact that Bismarck was forced to make a substantial shift away from his original ideas in the course of the battles over the drafting of the constitution. This was partly because of pressure from the parties and from public opinion, which would have been outraged by a half-baked outcome, and partly because he had to make tactical allowances for the south German states, which would have been loth to accept a much more markedly greater-Prussian solution. Furthermore, if he had not shifted his ground, his political goal of securing the ascendancy of the traditional ruling elites in alliance with sections of the rising middle class would have been unattainable. In the final analysis the position of the Reichstag was much stronger than Bismarck himself had foreseen, even though significant restrictions were placed on its legislative powers and the constitutional relationship between the government and Parliament was left obscure.

It is too easy, moreover, to say that the National Liberals were excessively compliant. The National Liberals in the North German Constituent Reichstag saw clearly what was at stake. If they were prepared to yield on the critical questions of ministerial responsibility and the size of the army and its budget (as Lasker was, in particular, who played a key role as leader of the party's left wing), this was partly because they were counting on progressivist constitutional changes in the future, but mainly because they were only too well aware of the limits to their power, especially as far as popular support was concerned. Lasker, especially, was guided by the conviction that if the constitution were adopted without liberal backing, or were simply imposed, then the liberals would disappear from the political stage and not return for a long time to come. Even when looking back in 1874, he took the view that there would have been chaos, and liberal aspirations would have been thwarted for half a generation, if the North German Constituent Reichstag had rejected the constitution.[24] Bennigsen offered his electors similar arguments when defending his policy of compromise with Bismarck[25]. The National Liberals took it as read that their own social base was fragile[26] and that they were right to be afraid of Bismarck, even though Bismarck at first was likewise obliged to set great store on achieving a *modus vivendi* with the National Liberals, particularly for reasons of foreign policy

In the following decade, too, the political fortunes of the National Liberals remained contingent, in considerable measure, on the maintenance of tolerable relations with Bismarck. If they had not had the advantage of playing the role of a quasi-governing party, their position within the party spectrum during the years 1871–79 would have been far weaker than it actually was.

A glance at some of the social statistics for the formative years of the

Empire shows why this was so.[27] The 1850s and 1860s are commonly regarded as the period of 'take-off' for the industrial revolution in Germany, but while this assumption may be true in a strictly qualitative sense, the impact of industrialization on the traditional social structure of Prussia and Germany, which was still to a great extent shaped by agriculture and the full range of pre-industrial trades, was very much slower than is generally realized. Industrial development was most evident in Saxony and in regional centres in the Rhineland; incomes among the top echelons of the middle class rose considerably during this period. There was not, however, a significant effect in society at large. In 1816 73.5 per cent of the population of Prussia lived in rural areas; the figures for 1852 and 1867 were 71.5 per cent and 67.5 per cent respectively. The decrease is not exactly spectacular, particularly given the sharp concurrent rise in the population. In fact, the number of people in agricultural employment did not decline at all in absolute terms, and fell only slowly in relative terms: according to Hoffmann, the figures are 51.6 per cent for 1861 and 49.8 per cent for 1871, the year of the establishment of the Reich, and the proportion was still as high as 48.3 per cent in 1882, eleven years later. Figures for 1867, covering the Reich as a whole, show that 2.3 million people were self-employed in agriculture, forestry and fisheries, and only 1.7 million in industry and the craft trades (*Handwerk*); the corresponding figures for 1882 are 2.6 million and 2.1 million respectively. Although we must exercise caution when evaluating statistics of this sort, it is clear that the agricultural sector, with its traditional leaning towards the Conservative parties, retained its preponderance, despite the fact that industrialization (as can be clearly seen from the available data on net output in individual sectors of the economy) was by now proceeding at a turbulent pace, in defiance of fluctuations in the business cycle. The significance for society as a whole of the industrial sector of the national economy should not, then, be overstated, for the Bismarckian era at any rate. There was, at most, an unstable parity between the agricultural sector, which was as powerful as ever in absolute terms, albeit unable to match the productivity increases of its competitors, and the industrial and commercial sector, which, while highly dynamic, was by no means dominant within society at large. At the same time, there was a broad central area of the economy consisting of people earning small-scale livelihoods within structures that were largely pre-industrial. Statistics of average sizes of businesses up to the mid-1880s similarly indicate a sizeable and as yet scarcely dwindling pool of small enterprises.

These statistical data are matched – if we follow Hamerow's analysis,[28] which is based on figures, admittedly not very detailed, for overall self-employment in industry, trades and commerce – by evidence that traditional trades, particularly the craft trades, far from undergoing an abrupt decline during the 'take-off' phase, actually made intermittent gains.[29] Moreover, craftsmen and those in related occupations, such as small merchants or innkeepers, who were faced in the medium term with a decline in their social status constituted a natural constituency for conservative policies, effectively until the First World War. The remarkable impact of the agitation by Hermann Wagener's Preußische Volksvereine (Prussian People's Associations), which, in contrast with the National verein, were not clubs for *Honoratioren* (prominent citizens) demonstrates that these groups were readily amenable to political mobilization in the anti-liberal cause.

The statistics available for the Bismarckian era do not enable us to give a precise account of the changes that took place in the socio-economic structure of the German Empire during the period. Using rough estimates, however, we can see that the agricultural sector, at a time when the number of self-employed was still rising, maintained an astonishing degree of stability until the 1890s, but also, more importantly, that structural changes involving other sectors of the economy did not bring about anything like as sharp a polarization between self-employed groups and the industrial working class as most of the recent research in social history has suggested. In fact, at first the number of self-employed rose much faster than the population as a whole, and it was not until the mid-1880s that the number of industrial workers conclusively overtook that of the self-employed in all sectors of the economy. In quantitative terms, the industrial working class posed no real threat to the middle classes until the 1880s.[30]

Until the mid-1880s, then, the great bulk of the population was affected only indirectly by industrialization. The period saw no drastic changes in most people's material living conditions, let alone in their way of life. Industrial development was concentrated at first in a small number of centres, and its effect on society as a whole was less pronounced than has generally been thought. By the same token, the rising entrepreneurial middle class, although giving the lead within the liberal movement generally, remained relatively weak in numerical terms.

It is apparent, in other words, that from a socio-economic point of view the position of progressivist groups in German society was fairly precarious during the first decade of the Bismarckian Empire, and indeed for a considerable time thereafter. If the broad mass of the population were to become politically mobilized, progressives certainly did not stand simply to gain. The liberals confidently assumed that the logic of history would be on their side, at least in the long run; in reality, however, the narrow base of support they enjoyed in society was being weakened rather than strengthened by the onward march of industrialization, despite the fact that the number of people with middle-range incomes was temporarily on the increase. Liberalism, particularly National Liberalism, mainly owed its relatively powerful political position during the 1860s and 1870s to the fact that a considerable section of the broad mass of the population was still largely passive in a political sense. The brusqueness of the liberals' response to the arrival of the Centre party was partly due to the fact that the

Centre, although led by a small group of aristocrats and middle-class *Honoratioren*, was the first party to rest on a mass popular base.[31]

Contrary to the expectations enshrined in liberal ideology, the process of industrialization did not lead to a strengthening of the position of the liberal middle classes in society, nor to a growing liberalization of political institutions.[32] Instead it fostered, indeed dictated, a merely piecemeal modernization of social institutions, including the law and the system of social-welfare provision, while the political order was left untouched. Such a policy of partial modernization was perfectly feasible within the existing semi-democratic system. Indeed, gallingly for liberals, it was in some ways easier to implement than it would have been within a fully-fledged parliamentary democracy.

These factors limited the political efficacy of all wings of the liberal movement from the start. By the same token, however, they were conducive to the aims of the social conservatives, to the extent that these involved partial and predominantly technical reforms. The great strides made by the Centre, which espoused an ideology of 'reconciliation between property, capital and labour', are not, therefore, surprising. Nor was it merely during the first decades of the Empire that conditions in society helped the social conservatives; they became even more favourable later. It was only the lack of direction shown by the Conservative parties in the years immediately following the establishment of the Reich that prevented them from fully exploiting these opportunities from the beginning.

Under these circumstances, Bismarck's decision to work with the National Liberals after 1867 takes on considerable significance. This move was far more than a piece of tactical finesse: it was a choice, above all, that gave the moderate progressive forces in Germany a strategic head start. It might be argued that what Bismarck, as a true conservative, did was to wrest from his own landed aristocratic class just enough by way of reform to ensure that the social system would remain stabilized on a new plane for decades to come. Yet Bismarck's action cannot be seen merely as an inspired strategy of anti-revolutionary modernization designed to serve the interests of the ruling class: the concessions he made to the rising middle classes were much more far-reaching than that.

Indeed, it is not surprising that the great majority of conservatives viewed Bismarck's policies after 1867 with mistrust and open animosity. For the most part they shied away from direct conflict, out of loyalty towards the monarch as well as prudence.[33] Conservative misgivings, however, were immediately transformed into overt hostility when the Chancellor, in the process of making common cause with the National Liberals in the early 1870s, began to encroach on institutions in Prussia that played a significant part in upholding the conservatives' social and political hegemony. Prussian conservatives were made extremely uneasy by the anti-clerical tones struck by Falk, the Minister of Culture, and by the *Kulturkampf* legislation, which seemed likely to affect, directly or

indirectly, the status of the Protestant as well as the Catholic church. The
Protestant pastor was an essential element in the pattern of traditional
authority centred round the aristocratic magnates in the countryside. These
paternalistic structures were still largely intact, despite the incursions made
by the money economy, and any weakening of the church's influence
constituted a threat to them in the longer term. Similar fears fuelled the
bitter struggle that was fought over the reform of local government in
Prussia (the so-called *Kreisordnung*), which Bismarck wanted to impose by
methods far more sweeping than any that the Prussian Ministry of State
was prepared to employ, a fact which impelled the Chancellor temporarily
to surrender the post of Minister President to Roon. After the economic
crisis of 1873 had seemed to demonstrate the complete collapse of the
liberals' economic policy, there were emotional outbursts in the
Kreuzzeitung against the 'era of Bleichröder, Delbrück, Camphausen and
the new German economic policy', protests symptomatic of the anxieties
felt by a large number of conservatives, particularly at the grass roots,
about the changes that had taken place in the economy since 1867.
Bismarck rightly took these events as a reflection both on his policies and
on himself. He publicly cancelled his subscription to the *Kreuzzeitung* and
called on loyal conservatives to do likewise; in turn, a considerable number
of members of the nobility signed a declaration opposing his action. This
outbreak of protest may have been ephemeral – not long afterwards, the
conservatives felt obliged to put a formal end to the conflict, since the only
way they could hope to do well in the forthcoming Reichstag elections was
by falling in behind the government – but it also illustrates the extent to
which the course of politics after 1867 was shaped by compromise on the
social front. At the same time, however, the dip in the fortunes of
conservatism that resulted from the alignment of political forces at the time
of the establishment of the Empire does not mean that the conservatives
then ceased to enjoy adequate mass support. Although they lost ground as
a result of the growing political mobilization of the masses and a
consequent loosening of paternalistic structures, they were perfectly able to
make up for this by appealing, in particular, to lower-middle-class groups
who could see their traditional status being threatened by the process of
modernization. After 1879 they had the bonus of constituting a quasi-
governing party on a permanent basis.

The social and political foundations on which the German Empire of
1871 rested were multiple and varied. In all of the political camps,
traditionalist views prevailed over progressive ones. Only on the left, in the
Progressive party and in the German People's party, were there any groups
seriously committed to a thorough-going democratization of the political
system. They, however, were comparatively uninfluential, as were the still
tiny workers' parties that combined to form the Social Democratic party in
1875. The main ideological opposition to middle-class liberalism came
from the conservative groupings, which not only sought to combat the

strengthening of the constitutional role of Parliament (still the common aim of liberals of all stripes) but also rejected the entire process of modernization that the middle classes consistently supported. The liberals also became embroiled in a battle of principle with Roman Catholics and the Centre party, which they regarded not only as a stronghold of reaction in social terms but as a source of dangerous potential rivalry in politics. The Centre, in its turn, although sympathetic towards the anti-centralizing doctrines of the conservatives, albeit on different grounds, was fundamentally at odds with them in being prepared to make full use of the constitution in pursuit of ecclesiastical and other interests – not, to be sure, with a view to making the political system more democratic, but in order to improve its own beleaguered position.

It is clear that this three-way political division (the Social Democrats were not yet strong enough to rank as a fourth force) gave enormous scope to the executive, which was able to exploit the interplay of political forces to the detriment of the Reichstag and of the parties represented in it. (The pattern was, to be sure, reversed after 1890.) Conversely, however, the Imperial government was dependent on majorities not only in the Bundesrat (the Federal Council) and in the Prussian Ministry of State (though this was not so difficult to achieve at first) but also in the Reichstag. Neither the Reichstag nor the government, each a pillar of the constitution with its own very distinctive basis and structure, was able to take positive action unless there was some degree of *rapprochement* between the two of them. The result from the outset was that substantial barriers were placed in the way of all attempts to bring about thorough-going changes to the system, whether of a progressive or of a reactionary nature.

Even if the liberals had not split up again into different factions in 1867 – a constitutional wing wedded to a dualist system and the principle of co-operation with the executive, and a wing firmly committed to parliamentary democracy – but had formed the united liberal bloc that Lasker, for example, ardently wished to see, there would have been precious little prospect of their securing any far-reaching liberalization of the political system. The array of conservative forces in society was far too strong, and the possibility that the liberals would be shown the door in the event of an open conflict with Bismarck was a real and vivid one to all concerned. It was, essentially, with these considerations in mind that the National Liberals, though not the Progressives, opted for the path of compromise in 1867, and certainly by no means out of mere blind loyalty to the Chancellor. Contrary to the crude accounts in the reference books, which maintain that the National Liberals now retreated into the protective arms of the authoritarian state, it is clear that in the early years after the founding of the Reich they consented for the most part only to short-term compromises, in the hope of being able to re-open the contentious questions at a subsequent stage when circumstances might be more favourable. There is no other way of explaining the National Liberals' political strategy, whether with regard to the accountability of the Chancellor or the army and its budget and, later, the Septennial Law (or in a sense even with regard to the Socialist Law). The fact that central questions such as the position of the Chancellor, budgetary powers and the scope of the Reichstag's jurisdiction over military matters had been only provisionally resolved, and were therefore being repeatedly re-opened (or were at least capable of being re-opened) injected a considerable degree of instability and uncertainty into the political system. Stürmer's description of the Septennial Law as a 'lever of internal stabilization' is correct only in a strictly limited sense; the Law was, in fact, the product of fragile domestic political compromise.[34] The leaders of the National Liberals took the sober view that their electoral support was far too unreliable to warrant going down the road of conflict. In April 1874 Bennigsen justified the compromise over the Septennial Law by citing the 'powerful popular movement that has swept the German nation in recent days and weeks'. '[...] in the purely political realm,' he said, 'there [had] not been so primitive and powerful a movement since the year 1848.' It had 'sprung from the urgent sense that now is not the time for the German state to tolerate a conflict between its government and the Reichstag on the matter of the army';[35] the two sides needed to reach an understanding.

At the same time, however, circumstances were not conducive towards openly reactionary Imperial policies either: that is, policies designed to eliminate or to curtail drastically the powers of Parliament and hence the supplementary role of parties within the constitutional structure. Bismarck certainly toyed repeatedly with the idea of making retrogressive changes to the constitution and undermining Parliament by establishing corporatist bodies representing occupational and economic interests, but he never dared actually to take practical steps in this direction. The crisis of 1890 was perhaps the only exception, since on this occasion he did seriously seek to provoke conflict, as Röhl has convincingly demonstrated.[36] But Bismarck's overriding concern, based on motives of true conservatism, was to seek political support that would be sufficiently broad while not simultaneously leaving him at the mercy of public opinion. It was for this reason that many of his political decisions were in the nature of compromises. They were indeed part and parcel of a conservative political strategy, but it was not a strategy that simplistically reflected the way in which the Prussian aristocratic ruling class perceived its interests. The great majority of substantive political decisions that Bismarck took were attuned far more closely to immediate circumstances than historians, pro- and anti-Bismarckians alike, have been willing to admit; they took remarkably close account of the balance of strength of the different social groups involved in each case. This was not a sign of opportunism, though historians have certainly always found it hard to explain how it was that Bismarck made a habit of simultaneously pursuing directly competing political courses of action and then opting with lightning speed for one of the competing alternatives when faced by a concrete situation. Rather, it was a consequence of the fundamental instability of the pluralistic system of power that had been institutionalized in 1871. Bismarck undoubtedly resorted regularly to high-handed methods in order to assemble majorities in the Reichstag, as he had done in the Prussian Chamber of Deputies. Nevertheless, the parties came to represent an increasingly independent factor in the political situation, if only because of the expanding role that was now being played by the state. Almost all of the significant pieces of legislation that were enacted during the Bismarckian era had been modified by varying constellations of votes in Parliament, sometimes to such an extent that the original intentions of Bismarck and his colleagues were no longer recognizable. For all the fact that the constitutional structure and the political environment in the Bismarckian Empire were highly authoritarian, the parties consistently exerted a strong and practical influence on events, and this influence steadily expanded.

We must, then – echoing Carl Schmitt – characterize the German Empire after 1871 as a 'system of skirted decisions'. This is not to say, however, merely that there was no clear commitment either to Prussian militarist authoritarianism or to middle-class party government.[37] Rather, the constitutional system was one in which individual centres of power existed cheek by jowl in relatively uncoordinated fashion, as Theodor Schieder has put it,[38] with each of the different dominant groups in society enjoying an ascendancy within its own domain. The aristocracy maintained its pre-eminence in Prussia, especially in the Chamber of Peers though also, and increasingly, in the Chamber of Deputies; in addition, and more significantly, it preserved its traditionally strong influence over the Prussian civil service, notably at the lower levels, although this hold was no longer quite absolute after 1872. The bourgeois parties, on the other hand, dominated the Reichstag and thus, within the limits imposed upon it, the legislature as a whole. In this way they were able to shape circumstances in their favour in the economic sphere and, in part, within the legal system. At the hub of the system was the state government bureaucracy, with Bismarck at its head. By constantly adjusting the thrust and direction of its policies the bureaucracy was largely able to retain the political initiative, and it played a crucial role in maintaining the balance of power, despite the fact that on many questions it was forced to seek compromises with party majorities in Parliament.

The fluid, indeterminate nature of the power structure was the central reason why German society underwent the process of modernization without, at the same time, undergoing a process of democratization. The growth of this unstable political system was not the effect of Bismarck's specific policies, which were designed to prevent the emergence of solidly based parties of whatever colour – though they failed to do so, despite the Chancellor's deployment of all the subtle tactical skills at his disposal. It was, rather, the effect of the changes in the structure of society that came about in the wake of the turbulent surge of industrialization that began at the start of the 1880s. The process of industrialization, in which (as Gerschenkron has shown) the dominant role was played by a comparatively small number of large enterprises closely allied with a few large banks, eventually led to the break-up of classical middle-class liberalism. The widening range of middle-class incomes, and the emergence of what Friedrich Naumann called an 'industrial aristocracy', together with its vassals and retainers, brought about the atomization of what is traditionally known as 'Besitz und Bildung' (the educated and propertied class) and gave rise to a growing diversification of vested interests and political aspirations within the middle class.[39] Middle-class liberalism began to lose its political momentum, and to do so, moreover, at the very time when the rise of the working class from the early 1880s onwards was starting to represent new and dangerous political competition. On top of this, the peculiarly German version of industrialization favoured the survival of a numerically substantial lower middle class. Both the Conservatives and the Centre party succeeded in projecting themselves as spokesmen for this social group, thereby securing a long-term role in the political structure in defiance of pronouncements by liberal and Marxist theorists alike that such a role was sure to be ephemeral.

Contemporaries (including both Bismarck and the liberal leaders) were by no means quick to discern these trends. This can be clearly seen if we analyse the events that preceded the great domestic political watershed of 1879. In the autumn of 1878 Bismarck was still proceeding on the assumption that it was impossible to govern without the support of the National Liberals and that they would therefore have to be assigned some share of responsibility for policy, albeit in a way that did not usher in genuinely parliamentary government.[40] He therefore decided to offer Bennigsen a Prussian ministerial post. His negotiations with Bennigsen were entirely serious, notwithstanding the stubborn resistance of Wilhelm I, acting as the mouthpiece of Prussian conservative misgivings. In a sense, the negotiations were the crowning moment of the era of liberal–conservative compromise; they were also the turning-point in the evolution of domestic politics in the Bismarckian Empire. It is notable that each of the two actors in the drama was convinced, at the time, that he had the other in the palm of his hand: Bennigsen perhaps more so than Bismarck. Bennigsen was certain that the National Liberals, by withholding their assent from the pending tax legislation, possessed a sure means of finally enforcing the transition to parliamentary government. Bismarck, for his part, calculated that if Bennigsen entered the cabinet it would be possible to swing the National Liberals (or at least the bulk of the party, minus the left liberals) behind the existing system, detaching them completely from the left wing. His purpose was to achieve popular backing for his future domestic strategy, which was to remain free of dependence on narrowly conservative influence while simultaneously forestalling possible changes to the system that might be expected to occur in the event of a change of monarch. His parallel efforts, however, to create a united front between industry and agriculture on the question of tariffs and taxes had advanced sufficiently for him to be able to present Bennigsen with the unwelcome demand that the latter make a break with previous liberal economic policy. Bennigsen's decision to remain 'firm' and, specifically, not to accept the Chancellor's financial proposals (which appeared to encroach, in particular, on the Reichstag's budgetary powers) led Bismarck, of course, to make a radical change of direction and seek to achieve his aims by abandoning the National Liberals. In the sequel the liberals of all stripes were strong enough to ruffle Bismarck's tax programme considerably and force him to make an uneasy compromise with the Centre, in the form of the 'Francken-stein Clause', which rendered largely nugatory the original purpose of his financial policy, namely the curbing of the Reichstag's budgetary powers; but they were unable all the same to exert any further substantive influence in the matter.

Liberal despondency did not descend overnight, but took the form of growing political fragmentation from 1880 onwards. The change in the character of the economy, which saw a growth in monopolistic structures side by side with a significant survival of traditional forms of economic activity in other sectors, proved an especially severe challenge for the National Liberals. The dynamic areas of the economy (heavy industry, the machine-tools industry and some parts of the textiles industry) were particularly in favour of protective tariffs and the abandonment of liberal economic principles, and believed that they had more chance of influencing government policy, particularly in the economic sphere, by the direct route offered through the new industrial associations than by the indirect route of the political parties and the Reichstag. The majority of banks, on the other hand, as well as commerce and those industries primarily concerned with the export trade, remained firm advocates of the 'international division of labour'. At the same time, the full impact of industrialization on the social structure was yet to make itself felt, and the great bulk of industrial and commercial activity was still being carried on in traditional small concerns: thus, in 1875 63.6 per cent of all businesses in industry and the craft trades employed five people or fewer, and in 1882 and 1895 the proportions were still 59.8 per cent and 41.8 per cent respectively. Seen within this context, Bismarck's conversion to protectionism did not so much trigger the political decline of liberalism as simply make it manifest or, at most, accelerate it. The National Liberals – after the defection of the Lasker wing, which first and foremost represented the commercial middle class – merely acted in their own clear interest when they moved sharply to the right after 1884. Bennigsen's language in defence of the Heidelberg Programme of 1884 was resigned: 'If we wish to achieve peace and stability in Germany, it is absolutely necessary for all liberal and moderate conservative elements to come together.'[41] This was, in a sense, an admission that the liberal movement was no longer capable, unaided, of securing the political changes that would help to bring about the domestic integration of the nation.

On the surface, Bismarck's switch to a policy of protectionism was a great success. It must be remembered, however, that 'gathering together the classes supporting the state' did not achieve the results for which he had hoped. In the short term the amount of new blood that was injected into the Prussian aristocracy from heavy industry and the upper middle class from the late 1870s onwards, while not considerable in quantitative terms, was sufficiently significant, in combination with the large retinue of conservatives in the lower middle classes and the intelligentsia, to protect the political system from any assaults from below. But this did not, *pace* Böhme's claim that the the switch to protectionism was a 'second founding of the Empire', provide a stable basis for the sort of social-conservative policies that Bismarck envisaged. Bismarck's attempts to carry out a sweeping reform of the political system along conservative lines, using an alliance of the agrarian aristocracy, heavy industry and the upper middle class, all came to naught. One exception, arguably, was the protection of the armed forces from parliamentary control by the Reichstag, but even this was achieved largely by indirect means, through a reduction in the powers of the Prussian Minister of War in favour of the General Staff and the 'royal power of command'. Bismarck's plan to create a corporatist system of representation based on occupational and economic interests, functioning in competition with, and (if the occasion arose) as a political alternative to, the Reichstag, did not get beyond the initial stages. His ambition to devise social legislation in such a way that workers would be under a direct obligation to the benefactions of the state was watered down by his own colleagues, who were well aware that the Reichstag would never give its consent. Bismarck was also unable to realize even partially the political goals of his taxation policy, namely to undermine the Reichstag's budgetary powers and to reshape the revenue system in such a way that the state would no longer incur the odium of being the visible collector of its citizens' taxes.

Bismarck's diversionary strategies – notably, the repressive legislation directed against the Social Democrats, though this was significantly diluted by the Reichstag from the outset; his exploitation of external crises for domestic political ends; even his colonial policy – were, at most, successful only in a negative sense. They no longer delivered the Chancellor reliable Conservative–National Liberal majorities that would support his policies without question. Even the elections of 1887, in which Bismarck deliberately played up tensions with France and constructed an electoral alliance of 'parties supporting the state', were only a limited victory. It should be recalled that in 1890 the 'Cartel Reichstag' rejected Bismarck's call for a renewal of the Socialist Law inclusive of the expulsion clause. This rebuff played a decisive part in Bismarck's political downfall.

In fact, the excessive emphasis that has commonly been placed, following Böhme and Stegmann, on the strategy of 'gathering together the parties supporting the state' tends to obscure the point that the old pattern of compromises over small questions accompanied by surviving disagreements over fundamentals – not only between, but also within, left and right – continued to prevail in the day-to-day politics of the 1880s.[42] The 'fault lines' in society became more numerous with the rise of Social Democracy; they certainly did not change beyond all recognition. The position of the conservative elites within the political system of the later 1880s remained an endangered one, even though the forces of the left were not strong enough to bring about a fundamental transformation. Bismarck's masterly skill in constantly changing direction and devising new diversionary tactics could not stem an imperceptible process of constitutional change that assigned the Reichstag, and hence the parties, mounting importance within a complex pluralistic system of division of powers and that had begun to undermine the dominant position of the old aristocratic elites in the civil service, in the military and in the party-political system itself. Although the internal conflicts within the political system of the German Empire continued to be resolved in the short term, and could increasingly be disguised by nationalist sentiment, they were also becoming more acute. To a very great extent the system was a reflection of the conflicts that were present within society; it was not a factitious instrument of Bonapartist rule. The process whereby a modern egalitarian industrial society was born from within an agrarian culture was a painful one throughout Europe, but in Germany the relatively weak position of the early-industrial *Honoratioren* middle class, the comparative strength of the aristocracy, and the rapidity of the process of industrialization itself (which was inimical to the principles of liberalism) exacerbated the conflicts and problems and made any sort of reformist or progressivist political solution all the harder to achieve. The political system created in 1871 was not a *monstrum* in Pufendorf's sense, as Sauer has claimed.[43] It was a 'system of skirted decisions', albeit one that possessed a remarkable capacity for integration, despite all the conflicts that beset it from within.

2

A delaying compromise: the division of authority in the German Imperial constitution of 1871

In recent decades it has become the prevailing view among historians that the founding of the German Empire was a 'revolution from above': in other words, that although it brought about national unity and thus fulfilled a central aim of the liberal and democratic movements of the time, it also served the purpose of stemming the tide of liberalism and democracy and diverting it into safe channels. Theodor Schieder's well-known thesis that Bismarck's policies were inspired not only by a *cauchemar des coalitions* but also – and, in the final analysis, more profoundly – by a *cauchemar des révolutions*[1] is now little disputed. That said, there are still many striking differences of emphasis among scholars, particularly with regard to the nature of the system of authority that was created with the Empire and the methods of exerting authority that were used by Bismarck himself. A size-able number of historians have tended, for varying reasons, to construe Bismarck's policies of the years 1862–71 as virtually a paradigm case of the 'Bonapartist' method of exercising power. On this view, Bismarck acted as a quasi-agent of the middle classes in carrying out the sweeping structural changes in society that were a necessary condition for the growth of the industrial system, but also created a system of authoritarian rule, legit-imized by spuriously plebiscitary means, that excluded the middle classes (to say nothing of the broad mass of the population) from true participa-tion in decision-making in the long run. Geoff Eley has gone furthest in this direction, uninhibitedly describing the creation of the Empire as the German equivalent of the 'bourgeois revolution', a revolution whose effects were essentially on a par with the achievements of the middle classes in western Europe.[2]

Other writers, however, notably Lothar Gall, have firmly rejected any Bonapartist interpretation of Bismarck's policies. They argue that the claim that Bismarck relied on such methods of wielding power do not stand up on empirical grounds, since the specific circumstances that might have made for policies comparable with those of Napoleon III did not apply.[3] It is certainly misleading to draw too close a parallel between Bismarck's rule and that of Napoleon III. On the other hand, that does not necessarily mean that it is inappropriate to use the model propounded by Karl Marx in *The Eighteenth Brumaire of Louis Bonaparte*, to the extent that the main emphasis in that model is on the long-term stabilization of a bourgeois system through plebiscitary means. There is no doubt, indeed, that Bismarck, faced with a dominant middle class and a political system that was still relatively undeveloped, pinned his faith on the loyalty of the broad mass of the population, as yet scarcely active in a political sense. Admittedly, the hope that the creation of a ramified system of Prussian Volksvereine (People's Associations) might provide a mass base for conservatism to match that enjoyed by the liberals was only partially fulfilled. Likewise, the timid attempts Bismarck made in the 1860s to attack the liberals at their most vulnerable spot, by introducing a state policy for social welfare for the working classes, were soon abandoned. By 1867, if not before, Bismarck was aware that if he were to outmanoeuvre the various brands of liberalism he would have to pursue a policy of flexibility and compromise with pointedly royalist overtones. Such a policy would give very free rein to the national aspirations of the liberal movement, while ensuring that the Crown and the conservative elites retained a considerable measure of real power. This can scarcely be called a Bonapartist strategy in the strict sense. Nevertheless, other weapons from the Bonapartist armoury were also called into play, notably that of universal, equal and direct suffrage, which the National Liberals, in particular, fought to have excluded from the constitution of the North German Confederation. Although the hopes that Bismarck invested in universal suffrage were not realized, the system of representation by middle-class *Honoratioren* (prominent citizens) was, to all intents and purposes, undermined, even if the result was not a straightforward gain for loyalist forces in society.

It is no accident that Lothar Gall, in his major biography of Bismarck,[4] comes somewhat closer to espousing the Bonapartist thesis than he himself is perhaps aware. He portrays Bismarck as the man who was able to steer a course between the dominant political and social forces and trends of his era and to translate into reality those ideas for which 'the time was ripe'. He also emphasizes, however, that the reason why Bismarck was particularly concerned to create a 'balance between the forces of the past and those new forces that were emerging as the result of a fundamental process of economic and social change' was that this helped both to preserve and to increase the authority of the state and to strengthen his own personal position of power.[5] This, though, can quite properly be said to have constituted a Bonapartist strategy. Gall is anxious throughout to cleave to a middle way between the view that Bismarck's handiwork essentially flew in the face of 'the spirit of the age' (as Ziekursch had earlier argued) and the view that the Empire was a thoroughly positive achievement if judged in terms of the circumstances of the period. Such an approach, however, is not without its difficulties. Hence we have the contradiction of the Bonapartist who, *ex hypothesi*, is not supposed to be anything of the sort: the masterly politician who repeatedly outwits his opponents and yet may never be described as a manipulative genius. Likewise, it is difficult to know what to make of an account which, on the one hand, sees the creation of the German Empire as essentially the realization of 'dominant and, in part, far deeper-lying, longer-term developmental trends',[6] but which, on the other hand, has Bismarck acting, from the very day of the founding of the Reich, in fundamental opposition to the spirit of the age until he is finally defeated by the selfsame forces that he had previously handled with such caution and prudence.

Lothar Gall is extremely anxious to rescue Bismarck from his grandiose reputation as the statesman of almost superhuman genius and to bring him back down to the workaday realities of political life. However, his thesis that Bismarck, at any rate before 1871, succeeded primarily in helping bring to fruition only those trends for which 'the time was ripe', by dint of a constant process of pragmatic compromise, merely serves to highlight the more important question, which is how the actual system of authority in the German Empire should be characterized. Was it an anachronistic structure that functioned primarily to defend the status quo, albeit by means of partial modernization?[7] Was it, to use a description I have employed elsewhere, a 'system of skirted decisions' that left crucial political questions unresolved?[8] Or was it, to follow Geoff Eley,[9] the product of a German variant of the 'bourgeois revolution', that is, did it provide a protective outer shell within which middle-class capitalism could develop unhindered and unharmed? I shall discuss this question, and seek to answer it, at least in general terms, by analysing the nature of the constitutional system that was created in 1867 and then modified and extended to include the south German states in 1871. I shall also say something about the broader social forces that lay behind the constitutional structure more narrowly defined – in other words, what Lassalle called the 'real constitution' of the German Empire.

Hitherto the debate about the nature of the German Imperial constitution has tended to be rather one-dimensional, concentrating mainly on the situation within Germany and paying little attention to contrasting constitutional developments in other countries.[10] Wolfgang Sauer's discussion of the 1871 constitution, in his well-known essay on 'The Problem of the German Nation State', draws parallels with Pufendorf's famous criticism of the old German Empire as a constitutional *monstrum*.[11] Hans Boldt shows how little the Imperial constitution owed to older German constitutional tradition, correctly pointing out that 'matters of sovereignty and government [were] deliberately left obscure'.[12] Other authors, partly echoing the penetrating criticisms of the constitutional apparatus of the Bismarckian

Reich that had been made by Max Weber, emphasize to a greater or lesser degree the 'pseudo-constitutional' character of the system and the strained attempt that was made to to disguise the *de facto* hegemony of Prussia. By contrast, Ernst Rudolf Huber, in particular, presents a reasoned case for viewing the Imperial constitution as an 'agreed constitution' that 'made the German nation state a reality', in its essentials at least, and that should be seen as exemplifying a fully distinctive, national type of constitutional order.[13] In response to such arguments, Ernst-Wolfgang Böckenförde maintains that the German model of constitutional government, with its dialectical opposition between executive and legislature, was essentially no more than a transitional phenomenon on the road to a parliamentary system and that the German Imperial constitution of 1871, in particular, was no exception in this respect.[14]

It cannot be disputed, certainly, that the establishment of the German Empire did not of itself bring about a German national state, let alone *the* German national state of the sort that liberals of all stripes had so ardently desired. It merely set up the political and legal framework within which the German Empire then in fact evolved into an integral nation state. In the course of this evolution some of the central elements of the constitution – notably the monarchy itself, but also the Reichstag in its role as the body representing the nation as a political (and, increasingly, as a politicized) entity – acquired considerably more weight than had originally been assigned to them.[15] This does not mean, however, that there was – as Manfred Rauh has argued, reviving an older line of argument – a more or less seamless and imperceptible transition towards parliamentary government within the Empire.[16]

One reason why it is difficult to give a precise account of the constitution of the German Empire primarily in terms of internal structural features is that the constitution contained a complex amalgam of both federal and confederal elements. Bismarck, indeed, addressed this point openly when preparations for the drafting of the constitution first began: [17]

> Formally speaking, we shall have to keep to a confederation [*Staatenbund*], while in practice giving it the character of a federal state [*Bundesstaat*], by using elastic and inconspicuous but very broad expressions. A Federal Diet [*Bundestag*], rather than a Ministry, will therefore serve as the central authority [. . .].

The specific circumstances that affected the drafting of the Imperial constitution – the need to preserve as much sovereignty for the individual states as possible, while at the same time meeting the national movement's demand for the creation of a unified nation state, at any rate in the spheres of foreign policy, military matters and the economy – have led Lothar Gall, invoking Bismarck himself, to regard as flawed any analysis of the Imperial constitution couched in more general terms. The strength of the constitution, Gall argues, was its very 'freedom from theory, system and dogma'.

'Any attempt,' he adds, 'to understate this freedom and to impose a systematic character upon the constitution which it did not possess is not only misleading but misses the essential point.'[18] It is surely permissible, all the same, using a comparative historical approach, to try to be more ambitious than this and to spell out the central features of the constitutional system. This is not to deny that the particular historical circumstances in which the Imperial constitution was drawn up were fairly unusual and make such a task a far from easy one.

The constitution of the German Empire was the product of three principal factors, which were quite distinct from one another and which differed, moreover, in relative significance at two separate stages of the constitution-making process, first, when the constitution of the North German Confederation was being drawn up in 1866-67 and, secondly, when this system was then extended to include the south German states.

1. The middle-class liberal movement, which was still the most active political force in Germany at the time, wanted a unitary nation state of a constitutional type. Liberals regarded this as essential both if the individual German states were to undergo fruitful economic and social development along middle-class capitalist lines and if Germany's position within the international system was to be strengthened.
2. The traditional elites in the state and in society believed that it was vital to preserve unhindered the existing authoritarian monarchical state in Prussia, which had made only partial concessions to constitutionality and liberalization. They saw this as crucial for the maintenance of their privileged position, at a time when the industrial revolution was getting under way and profound shifts in the pattern of distribution of national wealth were beginning to make themselves felt.
3. The policy of Prussia was to achieve final and unchallenged Prussian hegemony within Germany, by repulsing or even eliminating the influence of her competitor, Austria.

The middle-class liberal movement had, of course, failed at its first and only previous attempt to realize its goals, namely, in the revolution of 1848-49, which it had not, by and large, actively sought. Since the early 1860s, however, the national movement had become consolidated once again, to the extent that no realistic policy-maker could afford to ignore it. It was, above all, thanks to Bismarck's far-sightedness that the Manteuffel regime's attempts to stabilize the monarchical system by purely authoritarian means, using the traditional instruments of power – the Prussian monarchy, the army, the civil service and the higher nobility – were abandoned in favour of a flexible policy for rolling back the liberal movement. Despite the degree of comparative success that Bismarck enjoyed during the period of constitutional conflict in Prussia, it had become clear that there was no sense, in the long run, in simply continuing to ignore the liberal movement and trying to outflank the rising middle class by forging an alliance with the unpoliticized lower classes, broadly loyalist though the latter might still be. The pace of economic change, which had accelerated enormously in the industrial field since the 1850s, was sufficient in itself to rule out such an option. Nor could the national movement, which was largely a by-product of the economic advance of the upper middle classes, be neglected any longer. If the German question were not resolved, then the existing political and social order in Prussia-Germany could not be kept stable indefinitely. It was Bismarck's aim, accordingly, to deflect the energies of the liberal movement into safe channels by implementing some of its objectives, albeit by authoritarian means, and thus secure its commitment to the existing system. At the same time, the democratic left would be deprived of all chance of seeing its more ambitious ideas enacted in the foreseeable future.

Bismarck once said that his policy on the German question was simply a well-understood Prussian policy. Certainly, one reason why the goal of securing Prussian hegemony in Germany pointed to a partial rapprochement with the liberal movement was that Austria was sure to be marginalized as a result. The way ahead on the economic front had already been largely cleared, thanks to Prussia's policy of free trade; the case for realizing the goal in the political sense through a partial implemention of the liberal ideal of a German nation state seemed even more compelling. The settlement of 1866 opened the way forward to the creation of a 'little German' state in which Prussia would, of course, be the undisputed leader not only on matters of external relations but also on the crucial questions of constitutional and social policy.

The establishment of the North German Confederation cannot, admittedly, be seen as a mere transitional stage on the road to Imperial unity, even though this was how events in fact turned out. Anti-Prussian and particularist sentiments regained the upper hand in parts of the south German states after 1867, and it was only after nationalist enthusiasm had been whipped up by the Franco-Prussian War that these pockets of resistance were swept away and the south German states were integrated into the existing Confederation. Nevertheless, it is indisputable that when the constitution of the North German Confederation was being drawn up, the further goal of full German unification was never far from the minds of those involved. The consideration that the option should be held open for the south German states to accede under outwardly attractive conditions was clearly an important influence during the process of drafting. On this ground alone, the sovereignty of the individual states could not afford to be too drastically curtailed, at least in a formal sense. A non-revolutionary re-drawing of the political map of Germany would never have been feasible without the more or less voluntary consent of the German princes, even though Bismarck had no compunction in showing a complete disregard for the principle of monarchical legitimacy in particular cases.

The main reason, however, for the policy of providing as much protection as possible for the rights of the individual states, in line with relations
vis-à-vis the old Bundestag, was that the power and standing of Prussia herself had to be upheld at all costs. A stable Prussian state was the pillar that
supported the entire structure: it was therefore seen as imperative to ensure
that the newly created institutions of the Confederation, and then the
Empire, played as small a mediating role as possible. Indeed, the vested
interests of the Prussian aristocracy, and especially of the higher civil service, would have brooked no alternative. Moreover, it was only Prussia that
could be relied on to provide a stable counterweight against excessive parliamentary government. Given the teritorial, political and economic dominance of Prussia within the North German Confederation, no other
outcome was ever likely.

During the period of constitutional conflict the middle-class liberal
movement and the conservative Prussian aristocracy, along with the latter's
'camp followers' in the lower classes, had been caught in something of a
stalemate, albeit one in which Bismarck's Ministry and the Prussian state
bureaucracy occupied a pivotal strategic position. The transformation of
the situation after the battle of Königgrätz enabled Bismarck to go on to the
offensive on the domestic front. He decided on a partial rapprochement
with the liberals within the framework of a constitutional monarchy that
would remain authoritarian in structure. Apart from certain Old
Conservative groups, to which we shall return presently, the nucleus of the
liberal movement that was now taking shape as the National Liberal party
was the only serious oppostion in the parliamentary sphere that Bismarck
had to contend with in the period before 1867.

In 1867 the other political formations in Prussia-Germany (the Social
Democrats and the newly founded Catholic parliamentary group) had not
yet acquired sufficient political weight to be able to intervene significantly
in the process of drawing up the constitution. If we look at the level of
effective popular political mobilization that existed in the German states at
this time, it is clear that there were really only two dominant political
groupings within the 'political nation': middle-class liberalism and the conservative aristocracy. The latter in turn was able to count on intermittent
support from the lower classes, which were thought to be predominantly
royalist and loyally disposed towards authority; Bismarck himself, of
course, partly counted on being able to play this card. Wagener's moderately successful efforts to build up Prussian Volksvereine in the 1860s,
which have not been properly studied in the literature, are relevant in this
context.[19]

The working class did not pose a truly serious threat at this time, despite
some effective agitation, notably by the General German Workers' Union
(Allgemeiner deutscher Arbeiterverein). At the same time, middle-class liberal *Honoratioren* were well aware that encouraging the broad mass of the
population was not an expedient political strategy from their own point of

view. Later, indeed, it was the opinion of many within the National Liberal party that Bismarck made a cardinal error in 1867 by introducing universal, equal and direct suffrage for Reichstag elections and thus allowing the emergent lower classes to play a significant role in the major processes of political decision-making for the first time.[20] Those on the democratic (or, more properly, the radical) wing of the liberal movement, on the other hand, found themselves politically out-manoeuvred at this stage as a result of their failure in the constitutional conflict and Bismarck's triumph on the German question, which they had clearly hoped would be his downfall. Their political base in the population, moreover, was too weak for them to be able to play any further active role in the constitutional struggle. The same was true, perhaps in stronger measure, of the Catholic political movement, which found itself in a particularly unfavourable strategic situation. The mobilization of the Catholic electorate was still in its earliest stages, with Catholic popular support confined for the time being to groups and regions that had lost out in the settlement of 1866. Despite this, Windthorst came out with very explicit proposals for shaping the Imperial constitution that were couched in comparatively progressive terms. Both Bismarck and the spokesmen of the National Liberal party, however, were able largely to disregard them.

As far as the National Liberals were concerned, one of the principal reasons why they assumed a key role within the domestic political debate after 1867 was that Bismarck believed that he had little chance of making real headway with his policy towards the individual states unless he had the co-operation of the 'so-called National party, even though in truth it is irksome'.[21] The National Liberals were perfectly well aware that Bismarck's triumph in the field of external policy had left them in a poor tactical position in the short run and that compromises on the constitutional question were therefore quite inevitable. At the same time, however, they were conscious, and highly confident, of their own political strength. At this stage they certainly did not regard themselves merely as Bismarck's shield-bearers: they were an independent political force to whom, as they saw it, the future belonged, whatever the short-term dictates of *Realpolitik* might seem to be.[22] They recognized the present facts of power, which entailed that many of Bismarck's demands should be met: renewed conflict with Bismarck was out of the question. But they were anxious first and foremost that the constitutional questions should be resolved in a way that did not rule out liberalizing changes in the future, even if concessions might have to be made in the present. Johannes Miquel made this clear at the end of December 1866:[23]

Even though circumstances may not be such as to permit the full measure of popular rights to be achieved at a stroke, this should not make us indifferent to the development of civic freedom. We must therefore seek to ensure that the North German Confederation is built on foun-

dations that do not prevent from the outset the future growth, at
least, of a truly constitutional state.

At the same time, the constitutional aims of the National Liberals were
much less ambitious than is commonly assumed today. Their declared goal
was not the establishment of a genuinely parliamentary system on the
British model, but merely a firm guarantee of constitutional government.
For them, this meant a formal specification that the executive would be
legally responsible to Parliament: they themselves, however, regarded as
highly questionable the principle that the Chancellor should be accountable
to the Reichstag on specific matters, which would inevitably have led to the
emergence of genuine party government. There was certainly a widespread
sense that a parliamentary system on the British model might eventually
come into being, but even in the liberal camp there was by no means general agreement that such a development was desirable.

Recent work, guided by the conclusions of Otto Becker's major study,[24]
has generally portrayed the role of the National Liberals in the detailed
shaping of the constitution of the North German Confederation as a fairly
limited one. Only Ernst Rudolf Huber has remained firmly committed to
the view that the 'fact that the constitutional legislation of 1867 and 1870
represented a pre-emptive accommodation to the fundamental constitutional tenets of National Liberalism [... was] nothing less, in effect, than a
belated victory for the constitutional ideas of 1848-49'.[25] Lothar Gall has
also endorsed the view that the National Liberals' influence on the concrete
particulars of the constitution was minimal. Bismarck, he argues, allowed
himself to be pushed by the North German Constituent Reichstag, and
specifically by the National Liberals, into the course that he himself really
wished to pursue but had previously been unable to follow because of the
existence of separate state governments. Correspondingly, Gall comes to
the somewhat dogmatic conclusion – rather in defiance of his study's basic
thesis that the character of the constitution fully reflected the real forces at
work at the time – that 'the constitution of the new state that was accepted
by an overwhelming majority on 16 April 1867 [... was], in its most
important points, not a compromise but an unambiguous triumph' on
Bismarck's part.[26] In my judgement, however, this claim needs to be treated
with a certain degree of caution, since it leaves out of account the general
context within which the constitution took shape and the prevailing trends
within the political culture of the period. It is clear, first, that the constitution that actually came into being differed considerably from the original
drafts and, secondly, that the Reichstag parties eventually came to play
something of a parliamentary role in the major processes of political decision-making in a way that neither Bismarck nor the National Liberals had
foreseen, despite the existence of the numerous reserve provisions and the
checks and balances that had been built into the constitution in order to set
strict limits to the Reichstag's powers.

There can be no doubting the conservative nature of Bismarck's political goals as such. From the moment he embarked on his policy of establishing the Reich, he made it absolutely clear that 'our great aim' was to 'promote the conservative interest' and that he was opposed to the attempts of the statesmen of the central states to court the favour of 'democratic parliamentary majorities'. 'If we wished to be untrue [. . .] to the conservative cast of our domestic policy,' Bismarck said in April 1865, 'then we would be capable of turning the weapons of revolution on our adversaries themselves, and to much greater effect.'[27] The question, however, is whether Bismarck, in conjunction with the National Liberals, did not subsequently make rather too ample use of the revolutionary weapons of his adversaries. That is to say, we have to ask whether his attempt to consolidate the Prusso-German policy on a new basis by borrowing some of the political ideas of his antagonists did not lead to a constitutional structure that actually made it extremely difficult to preserve the political and social status quo without deploying every available weapon of authoritarian rule, along with a dose of skilfully administered nationalism. To put it the other way round, it can be asked whether the National Liberals' strategy of seeking to keep open the possibility of liberal reforms of the Imperial constitution in the future, while being prepared to make all manner of compromises in the short run, was in fact as great a failure as writers of varying persuasions have repeatedly claimed.

Whatever our verdict on these questions, the fact is that Bismarck, in the course of his dealings with the separate state governments and with the Reichstag majority, was swept a long way forward from the position he originally adopted. His first scheme was for a fairly powerless Reichstag, which could safely be permitted to be elected on the basis of universal, equal and direct suffrage. (Later he was occasionally to consider other options, involving the combination of a franchise biased heavily in favour of the wealthy and corporatist forms of representation based on occupational and economic interests.) The aim was that the agencies of the executive should be kept at arm's length from the Reichstag, so firmly anchored in the Prussian Ministry of State and in the committees of the Bundesrat (or Federal Council) that the Reichstag parties would be able to exert little influence over them. This would have made it extremely difficult for Parliament to exercise control over the policies of the 'Confederated Governments' (to be implemented by the Presidency), let alone for a parliamentary majority to play an active part in shaping policy, unless the party leaders themselves were conceded the chance of being appointed as delegates to the Bundesrat. The liberals quite properly put their finger on the most serious shortcoming of this constitutional draft, which was that the precise legal status of the executive within the overall constitutional structure was left undefined. Without such a definition the executive could not be held to account if the need arose.[28] The National Liberals themselves, however, by rigidly insisting on a rather bureaucratic solution (namely, a collective Reich Ministry) helped to blur the questions at issue and made it significantly easier for Bismarck to resist analogous proposals put forward by individual heads of federal state governments, including the Grand Duke of Oldenburg and the Crown Prince.[29] Rather, Bismarck stuck stubbornly to his original intention of governing the North German Confederation, and then the Empire, essentially on the basis of subsidiarity – in practice, from Prussia – and of dispensing with formal Reich ministries altogether, even after it had become clear that pressure from the parties and from public opinion had caused the balance to shift increasingly in favour of enhanced powers for the Confederation.

Bismarck's overriding idea was that the business of the Empire should essentially be conducted from Prussia, with the Bundesrat serving in an intermediary role as the representative of the governments of the federal states. The Bundesrat was conceived as both an organ of the legislature and a part of the executive, and in theory – by virtue of representing the 'Confederated Governments', which in Bismarck's eyes were jointly sovereign – had a pivotal role within the constitutional structure. The committees of the Bundesrat were intended, at any rate in the original scheme, to function somewhat in the stead of accountable federal ministries; the executive, represented *vis-à-vis* the Reichstag through the Chancellor alone, would operate, formally if not in fact, more or less as an instrument of the Bundesrat.

The advantages of this complicated pluralistic system of shared authority are obvious. Prussia's position of hegemony within the structure could be cemented in relatively unobtrusive fashion; the higher ranks of the Prussian bureaucracy became, *de facto*, a vital component of the power structure. For one thing, the Prussian delegates to the Bundesrat found it easy, given the support of the small north German duodecimo states, to control that body in exactly the way the Prussian state government – that is, the Prussian Foreign Minister and Chancellor – wished. In addition, the Bundesrat was totally dependent on the administrative groundwork and support provided by the Prussian ministries and, later, by the Imperial Home Office.[30] However, the system possessed a further feature, one which Bismarck himself regarded as crucial: it enabled a permanent and insurmountable barrier to be placed in the way of the ambitions of the Reichstag.[31] As is often pointed out, Bismarck did all he could – and not only during the period while the Empire was being established – to sustain the legal fiction that the Reichstag parties were dealing, not with an Imperial government, however made up, but with the 'Confederated Governments'. Using similar logic, he sought to place the narrowest possible construction on the constitutional prerogatives of the Chancellor as an 'official of the Presidency' and to locate the responsibility for legislative decision-making entirely with the delegates to the Bundesrat, acting under the instructions of the individual governments. The role that the Chancellor played within the legislative process, he once claimed (in April 1869), was 'precisely nil'.[32] Even allowing, however, for the fact that there were power-ful reasons at the time for preserving the façade of active participation by the federal state governments in the business of the North German Confederation, this claim is an astonishing one and was grossly at odds with the true state of affairs. It is quite clear that the exercise primarily served a domestic political purpose. The aim was to conceal, as far as possi-ble, the real relationship of the Reich executive *vis-à-vis* the Reichstag and the parties, behind the formalism of representation of the 'Confederated Governments', in order to protect the executive from direct Reichstag con-trol. The result was that the executive, well shielded from the Reichstag, enjoyed a remarkable degree of freedom of manoeuvre in its relations with competing bodies within the constitution. There can be no doubt that the fact that the legal basis of the government of the Empire lay in the Bundesrat, even though the principle was quickly seen to be a pure fiction, remained a severe impediment to the introduction of parliamentary reform into the constitution right through until September 1918.

This structure was, obviously, purpose-built to serve the interests of con-servative power. In many ways, however, the solution (which has no paral-lel among other European constitutions) must be regarded as a pyrrhic victory. The Bundesrat was permanently relegated to a shadowy exis-tence.[33] On the one hand, it was the body in which, formally speaking, sov-ereignty was jointly vested, and hence was seen, first, as the possible starting point for an anti-parliamentary solution of the German question and, later, as the possible vehicle for a coup. On the other hand, however, it had the drawback in practice of leaving the Chancellor quite isolated when standing up against the other constitutional bodies that played a significant role in the decision-making process: the Crown, the Prussian Ministry of State and the Reichstag. For Bismarck, with the enormous prestige that he could bring to bear, this did not matter so much; for his successors, though, it was to become a problem. During the First World War Bethmann Hollweg made some attempts, by activating the Bundesrat committee for foreign affairs, to create a political power base among the central German states that would act as a counterweight to the intransigence of the Prussian Ministry of State and the two houses of the Prussian parliament; but the attempts ended in failure.

Altogether, what seemed to be the ideal solution at the time, namely the informal underwriting of Prussian hegemony, had highly ambivalent conse-quences in the long run. The running of the Reich became the structural responsibility of the Prussian state government, and this served to weaken the power and position of those Chancellors who succeeded Bismarck. The system favoured the Chancellor only if he was simultaneously undisputed master of the Prussian higher civil service. After Bismarck, however, Imperial authority fell victim to growing conflict between the Empire and Prussia, and this conflict was the main reason why the system of govern-ment in the German Empire became stalled – to fateful effect – after 1912.[34]

A similar point applies to the make-up of the federal executive, which has probably been the most hotly disputed of all the questions involving the constitution. Bismarck originally wanted the office of federal Chancellor to be merely a subsidiary function of the office of the Prussian Foreign Minister, clearly hoping that its political significance could be kept as small as possible. This idea, however, soon proved to be unworkable. Instead, even during the preliminaries to the constitutional deliberations proper, the role of the Chancellor was amended so that it became, *de facto*, the focal point at which all threads of power came together, with the result, in turn, that Bismarck himself became the only person who could be considered for the post. There is disagreement about the extent to which these changes came about as a result of pressure from the liberal movement, which had been calling, very reasonably, for a clear constitutional definition of the role of the executive. Otto Becker and, following him, Lothar Gall have argued strongly, as we have said, that Bismarck merely let the National Liberals push him in the direction in which he intended to go anyway. However, this is true only in a strictly limited sense. Although Bismarck, in being forced to accede to an enhancement of the role of the federal Chancellor within the constitutional structure, may also have been acting in a way that suited his own personal desire for power, the effect was nevertheless to create areas of institutional vacuum that Bismarck himself was then soon forced to fill, against his original wishes, by building up his own ramified apparatus of Imperial administrative departments – departments which then inevitably came into competition with the corresponding ministries in Prussia.

On the other hand, the National Liberals' pressure for a clear constitutional definition of the functions of the executive brought only a few positive gains. This was particularly the case with regard to the central political question of the Chancellor's accountability. As has already been mentioned, it was certainly not the National Liberals' aim to bring about parliamentary government on the British model. Their main preoccupation was to establish the general principle of constitutionality on a secure basis: partly because the period of constitutional conflict, only recently concluded, was still fresh in their minds, and partly because they were anxious to forestall the danger that the numerous questions that had remained open during the negotiations on the constitution (for example, budgetary powers, or the scope of press freedom) might later be resolved to their own disadvantage. When Wagener objected that the right of impeachment had fallen entirely into disuse within the British parliamentary system, Miquel made a point of insisting that the situation in Germany was different from that in Britain, where 'constitutional government [had] become party government' and 'Parliament completely [dominated] the executive'.[35] By contrast, the liberals did press for greater clarification of administrative technicalities with regard to the organization of the executive. However, although Article 18 of the constitution of the North German Confederation specified that the Chancellor was answerable for all actions of the Presidency, the hope that this principle could be given substance in the form of legal accountability fell by the wayside, to say nothing of the broader demand for a collective Ministry combined with individual ministerial accountablity for separate portfolios. This first version of the constitution, in other words, left crucial questions unresolved, with concrete answers being made to wait on future developments.

In a sense, the demand of the National Liberals for the creation of Reich ministries was actually met later on, though only by the back door and in incomplete form. However, the rejection of attempts to define the status of the federal and, later, the Imperial executive in formal constitutional terms was only one of numerous essentially negative decisions that left the actual point of issue in abeyance. Subsequently the relationship between the Imperial bodies (which, of course, lacked any administrative support structure of their own) and the Prussian ministries was to become a frequent source of conflict: indeed, the exact constitutional balance between the two sets of institutions was never definitively spelled out. Whether, though, this served unequivocally to bolster Prussia's position of dominance, as had originally been intended, is actually very doubtful. The assumption of Imperial responsibilities by the Prussian authorities led to an intertwining of the Imperial and the Prussian bureaucracies from which Prussian interests did not always emerge victorious. Karl Erich Born speaks, with some justice, of the 'Imperialization' of Prussia in this respect.[36] A similar result arose because of the special prerogatives of the Prussian Crown, specifically with regard to military matters. The considerable degree of protection from parliamentary control that was accorded to the military, by virtue of the special status of the Prussian War Minister and the quasi-autonomous position of the officer corps *vis-à-vis* both the Reichstag and the 'civilian' Imperial government, by no means had the effect of straightforwardly strengthening state authority, as was to become only too plain to Bismarck himself. The constitution did not foresee 'personal rule' by the monarch, but it certainly created the opportunity for such a regime to come about.

All told, the constitution of the North German Confederation, far from providing definitive answers to all questions, left a considerable number of them dangling in mid-air. This was in part due to the particular circumstances of its origin. Bismarck himself was quite prepared to accept criticism on this count. 'I readily admit,' he said in the Reichstag on 16 April 1869, when the National Liberals were making a renewed attempt to introduce accountable federal ministries, 'that the federal constitution is incomplete. It was not merely created in a hurry: it was created at a time when the building land was very difficult to work, when the terrain was rough – but when the land absolutely had to be used.'[37] On the other hand, Bismarck made it quite clear that there were no circumstances in which he would be prepared to contemplate a revision of the constitution. This was particularly true, of course, of the phase when the Empire was being founded in the strict sense. In theory there might have been an opportunity to carry out a thorough-going overhaul of the constitutional apparatus at the moment when the south German states joined the North German Confederation and the latter was then transformed into the German Empire. The only changes that were made, however, were to matters affecting the relationship between the south German states and the Reich, the position of the Emperor and the role of the army. Bismarck firmly resisted any alteration of the constitution's complex structure, and specifically of the crucial formal role of the Bundesrat. He even opposed the suggestion that the Bundesrat be renamed the 'Reichsrat', since this would have called into question its character as the body representing the federal states.[38] The constitution of the North German Confederation, in other words, was merely adapted to the new situation; it was not subjected to fundamental change. For their part, the National Liberals desisted from renewing their pressure for ministerial accountability, while the attempts by the Centre to achieve basic protection against the arbitrary exercise of state power through the inclusion of legal safeguards, modelled on the Prussian constitution, came to nothing. The negotiations with the Constituent Reichstag over the recasting of the constitution did lead to the adoption of a number of new provisions, but the constitution's general character remained largely unaltered. Indeed, on several counts its principal feature – the fact that it steered clear of any clear-cut definition of the spheres of jurisdiction of different centres of power, and left contentious questions unresolved – was actually further reinforced. This was the case not only with regard to the institutional structure of the Imperial executive and the relationship between the executive and the federal governments (in particular, the Prussian Ministry of State), but also to a considerable number of other matters, notably the question of the military budget. Here the only solution was a compromise limited to three years, followed by another temporary expedient in the form of a septennial review.

It has often been said that the constitution of the German Empire was conceived in such a way as to rule out any evolution in the direction of greater liberty and parliamentary accountability. It is undeniably the case that Bismarck was anxious from the start that there should be numerous built-in safeguards against the ambitions of the Reichstag and the political parties. The real weakness of the constitution, however, was that it left too many questions undecided, not too few. At first this worked to the Chancellor's advantage, as he made masterly use of the opportunities the constitution gave him to reinforce his own power. However, shrewd observers were quick to see that the solution was double-edged. Constantin Frantz, for example, anxiously posed the question: 'How much vital energy can we expect of any design that depends in reality on one pair of eyes alone?'[39] The constitution was a compromise not only in the sense that it embodied distinct, barely reconcilable constitutional traditions but because it was a 'system of skirted decisions' in which numerous questions remained unresolved, the answers left to wait upon future events.

It was, nevertheless, this very fact, as much as any other, that made the constitution acceptable to the principal parties engaged in the negotiations over its contents. The constitution granted Bismarck wide scope to build up an informal system of personal plebiscitary rule, an opportunity which he did not shrink from exploiting ruthlessly; in the eyes of contemporaries, at least, he emerged as the clear victor of the negotiations. From the National Liberals' point of view, the result fell some way short of the pure, unitary constitutional system they had hoped to achieve, and yet they were confident that the road towards such a system was not blocked.[40] It would soon become clear, of course, that this judgement was too optimistic. Indeed, the liberal parties quickly found that they had become trapped inside an artfully constructed pseudo-constitutional structure that crushed most of their political aspirations, even while it enabled many of their economic goals to be realized and allowed many of their social policies to be implemented at a local level.

As far as the ruling conservative elites were concerned, the constitution certainly gave Prussia undisputed supremacy within, or dominion over, Germany for the foreseeable future and concentrated an exceptional amount of power in the hands of the Prussian monarchy. In addition, vital areas of the executive were kept more or less intact from party-political control, despite the fact that the scope of the Reichstag's authority had turned out to be be much wider than Bismarck had originally envisaged. National Liberalism, representing the rising strata of the middle class, seemed, for the time being at least, to have been successfully locked into a system of rule that remained essentially authoritarian. There was, nevertheless, still the nagging question: would it be possible to keep the power of the Reichstag within bounds in the long run? This fear soon sparked off 'domestic preventive wars' once it became apparent that universal, equal and direct suffrage was leading to the emergence of mass parties of a new type, which were ready to jettison the old rules of the game of domestic *Honoratioren* politics. The anxieties of Prussia's ultra-conservatives that Bismarck's strategy, despite its ostentatiously greater-Prussian character, would nevertheless cause Prussia eventually to lose her position of dominance were by no means unfounded. These anxieties were reinforced by the fact that modernization was meanwhile being allowed to proceed largely unchecked, at the expense of particularist interests, notably those of the aristocracy.

On the other side, the Centre's opposition to the design of the Imperial constitution, the provisions of which it saw as comparing badly with those even of the constitution of Prussia, was entirely comprehensible. Paradoxically, though, it was the Centre that was subsequently most adept at exploiting for its own purposes the opportunities that the constitution created. The democratic left, by contrast, and *a fortiori* the embryonic Social Democratic movement, not surprisingly derived no advantages whatever from the new constitutional structure, which they regarded in any case as a calamitous dilution and distortion of the great democratic constitution of 1848–49.

In social terms the Imperial constitution of 1871 was a delaying device: a compromise in which authority was divided between the traditional ruling elites and the rising middle classes. The compromise was complicated by the constitution's federal structure, though this was in fact federal only in a nominal sense and in practice ensured Prussia's long-term hegemony. The constitution created a pluralistic system of power, the centrifugal tendencies of which were held temporarily in check by Bismarck's ability to exert a unifying force by personal plebiscitary means.[41] The power of the conservative aristocracy was left largely untouched; indeed, through the incorporation of sections of the rising middle class, the nobility was given something of a new lease of life. The army and the officer corps were shielded, for the time being at least, from the encroachments of democracy, the officer corps in particular retaining a guaranteed position of privilege within society under the aegis of the so-called royal 'power of command' or *Kommandogewalt*. In the spheres of economic and social policy, on the other hand, the middle class was given free rein to modernize the economic and legal infrastructure, albeit on condition that the specific prerogatives of the monarchy were not violated. The higher civil service, particularly in Prussia, acquired a key role within this semi-constitutional structure, since it was generally able to dictate the agenda to the Reichstag and the parties. The unifying power of the throne also played a part in subduing the parties' political energies and safeguarding the considerable room for manoeuvre that the executive enjoyed.

Of course, as new sections of society became politically active – notably the working class, but also the lower middle class and the peasantry – this division of authority was eventually to prove a fragile one. It created the framework within which the remarkable modernization of German society took place, but it did not enable the broad mass of the population to play a steadily increasing part in the political process, and in due course this fact was to become a significant source of instability.

It remains for us to categorize the German Imperial constitution in comparative terms. Within the context of the European continent as a whole, it was midway in character between, on the one hand, the more advanced constitutions of western and parts of southern Europe and, on the other, the incomparably more authoritarian systems of the east and south-east. At first sight at least, it was strikingly progressive, inasmuch as it enshrined the democratic principle of universal, equal and direct suffrage and the secret ballot. In this respect, although the full effects of 'one man, one vote' were muted by the fact that members of the Reichstag were prevented from receiving remuneration (and later also by the *Kulturkampf* and the Socialist Law), the constitution of the German Empire was one of the most advanced of its era. By contrast, the suffrage in Great Britain remained extremely circumscribed, even after the electoral reforms of 1884 and

1885, while in the France of Napoleon III the franchise heavily favoured the wealthy (although a modern democratic franchise with few restrictions was introduced later). In most of the other European constitutions, such as that of Italy, there were far stricter limits on active citizenship than was the case in Germany.

On the other hand, the scope for parliamentary bodies to exert effective influence over policy decisions was much wider in those countries than it was in the German Empire. Despite, or perhaps because of, the fact of democratic suffrage, the German constitution retained a firm central core of authoritarian institutions of government, in this sense resembling more closely the highly antiquated constitutional systems of Austria-Hungary and Russia. The Emperor and King of Prussia was entitled to exercise a plethora of rights that were immune, either in whole or in part, from parliamentary control. More significantly, the running of the executive was placed in the hands of a Chancellor who, while formally 'accountable', functioned in constitutional terms as the authorized agent of the Bundesrat, which was not subject either to political or to legal constraints: the Chancellor was therefore not dependent on majorities in the Reichstag even in a non-formal sense. As we have seen, the federal structure of the German Empire served partly to safeguard the independent status of the federated states (although their rights to an effective share in the running of the Empire in fact remained largely nominal) but its primary purpose was to curtail the power of the Reichstag and the parties.

The fact that the Bundesrat, as the body representing the 'Confederated Governments', was beyond the reach of the Reichstag parties, while, at the same time, central elements of the activity of the state (notably the role of the army) were partly shielded from parliamentary control, is the principal reason for saying, with Max Weber, that the Imperial system was only 'semi-constitutional' or even 'pseudo-constitutional'. That the Bundesrat was generally overshadowed by the Imperial Chancellor, and that in practice the Prussian ministries (and later the Imperial departments) played the decisive role in the preparation of legislation, is not the real point. The executive was able to exert far-reaching control over the Bundesrat through the Prussian federal delegates who took instructions from it, and through the delegates of the smallest states: it was generally able to get the Bundesrat to serve as an unresisting instrument of Imperial policies. It was this that enormously strengthened the hand of the executive *vis-à-vis* the Reichstag, making the system a highly bureaucratic form of government, despite its parliamentary trappings.

The constitutional obstacles that stood in the way of the emergence of true parliamentary democracy in the German Empire were, in other words, substantial. It was no accident that Max Weber, deliberating after 1906 on the best way in which the Imperial constitution might be reformed, seriously considered whether the influence of the political parties should be strengthened, not by making the position of the Chancellor formally dependent on a majority in the Reichstag, but by turning the Bundesrat itself into a parliamentary body. The leaders of the parties would be admitted to the Bundesrat either as delegates of the Empire or, if appropriate, as representatives of the balance of political forces in the parliaments of the individual states, and would determine Imperial policy, from the centre outwards, in line with their parties' wishes. Weber accordingly set great store by ending the bar on simultaneous membership of the Reichstag and the Bundesrat. (In the first draft of the constitution of the North German Confederation, incidentally, simultaneous membership had not been ruled out.)[42]

In substantive terms, the Bundesrat assumed only a marginal role in the process of political decision-making, although not an entirely nominal one. The structure, however, created the basis for the informal dominance of the Prussian machinery of rule, and it gave the Prussian higher civil service a pivotal role in the system. The civil service, in turn, was not only closely intertwined with the ruling aristocratic elites, in both personal and material terms, but had a vested interest in the maintenance of a system of division of power within which it possessed room for virtually unimpeded manoeuvre. It is this fact, in particular, that makes the constitutional system of the German Empire akin to those of Russia and of the Cis-Leithan part of the Austro-Hungarian monarchy, which in other respects were markedly more authoritarian. The Russian regime was an autocracy; the Habsburg monarchy was underpinned by a German-speaking bureaucracy; and in all three cases the army constituted an additional pillar of monarchical authority, largely protected from civil control.

From the start, the unusually strong position of the civil service (socially very homogeneous, and closely bound to the throne through the oath of office, tradition and recruitment) within what was otherwise in large part a constitutional system of government substantially reduced the likelihood that the German Empire would gradually evolve towards parliamentary democracy. There was a second reason too: namely, the state of hostility and confrontation that existed between the legislature, in the form of the Reichstag, and the executive. The gulf between the ministries, which were responsible for preparing parliamentary bills, and the parties in the Reichstag was extremely wide and did not become any narrower as the activities of the state gradually expanded into new areas of society. Under such circumstances the efforts of the Reichstag were principally confined to a negative form of politics, with harmful consequences for the standards of its work and the vitality of its members, as Max Weber pointed out. The constitution created a fundamental structural division between the two political elites of the Empire: between making a career in Parliament and making a career in government. With a tiny number of exceptions, candidates for ministerial office were selected, as they had previously been, from members of the ruling aristocracy and their kinsmen in the higher civil service; members of Parliament, on the other hand, had little prospect of ever becoming accountable as ministers. There were very few instances – and no successful ones – in which the gap between Reichstag and ministerial office was bridged, with the exception of the brief interlude when Count Hertling served as Chancellor in 1917-18.

On this score, the constitutions of Great Britain, France and Italy, while much less democratic in electoral terms, differed fundamentally from that of the German Empire. Although the proportion of people in these countries who were entitled to participate directly or indirectly in major political decisions was much more tightly circumscribed, both in law and in practice, there was constant mutual interaction between the executive and legislative arms of government. At the same time, moreover, there was a much higher level of circulation within the ruling elites in the narrower sense. In Germany, on the other hand, a two-tier system of political leadership emerged that never really broke down except in a few individual cases (such as the rise of Miquel to become Prussian Finance Minister). Members of Parliament and the governing bureaucracy had relatively little in common. Admittance to the latter was mainly reserved for the traditional aristocratic class, although it became increasingly difficult to exclude middle-class professional people. Leading party-political figures, on the other hand, generally stood no chance of implementing in government the policies for which they campaigned in Parliament, and if they did, it was on condition of giving up their parliamentary power base and their party position. This feature of the German Imperial system was the main reason why there was no smooth transition to parliamentary government of the sort that happened in most other comparable countries.

On the other hand, the bureaucratic nature of the system had the effect of radicalizing the parties, causing them to adapt increasingly to the principles of popular sovereignty, even though there was no outlet for such principles within the constitution. By the same token, it served to intensify party-political conflict. The fact that the design of the constitution was biased against the parties did not itself prevent further power from accruing to the Reichstag as the functions of the state expanded, in accordance with what can be seen as a general long-term trend of the later nineteenth century. To this extent it is no contradiction of the thesis of 'semi-constitutionality' to note that in the course of time the Reichstag steadily found itself being pushed into overstepping the prescribed limits of its role within the constitution. Instead of confining itself to legislative matters, it began to seek to influence the concrete policies of the government, using all means that lay at its disposal. Usually, however, it could do so only in a negative sense, with the result that the gulf between the government and the parties (the former remaining bureaucratic in cast, the latter increasingly seeing themselves as democratic) grew ever wider. By the end of Bismarck's tenure of power there were already early signs that the German Empire was becoming ungovernable. The fall of Bülow over the question of Imperial financial reform in 1909 marked the beginning of the death-agony of Bismarck's constitutional structure, and this in turn eventually helped to drag Europe into war. It was only under wartime conditions that long-overdue changes were made to the constitution, to adapt it to a society that had profoundly altered. By that stage, however, it was too late to prevent the collapse of the Empire altogether.

3

The Prussian conception of the state and the German idea of Empire: Prussia and the German Empire in recent German history

The remarks that follow are concerned mainly with the period after 1866,[1] since it is the changes in politics and society which took place after the mid-point of the nineteenth century, and reached their culmination in the First World War, that have been the principal reason why the image of Prussia in German and European history has been, on the whole, a sombre one. The period of the Weimar Republic, incidentally, seems to me – and here I differ from Karl-Dietrich Bracher[2] and, in some measure, from Horst Möller – to have constituted the final stage in the decomposition of the Empire, rather than a truly new beginning. I agree with Bracher that the so-called Papen putsch of 20 June 1932 should be regarded as the real end of Prussia, in the sense of representing the demise of a specifically Prussian conception of the state.[3] The major events that determined the course of Prussian history, however, occurred much earlier, in the second half of the nineteenth and the early years of the twentieth century. It was this period that saw the dissolution of the Prussian conception of the state and the emergence in its place of the nationalistic 'new German' idea of Empire, which drove the independent Prussian tradition – to the extent that it survived at all – into a purely defensive posture and deprived it of the highly integrative force it had originally exerted.

My thesis, couched in ideal-type terms, is that the supersession of the Prussian conception of the state by the nationalist Imperial ideology of the new Germany (the latter first making itself felt in the age of Bismarck and then reaching its zenith in the Wilhelmine era) had the effect of reinforcing the shortcomings of each of the two political traditions, while at the same time crucially weakening, and eventually distorting beyond recognition, the virtues that each tradition also possessed. It is particularly important, in my judgement, that the relationship between Prussia and the German Empire of Bismarck and Wilhelm II should be considered from this point of view (that is, from the point of view of social and intellectual history) and not just on the level of institutions (which in any case have been examined very expertly by Lothar Gall).[4]

According to the 'Borussian' interpretation, Prussia's role during the establishment of the Empire and her subsequent position of hegemony within the Imperial political system were merely the fulfilment of an historic mission that had always been inherent in Prussian history. Hans Joachim Schoeps, however, pointed out (though without doing much more than arouse polite interest) that the creation of the Empire had effectively put an end to the Prussia of the past. In a sense, Schoeps was echoing the verdict of the Old Conservatives: in his view, their resistance to Bismarck's policies in the first decade after the founding of the Reich had been entirely logical, since the new system was bound eventually to leave Prussia in a subordinate position. And today, indeed, it can no longer be disputed that although the system of authority that was created in the Bismarckian empire was a complex and many-layered one, the status that was granted within it to the middle class was secure enough to mean that the displacement of the old Prussian conservative elites would only be a matter of time. There is ample evidence to show that the only way in which the pre-eminence of the Prussian aristocracy within the state and society could be sustained in the new era of what Morazé calls 'les bourgeois conquérants' was by dint of the 'conservative revolution from above' that Bismarck set in train during the period when the Empire was being established.

At the same time, however, we should not ignore the fact that the new political system was founded on a compromise. It debarred the liberal middle classes from playing an active role in the political process, whether through parliamentary or, failing that, advanced constitutional government, even while it also gave them considerable scope for implementing their principles in the spheres of economic and social policy and at local-government level. The political system of the German Empire was devised, from the first, so as to give maximum protection from parliamentary influence to those institutions that had always been the particular preserve of the conservative elites – the army, the civil service and, above all, the leading agencies of foreign policy – by making them subject to the exclusive prerogative of the King and, later, the Emperor. Bismarck devoted considerable energy to achieving this result, and during the reign of Wilhelm II repeated attempts were made to extend further the sphere of the so-called royal 'power of command' (*Kommandogewalt*), in order to shield the army and the officer corps as much as possible from the encroachments of Parliament and the pressures of public opinion.

All of these arrangements were expressly regarded as conforming to the

Prussian conception of the state – or rather, what was perceived as such. From the time of the Prussian constitutional conflict of the 1860s, if not earlier, it had been an uncontested axiom of Prussian state doctrine that parliamentary institutions should not intervene in the direct relationship between the monarch and the army; in particular, the bond of loyalty between the Crown and the officer corps should not be weakened. The same principle was deemed to apply to the higher civil service, which was extremely conscious of its obligations to the monarch, who made all higher administrative appointments in person. Foreign policy was regarded as the most important Crown prerogative of all – not least, in Bismarck's day, because of the debatable assumption that as the 'art of the possible', it could be conducted only at a far remove from the pressures of public opinion. Under Wilhelm II, of course, this practice degenerated into 'personal rule' by the Emperor, with the monarch intervening high-handedly in the conduct of foreign policy, often precisely in order to pander to public opinion as he perceived it. Even though homage continued to be widely paid to the constitutional fictions of the Prussian conception of the state, the eventual reality was something quite different. Governments were swept along on a current of popular, imperialist nationalism that became increasingly blind to the realities of international relations.

Traditional conservative militarists had favoured an army that would be relatively small but would be led by a largely aristocratic officer corps, imbued with monarchist sentiments and the ideals of Prussian statehood, and would be quite capable of dealing with internal enemies such as the Social Democrats. Increasingly, however, a new middle-class militarism began to come to the fore, eager to make full use of German military strength and do away with antiquated aristocratic customs in order to realize Germany's potential on the world stage.[5] The most significant spokesman of such attitudes on the General Staff was the middle-class parvenu Ludendorff, whose fervent campaign, backed by sections of middle-class opinion, for the creation of three additional army corps led to his transfer to a regimental command in Düsseldorf in 1913. On the civilian side, political pressure groups such as the Army League (Wehrverein) and the Navy League (Flottenverein) emerged as mouthpieces for a policy of all-out armament-building on land and sea, and even flirted openly with the notion of preventive war. In Parliament the bourgeois parties at the centre of the political spectrum, most notably the National Liberals, made a provocative 'Weltpolitik', or 'world policy', the centrepiece of their programme and pressed for Germany to exploit her superior weapons as bargaining tools and, if necessary, not to flinch from using them in action.

In view of these latter facts, it is a mistake to hold the traditional Prussian ruling elites primarily responsible for the fact that the German Empire (which in Bismarck's day essentially pursued a policy designed to preserve the peace) was subsequently led astray into the pursuit of an aggressive brand of imperialism that in due course, partly against the better judgement of the statesmen responsible, led to the outbreak of the First World War. The pattern of wrong turnings and unhappy decisions in German history is much more complex than many proponents of a revisionist German historiography are prepared to admit – justifiably anxious though they have been to counter the glossed-over accounts that still characterized national-liberal scholarship in the 1920s and early 1930s. Rather, two factors were jointly responsible for the policies that finally led to the collapse of the German Empire. One was the Prussian conception of a powerful state, espoused by a governing elite which, by virtue of Prussia's position of hegemony within the Empire, played a pivotal role in the formulation of policy. The other was the naive nationalism, largely untroubled by any real knowledge of the facts of the international system, that was adopted by the rising middle classes. It is only fair to point out that in many cases the Prussian conception of the state was invoked by figures who were actually spokesmen of the 'new German' nationalism, such as Heinrich von Treitschke and, later, Friedrich von Bernhardi, in support of a supposedly Prussian doctrine of world-wide power politics that in reality had virtually nothing in common with the views of the traditional aristocratic governing elites.[6] Conversely, when Bethmann Hollweg, for example, during negotiations over the reform of Prussia's three-class electoral system in 1911, appealed to 'divinely ordained relations of dependence' that no constitutional reform could erase, it is arguable that what he was seeking to do was to protect his own weak bargaining position rather than defend the traditional pre-eminence of the aristocracy in Prussia.

Leaving aside specific questions, it is undeniable that in the eyes not only of committed German liberals but of opinion abroad, the blame for the shortcomings of the German political system has been attributed mainly, though not entirely, to the continuing dominance of Prussia within Germany. The most important aim declared by the British government under Asquith at the start of the First World War was the elimination of Prussian militarism and, as a corollary, the removal from power of the Prussian governing elites. Similarly, during the Second World War the Allies speedily agreed that Prussia as a state had to disappear for good, come what may, since she was the repository of aggressive militarist and anti-democratic traditions that had to be expunged if lasting peace in Europe were ever to come about.

To an important extent, however, these verdicts have rested on an historical misunderstanding. The truth is that the rising middle classes in Prussia and Germany bore a greater responsibility for the expansionist policies of the era before 1914, and also for the radical revisionism of the period between the wars, than did the Prussian ruling elites in the narrower sense. These misconceptions show, I believe, that for a long time the real Prussia had been largely lost to view behind the constitutional structure of the

Empire, a structure that unquestionably acted as a retarding factor throughout the Empire's lifetime.

By comparison with Germany as a whole, in fact, Prussia was far from being simply reactionary, certainly before the 1860s. In the judgement both of contemporaries and of present-day historians, the Prussia of the first half of the nineteenth century was very much a modern state, embracing and profiting from the cause of progress, albeit within certain characteristic limits. The modernization carried out in the Prussian state and in society by the Prussian reformers may have been cautious, but it pointed in the right direction and in several respects went further than did reform in many, if not most, of the other German states. This applies particularly, as Thomas Nipperdey has impressively demonstrated, to the establishment of the new university system, in which research was given pride of place.[7] Similarly, Prussia became a pioneering campaigner for the principle of free trade, even though the business community itself was not always wholly enthusiastic. It is certainly the case that during the revolution of 1848–49 Prussia proved a bitter disappointment to her friends, both inside and outside her borders, who had seen her as the most modern of the German states and hence obviously equipped to take the lead on the German question. Prussia failed to rise to the occasion, ignoring the middle classes' call for national unity and constitutional freedom. Nevertheless, the Prussian constitution of 1850, while falling short in certain respects of the modern constitutions of western Europe – such as that of Belgium, on which it had ostensibly been modelled (comparisons with Great Britain are not appropriate) – was perfectly fitted to evolve along liberal lines.[8] As Friedrich Naumann repeatedly stressed, it was the first enacted German constitution to contain a catalogue of basic rights. Indeed, the main strategic tenet of the German middle class in the 1850s and 1860s was that if Prussia, which was already progressive in terms of domestic policy, were to adopt the principle of constitutionality in a whole-hearted manner, she would inevitably assume the undisputed 'moral leadership' of Germany as a whole. It is fair to say that in this period Prussia had the chance of becoming a liberal state on the English Whig model.

It is also a mistake, incidentally, to accuse the Prussian ruling classes, without further examination, of being highly exclusive by the standards prevailing in Europe at the time. This was not true even of the Prussian nobility in the strict sense. It is certainly the case that Prussian aristocrats constituted a closed caste in comparison with the 'open aristocracy' of Great Britain, which had a remarkable capacity for assimilating new varieties of political opinion and was cross-fertilized by leading middle-class families from finance and industry. The Prussian aristocracy had also partly lost its social autonomy by declining, by and large, into a *Dienstadel* (deriving its titles from service to the king), since the big agricultural estates had never been sufficiently productive on their own account to provide their owners with a standard of living on a par with their social status.[9] On the other hand, in contrast with, say, the position in Austria, restrictions on intermarriage between the middle class and even the higher nobility were remarkably slight.[10] Similarly, the transformation of the aristocratic landowning class into a body of agrarian entrepreneurs with a rising proportion of middle-class members had begun to take place at a relatively early date.

The educated elite also played a sizeable role in the Prussian state civil service, although there were admittedly only intermittent occasions when it turned this position to modestly progressive account, as during the reform era and, later, on the question of Prussian higher education during the Wilhelmine period. In a sense Prussian reformism should be interpreted as a belated instance of enlightened despotism and not, as it often is, as an instance of bureaucratic liberalism.[11] Civil servants regarded themselves as agents neither of the aristocratic elites nor of the rising bourgeoisie, but as a class owing its allegiance to the Prussian state as such. With good reason, Hegel described the civil service as a 'universal estate' (*allgemeiner Stand*), by which he meant that it was not tied to a particular sectional interest: by contrast with the position in the British parliamentary system before 1832, it was fitted to promote policies that were not class-bound in the narrow sense. The Kantian ideals and virtues to which the administrative class subscribed undoubtedly sprang from more than mere political vested interest, although motives of such a sort did play their part; indeed, these qualities remain an essential element of our conception of the functions of a modern state civil service, dedicated to the public interest for its own sake.

We can say, then, that until the 1860s, events in Prussia (despite the restorationist policy adopted during the revolution of 1848–49, and despite the subsequent period of reaction) did not lead in one direction and one direction alone: namely, towards conservatism and away from liberal middle-class constitutionalism. They did not, that is, mark out a German 'Sonderweg', a peculiarly German path towards semi-constitutional government. The constitutional conflict of the years 1862–66, however, was a major watershed in this respect; and it was recognized as such by both parties to the conflict. We may recall Bismarck's provocative words, uttered at an early stage of the constitutional crisis: 'The Prussian monarchy has not yet completed its mission: it is not yet ready to become a mere ornament on your constitutional edifice, not yet ready to be inserted as a dead component into the machinery of the parliamentary system.'[12]

Bismarck's triumph in 1866, indeed, was not followed by a simple extension to the North German Confederation of the moderate constitutionalism that had characterized the system of government in Prussia. It led instead to the creation of a pseudo-constitutional system, albeit one with marked supplementary parliamentary features. The Prussian institutions were turned into mere instruments of the Imperial Chancellor's *de facto* Caesarist rule, while at the same time all major decisions – on questions such as the Reichstag's budgetary powers, or the structure and role of what was later to be called the 'Reichsleitung', i.e. the Imperial government – were actually left in abeyance.

The role of Prussia within the constitutional structure of the Bismarckian Empire is generally characterized as one of hegemony. Prussia is seen as holding many of the reins of power, as a result of the symbiotic relationship between the royal throne of Prussia and the Imperial throne of Germany, of the fact that the Chancellor was also Prussian Minister President (or at least Prussian Foreign Minister), of the extensive overlap between Prussian ministerial departments and Imperial ones, and of the dominant status that Prussia enjoyed within the Imperial structure as the instrument of the Prussian governing elites. This was, indeed, the way the system was originally devised, even though from the start, as a result of National Liberal pressure, there was a shift (which Bismarck nevertheless managed to prevent from being legally enshrined in the constitution) towards a nation-state system in which the Chancellor, and the Imperial government in general, assumed accountability in their own right to the Reichstag, as the body representing the interests of the German nation. The clearer it became, however, that the Empire was a political entity with an undreamed-of new dynamism, the more the initiative in the major realms of policy passed to the Empire's own institutions: specifically, to the Chancellor and to the major political parties – even though the latter were restricted (in their case, by technical constitutional constraints) to practising what Max Weber called 'negative' politics. The Prussian ministries, and to a degree Prussian policy itself, became mere tools of Imperial policy, as during the *Kulturkampf*, for example.

In this sense, Prussia's position of hegemony within the German Empire gradually proved to be a mixed blessing, since it served to undermine Prussian policy and deprive it of much of its independence. As the role of Parliament within the Empire expanded, so Prussia increasingly came to function merely as a retarding factor within the political system. It is true that the social-insurance legislation of the 1880s, for example, which is commonly agreed to have led the way in Europe, owed its inspiration to the Prussian tradition of state assistance for the poorer classes – specifically, to Bismarck's aim, originally based on paternalistic motives, that the state should make a much greater direct contribution to welfare benefits. The legislation, however, was enacted at Imperial level and, characteristically, was amended along liberal lines. Prussia herself was called in only when the Reichstag failed to deliver a specific piece of repressive legislation: she lost her hereditary role as the seedbed of new political initiatives and state-led reform. Indeed, since the Reichstag had now become the outlet for all progressive political trends, the political pressure was now, in the main, on Prussia to adapt to the new circumstances within her own political system. It was at this stage that Prussia took on the political coloration that has so significantly helped to define her image ever since. To overstate the case somewhat, from now onwards Prussia degenerated into a welfare agency for needy landowners, wielding her political influence within the Empire in two principal ways: first, by seeking to obtain preferential treatment for her agriculture, notably in the form of high tariffs to protect it against foreign competition; and secondly, by doing her utmost to stem the advance of reformist Imperial policies or, if this was not possible, to shield her own power and position from the effects of political change.

No less a figure than Max Weber extolled the *Junker* class for having developed the outstanding political skills without which first Prussia and then the Empire would never have become a great power. But he also pointed to the profound social changes that permanently destroyed the economic foundations on which the aristocratic landowning class had been built. He described the great East Elbian estates as 'local centres of political authority' which, 'according to the traditions of Prussia', had been ordained to 'provide the material basis for the livelihood of a section of the population that the state had been accustomed to entrust with the responsibility for exerting political authority and for representing its military and political power'.[13] Times, however, had changed radically. 'Political power can no longer derive from a protected material foundation; on the contrary, it must be placed at the service of economic interests.'[14] Since the *Junker* class had lost its economic independence as a result of the decline in agriculture, so the case for its retention of political privileges had also collapsed. [15]

> The last and greatest of the *Junker* stood at the pinnacle of the country for a quarter of a century, and posterity will surely judge that for all the incomparable greatness of his career as a statesman, the tragedy that attached to it, and that many still fail to perceive today, was that under his leadership the nation that was his handiwork, the nation that he had united, underwent a slow, irresistible change in its economic structure and became something different – a people that was compelled to demand different arrangements from those which he could provide and to which his Caesarist nature could adapt.

The needs of the industrial society that had begun to emerge in the German Empire in the 1880s were, simply, not compatible with the continuing dominance of a purely agrarian elite. The Prussian state had done a great deal to pave the way for industrialization (although its contribution can be exaggerated, as Wolfram Fischer[16] has convincingly shown). The result, however, was that from the 1890s onwards it found itself at odds with the structural principles on which its own existence was based. The political system and the economic structure were in conflict with one another. This clash was masked by the fact that for the time being the official semi-feudal political culture survived unaltered, the reserve-officer ethos and the student duelling corporations continuing to cast their spell over large sections of the educated elite and the highest echelons of the middle class. The tension could not, however, be kept concealed indefinitely; and in the political sphere its effects became rapidly apparent.

The later phase in the evolution of Prussia, from the fall of Bismarck onwards, was dominated by mounting strains between the Prussian aristocracy, which now did its best to forge an alliance with heavy industry, and the political forces represented in the Reichstag, which had acquired greater influence as a result of the imperceptible shift of balance in the Empire's complex constitutional structure. As an assemblage of moderately progressive bourgeois parties took firmer shape in the Reichstag, so those in the conservative camp – knowing that the three-class electoral system would deliver them safe majorities – grew steadily more disposed to take refuge in their Prussian redoubt and use it as a base from which to forestall any reformist Imperial measures. The most telling instance of this attitude was the systematic undermining between 1892 and 1894 of the position of the Chancellor Leo von Caprivi, perhaps the only German Chancellor before 1914 to pursue a realistic foreign policy that might, in combination with his attempt to achieve co-operation among the warring bourgeois parties, have led the Empire out of the cul-de-sac of the German 'Sonderweg'. Another example was the Prussian conservatives' response to the question of constitutional reform for Alsace-Lorraine in 1911, although in this case their only reward was to become severely isolated in Parliament. In 1913 the ultra-conservative tendency in Prussia found its clearest expression of all, in the founding of the 'Prussian Alliance' (Preußenbund), dedicated to the 'maintenance and consolidation of the distinctive character of Prussia in the state and in the life of the people'. In practice, this organization served to defend, not the Prussian conception of the state, but merely the privileges of the beleaguered Prussian aristocracy within a society that was inexorably becoming more democratic.

To the extent that we can nevertheless speak of a persisting Prussian view of the state among the highest Prusso-German officials in this period (figures such as Theobald von Bethmann Hollweg, for example) this view was in conflict, overt as well as latent, with the basic political thrust of the conservatism of the time, both that of party politicians and that of the big landowners, for whom conservative principles had declined into the mere defence of a vested interest. The fundamental Prussian virtues – duty, justice, accountability 'before God, country and history',[17] unconditional loyalty to the throne even if the monarch's own wilfulness was doing serious damage to the conduct of policy – are, indeed, well exemplified by Bethmann Hollweg himself. The dedication and sense of duty displayed by the Prussian higher civil service, not least during the final years of the Empire, unquestionably deserve acknowledgement and a considerable degree of respect. Under the circumstances, these officials sought to do the best they could, without allowing a fundamental shift of political power in favour of the bourgeois parties to take place, especially bearing in mind the fact that the rise of Social Democracy as the major force on the left meant that it was impossible after 1912 for any workable majority in the Reichstag to be assembled.

All the same, while we should recognize that the conservative public officials of the Empire strove hard, within the situation in which they found themselves, to follow the path of political compromise and social conciliation, keeping their distance from the extremes on both the right and the left, it cannot be denied that the effect of their efforts was to promote a fatal process of bureaucratization in political decision-making, and that this process increasingly militated against the development of true political leadership.

Indeed, it is arguable that the Prussian state tradition played a crucial part in causing the system of authority in the German Empire during the post-Bismarckian era to degenerate steadily into a form of mere rule by officialdom, largely lacking the breadth of vision and political leadership that the Prussian aristocracy had originally demonstrated. Max Weber, in particular, held this view.[18] He wrote:

> Germany was governed, after the resignation of Prince von Bismarck, by 'officials' [*Beamten*] (in the true sense of the word) [...]. Germany still retained the military and civilian bureaucracy which, in its integrity, education, conscientiousness and intelligence, was the most distinguished in the world. [But] affairs of state lacked the guidance of a politician.

Weber's criticism may be overstated, but a brief glance at the circle of individuals from which Imperial Chancellors and ministers were recruited before 1914, in accordance with a long-standing tradition that was defended as Prussian in the best sense, certainly shows that political horizons had become much narrower than they had been in the old Prussia. What had once been a powerful political governing class was now clearly in decline, and there was no readiness – leaving aside isolated cases such as the appointment of Miquel as Prussian Finance Minister in 1891 – to breach traditional barriers and promote representatives of the political parties into senior positions of leadership.

To a certain extent this gradual shrinking of the recruitment pool for ministers and other senior figures in both Prussia and the Empire before 1914 reflected the social situation in which the conservative Prussian aristocracy now found itself. Whereas in Britain the aristocracy had gradually been merging with the highest strata of the middle class, to form a new upper class displaying a fairly homogeneous common life-style, in Prussia the landowning aristocracy shut itself off against the rising middle classes and forfeited the opportunity of becoming a part of Germany's emergent modern industrial society. It is therefore not surprising that questions now began to be raised, even within the conservative camp itself, whether the governing class and the higher civil service in Prussia should continue to be selected primarily from the aristocracy. Gustav Schmoller, a social scientist of firm conservative convictions, felt obliged to defend the prevailing practice of giving preference to aristocratic candidates for high public office by maintaining that once in place, they would soon be forced to steer a middle course or would even become liberals: 'The goal of a sound policy should not be to drive our eastern manorial knights out of the civil service, the army and local government, but to improve their political understanding.'[19]

In point of fact, for some time the balance within the higher bureaucracy and the officer corps had already been shifting in favour of what was then called the *gebildetes Bürgertum*: the 'educated' – that is to say, university-educated – middle class. In many ways Gustav Schmoller was a public champion of this new conservative civil-service elite, which differed from the landed aristocracy in its attitudes as well as in its material circumstances. In a sense it was the members of this caste who now preserved the legacy of the Prussian idea of the state, in the face of the opposition of the Prussian landed nobility. They sought, from conviction, to promote policies which, while essentially based on authoritarian principles, were nevertheless intended to benefit all classes equally: on the domestic front, policies designed to create social equilibrium; in foreign relations, a vigorous yet cautious approach. It is not this administrative elite that should be held principally responsible for the wrong turnings in domestic and foreign policy that were taken during the Wilhelmine period, although its members were certainly very slow to realize that there was no need to repress the Social Democratic movement by all available means and, indeed, that there was a strong likelihood that the Social Democrats, being thoroughly committed to the national idea, could gradually be integrated into the existing political system. Rather, the group that introduced a new aggressive tone into German politics was the rising middle class, as it embraced the 'new German' notion of Empire with its blend of nationalist sentiment and naive faith in Germany's power. In the vanguard of this new integrative nationalism were the nationalist propaganda associations, which, though they did not recruit very large numbers of members, nevertheless became the voice of significant sections of society that had previously been on the margins of politics. The direct influence of these pressure groups on politics proper was only intermittent, and they were not regarded as serious organizations by the political parties themselves. All the same, when the bourgeois parties and, after 1912, the Conservative party found themselves vying hard to assert their own credentials as the most effective mouthpiece for a strengthening of Germany's standing in the world, part of the purpose of this tussle, expressly acknowledged, was to make a home within the party-political system for this new constituency on the right.

The new idea of Empire, which steadily gained ground – even among the governing class in Prussia and Germany – as the Prussian conception of the state retreated, was entirely centred on the new nation state that had developed from the 1870s onwards, with its wide-ranging powers and its strongly military stamp; nationalism in the cultural sense played a relatively minor role. It also sprang from a strong sense of pride in the great economic achievements of the preceding decades, together with displeasure that Germany's power in the world lagged even further behind these achievements than ever. It has often been said that Germany before 1914 was a feudalized society, yet if anything the contrary was the case. Germany's political culture was becoming increasingly middle class – unhappily, however, not because it was becoming more liberal but because it was becoming permeated by a simplistic and often quite unthinking brand of integrative nationalism. To a certain extent this nationalism constituted an emancipatory ideology for the middle classes, although it existed, of course, within a political system that was distorted by authoritarianism and that barred any direct realization of the middle classes' political and social aspirations. It is not surprising to find, accordingly, that middle-class nationalism increasingly presented a challenge to the dominant position of the great Prussian landowners within the civil service and the army, while at the same time not going so far – given also the ostensible threat to society posed by the Social Democrats – as to provoke any real change in the constitutional structure. Indeed, as a protection against Social Democracy, the existing authoritarian state fitted the bill exactly. Similarly, the nationalist camp was content to push the governing elite into an ever more aggressive posture on the international stage, but without having any clear vision of the consequences. The imperialist nationalism that held large sections of the middle classes in its grip in the decade before 1914 was, in a very literal sense, irresponsible: its leading exponents were not integrated into the institutional structure of the political system and were not accountable in a formal sense for the political effects of their actions. They operated beyond the margins of Parliament and exploited the strategic advantages of their position to the full.

The crucial failure of the conservative public officials who were responsible for every significant decision in Prusso-German history during these decades was that they did not hold out firmly against this new nationalism, which at bottom was diametrically opposed to the political traditions of Prussia. Instead, they partly tried to exploit it for the sake of maintaining their own grip on power, and partly let themselves be carried along by it, thereby giving it the seal of respectability. The great majority of the statesmen and diplomats who guided the Reich's fortunes after the fall of Bismarck were not actually in favour of a vigorous foreign policy and were certainly not enthusiasts for an expansionist 'Weltpolitik'. With the possible exception of Bülow, they were at best reluctant imperialists, like their British counterparts. Moreover, Bülow himself embarked on his 'Weltpolitik' solely for domestic political reasons, calculating that it would reconcile the middle classes to the Imperial government and 'gather them together' in a combined front against the Social Democrats. Bülow, incidentally, bears the primary responsiblity for allowing Wilhelm II's 'personal rule' to take on the dimensions it did. Taking a leaf from Disraeli's book a generation earlier, he hoped that by encouraging Wilhelm to front the new foreign policy he would be able to exploit the Emperor's prestige for his own political purposes. Wilhelm II, for his part, saw himself as standing squarely in the tradition of the Prussian monarchy and became intoxicated with his position as sovereign 'by the grace of God',[20] though it need hardly be said that such a claim actually had precious little basis in Prussian history, as a comparison with Frederick the Great, whose view of Prussian kingship was a far more modest one, would readily have shown.[21] In practice, all that Wilhelm II ever really wanted to do was gratify public opinion – for the vagaries of which he certainly had a sharp sense – and, in particular, win the plaudits of the middle class and the intelligentsia. Wilhelm's need to deck himself out ostentatiously in the insignia of the Prussian monarchical tradition, without recognizing that these symbols had largely become anachronistic, served increasingly to damage the image of Prussia in the eyes of German public opinion. This happened despite the fact that he was anxious for his government to seek support from the bourgeois parties rather than from the traditional conservative classes, and that after 1901 he broke off all social contact with the leaders of the Conservative party.

Contemporary evidence clearly and consistently reveals the conflict of loyalties that the monarch's obvious shortcomings created among the members of the Prusso-German governing elite. Should they do their best to cover up the Emperor's misguided actions and protect the public from their consequences, in the interest of upholding respect for the authority of the Crown? Or should they resist, however decorously, even though to do so was bound to encourage the trend towards parliamentary democracy? Prussian tradition required unconditional loyalty to the monarch, but it also required that public officials should act responsibly in the interests of the nation, as Count Yorck had done a century earlier when he concluded the Convention of Tauroggen in 1812 against the express orders of Friedrich Wilhelm III.[22] In the event, Bülow and, later, Bethmann Hollweg opted to steer a middle course, with the result that the Emperor's 'personal rule' was never really eliminated.

Much the same was true in the realm of foreign policy, where the conservative governing elite, quite against its own better judgement, allowed itself to be swept along into a policy of aggressive imperialism. As in the military sphere, those who were keen that Germany should go on to the offensive in international relations did not hail from the Prussian state tradition. Kiderlen-Wächter was a Swabian, tough-minded and inclined towards a Machiavellian cynicism; Zimmermann, who was the real firebrand at the Wilhelmstraße during the crucial phase of the July crisis in 1914, was from Franconia. The great error that the members of the conservative elite committed was to accede to such a policy against their own better judgement, partly out of a misconceived sense of duty and partly out of an unacknowledged need to respond to public pressure for a 'strong' national foreign policy in order to preserve their increasingly shaky hold on power. A further factor was that Prusso-German tradition seemed to dictate that the advice of the military should be followed in the event of doubt and that military considerations should take precedence over considerations of politics and diplomacy, at least at times of crisis. But it was precisely on the General Staff itself, and in the military leadership generally, that the representatives of the Prussian tradition – who had tended to believe that the army, as an arm of the Crown, should be employed with a degree of caution – had steadily been losing ground to those espousing the newer middle-class militarist attitudes.

Such were the circumstances when the Imperial government staged its fateful diplomatic offensive in July 1914, hoping for success even while itself regarding the move as a 'leap in the dark'. The fact that the government counted on being able to satisfy both the military leadership and the bourgeois and Conservative parties, which were demanding that Germany take a strong line, played a critical part in its decision. Bethmann Hollweg had made the prophetic comment, at the beginning of July, that a war would enormously increase the strength of Social Democracy and topple a number of thrones.[23] In the event, the battles of the First World War brought about the demise not only of the German Imperial monarchy but also of the final remnants of the great political traditions of Prussia.

During the Weimar period these traditions, *qua* norms of behaviour, continued to exert some measure of influence within the officer corps and the higher civil service. The Prussian official class's conception of public service proved hardy enough to be capable of transplantation into post-revolutionary, democratic Prussia. It would be wrong, however, to imply that Prussian traditions survived unaltered amidst a dramatic reversal of political circumstances. What had happened, rather, was that the political attitudes of the higher public-service class had already become significantly detached, during the final phase of the monarchy, from the traditional Prussian conception of the state, with its inescapably authoritarian and aristocratic cast. These attitudes had become redefined into a more pragmatic outlook, yet one in which the classical Prussian virtues of devotion to duty, loyalty to the state and the people, and commitment to justice and conscience remained as binding as they had been before.

Let us conclude by returning to our central question: the role of Prussia in German history. It is clear that there can be no going back to the Prussian tradition as a substitute for the idea of a unified Germany based on the Bismarckian nation state, an idea that has itself lost something of its binding force as a result of the division of Germany after 1945. Until the middle of the nineteenth century Prussia was one German state among many: not progressive, but modern and, in broad European terms, by no means particularly reactionary. Indeed, its higher administrative class, well educated by the standards of the time, was actively concerned to promote modernization, despite the fact that in the long run the inevitable result would be to exacerbate the deep-seated structural tensions that existed between the western parts of the state, which were middle-class and industrial, and the agricultural provinces in the east. Nevertheless, the opportunity of overcoming these manifest and latent social tensions by moving gradually towards a liberal and then parliamentary form of government, of the sort that was established – albeit under more favourable circumstances – in other in other European states, was missed on two occasions: first in 1848–49[24] and then, again, in 1862–63. Instead, the German Empire was established, the product of Bismarck's 'Caesarist' policy[25] of forcibly combining heterogeneous constitutional principles into an impressive but self-contradictory whole. At first this structure proved an effective means of maintaining the dominance of the traditional governing elites in a new era of bourgeois politics, providing defence in depth against incursions by the forces of liberalism and democracy. In the long run, however, the advance of the middle classes could not be halted. Since, though, the system was only semi-constitutional, albeit with supplementary parliamentary features, the middle classes were deflected into an aggressive form of nationalism that became ever more detached from its original liberal roots and assumed an increasingly authoritarian and militarist (though not 'Prussian') character. The new middle-class Imperial idea, with its nationalist thrust, gradually displaced the older Prussian conception of the state. The members of the Prussian ruling elites either were forced on to the defensive, or made their own accommodation with the new *Zeitgeist*, coming down on the side of a symbiotic linkage between Prussia and the Reich that nourished the vices of the two political traditions while largely allowing their virtues to atrophy and disappear. The higher Prusso-German bureaucracy ended up having to defend the remnants of the Prussian political tradition against a monarch who was unequal to the responsibilities of his office and against aristocratic Prussian large landowners who now exploited their inherited political privileges ever more nakedly as their economic position became ever more precarious. To a degree, the bureaucracy found itself being driven to protect the inheritance of the old Prussia even against the conservative political camp. During the difficult two decades before the outbreak of the First World War, however, it became increasingly unequal to the task as it came under mounting pressure from nationalistic currents of opinion in the middle classes.

In the final analysis, the German Empire, far from being an arrangement serving to strengthen, indirectly, the power of Prussia, hastened the inescapable decline of Prussia as a unique, independent political system. Prussia was incorporated into the structure of the Empire as a mere conservative bulwark, debarred from pursuing progressive reforms on its own account. Conversely, the Empire's authoritarian traditions, which sprang indirectly from Prussia's position of hegemony, and its official political culture, which strongly proclaimed itself as Prussian, contributed significantly to the system's collapse, with consequences that stretched to 1933 and beyond.

As Germans, we have no reason to be ashamed either of the historical

Prussia or of the Empire. All things considered, the two states were no worse, though also no better, than comparable political systems in Europe during the nineteenth and twentieth centuries. And yet the combination of middle-class liberalism and Prussian conservatism that found its expression in the Empire proved to be an ill-starred one. The weaknesses of each tradition were magnified, rather than their strengths.

It is often said that with the establishment of the Federal Republic there is no longer a need in Germany to look exclusively to German history for political values and exemplars. The Federal Republic has become part of the western world; its vital intellectual roots lie in western political traditions in general, and not merely in the vicissitudes of Prussian and German history. Nevertheless, the fate of Prussia remains instructive. It serves to remind us that a retreat into narrowness and isolation by a class that has previously been politically and socially dominant is always a symptom of decline. It also shows that if such a class attempts to preserve its power by exerting authoritarian rule, rather than allowing competing social interests to be accommodated openly within the framework of a liberal system governed by the rule of law, then it may unleash destructive forces that will eventually run out of control, endangering not only the state itself but also the entire international system.

4

Society and state in Europe in the age of liberalism, 1870-1890

Periodization in history always causes problems. Any particular demarcation of a historical period that we choose to make will reflect prior interpretative decisions and specific sets of assumptions. Only rarely will our choice be fully satisfactory in the light of a range of different points of view, although thinking about periodization may certainly help the historian to get to grips with the central questions. These considerations certainly apply to the subject-matter of the present essay. The years between 1870 and 1890 cannot be seen, without qualification, as a unified era of European history. In several respects the changes that occurred in the states and societies of Europe during those years were out of phase with one another; equally, quite disparate developments took place concurrently.

On a number of counts the history of Europe in the nineteenth century can be seen to have followed a consistent pattern of development, with the direction of change running strongly from west to east, albeit subject to many regional variations. Great Britain, France, Belgium and (after only a small time-lag) the Scandinavian states took the lead in the establishment of constitutional democracy – the crowning achievement of an era of liberalism and, from the 1880s onwards, of increasingly representative politics. The German states, Italy and – likewise with a characteristic time-lag – Austria-Hungary were next to follow. Tsarist Russia, on the other hand, despite having been subject to equally far-reaching change, remained a bastion of authoritarian, indeed repressive, rule. The process was similar in the economic and social spheres. Britain again was the chief pioneer, and was fairly closely followed by Belgium and France, although the latter countries did not experience an industrial revolution of the same degree of magnitude – indeed, France's industrial development, in particular, proceeded at a much more leisurely pace. Germany did not feel the real effects of industrialization until the 1850s, and did not undergo her industrial spurt until the 1880s, though thereafter change was very rapid. Even then, however, the transformation of Italy and Russia into industrialized states had scarcely yet begun. Austria-Hungary too, with her great diversity of territories, was slow to be swept along by the tide of industrial change, and when industrialization did get under way it was subject to considerable regional variation.

Apart from the specific economic advantages and disadvantages (and the differences in industrial structure) that resulted from being either in the vanguard of industrial change or from experiencing what Gershenkron calls 'the advantages of backwardness', the drive towards industrialization also had highly varied social effects in the countries of Europe during the period under discussion. France responded very cautiously to the modernizing forces associated with industrialization and until well into the twentieth century retained her system of rural and small-town politics dominated by local dignitaries and her rather traditionalist, specifically *bourgeois* social structure. In Britain and Germany, by contrast, extensive social changes took place: in particular, the old pre-industrial middle strata of society were largely displaced by the 'new middle class'. Belgium, or the Walloon region at any rate, developed relatively early into something of an offshoot of the British industrial system. In the case of Germany the second industrial revolution followed virtually on the heels of the first. Countries such as Austria-Hungary and Italy, however, were drawn into the orbit of the new industrial system only on a sectoral basis, while Tsarist Russia remained outside the system altogether during the years in which we are interested. What we find in this period, in other words, is that within each individual country there were quite different blends of agriculture, small business, large-scale industry and tertiary-sector activity: each society, in other words, was passing through a different stage of the process of modernization. It is not surprising, accordingly, that liberal principles and, in their turn, democratic institutions stood a very different chance of being eventually enshrined in society and the state in the different regions and countries of Europe.

We must, then, bear in mind the essential fact that different countries were out of phase with one another with regard to the process of political and social modernization. At the same time, however, various overarching trends affected Europe as a whole during this period, irrespective of the great variations in the level of development that prevailed within individual countries; and these trends also had a vital bearing on political and social conditions. In addition, there were close contacts between individual European societies, sometimes resulting from episodes in foreign policy that caused political or economic ideas and practices to spread very rapidly across national boundaries. During the later part of the nineteenth century Europe enjoyed a degree of freedom of movement that we have now lost, as well as a system of 'public opinion' which, though it may have encompassed only a narrow group of influential figures within each individual society, was nevertheless remarkably supranational in character.

The most notable feature of the period between 1870 and 1890 was the triumph of the *constitutional nation state* over competing types of political system. The Franco-Prussian War of 1870–71 created the political conditions that led to the formation, under Bismarck's leadership, of the 'little German' nation state – or, as one is also tempted to put it, to a conservative 'revolution from above' and the birth of a powerful nation state headed by conservatives in a partial alliance with the liberal movement. In Italy, too, the taking of Rome marked the – provisional – completion of the grand design of the Risorgimento and the unification of the nation state. In France the collapse of Napoleon III's Bonapartist system opened the way for a parliamentary republic that in many respects represented the final emergence of the French constitutional nation state based on liberal principles. These events provided a model for the nationalist movements in eastern central and south-eastern Europe that were now pressing vigorously for the establishment of nation states of their own.

Of course, Mazzini's vision of a Europe of free peoples organized into nation states had been only partially realized, and only in western and central Europe at that. The movements of national emancipation in the Balkans could at best claim some patchy initial gains, while the Polish nation was totally crushed by the competing nationalisms of other European states. Furthermore, scarcely any of the new nation states conformed wholly to Mazzini's conception as far as their internal political systems were concerned. This was particularly true of Germany: the German Empire that was founded in 1871 was not, in fact, so much a nation state as an outer shell within which the Germans had yet to come together as a nation. Its central structural features were authoritarian, not liberal, and deep 'domestic political fault lines' (to use Theodor Schieder's terminology) were soon to become apparent. Even the French Third Republic at first lacked secure political foundations and was at risk from reactionary attacks by right-wing conservatives and, indeed, by royalists until 1876. The administration of the French state, moreover, remained heavily influenced by the authoritarian and bureaucratic constitutional system of the Napoleonic era. In Italy, and even more so in the Iberian peninsula, the liberal constitutional order was dominated by narrow middle-class elites, while the mass of the population either played little part in politics or willingly consented to serve the interests of particularist groups that generally draped themselves in nationalist colours.

One thing, however, was clear: any notion that there could be a return to the system of conservative monarchical states of the Metternich era was now quite out of the question. All of the European states, including those governed on authoritarian lines, had to make an accommodation, to a greater or lesser extent, with the liberal movement – even if only an accommodation that was sometimes more apparent than real. No regime could completely shut its eyes any longer to the dominant political principles of the time: in particular, the demand for constitutional government, the call for guaranteed civil liberties, the belief in the primacy of public opinion, and the liberal axiom that social problems were best resolved by free joint action on the part of the individuals directly concerned. In this sense, it is fully justifiable to describe the period between 1870 and 1890 as the age of liberalism.

In Great Britain, France, Scandinavia and Italy liberalism had swept the board, though its victory was actually much less conclusive than was at first thought: even in these countries the forces of conservatism had merely been temporarily ousted from power rather than smashed. In central Europe, by contrast, liberals had been forced to make all manner of igno-minious compromises, while on the eastern and south-eastern margins of the continent they were still debarred from entering the political system altogether. And yet liberalism had become a force that could no longer be ignored in any part of Europe, especially since it went hand in hand with the idea of national identity. At the same time, this statement must immedi-ately be qualified. Although the liberal movement had prevailed over tradi-tional forces throughout most of western and central Europe, or at least had largely succeeded in dictating terms to its opponents, it was not totally triumphant. Its victory had been at best partial, and in some respects even pyrrhic.

In Great Britain, which had set the pace of change in any case, the Con-servative party under Disraeli's leadership effectively cut the ground from under the Liberal party's feet in 1867 by adopting a line on electoral reform that was actually much more radical than that of its opponents. It carried out a dramatic extension of the suffrage, finally ending the dominance of the gentry and obliging both parties to obtain broader support among the electorate. Gladstone's Liberal government of 1868–74 found it increas-ingly difficult to stay loyal to its slogan of 'peace, retrenchment and reform'. In France Adolphe Thiers's cautious tactics made possible the establishment of the Third Republic, in the face of resistance from the forces both of social revolution and of restoration, though in the short run the new order was far from proof against pressures for a return to the monarchy. In the German Empire the National Liberals, in conjunction with Bismarck (who needed an ally against the dynasties of the individual states and the forces of the far right in Prussia) succeeded in realizing some, at least, of their political aspirations. The Imperial constitution of 1871 cer-tainly left vital questions unresolved and was, to that extent, a 'system of skirted decisions', but it was, equally, the product of a compromise between conservative and liberal principles. For more than a decade the National Liberals functioned as the 'governing party', despite also being in a sense dependent on Bismarck's good graces, and they were responsible for usher-ing in a number of important liberalizing domestic measures. Conditions in Italy enabled the liberals to achieve much more, since for over thirty years they were the only effective political force in a country that remained deeply divided against itself. In the states of northern Europe the position was more favourable still, with liberal constitutional movements on the

English model coming to the fore throughout. On the other hand, in eastern central and south-eastern Europe the time was not yet ripe even for a partial implementation of liberal reforms. Here the liberals' only real option was to ally themselves with sections of the traditional governing elites or with the traditional apparatus of state, and to exert a liberalizing influence from above. Austrian liberals had a certain measure of success in this way, though on a severely restricted range of questions; in Russia, liberal forces at best established a weak foothold through the setting-up of the *zemstvo* system. South-eastern Europe was dominated by the competition between Russia and Austria-Hungary for control of the territories that were slipping away from the authority of the Ottoman Empire. Where liberal movements took root and constitutional nation states were established, as in Serbia and Bulgaria, the new states became caught up in this struggle between the rival great powers.

To a degree, then, we can say that middle-class liberalism enjoyed a position of *political* dominance in the period after 1870: the older authoritarian forms of state organization had gone on to the defensive, while political movements on the left – democratic radicalism and the socialist labour movement – did not yet present the liberals with serious competition. It is also clear, however, that the *social* foundations of middle-class liberalism were extremely flimsy. In the great majority of those European states whose constitutions had been modified in response to the liberal *Zeitgeist*, the right to vote remained conditional, to a greater or lesser degree, on property and educational qualifications; only the educated and the wealthy had any effective say in the system. Thus in Italy, the Netherlands and Belgium, the franchise was fairly restrictive and ensured that the middle classes dominated the political process. In the mid-1880s Great Britain took a significant step towards making her political system genuinely democratic, the Reform Act of 1884–85 giving the vote to all adult male householders, but full popular sovereignty in the sense of universal, equal and direct suffrage remained some way off. Gladstone said openly that the legislation had been deliberately devised so as to exclude people without property or settled employment from active participation in the political process. In the German Empire, universal, equal, direct and secret suffrage was introduced at the outset, but the only reason why Bismarck, in his words, 'threw it in' as a device for frustrating Austria was that he was convinced that it would generate conservative majorities – as, indeed, it did, at least in the beginning. Moreover, the democratic effects that began to flow from universal suffrage by the end of the 1870s, with the emergence of the Catholic Centre and the Social Democratic movement as mass parties of a new type, were effectively thwarted by virtue of the hegemonic position of Prussia within the constitutional structure of the Reich, since the three-class electoral system in Prussia guaranteed conservative majorities there from the 1870s onwards. Italy's electoral reform took place much later, in 1882. The size of the electorate was tripled, but since it had previously encompassed only two per cent of the population the gulf between the *pays légal* and the *pays réel* remained wide, and the reform did not amount even to a partial democratization of the system. In fact, the only state to possess a truly democratic franchise from the 1870s onwards was the French Third Republic. The initial effect of the franchise, however, was to threaten the Republic's survival, as both Bonapartists and Orleanists sought to exploit the new dispensation for their own purposes, and it was only after the miserable failure of Boulangism in 1889 that plebiscitary methods of rule finally ceased to represent a serious danger. France also experimented with a wide variety of electoral systems, in an attempt to prevent the full impact of the universality of the suffrage from being felt and to uphold, as far as possible, the supremacy of the middle class. (We need not concern ourselves in this connection with the position in the big semi-authoritarian states of the older type: Tsarist Russia, the Habsburg monarchy, and the rapidly declining Ottoman Empire.)

In general, then, we can say that even in countries where the electoral system was coming closer to conforming with democratic principles, the broad mass of the population remained largely outside the political process. Often (as in Britain, for example) the results of elections were determined by the battle to get groups of loyal voters on to the electoral roll, and not at the ballot box itself. In other words, the fact that the liberal middle class occupied a key position in most of the European states from 1870 onwards had come about primarily because large sections of society had not yet become politically mobilized. This meant that the potential existed for conservative forces to regroup, as indeed they commonly did later on. It also left open the possibility that Catholic or socialist mass movements might eventually be able, so to speak, to dislodge the liberal parties from below.

There was a further danger for the liberal movement: at the very moment when its battles against authoritarian tyranny or feudal privileges seemed to have been won, it was beginning to lose its political cohesion and its ideological appeal. It could no longer be seen, as it had still been seen in the 1860s, as an emancipatory movement pure and simple, acting on behalf of the interests of the nation as a whole. On the contrary, it was gradually settling into a state of mind where what mattered most was preserving the status quo and passing liberal economic legislation directed against both the right and, increasingly, the left, rather than defending, or indeed extending, what had been achieved in the constitutional sphere. In so doing, liberalism lost its force as a moral cause and became, ineluctably, a mere class-based movement, not only in an 'objective' sense but in the eyes of liberals themselves. The liberal constitutional programme, significant though it was, ceased to be sufficiently attractive in its own right to win over large groups of voters to the liberal ranks, and even the magic weapon of 'public opinion' began to lose some of its lustre once the new mass-circulation newspapers set about manipulating it at will.

From about 1880 onwards, liberals became increasingly concerned that the level of participation by citizens in the processes of political decision-making might be going too far and might lead to a new despotism. At root, their fear of being dislodged from below had had a significant effect on their behaviour since the time of the revolutionary movements of 1848–49, if not earlier. By 1859 John Stuart Mill was voicing the anxiety that the very success of liberal reform movements had put the principle of freedom itself in jeopardy. Whereas the earlier concern of liberal reformers, he wrote, had been to set limits to the power of government by means of constitutional procedures and parliamentary institutions, more recently it had been urged that the people should issue their rulers directly with goals and instructions: 'This mode of thought, or rather perhaps of feeling, was common amongst the last generation of European liberalism, and in the continental section of which it still apparently predominates'.[1] Among moderate liberals, at any rate, there was now a renewed stress on the older view that the primary aim of liberal policy should be to create social equilibrium and ensure that changes in social relations evolved on a stable basis. In parallel, liberal enthusiasm for the principle of free trade began to weaken, as, generally, did the belief that society should cast off the leading-strings of the state and place its trust in the self-regulatory functioning of market forces. Instead, the middle classes started to swing towards the idea of a strong nation state, not only as a means of protecting society from external threats but as an instrument for dealing with internal pressures from groups lower down the social scale.

In keeping with this change of attitude, the idea of the nation was now ceasing to stand, first and foremost, for policies of emancipation directed against traditional authoritarian regimes and was increasingly being enlisted as a way of asserting and upholding status. This applied both on the domestic front and in states' external relations. Unpopular marginal groups in society began to be isolated in the name of national identity. The idea of the nation was put to particularly effective use against the internationalist ideology of the labour movement and its organization, the Second Socialist International. More perniciously, it was used against ethnic minorities. The notion that an ethnically and culturally homogeneous nation state should be the measure of all things led to attempts to enforce uniformity on ethnic minorities, either through the use of authoritarian educational policies or through administrative measures, and also to active settlement policies, as when Bismarck, at the urging of the National Liberals, brought in the Settlement Law covering the East Elbian regions of Prussia in 1886. The most blatant application of such policies occurred in Hungary, where the Magyar ruling class used every means at its disposal of assimilating the majority Slav ethnic groups within its territories. The end of the 1880s also saw the first signs of moves to reverse the classic liberal policy of Jewish emancipation.

The concept of the nation was changing. It was not only losing much of its original emancipatory thrust, as we have said, but was gradually acquiring new connotations of state power and, ultimately, of aggression. Jacob Burckhardt voiced his concern in his *Weltgeschichtliche Betrachtungen*: 'Primarily, however,' he wrote,[2]

> the nation – either apparently or in fact – seeks power above all else [...] There is a desire to belong only to something that is great, which reveals clearly that power is the primary goal and that culture is at best a quite secondary one. Above all, there is a desire to assert the general will externally, in defiance of other peoples.

The idea of the nation increasingly became a central element of the political consciousness of the rising middle and lower-middle classes. Identification with the nation as an entity was a reflection of the growing pride of the middle classes in their own achievement and in their importance within society. At the same time, it became particularly pronounced in states where the middle classes remained debarred from exerting significant influence on actual political decisions.

And yet although the primarily middle-class concept of the nation united within its own state had great cohesive force, the gradual erosion of liberalism as a unified political movement, which had been under way since well before 1870, now entered a critical phase. The year 1879 can be seen as something of a watershed. Hitherto the liberal camp had merely been divided into moderate and much more markedly reformist tendencies, the two groups more or less managing to operate in tandem despite their various differences. From the late 1870s onwards, however, the liberal camp as a whole began to weaken. Leading sections of the movement, in particular the remnants of the liberally minded nobility and the *haute bourgeoisie*, started to gravitate towards the right. In Great Britain, this trend was exemplified by the secession of Chamberlain's Unionists from the Liberal party in 1886. In Imperial Germany the National Liberal party moved to the right after 1879, subsequently adopting the 'Heidelberg Programme' in 1884. The corresponding event in Third Republic France was the split of the republicans into Opportunists and Radicals. In Italy the election victory of the 'left' in 1876 marked the supersession of the older liberal leadership, landed and partly aristocratic, by a new elite based on the professional classes, and there was no immediate liberal swing to the right. A clear rightward shift took place over the course of the following generation, however, first under Depretis and then under Crispi, although the liberal bloc retained its pre-eminence.

At the same time, however, the leading elements among progressive liberals were now preparing to take the plunge to the left, in the cause of greater democracy and social reform. Whereas older, 'classical' liberals were tending to end up in the neo-conservative camp, out of fear of the rising lower classes, radical liberals began to look for a new political base among the broad mass of the population, abandoning the traditional liberal structures based on prominent figures. On the whole, though, they met with only limited success. It became increasingly clear that many of the expanding 'new middle class' of upwardly mobile white-collar workers and clerks who in theory might have been expected to throng to the progressive liberal colours were, instead, turning in large numbers to a revitalized, nationalist brand of conservatism. The emergence of this 'new right', or of 'integrative nationalism', in France and in the German Empire in the years around 1890 was symptomatic of this trend; so was the contemporaneous growth of radical nationalism among the educated class in Italy. In addition, there could be no overlooking the competition now coming from the political labour movement: it was the organized working class, and not progressive liberalism, that was becoming the standard-bearer of radical change in politics and society. From the turn of the century onwards, progressive liberalism was caught between the twin millstones of resurgent nationalist conservatism and the socialist labour movement.

The period between about 1870 and 1890 must be seen as the final phase in the history of bourgeois liberalism, at any rate at the level of the state. If the period between 1848 and 1870 had been what Charles Morazé calls the age of 'les bourgeois conquérants', and what Eric Hobsbawm calls the 'era of the triumphant bourgeois' (while also conceding that the era was unstable and short-lived),[3] then by the 1870s the dynamic thrust of liberalism had been checked and its decline had set in. The pattern of state politics began to shift accordingly. In Great Britain, after more than two decades of almost uninterrupted rule, the Liberals fell from power in 1874 and made only a partial comeback between 1880 and 1885; this interlude was followed in turn by a long period of almost continuous Conservative party domination. In the German Empire the liberals' dominance ended abruptly in 1879 and the political system went on to a new and far more conservative footing, with the forging of an alliance of self-interest between agriculture and heavy industry, together with their auxiliary troops in the lower middle class. There were no directly comparable developments in the Romance countries, where clear-cut political dividing lines were not drawn, but the social foundations of liberal government in those countries were nevertheless subject to a process of steady erosion. The relatively rapid turnover of governments frequently concealed the fact that real power remained the preserve of fairly small groups of politicians. Government posts rotated among this largely closed set of leading political figures, who in turn were the representatives of a quite narrow elite, while genuine participation in political decision-making by the broad mass of the population was still as limited as ever.

From the end of the 1870s onwards a clear change was in train. In Imperial Germany, Belgium and the Netherlands, Catholic parties were formed, not based on small numbers of prominent people but seeking to mobilize mass constituencies of voters. The harsh anti-Catholic *Kulturkampf* that was launched in Germany – and similar, if less drastic, attempts to stem the political influence of the churches that were made in other countries –

served if anything to strengthen this trend rather than weaken it. A new kind of political grouping became feasible: an alliance between these Catholic parties and traditional conservatives, joined in some instances by members of the upper middle class who had begun to drift to the right. This new pattern did not come into being overnight (in the German Empire there was a spell after 1887 when Bismarck ruled with the backing of a 'Cartel' of markedly authoritarian parties) but Bismarck's fall in 1890 ushered in a period during which the Centre party was almost permanently the dominant member of a succession of varying parliamentary alliances. In neighbouring Belgium and in the Netherlands similar patterns had already emerged. In Italy the only reason why the formation of a Catholic party was delayed was that the circumstances surrounding the founding of the Italian nation state had led the great majority of Catholics to keep aloof from politics altogether. It was not until the Giolitti era that a Catholic-based party of the right was established.

More momentous still was the rise of mass socialist parties across the whole of continental Europe. Only in Great Britain did the Liberal party succeed for any length of time in stemming the advance of an independent workers' political party, by giving working-class leaders a measure of indirect representation; but even in Britain an era ended in 1900 with the founding of the Labour Representation Committee. In Germany, Italy and Austria powerful socialist parties emerged; the socialist Second International was founded in 1889. In France and other Romance countries a strong anarchist tendency remained significant for a considerable period.

What these developments showed, of course, was that whereas the great mass of the population had previously been fairly apathetic about politics – even allowing for the many and varied restrictions on the suffrage that still existed, turn-outs in elections were low and there was a lack of eagerness even to register to vote – this indifference had now begun to disappear. The dominance enjoyed by prominent local individuals was coming to an end, and the consequences even for internal party organization were to be dramatic. The entry of the masses into politics had finally begun, and it was clear that the process would gather pace.

The informal hegemony that middle-class liberals had hitherto exercised in Europe, in conjunction with the aristocratic elites, had been broken: a new, democratic age had arrived. The question now was whether there was any prospect that liberalism might recapture, under these changed circumstances, the pivotal political position that it had been almost universally forced to surrender to conservative or conservative-clerical coalitions by the end of the 1880s. Progressive liberals argued that what was now needed was a whole-hearted effort to forge links with the left and press for democratic reforms and systematic policies of social welfare. But events were to demonstrate that such a tactic would not resolve the problems that the liberals faced. The outlook for progressive reformist politics in 1890 was unpromising throughout Europe. The new 'integrative nationalism', and the more heated popular mood, sometimes boiling over into jingoism, were more likely to strengthen the hand of conservatives, particularly when, as in Germany under Bismarck and Wilhelm II and in Italy under Crispi, there were also moves to stem the rise of the political labour movement by the use of repressive legislation. The Dreyfus affair in France threw into stark relief the strength of the anti-liberal and anti-democratic forces that had come the political forefront, even in a country as democratic as Third Republic France.

The fact that the final flowering of liberalism in the years between 1870 and 1890 coincided with the formation of new parties and party combinations, both of the conservative authoritarian right and of the radically democratic or social democratic left, was, of course, bound up with fundamental changes that had taken place in economic relations and, indirectly, in social structures. To these we shall now turn.

In economic terms, the period between 1870 and 1890 was marked by the 'Great Depression' of 1873–96, which followed a protracted spell of unparalleled economic growth from 1859 onwards. In Germany the event that made the strongest impact on the public mind was the crash of 1873, which brought the *Gründerjahre*, with their hectic speculation and feverish business expansion, to an abrupt end. This was the first time, in fact, that the previously unbounded confidence of economic liberals in the self-regulatory powers of a capitalist free-market economy had suffered a reverse. A great chorus of voices suddenly arose, not just from the far left but among conservatives too, criticizing capitalism and attacking what was held to have been irresponsible speculation on the part of the entrepreneurial middle class at the expense of the general good. And yet although the slump was a severe one, particularly in Imperial Germany (from where it spread rapidly to the other European economies) there was no question of a real crisis of the capitalist system as such. The 'Gründerkrise' was merely the pivotal moment of a long-term cycle of economic activity, made the more dramatic by speculative over-expansion, particularly in railway construction and in the iron and steel industry. A period that had seen comparatively high rates of growth was followed by a long spell of much slower expansion, interrupted in 1885–86 and 1891–94 by new and fairly severe recessions. There was an almost continuous fall in prices, not only of raw materials and agricultural products, but also of capital goods and of industrial products generally. Money wages declined, although real wages continued to edge upwards, if at a slower rate, mainly as a result of the fall in prices. The new conditions, particularly those facing firms and the social groups dependent on them, created a perception of economic crisis. It was no longer an era of quick profits, made possible by heavy reinvestment from current returns. Net yields fell sharply in comparison with the previous period, and interest rates rarely rose above 3.5 per cent.

In reality, what the crisis showed was that it was necessary to adjust to new circumstances: to the enormous expansion of home markets that had taken place, and to the great intensification of international competition, both at home and in export markets. With the world being opened up by new modes of transport, in the form of railways and steamships, the nature of economic enterprise had changed fundamentally from the era of early capitalism. Investment was now likely to be profitable only if market conditions had first been carefully assessed. The days of easy markets, when pre-industrial products had been effortlessly superseded, were gone, and so too (with certain exceptions) were the days of huge monopolistic profits. At most, large gains could still be made outside Europe, through speculative investment in colonial or, preferably, semi-colonial territories. Hence the enthusiasm among sections of the public for policies of imperialist expansion.

On the one hand, the development of a multilateral system of world trade, in which Great Britain no longer occupied a monopoly position, held out the possibility of an extraordinary quantitative increase in industrial production and, accordingly, continuous economic growth. On the other hand, the individual entrepreneur was exposed to more intensive competitive pressures, to which he was forced to respond with rationalizing measures, innovative investment decisions and rigorous calculations of prices – unless, of course, he had the opportunity of protecting himself from unwelcome foreign competition by means of tariffs or cartels.

For the more advanced industrial countries, like Britain, France, Belgium, Germany and the Bohemian lands of the Habsburg Empire, these changes were, on the whole, beneficial. They were a sign that the industrial system was beginning to mature; they did not indicate a long-term crisis, even if some entrepreneurs felt that harder times presaged just this. For the less developed states, however, the outlook was not so favourable. Their industries were still in their infancy and before they had become properly consolidated they were being exposed to mounting competition from industrial economies whose technology and banking systems were also more advanced. In many of these countries the effect was to delay yet further the achievement of independent industrial growth. Indeed, this period saw a significant widening of the gaps that already existed between west and east, and between north and south. Many states, including Italy and Russia, attempted to get to grips with the situation by imposing protective tariffs, only to find that tariff walls could be erected against them in return.

Conditions were aggravated by the fact that this phase of faltering economic growth – accompanied by excess supply and falling prices and yields, and occurring at a time of increasingly intense international competition – also saw a severe crisis in agriculture. (Admittedly, the low point of the agricultural crisis came in 1896, after the end of the period we are discussing.) Although the long-term decline in farm prices was due in considerable part to technological progress in agriculture, an additional marginal factor was competition from overseas, which was now a powerful force in European markets. In some countries (in the German Empire, for example) the effects of competition, especially on grain prices, were cushioned by agricultural tariffs, but essentially farming was now under economic pressure both in Germany and elsewhere. The symptoms were a fall in the price of farmland, rising levels of indebtedness, particularly among large agricultural landowners (although other factors also came into play here, such as the high social value placed on agricultural property), and growing distress among peasant farmers and agricultural workers, large numbers of whom continued to stream from the countryside into the rapidly growing cities or to emigrate abroad.

These economic changes had important effects on social structures. Since almost all of the countries of Europe were still predominantly agrarian, even those that had made considerable progress in building up an industrial base, problems were inevitable. The demand structure of the European economy was altering rapidly in favour of the new urban centres; this gave added impetus to the rural exodus that was under way in any case. At the same time, there was a shift in relative incomes, to the disadvantage of the rural populations, including large landowners, and in favour of the middle classes, particularly the *haute bourgeoisie* and the professions. On the other hand, the migration of rural workers on to the urban labour market was also highly detrimental to the position of the industrial working class. Only the elite within the working class (Lenin was later to borrow the concept of an 'aristocracy of labour') was able to improve its economic position to any substantial extent. The great mass of workers, particularly in non-industrial occupations, benefited very little from the rise in output. Labour remained relatively cheap, despite the fact that the labour force was becoming increasingly differentiated, both with regard to job skills and, in consequence, to wages. Admittedly, the establishment of 'new unions' (trade unions based on mass membership) which took place almost simultaneously in Great Britain, France and Germany at the end of the 1880s, sent a signal that rank-and-file unskilled workers were no longer prepared simply to acquiesce passively in their fate. But early attempts to organize these groups of workers into effective mass unions and to wring decent wage settlements from employers made little headway. The trade unions promptly found themselves subjected to a combined barrage from the newly founded employers' organizations, the courts and the state, and the existing wage system, under which only the top echelons of workers earned an adequate living, remained largely intact for the time being. On the other hand, the labour movement made permanent gains on an organizational level.

Although there is no denying that the position of the working class improved significantly during the years of the Great Depression as a whole, it should be borne in mind that there were substantial differences in the extent to which different groups within the lower social classes shared in the growing prosperity of the period. As Charles Booth demonstrated to devastating effect in the case of London in the early 1890s, and as similar studies of domestic workers in the German Empire also showed, there were still large numbers of people, even in those countries where industry was furthest advanced, who were living on the margins of subsistence because of periodic or long-term unemployment or cyclical changes in the economy. The establishment of trade unions or of state systems of social insurance did little to remedy matters in the short run, since these institutions were primarily concerned to assist workers who were healthy, able-bodied, adult and in work. Mass poverty was still a familiar feature of everyday life in Europe, not only in countries with less highly developed economies but also in the industrial nations. The axiom of classical liberal economics that rising living standards would lead to the integration of the poor (with the exception of the supposedly work-shy and of the physically incapacitated) was gradually abandoned in face of a growing recognition that the state had an obligation to intervene and regulate. On the whole, liberals fought to impede rather than encourage progress on these fronts.

Economic and social conditions in the transitional phase from the 'triumphal age of liberalism' to our own 'post-liberal age' (when the state has sought to regulate the capitalist market economy either through interventionist planning, or by creating a comprehensive system of social security, or by means of direct state and local-government participation in production) certainly served at first to consolidate the position of the industrial and commercial middle class at the lower levels of the political structure, particularly in local government. Even though middle-class liberalism did not occupy the commanding heights of the state, the middle classes not only retained both social and political power in towns and cities between 1870 and 1890 but managed significantly to strengthen them. An important reason for this was that at local-government level the old electoral rules, linking the right to vote to the ownership of property, remained largely unaltered. In the German Empire the three-class system of suffrage for local government ensured stable middle-class majorities in urban areas; only the Centre party was able to offer the liberals any serious political competition. Municipal authorities did not begin to fall under Social Democratic control for another decade or more, and then only as an 'amusing' exception. We find a similar pattern in Britain, where, although the size of the electorate for local-government elections was significantly increased by the Assessed Rates Act of 1869, and women were given the local vote provided that they owned property in the area in question (and provided also that they were unmarried), voting rights essentially remained governed by a substantial property qualification until 1894. This ensured that the middle classes were not subjected to any effective pressure from lower down the social scale: in Birmingham, for instance, high-ranking businessmen and industrialists generally called the tune in local government. The proud municipal buildings and institutions, dating from this time, that can be found in all of the large cities of Europe are testimony to the remarkable confidence of the middle-class figures who guided the destinies of their communities. Cities became centres of a new, self-assured middle-class culture. Museums, theatres, zoological gardens, amusement parks, schools and many other kinds of educational establishment came into existence as a result of active promotion by local authorities. As David Blackbourn and others have shown in the case of Germany,[4] these institutions symbolized a specifically middle-class, liberal life-style that contrasted sharply with the previous traditions associated with authoritarianism and the nobility.

In local communities, then, and to some extent on a regional level, liberalism maintained its hegemony. At these lower levels of the political structure, and particularly within the cities, liberal principles continued to impart their own modernizing thrust to the societies of Europe – sometimes with, but also sometimes without, the backing of the central institutions of the state. At the same time, however, in many spheres, particularly those of health and social welfare, central institutions were beginning to dictate the actions of local authorities. Indeed, the greater the amount of progress there was on such matters, the less appropriate it became for local control by middle-class liberals to remain the basis for national policy. It is worth noting, however, that the politicians who were most prepared to support policies of constructive social reform, in breach of the older principles of Manchester liberalism, and to attempt to integrate the working class into the system were actually middle-class liberals who had risen from local to national government. The 'radical programme' proposed by the British politican Joseph Chamberlain in 1886 was a landmark in this respect.

There was a widespread desire, of course, to seek to achieve these aims by means of a policy of imperialist expansion rather than by imposing new burdens on tax- or ratepayers in the cities. At first it seemed that it would be feasible to displace social problems by founding resettlement colonies for what were held to be surplus groups in the population: Friedrich Fabri, for example, campaigned for such a policy in Germany, as did Paul Leroy-Beaulieu in France. Imperialist expansion also seemed to promise the creation of new markets, and thus of market-neutral sources of taxation that could be used to finance social policies. It was this prospect, in particular, that caused Joseph Chamberlain to convert from radicalism to imperialism, becoming perhaps the strongest proponent of an ambitious imperialist policy in Britain during this period. But in other countries too, such as Italy, there was a popular belief that the acquisition of a colonial empire would act as a safety valve and protect society from being swamped by under-employed members of the proletariat.

To some extent, the argument of the social imperialists for a policy of extensive colonial expansion was merely a device to give respectability and political legitimacy to the much more palpable material interests of those groups that had a direct stake in colonial ventures. The change to an official and avowed policy of imperialism, however, which occurred in all of the major European states from about 1881 onwards (beginning with France's annexation of Tunisia in that year and Britain's occupation of Egypt in 1882) had many causes, including power-political, economic and 'peripheral' factors. The immediate trigger was the fact that crises on the 'periphery', which led to the collapse of collaborative local regimes and direct intervention by the European powers, coincided with a period of intensifying great-power rivalry. The background cause, on the other hand, was an expectation that the acquisition or development of overseas possessions would create new opportunities for growth within domestic national markets at a time of relative economic stagnation. In the first instance, admittedly, it was 'strategic cliques' (in Gilbert Ziebura's phrase) and individual groups of entrepreneurs bent on acquiring the spoils of monopolisitic control, rather than significant economic interest groups (let alone large-scale capital as such) that took the lead in campaigning for imperialist policies. An initial phase of hectic territorial conquest, in the first half of the 1880s, was followed by a comparative lull as it became clear clear that much of the land in question would not give an economic return commensurate with the effort that had been expended on acquiring it. Nevertheless, in each of the leading European nations a section of the public soon began to demand that the state, rather than the economy, should lead the way on the matter of overseas colonial acquisitions – 'in order to peg out claims for posterity', as Lord Rosebery put it, in an unsurpassed formulation closely echoed by Chamberlain.[5]

Classical liberals had been all in favour of the methods of 'informal imperialism', with the flag following trade if it was clear that that was indispensable. In general, however, they favoured the principle of free trade and believed that it was inappropriate for the state to pursue a policy of colonial conquest, with the sizeable investment of military and administrative resources that such a policy would entail. After 1880, however, circumstances were altered. 'Informal imperialism', the main object of which had been to exploit overseas territories economically while employing only indirect forms of state control or a minimum of of direct control, steadily began to give way to 'formal imperialism': that is to say, states increasingly began to use their power and resources in order to make pre-emptive annexations of territory, on the assumption that the new colonies would be capable of exploitation at some time in the future. This amounted to a jettisoning of classical liberal principles on several counts. Market freedom was made subordinate to state control; the principle of free trade was, at the very least, seriously thrown into question; and there was no longer any thought of keeping the state's role in the economy and society to a minimum and of holding taxes as low as possible. A retrenchment of state activity was questionable in view of the rising cost of administering overseas possessions and providing them with military protection in an age of mounting rivalries between the powers.

This new, aggressive form of imperialism did not, in fact, emerge full-blown until the 1890s. By then, however, even dedicated liberals were finding it far from easy to dismiss 'formal imperialism', on Cobdenesque grounds, as misconceived. Indeed, in deference to the changing temper of the age, a specifically 'liberal imperialism' began to be propounded. The main difference between this and the popular imperialism of the new right that had been put to such fertile use by conservative parties and governments was that it went together with a progressivist demand that the lower and working classes be given a steadily expanding role in society. In several respects, however, 'liberal imperialism' was tantamount to a repudiation of liberal ideals. Moreover, whether its adherents called it 'sane imperialism' or a 'progressive "Weltpolitik"' (to distinguish it from the 'land-grabbing jingoism' of the new nationalism) it did not succeed in shoring up the endangered position of liberals within the political system in any of the countries of Europe: on the contrary, it eventually played into the hands of liberalism's enemies. Nevertheless, the fact that the new imperialist ideology possessed clear anti-conservative features should not be ignored. The main proponents of this new nationalist form of imperialism were not the traditional aristocratic elites, but the rising middle class. In some ways, in fact, imperialism can almost be seen as an integrative middle-class ideology that helped pave the way for a fusion of the old leadership elites, still dominated by the aristocracy in most of the countries of Europe, with leading middle-class groups.

By way of conclusion, let us try to restate some of the overarching trends that gave the period 1870-90 its distinctive character.

The most significant phenomenon of the period, without a doubt, was the fact that middle-class liberalism steadily lost its key role within the social systems of Europe and split into two bitterly opposed camps. One tendency shifted to the right and made common cause with the forces of conservatism; the other, on the left, set itself up as the champion of constitutional reform and interventionist state policies of social welfare, though it failed in the short run to capture any significant amount of new political territory. Radical groups and the socialist labour movement were still too weak to bring about any truly thorough-going democratization of the societies of Europe; but fears of democratic mass rule and of the 'red peril' were sufficiently powerful to induce the middle-class and conservative elites to draw closer together. In those states, such as Prussia or Austria-Hungary, where the aristocracy could not quite bring itself to make a rapprochement with middle-class groups, future conflict and political and social immobility were more or less pre-ordained. In Russia the aristocracy proved even less adaptable, after Tsar Alexander II's wary programme of liberalization in the 1860s and 1870s failed to yield the immediate benefits that had been promised; the liberalization of Russian society accordingly came too late to ward off revolutionary upheaval.

Industrial development and the growth of a multilateral system of world trade had subjected Europe to a continuing process of transformation, characterized very inadequately by the shorthand term 'modernization'. And yet the societies of Europe had by no means become more alike. On the contrary, in many ways the disparities between those countries that

were economically advanced, and those that were less developed, had
become even more prononunced. Great Britain had largely lost her monopolistic economic position, but she was also in the process of seizing a new
advantage in the tertiary sector of capital exports and the exporting of
'know-how'. On the continent, the tension between agriculture and the rising middle class was a potential source of conflict, contributing to the gradual undermining of the position of the traditional elites. The continuing
crisis within agriculture itself was an additional threat to political stability.

At the start of the 1870s many liberals still believed that it would be possible, by putting an end to rule by narrow privileged elites and non-
accountable monarchical regimes, to roll back the powers of the state and
allow the forces of society full expression on the basis of the free association of citizens in pursuit of common goals. Gladstone in Great Britain, and
Sella in Italy, sought to curtail the role of public authorities and reduce the
amount of revenue the state raised by taxation. They were soon overrun,
however, by new ways of thinking. Times were changing in favour of a continuous expansion of the role of the state in society, as people began to conclude that the urgent problems of the day could not be solved without
public intervention. The new imperialist trend in foreign policy also played
its part, in the form of constantly rising military expenditures. The challenge posed by the forces of democracy, especially those within the political
labour movement, led to the reform of the old system of the poor law and
the workhouse, which had been based on the assumption that the victims
of poverty and unemployment were to blame for their own misfortunes.
This meant more state intervention, not less (contrary to the predictions of
classical liberalism). By 1891 Johannes von Miquel, who had been a leading member of the first generation of National Liberals in Germany, found
himself compelled to undertake a comprehensive reform of the Prussian tax
system, which had become anachronistic as a result of the enormous diversification of income structure that had been created by industrial change.
He embraced a new principle of taxation, namely a (very mildly) progressive income tax, which for the first time called upon the wealthy to make
much higher payments than had previously been thought feasible. It was a
first, if mild, foretaste of the interventionist and redistributive state of the
future, and a sign that the age of middle-class liberalism was finally drawing to a close.

5

The causes and objectives of German imperialism before 1914

The German Empire was comparatively late in joining the ranks of the imperialist powers. Bismarck's sudden and somewhat unexpected conversion to an active colonial policy in the mid-1880s proved to be a mere passing phase. The policy was abandoned fairly soon afterwards, and by the end of the 1880s and the early 1890s official attitudes towards further colonial acquisitions had become rather cool. In Caprivi's view the recovery of Heligoland was far more important than the upholding of German claims to Zanzibar, despite the fact that these claims – somewhat dubious if judged by present-day criteria – were thought well-founded according to the international conventions of the time. In the later 1890s, however, this period of colonial self-denial came to an end almost overnight. Under the leadership of Bülow and Tirpitz an energetic 'Weltpolitik', or 'world policy', was set in train, a policy that consisted, admittedly, more in sonorous rhetoric directed at German public opinion than in actual deeds. Then, in 1905, Germany began to embark on more sizeable imperialist undertakings, with the purpose of assuming at last her place among the imperial powers. And yet despite this general change of direction, German policy on imperialist matters remained far from consistent: indeed, it remained in a state of continuous flux.

Like Italy, Germany was a straggler in the race to acquire overseas possessions. By the turn of the century, when, more or less simultaneously, Joseph Chamberlain in Great Britain, Paul Leroy-Beaulieu in France and Heinrich von Treitschke in Germany were arguing that any power wishing to avoid dropping down to the second rank would have to pursue a policy of imperialism, Germany (unlike the great majority of her competitors) still had very few foreign outposts to her name. The handful of colonies that Germany did possess were far from prosperous and did not appear to offer a particularly suitable foundation on which an extensive imperial structure could be erected. The 'peripheral' theory of imperialism, then, is not applicable to the German case, or is relevant only in an indirect sense. In addition, Germany's imperialist ambitions had to contend with the joint resistance of the incumbent powers, which, unsurprisingly, were not enthusiastic at the prospect that their own imperial possessions might be threatened, or destabilized, by a rival power that had only recently entered the imperialist arena. This latter consideration loomed all the larger in German minds for coinciding with doubts whether imperialist expansion was actually worth the great expense that it would entail. Imperialism certainly created exceptional profits for a small section of society; but it also made for a rising tax burden, and thus represented a clear cost for the population as a whole.

German imperialism (undisguisedly aggressive on the one hand, inconsistent and constantly in flux on the other) has been, and remains today, a controversial subject among historians. At first sight, the 'Weltpolitik' of the 1890s would seem to have been a direct descendant of the belligerent German nationalism that had emerged during the nineteenth century and that had finally found such powerful embodiment in the German Reich. But this view really only replaces one metaphor with another; and in any case, the attempt to attribute the root causes of political processes to specific qualities of national character has long, and rightly, been seen as inadequate. Thirty years ago Fritz Fischer re-opened the debate about the character of German imperialism before 1914 with the argument that the German people as a whole (all social classes, with the exception of large sections of the Social Democratic movement) was driven by an untrammelled urge for world power, springing from the nationalist traditions of German political thought and reinforced by the anachronistic nature of Germany's semi-constitutional political system. But even though this thesis may be correct in broad outline, a close inspection of the facts shows that it does not provide a sufficient explanation of German imperialism before 1914, which was a highly complex phenomenon and by no means entirely self-consistent.

The same goes for orthodox Marxist interpretations of German imperialism, which continue to be published in a steady stream, notably by historians in the German Democratic Republic. These studies see Bismarck's colonial policy, and Bülow's later 'Weltpolitik', as a direct reflex of powerful economic interests that had developed in the course of the rapid emergence of a capitalist economic order. It should be pointed out, however, that the economic interest groups that had a direct stake in Bismarck's imperialism were marginal, at best, and that much the same was true as far as the policies of the 1890s were concerned, with the possible exception of the naval building programme. The great majority of businessmen and industrialists had little to do with the aggressive imperialist ideology that took shape in the 1890s and that was soon to become a crucial factor in shaping Germany's foreign policy. The specific imperialist goals that they did come to support tended to be distinct both from the aims of official government policy and from the demands of the Pan-Germans. It is true that heavy industry and the great landowning aristocracy built up a considerable degree of co-operation, and that each of these groups had an interest in the preservation of the existing socio-economic order; but neither group had a direct vested interest in imperialist ventures. On the whole, in fact, the driving force behind German imperialism came from a different area of society – from the rising middle classes and the intelligentsia. Economic considerations played at most a secondary role.

A number of currently influential historians regard German imperialism before 1914 as a primarily defensive strategy, adopted by the ruling classes as they saw their position of dominance within society and the state come under threat from the processes of modernization and democratization. It is certainly the case that the German Empire, despite its semi-authoritarian structure, registered the impact of the general thrust towards democracy that took place throughout Europe before 1914, even though the effects in Germany were mainly indirect and imperceptible. According to this group (following in the footsteps of Kehr), Germany's 'Weltpolitik' was in reality a brand of social imperialism, the purpose of which was to deflect the effects of acute social tensions from the centre to the 'periphery' and to create conditions that would permit the prevailing division of social and political power in Wilhelmine Germany to be maintained. Hans-Ulrich Wehler and Volker Berghahn, in particular, have argued strongly that German imperialism was the product of a deliberately manipulative strategy on the part of the ruling elites as well as a symptom of a political culture that was still heavily dominated by traditional values and that glorified power politics for their own sake. In similar vein, Arno Mayer has maintained that beleaguered elites always tend to resort to policies of aggression and, in extreme cases, diversionary war in order to uphold their ascendancy *vis-à-vis* the rising forces of democracy and socialism.

Despite its obvious shortcomings, the thesis of social imperialism still provides the best framework for explaining German imperialism before 1914. It enables us to bring together a variety of competing interpretations of modern imperialism, both those that emphasize economic or socio-political factors and those that look to international relations (although analyses of the latter type have lost ground in recent years – and with good reason, given that statesmen throughout Europe, with a few exceptions, proceeded very cautiously on imperial questions). The motive force behind the emergence of imperialist policies must be sought either in events on the 'periphery', following David Fieldhouse's innovative suggestions, or in the social and political processes that were at work within the societies of the home countries themselves, and the thesis of 'social imperialism', though it has its shortcomings, is undoubtedly a fruitful new approach from this point of view.

That said, however, there is much evidence to show that the thesis in its purest form needs to be considerably modified if it is to provide a satisfactory explanation of the distinctive character of German 'Weltpolitik' before the First World War. In the first place, the conservative aristocracy was certainly not the spearhead of the imperialist movement. On the contrary, in the eyes of the aristocracy, imperialism was linked with accelerating industrialization and a weakening of the position of the agricultural sector. Conversely, and not by coincidence, the ideological advocates of imperialism believed that the notion of a strongly assertive German 'Weltpolitik' went hand in hand with ideas that were little calculated to appeal to the landed aristocracy: for them, an effective imperial policy entailed the comprehensive modernization of the social and political system, including a degree of constitutional reform. In the second place, the new 'Weltpolitik' and the expansion of the navy that were inaugurated in 1897 robbed the army of some of its public prestige and, perhaps more important, meant that it no longer took precedence in the allocation of state funds. The army, though, was the state institution most closely associated with the aristocracy and was an important agent in the transmission of traditionalist and, specifically, aristocratic values within Wilhelmine society. Finally, we should note that the new nationalism that was being boosted, in particular, by propaganda organizations such as the Pan-German League (Alldeutscher Verband) and the Navy League (Flottenverein) – later joined by the Army League (Wehrverein) – was far from being simply a product of clever ideological manipulation on the part of the ruling elites or the government. Rather, it sprang in large measure from a new political activism among sections of the lower middle classes. Nationalist propaganda was directed not only against the left but against the established elites, both within government and in the bourgeois parties. Indeed, the nationalist propaganda organizations claimed that they had greater popular backing than either the Conservatives or the National Liberal party. This claim was by no means baseless, although we should also add that the nationalist bodies were, by their nature, run by very small groups of activists and ideologues who constituted their own self-appointed elite. That elite, however, was able to operate successfully only because the government and the established parties had helped to create something of a political vacuum which the nationalists were then able to fill. At root, the nationalist phenomenon was a by-product of the change from a traditionalist politics based on *Honoratioren*, or prominent personalities, to a modern mass politics – a change whose effects the established parties had not yet properly understood.

These considerations aside, however, the explanatory models we have mentioned so far cover only a part of the domain that is nowadays generally regarded as connoted by the term 'imperialism'. In recent decades the concept of imperialism has widened significantly. It now refers to a variety of types of both formal and informal control, of which formal political rule enshrined in a state colonial administration is only one. If we employ these broader criteria, we find that German imperialism before 1914 becomes a many-faceted phenomenon indeed. We can identify within it at least three different sub-trends, which were frequently at odds with one another but which at other times combined to produce catastrophic consequences. These trends were *governmental imperialism*, commonly referred to as 'Weltpolitik'; the *radical nationalist imperialism* advocated by the propaganda organizations and, later, by sections within the bourgeois parties; and the predominantly *informal economic imperialism* that was part and parcel of the functioning of the German economy. Only if the overlapping operations of these different types of imperialism are clearly distinguished can we arrive at a coherent interpretation of German imperialism as a whole. What is needed is a functional explanatory model that takes account of the social and economic factors that were present in the various sub-systems of German society, and that relates them to the semi-constitutional nature of the German Imperial system, which prevented the clashes between competing political and economic interests from being resolved in an open manner. The central question that has to be answered is why, in the German case, imperialist pressures accumulated to the point at which they eventually brought about the self-destruction of the political order. We can say at the outset that German imperialism was, in part, the product of a policy of crisis management that went disastrously wrong: that is, one of the factors determining the course of events after 1907 was the weakness of the traditional ruling elites in the face of a spate of ill-defined emancipatory movements couching their demands in the language of nationalism and imperialism. The discussion that follows will seek to pinpoint these various tendencies that were continually at war within German imperialism and that had the effect, in combination, of injecting a quality of belligerence into German foreign policy that kept mounting until ultimately it went quite out of control.

First, however, we must look briefly at Bismarck's policy of overseas territorial acquisition. Hans-Ulrich Wehler has demonstrated in detail that Bismarck's colonial policy was an example partly of informal imperialism and partly of a pragmatic type of imperialism motivated largely by domestic factors (though considerations of classical international power politics also played a clear part in Bismarck's decision to adopt an imperialist course). When he made up his mind to press hard for the establishment of German protectorates in different parts of Africa, Bismarck had no intention whatever of involving the German Reich in the process directly: the costs and risks of the policy were to be borne almost entirely by private colonial companies. These would be given Imperial backing, in the way that the many British colonial companies had been granted royal charters by the British Crown, but would have exclusive responsibility for the administration of the territories in question, including the maintenance of public order; the government at home would have no immediate influence or control. It is well known that Bismarck himself doubted whether the German civil service would be capable of administering colonies and, for this reason if no other, decided that the job should be done either by the 'men on the spot' or by the businessmen and financiers who were sponsoring them.

When the German Empire was forced a few years later (after the financial and political failure of the colonial companies in German South West Africa, the Cameroons and German East Africa) to take these companies under Imperial control and set up a state colonial administration in the territories concerned, Bismarck lost all further interest in overseas exapnsion. He declared in 1887 that Germany had 'had its fill'. During his last years as Chancellor and during the four years of government of his successor General von Caprivi, Germany largely refrained from pursuing an imperialist policy. Caprivi's handling of the exchange of Zanzibar for Heligoland, however, set off a sudden and massive eruption of colonialist propaganda activity. The newly-formed Pan-German League denounced the Heligoland-Zanzibar treaty of 1890 as a 'colonial sell-out'. Within a few years public opinion had been swept by a wave of enthusiasm at the prospect of the benefits that would supposedly flow from colonial expansion. The Emperor himself, who was driven by a genuine if somewhat naive need to be universally liked, discovered an interest in imperialism and in the acquisition of overseas possessions.

It was not until the 1890s, then, that imperialist ideas made a serious impact on German public opinion. Before then they had been advocated only by comparatively minor groups within Germany, notably by the Colonial Union (Kolonialverein), which had a rather disparate membership of businessmen, academics, former senior civil servants and moderately high-ranking aristocrats. Now, however, a far larger body of opinion was caught up by the new imperialism. Men such as Max Weber and Friedrich Naumann played an important part in disseminating the idea of a German 'Weltpolitik' among the middle-class, and especially Protestant, intelligentsia.

The fact that imperialist ideas had become popular in many different sections of society seemed to offer a suitable opportunity for trying to halt the swing to the left that was deemed to have begun under Caprivi and to have been accelerated by the ineptitude of the Hohenlohe regime. A campaign for a policy of governmental imperialism would, it was hoped, eventually bring the bourgeois parties back into government while at the same time impeding the rise of the Social Democrats. When Bülow made his famous proclamation of a German 'Weltpolitik' in the Reichstag on 6 December 1897, demanding that the Germans also had a right to a 'place in the sun', he did so on the assumption that his call would be a battle-cry that would rally the middle classes as well as the Conservatives. Bülow's move offered the government an opportunity of re-emerging from the severe domestic crisis that had beset the Reich ever since Caprivi had suffered a Conservative rebellion against his policy of free trade and been forced into a premature resignation. In private discussion Bülow made it quite clear that his initiative had been undertaken primarily for domestic political reasons: 'I am putting the main emphasis on foreign policy. Only a successful foreign policy can help to reconcile, pacify, rally, unite.'[1] In this sense Bülow's brand of imperialist policy can certainly be seen as an instance of social imperialism. As Geoff Eley has shown, the new imperialism was intended to supplement, and at least partly replace, the strategy of 'Sammlung', or of 'gathering together' the elements 'supporting the state', which by now had become somewhat old-fashioned.

In its content, Bülow's 'Weltpolitik' had much in common with the Tory imperialism that Disraeli had launched a generation earlier in an attempt to strengthen the constitutional role of the Crown. Bülow was similarly careful to bring the Emperor into the equation: Wilhelm II was designated to act as the spearhead of a populist form of imperialism that in theory would benefit all classes of society equally, though in practice it was designed to swing the conservatives and the middle classes back behind the government. Only two years later, Friedrich Naumann, who had a great knack for detecting new trends in German public opinion, published a book entitled *Demokratie und Kaisertum* (Democracy and Empire), which became an immediate bestseller. It was a call to Wilhelm II to establish a form of plebiscitary imperial rule, deriving its support not from the traditional elites but from the mass of the people, especially the rising middle classes. Bülow was moving in effectively the same direction, and for similar reasons. In order to promote his policy, he exploited the Emperor's personal prestige in a great variety of ways, encouraging Wilhelm to assume the public role of a man equipped by nature to lead the German nation into a new imperialist future. For doing this, Bülow himself must be assigned a significant share of responsibility for the naive, bragging language that Wilhelm adopted and that later damaged Germany's international standing, to say nothing of discrediting the Emperor himself.

A careful analysis of the motives underlying Bülow's foreign policy in this period shows that his primary aim was to blazon a message to the German nation, rather than to other countries, that the German Empire really was a world power in its own right and therefore fully entitled to have its say in international affairs. He hoped that by mounting a programme of governmental imperialism he could woo the bourgeois parties, especially the Centre, and halt the continuing rise of the Social Democrats; and he did, in fact, succeed in re-establishing something of a *modus vivendi* with the Reichstag, which had largely disappeared during the preceding years. More generally, by creating a pseudo-plebiscitary regime, with Wilhelm II at its head, he counted on being able to restore the government's authority. This would enable him to make some concessions to the Reichstag, while not undermining the rights and privileges of the Crown and the Imperial government.

The fact that the programme of governmental imperialism had been set in train primarily for domestic political reasons is reflected in the hollowness of the rhetoric with which German diplomacy went about pursuing its 'world-political' goals. The Bülow government actually had no clear conception of the specific objectives it wished to attain on the international stage, and was also very uncertain as to those parts of the world in which it ought to intervene and those in which it ought not. Eugen Richter summed up Bülow's foreign policy sarcastically but accurately when he said that whenever something was happening, anywhere in the world, Germany had to be there too. The policy, in other words, was concerned first and foremost with spectacle and only secondarily with concrete practical results, whether in the form of territorial acquisition or the staking out of specific economic spheres of influence. Bülow evidently regarded it as more important to demonstrate that the German Empire had a right to join the debate on any colonial question, in any part of the world, than to concentrate on obtaining particular colonial territories at the cost of forgoing other possible objectives. Accordingly, he made forays in rapid succession into regions as disparate as Samoa, Angola, Mozambique, China and Morocco, while in no case displaying total commitment and resolve. What generally happened was that as soon as the situation threatened to turn into a crisis, Germany drew in her horns again and remembered that her overriding aim was to preserve her position of dominance on the European continent. In a sense even the naval programme, planned in masterly fashion by Tirpitz and launched with a cleverly orchestrated propaganda campaign, was inconsistent with a policy of colonial expansion. Indeed, Tirpitz told Bülow more than once that colonial expansion would have to come to a halt until the fleet was strong enough to warrant the risk of a conflict with Great Britain; and this, in all likelihood, would take twenty years.

Volker Berghahn has argued very forcefully that the primary purpose of the naval building programme was to overcome the Empire's internal crisis and stave off the introduction of greater democracy into the Imperial constitution. But although it is undoubtedly true that Tirpitz and Bülow were anxious to curtail the influence of Parliament in military and political affairs, this thesis is surely overstated. Indeed, the new naval policy could never have been carried out at all if there had not been some degree of rapprochement with the bourgeois parties, in particular the National Liberals and the Centre. Tirpitz's wheelings and dealings with the political parties actually served somewhat to strengthen the position of the Reichstag within the constitutional system, although the Centre and the liberal parties also consented temporarily to accommodate themselves to the prevailing balance of political power.

It was not surprising, therefore, that the Conservatives viewed the naval programme with deep antipathy, although they were reluctant to come into direct confrontation with the government on the matter (or indeed on other questions). They quickly realized that the inevitable effect of Bülow's 'Weltpolitik' would be to broaden the government's parliamentary base somewhat, at the expense of the dominance of the Conservative party. Until this point the Conservatives had largely called the political tune, partly thanks to their close links with senior government figures. The new policy induced in them a mood of anxiety and misgiving from which they were never to recover. It made them even more determined than before to use all of the parliamentary and constitutional means at their disposal to wring concessions for agriculture out of the government. Such concessions, in their view, would be a form of compensation for their assent to the naval programme, which effectively entailed a speeding-up of industrial growth at the expense of the agricultural sector of the German economy. They made their support for the government on naval questions increasingly conditional on such concessions, in the end not shrinking even from a personal confrontation with the Emperor on the matter of the Mittelland Canal in order to demonstrate their unhappiness at the social consequences of the government's new course.

In addition to governmental imperialism, and partly interlinked with it, a new populist form of imperialism began to emerge. This was mainly an extra-parliamentary phenomenon, promoted particularly by the nationalist propaganda bodies such as the Pan-German League and the Navy League. These organizations boasted their own independent base of popular support and claimed to speak on behalf of the people as a whole. The main thrust of their campaigning was directed against politicians of the *Honoratioren* sort, but their sights were also set on the national government. The government in turn soon concluded that they were rather questionable allies and that a coherent foreign policy could not be pursued in tandem with them. Eley has recently shown that although these bodies had the active backing of sizeable numbers of members of the traditional elites, many former senior civil servants and various aristocrats, their leading figures were for the most part upwardly mobile people from a middle- or lower-middle-class background who were hoping to make their way up the social scale by opposing the established *Honoratioren* system within the bourgeois parties. Neither the Imperial government nor the existing parties had become fully alert to the new political conditions that had been created by a mass society. By contrast, the pressure groups succeeded in building up political support among sections of society that had previously been unpolitical or had remained on the margins of politics. In other words, the old political system, rightly described by Max Weber as pseudo-constitutional, had given rise to a political vacuum within which the nationalist organizations were well placed to operate. They were able to solicit the support of broad groups within the population and to question the authority of the ruling political elites, both in Parliament and within the government. Circumstances, indeed, conspired to give them a measure of influence that was quite disproportionate to the level of popular support that they actually were capable of mustering. The small, self-appointed groups of people who headed these organizations managed to subject the great bulk of the membership to an astonishing degree of political manipulation. The rank and file were far more divided over specific objectives than their leaders ever admitted.

The new imperialism represented by the Pan-German League, the Navy League and other organizations was intemperate, strident and radical; it was almost inherently lacking in realism or discernment. Driven by the need to win over broad sections of the population, its spokesmen found themselves outbidding not only the government and the bourgeois parties but also, to a large degree, one another, as they came out with ever more inflated aims. Their outlook rested on a narrow-minded populist national- ism that had no comprehension of the legitimate interests of other European nations, let alone of the indigenous populations of the colonial territories outside Europe. Though not racist in the strictest sense, it was a brand of nationalism that undoubtedly came very close to racism, and as time went on it crossed the line with growing frequency. It was an ideology intrinsically incapable of tolerating restrictions on its ambitions. In a sense the new right wanted, to use Schumpeter's term, a policy of 'expansion without any definable limits': in this respect, at least, radical nationalism was a precursor of fascism in its various forms.

Given this basic outlook, the advocates of this sub-branch of German imperialism increasingly lost any sense of what could and could not be achieved by foreign and colonial policy within the constraints of the inter- national situation. Not surprisingly, therefore, the governing elites refused to regard the Pan-Germans (and, to a lesser extent, the leaders of the Navy League) as operating on their own political level. All the same, the national- ist organizations were given a largely free hand to campaign for their cause, not least because both the government and the Conservatives and National Liberals, not to mention those industrialists whose interests were directly at stake, repeatedly found it advisable to co-operate with them on specific questions. The nationalists' claim that they, and not the government or the established parties, were the true voice of the people was never properly put to the test; but then, given the semi-constitutional nature of the political system, there was no way in which such a test could have been conducted.

Official governmental imperialism and the radical nationalist imperial- ism of the militant pressure groups both purportedly had the interests of German foreign trade and German industry at heart. On closer examina- tion, however, it is evident that neither brand of imperialism had much rele- vance to Germany's real economic interests. Few businessmen could realistically hope to profit directly from any imperialist ventures over and beyond the general encouragement of German external trade. Although heavy industry, for obvious reasons, at first gave strong backing to the activities of the Navy League, relations soon became strained. It has been shown that most of the nationalist organizations financed their opera- tions primarily through members' contributions, although they did also receive donations from industry and commerce at particular times and for particular purposes. Likewise, the government's 'Weltpolitik' promised industry few immediate economic benefits, except in a handful of individual cases.

During the period under discussion the German economy was undergoing a process of rapid change and dramatic expansion, interrupted by fairly brief and relatively undamaging intervals of recession. From the early 1880s onwards a strong, highly export-orientated industrial system had developed, which, thanks in particular to advanced technology, was achieving an increasingly powerful position in world markets with only a minimum of government backing. The great majority of industrialists and manufacturers (apart from those in heavy industry, whose concern was mainly with the domestic market) favoured a policy of free trade. This certainly did not mean that they regarded Germany's international economic expansion as unimportant: on the contrary. It was the prevailing view in business circles, however, that the penetration of world markets by German products and German know-how would be hindered, rather than helped, by a policy of formal imperialism. In many ways, in fact, Germany's economic expansion in the two decades before 1914 can be seen as a form of informal imperialism that had little connection with official colonial policy.

This was true, admittedly, only in the specific sense that the expansion was in very great part achieved by market forces rather than through the exploitation of monopolistic opportunities or through massive assistance from the government; heavy state support was provided in only a few cases, notably with the project to build the Baghdad Railway. There were important respects, however, in which the policy framework helped German business to get a foothold in the world economy. For one thing, the system of high protective tariffs for both industrial goods and agricultural products ensured that German industry was pre-eminent in the domestic market, which in turn gave firms a base from which to compete successfully in markets abroad. This applied particularly to heavy industry: secure behind the tariff walls that had been erected in 1879 (they were partly dismantled by Caprivi, but then rebuilt on a larger scale in 1902) heavy industry underwent an extensive process of vertical concentration, especially in mining and in iron and steel. Moreover, cartels were formed which made it possible for industry to exert a certain degree of control over home markets and thus sell its goods, at least in the short term, at significantly higher prices than would have been possible under free international trading conditions. This, of course, in turn also helped industry to hold its own reasonably well against competition in external markets, since – again, on a short-term basis at least – goods could be exported at cost price or even more cheaply still. There was relatively little dumping in the strict sense, despite the mythology on this score that still persists to the present day, especially in English-language textbooks. But it can certainly be said that German heavy industry, by virtue of its privileged position in the home market (which, to repeat, would not have been possible without political backing by the state) started from a somewhat more favourable position than did, say, the British mining and iron and steel industries. By the turn of the century Germany had begun to export coal and steel to Great Britain.

By and large, however, it was not heavy industry that gave Germany such a powerful (if not quite the dominant) position in the world economy, but machine tools, manufacturing and, after the turn of the century, the electrical and chemical industries. None of these industries benefited greatly from tariffs. They owed their success to genuine innovations in technology and organization, not (or only to a very small extent) to political advantages of any sort. It should also be emphasized that Germany's existing colonies played an entirely subordinate role here. Exports to the colonial territories of other powers (for example, to India or later to Egypt) were by no means insignificant, but this was not the case with the German colonies themselves, since their economic potential, at any rate at this time, was extremely low. The main thrust of Germany's economic expansion was directed towards countries with well-established, advanced economies of their own: not, or not in any great degree, towards undeveloped or semi-developed countries. German economic success was based, in short, not on the exploitation of monopolistic concessions of the sort available in undeveloped and colonized countries, but first and foremost on the exploitation of market opportunities within an increasingly competitive international economy.

We should note in addition that there was no special drive within the German economy (with the exception of heavy industry) to acquire exclusive sources of raw materials, provided that these were relatively freely available on world markets. Nor did overseas investment, which Hobson and Lenin saw as the great driving force behind both formal and informal imperialist expansion, play a crucial role. Neither German bankers nor German industrialists were particularly interested in speculative overseas enterprises, which, as well as holding out the possibility of high profits, also carried high risks. In any case, there was never a surplus of investment capital in Germany. On the contrary, the German economy suffered from a chronic capital shortage, which forced large concerns, whether operating at home or overseas, to resort to the international money markets. This fact alone limited the banks' willingness to make money available for formal imperialist projects.

Wilhelmine Germany is commonly regarded as the classic instance of a finance-capitalist economy or, more precisely, as a form of capitalist economy heavily, though not totally, dominated by high finance. According to Gerschenkron, this form of economic organization was typical of economic systems that were late to develop and thus were able to make full use of the specific advantages that flowed from adopting already developed technologies and applying them on a large scale. As early as 1913 Hilferding put forward the doctrine that it was the domination of industry and politics by finance capital that was the true root of modern imperialism. Modern scholarship, however, has considerably undermined this picture of the supremacy of high finance within the German economy before 1914. In reality, the big banks were not nearly as powerful as either Hilferding or – writing under quite different assumptions – Gerschenkron maintain. The German universal banks did not, as has commonly been thought, simply dictate terms to industry. In so far as it is possible to come to any verdict on the matter, the reverse seems to have nearer the truth. There were exceptions, but they serve only to prove the rule. Mannesmann, for example, was taken over by the Deutsche Bank in 1893 and was directly controlled by it for a considerable period of time, but this situation arose largely because the manufacture of seamless steel tubing had not yet been fully developed and at first gave rise to serious financial setbacks. In the majority of cases the German banks were far too short of capital to be able to act in such a way. If anything, the big industrial combines that had emerged in the course of the 'second industrial revolution' were able, up to a point, to impose their own policies on the banks. For the most part they could select those banks that were most willing to fall in with their requirements, using them almost as private banks. Quite often they placed their own trusted appointees on the boards, so as to have some guarantee that the banks would continue to support their commercial policies.

By and large, the banks were perfectly willing to make substantial amounts of capital available for industrial development. In contrast with the pattern that prevailed in Britain and France, they operated from the outset as universal banks – in other words, combining the provision of both deposit and investment business. They consistently regarded it as one of their essential tasks to facilitate the growth of German exports, either by granting appropriate credits or by providing sufficient capital for the establishment of branches and subsidiaries overseas. As time went on they proceeded to set up their own branches in the major world trading centres, and later followed suit in most of the countries of the Third World, concentrating particularly on South America. The development of a system of overseas banking branches played a crucial role in strengthening the position of German commerce and German export industries. On the other hand, the German banks did not reach the point of being able to compete on equal terms with the British overseas banking system. Nor were they ever able to generate anything approaching the quantities of funds for major industrial investment that were provided by, say, the French international banks.

The major German banks rarely succeeded, therefore, in establishing any effective kinds of long-term control, either formal or informal, with respect to large industrial projects in foreign countries. The few exceptions were, admittedly, important ones, notably the Baghdad Railway scheme, which was perhaps the only really substantial example of German high-financial imperialism during the period. Instead, the big German banking concerns practised their own version of informal banking imperialism by founding banks in other European countries, such as the Handelsbank in Vienna, which soon became one of the most important banks in the Austrian econ-

omy, and the Banca Commerciale in Milan. This was less a matter of capital investment, however, than of the export of know-how and banking
skills, together with the appropriate specialist personnel. The banks rarely
retained control over their subsidiaries for any extended length of time. The
Banca Commerciale, for example, was still headed by directors of German
origin in 1913, but the greater part of its capital had long been in French
hands and the role of German capital was merely subordinate.

Otherwise, though, the German banks were somewhat wary of imperialist ventures, both of a formal and of an informal nature. In general they
were prepared to invest in designated German spheres of influence only in
response to heavy pressure from the government, and then usually only if
sizeable interest payments in the form of an Imperial guarantee had first
been promised. The Baghdad Railway was a major exception to this pattern. The Baghdad Railway Company was a subsidiary of the Deutsche
Bank and was fully controlled by it. Even in this case, though, it should be
noted that the company would never have achieved what it did without the
close co-operation of international banks – in particular, the Banque
Impériale Ottomane (the capital of which was mainly French-owned) and
the Caisse de la Dette Publique Ottomane (the international debt adminis-
trator that exerted substantial control over the public finances of the
Ottoman Empire, and that also came under decisive influence from French
and British capital). It was no accident, in fact, that the Deutsche Bank had
originally hoped not to operate on a narrowly nationalist basis with regard
to the Baghdad Railway but, if possible, to collaborate with international
finance: partly in order to attract capital from other countries, notably
France, since its own assets were not large enough, and partly in order to
avoid, as far as was feasible, the political conflicts that might result from
the railway's construction. The fact that the Baghdad Railway became a
focus of disagreement among the rival imperialist powers – and German
diplomacy and public opinion also both played their part here – was, from
the bank's point of view, regrettable. Hence, although the Baghdad Railway
Company naturally welcomed the support of the German government, relations between it and the government were by no means always easy.

It would, of course, be quite misleading to assume from this discussion
that German high finance was not involved in other large-scale imperialist
financial ventures. There was substantial German investment, for example,
in South African gold mines and in mining and other industrial enterprises
in South America. German funds also went ito the oil business, albeit usually again in a role subsidiary to British investment. In 1913, for example,
the Deutsche Bank was assigned a 25 per cent stake in the share capital of
the Turkish Petroleum Company (later to be incorporated into Shell),
which was active in developing oilfields in Mesopotamia and Anatolia. The
First World War put paid to these German holdings, however, and they
were never recovered. In Romania, on the other hand, German banking
capital came up against superior opposition not only from France but also

from the United States. Investment activity in China, again conducted in collaboration with British banks, fared more promisingly, yet here too failed to evolve into a system of local hegemony.

The position as far as industry was concerned was essentially similar. In general, apart from certain economic sectors where there was a direct interest in the acquisition of specific economic concession overseas, industrialists were not particularly keen to exploit monopolistic concessions, at any rate while raw materials remained available at reasonable prices on world markets. Once more, however, there were notable exceptions. From the turn of the century onwards, for example, in keeping with the trend towards vertical concentration in mining and steel, heavy industry began to extend its reach across the frontiers of the German Empire into Belgium and northern France. German concerns steadily acquired a considerable number of majority holdings in iron and coal mines in these regions. Indeed, the scale of the commitment of German heavy industry in Belgium and northern France looks almost like a prefiguration of the plans for the formal territorial annexation of these regions that later surfaced among German war aims during the First World War. On the other hand, it should not be forgotten that this informal economic expansion was entirely the product of market forces, and that remained the case even after the French government decided in 1909 to do everything it could to block it, placing legal obstacles in the way of German investment within France and of foreign acquistion of interests in French companies.

The sort of expansion that was undertaken by German heavy industry can, therefore, be classed as an example of informal imperialism only in a qualified sense. It can equally be seen as a first step on the path towards the creation of multinational corporations, as companies sought to free themselves from the shackles of an economic system that had hitherto been confined entirely within the borders of nation states.

Of greater relevance in our present context were the efforts that were made by heavy industry, with political backing, to develop various specialized categories of export opportunities, particularly in the field of weaponry. This was done through the granting of loans to smaller countries that would otherwise have been quite unable to undertake ambitious armament programmes. Before 1914, state loans were granted almost exclusively on the condition, formal or informal, that the bulk, at least, of the imports that would be bought with their help would be supplied by the country making the loan. Characteristically, however, the big German banks were generally rather disinclined to issue such loans, since from a purely commercial point of view they were relatively risky and not very lucrative. Not even active intervention by the government was always enough to overcome their caution. It was no accident, therefore, that relations between the firm of Krupp, for example, and the major German banks, especially the Deutsche Bank itself, were less than cordial.

The electrical industry was in a different position. It was the big success story of the 'second industrial revolution'; its great technological lead had enabled it to gain informal dominance in many foreign markets, both in developed and in relatively undeveloped countries. Since the amount of capital expenditure involved in building up the infrastructure necessary for electricity supply was usually very considerable, the electrical industry was anxious to fend off foreign competition as much as it possibly could, and it was therefore often keen to obtain diplomatic support. On the other hand, even this industry was totally opposed to all methods of formal control.

It is not surprising, therefore, that the notion of creating a central European economic association, with common external tariffs, was well received in such circles. In the years leading up to the First World War the model of an exclusive central European economic zone was often seen as the only realistic alternative to the old-fashioned acquisition of colonies, which was regarded as no longer in tune with the economic necessities of the age. In 1913 Walter Rathenau put forward a plan for a central European customs union, to serve as the nucleus for a future European economic community. Such a community would act as a bulwark against future economic domination by the United States, and at the same time provide a constructive alternative to outmoded traditional forms of colonialism. Rathenau, however, was far from regarding his scheme as a form of indirect imperialism. On the contrary, he was convinced that it would lead to a lessening of international conflict. 'It does not mean world peace,' he wrote, 'or disarmament, or enervation; but it does mean an easing of conflict, and a saving of effort, and the solidarity of civilization.'[2]

It is clear, then, that German finance and German industry were not, on the whole, particularly interested in the formal imperialist acquisition of territory. They were, however, quite prepared to take part in a wide variety of informal imperialist initiatives, no matter whether active government backing was forthcoming or not. Bethmann Hollweg's attempts to start building a German presence in central Africa (as a positive alternative to Bülow's ill-focused 'Weltpolitik') were generally viewed with scepticism by industrial and financial leaders. Industrialists felt, for example, that the contemplated acquisition of parts of Mozambique and Angola would be of little economic consequence; these territories, it was said, were 'in the back of beyond'.[3] German industry did have real overseas interests, but these lay elsewhere: particularly in the Balkans, the Near East and, importantly, in South America. All told, we cannot say that pressure from within the German economy was a principal motive force behind the official 'Weltpolitik' that was inaugurated by Bülow in 1897 and continued, on a comparatively more rational basis, by Bethmann Hollweg from 1909 onwards.

Accordingly, one of the key problems that arise when we look at German imperialism before 1914 is that of explaining why there was such a wide disparity between the goals of the semi-official imperialist policy that was pursued, with differing degrees of emphasis, by the governments of Bülow and Bethmann Hollweg (to say nothing of the feverish integrative imperialism of the nationalist pressure groups) and the actual needs of the German economy.

During the final decade before 1914 many journalists and academics, and some industrialists, became exercised by a fear that the system of virtually barrier-free world trade which had evolved since the 1860s – and which, broadly speaking, had functioned well, despite the protectionist policies pursued by certain countries – might not have much life left in it. They foresaw a division of the world into a number of economic spheres of influence, each more or less well shielded against external competition by means of high tariff walls. The German business community, on the other hand, for the most part remained fairly buoyant. A flavour of the prevailing mood is given by an exchange between Hugo Stinnes and Heinrich Class, the leader of the Pan-German League, in the autumn of 1911. Class took the view that the German Empire would sooner or later be forced to go to war in order to assert its place in the world beside Great Britain and France. Stinnes, on the other hand, argued strongly for a policy of patience:[4]

> Give us three or four more years of peaceful progress, and Germany will be the undisputed economic master of Europe. The French are lagging behind us: they are a nation of small *rentiers*. And the English dislike hard work and lack the mettle for new ventures. Apart from them, there is no one in Europe to compete with us. Three or four years of peace, then, and I assure you that Germany will secretly come to dominate Europe.

Class for his part was horrified that a figure so prominent within the German economy could be 'labouring under such delusions'.

The disparity between the imperialist designs that were harboured in nationalist circles and the strategies of economic expansion that can be termed informal imperialism by economic means never disappeared: not even in the final years before the war, when the Reich government showed itself more ready to fall in with the needs and wishes of finance and industry. Nevertheless, the extreme nationalism that was preached by the Pan-German League and the other nationalist organizations received active support from a considerable section of the business community, winning widespread sympathy, even if not outright approval. The Mannesmann brothers gained strong political backing for their interests in Morocco, rallying the Pan-German League behind their complaint that their mining concessions had been completely neglected by the Reich government in the negotiations leading to the Franco-German pact on Morocco of 1909. This situation may well seem somewhat baffling. To explain it, we need to consider the political and social conditions within which the political parties and the nationalist organizations were operating at this juncture in Wilhelmine history, and the obstacles that hampered political decision-making during what was a transitional stage from a system of *Honoratioren* politics and rule by bureaucracy to a system in which the broader mass of the population would play a more active part in the political process.

Before we go into these questions, however, we need to look in greater detail at Germany's imperialist policy before 1914. Leaving aside Bismarck's 'imperialism' as *sui generis*, we can distinguish three phases of German 'Weltpolitik': the Bülow era, from 1897 to 1909; a period of cautious disengagement between 1909 and 1911; and a period of more intense imperialist activity from 1911 to 1914.

Bülow's 'Weltpolitik' ended in a series of errors, some more spectacular than others. This was partly because the government had not taken proper account of the true nature of the international situation, and partly because the various objectives of the policy – the establishment of reversionary rights over parts of Angola and Mozambique, international recognition of an exclusively German economic sphere of influence in China, the protection of possible future German interests in Morocco against the growing influence of the French – were only half-heartedly pursued. The agreement with Great Britain over the division of Angola and Mozambique fell through, largely as a result of what was seen as double-dealing on the British side. Bülow's China policy also failed to deliver any convincing gains in the end, in part because Bülow retreated when it became clear that its effect would have been to tie Imperial Germany's destiny directly to that of Britain, with the additional risk of worsened relations with Russia. The Moroccan venture of 1905 ended in disaster because it was not prosecuted with firm resolve but was merely an attempt to keep the door open for the future: the outcome was almost total German isolation at the conference of Algeciras. By 1908 it had also become clear that the naval programme was not going to yield the result that Tirpitz had been hoping for, namely a German fleet strong enough to force Britain to surrender some of her own overseas possessions through negotiation. The glorious expectations that had been invested in the naval programme proved to have been largely unfounded.

Theobald von Bethmann Hollweg, who was appointed as Bülow's successor in 1909 (despite lacking all experience of foreign affairs) had some grasp of the nature of the situation and decided to tone down Germany's international ambitions and work for détente with France and Great Britain. The Franco-German pact on Morocco that was reached in 1909 effectively conceded priority in Morocco to France; in return, however, France pledged herself to allow German industrial enterprises with interests in Morocco to operate there on equal terms. This suited the firm of Friedrich Krupp, which had joined forces with a French group in order to exploit ore deposits in Morocco; the Mannesmann brothers' mining rights, on the other hand, were simply ignored. Bethmann Hollweg also made a somewhat half-baked attempt to persuade Britain into entering into a neutrality agreement and making colonial concessions in return for a gradual slowing-down of the German naval building programme. The British rightly saw this as far too meagre an offer to warrant such a drastic shift in their foreign policy.

None of these endeavours was successful, and the small amount of good will that they helped to generate was promptly forfeited once more as a result of Kiderlen-Wächter's ill-planned, and ill-fated, despatch of the gunboat *Panther* (the 'Panthersprung' or '*Panther*'s leap') to Agadir in 1911. Instead of reducing the *entente cordiale* to a meaningless piece of paper, as Kiderlen-Wächter had hoped, and forcing France to hand Gemany the whole of the French Congo, the Moroccan initiative led to a sharp worsening of the international position of the German Empire. At the same time, however, it jolted the government's already shaky relationship with the parties and with public opinion. There followed an eruption of nationalist sentiment which the government was to prove quite incapable of repressing or subduing.

From this point onwards, the Bethmann Hollweg government found itself increasingly on the defensive. Public opinion (or, at any rate, the publicly voiced opinions of those sections of German society that were politically active) began to push the government into adopting an aggressive foreign policy quite contrary to its own inclinations. At the same time, the international situation was deteriorating rapidly as a result of the Balkan wars and of exacerbated rivalry with Russia, fomented by German activities in the Ottoman Empire, and this redoubled the government's difficulties.

None the less, the Bethmann Hollweg government tried to construct a rational imperialist policy fundamentally distinct from the irrational – indeed irresponsible – nationalist programme of the agitators of the new right. It did so even though, to its annoyance, nationalist sentiments were now also being expressed by the Conservatives, albeit mainly for tactical reasons. The government's project was to consolidate Germany's existing territorial possessions in Africa by acquiring parts of Angola and Mozambique as well as of the Belgian Congo, with the eventual aim of creating a central African colonial empire. In addition, it made an express decision to seek political backing for Germany's economic penetration of the Ottoman Empire and to protect the German presence there from intervention by other powers. Bethmann Hollweg hoped to be able to count on British support, in particular, in carrying out this programme: in a sense, Berlin believed that it would be able to act as London's junior partner on these questions.

Time and patience were needed if such aims were to be achieved: the government could not afford to let noisy public demonstrations and outbursts of populist Anglophobia derail the secret diplomatic approaches that were required. Accordingly, it kept a clear distance between itself and the nationalist pressure groups, and generally did everything it could to avoid joining in the public imperialist debate. But although the policy produced some initial results that made it realistic to think that in the long run the Reich might acquire a reasonably sized colonial empire, there were no immediate spectacular gains. There was therefore little chance of assuaging public opinion, already inflamed as it was, or of damping down the nationalist and imperialist agitation to which the parties of the right were now increasingly adding their voice – to say nothing of the irresponsible demagogy that was was being practised by the nationalist organizations.

We can say without qualification that during this period the statesmen were, at most, reluctant imperialists. The Bethmann Hollweg government was steadily being driven by influential political groups and by public opinion into adopting a more forceful foreign policy. None the less, the government did not believe that a war would be an appropriate way of realizing its imperialist aims. It was certainly prepared to resort to war if, contrary to expectation, the Ottoman Empire were to break up and Germany were not offered an adequate share of the spoils. This, though, seemed fairly unlikely, especially since the policy of preserving the political status quo in Turkey was also in the interest of Great Britain. The 'civilians' within the government, at least, did not believe that Germany's drive for world power, in Fritz Fischer's phrase, either needed to be, or could be, fulfilled by means of war, though they were becoming steadily more disposed to the view that other powers should take notice of German interests by being reminded, if necessary, of Germany's military potential.

At the same time, however, Berlin was becoming increasingly concerned, not only by the growing isolation of the Central Powers and the obvious weakness of Austria-Hungary, but also, most especially, by the rapid military resurgence of Russia, who now appeared to pose a direct threat to the security of the German Empire. Hidebound by narrow military preconceptions, but also heavily influenced by the rising tide of propaganda to the effect that Germany would not be able to join the ranks of the world powers except through war, even leading military figures now began to press the Chancellor and the Foreign Office to consider the advantages of a pre-emptive strike. Bethmann Hollweg found it increasingly difficult to stem the mounting influence of the military and of certain conservative groups at the Emperor's court, and his task was made the more difficult as his position *vis-à-vis* the Reichstag and the parties became more precarious. Circumstances conspired to make even greater the gap between the expectations of conservative and middle-class groups on imperial questions and the actual options that were offered by a policy of realism and moderation. Since the government could not yet point to any positive achievements in foreign affairs, it did not even attempt to amend this threatening situation. Instead it watched passively as nationalist expectations among the middle class kept rising, even though inaction left it with less and less room for manoeuvre.

What made the government's dilemma even more acute was the fact that demands for an active imperialist policy were now coming not only from those sections of the population that had originally been mobilized by the militant nationalistic campaigning of the Pan-German League and other pressure groups but also from significant numbers of political supporters of the established bourgeois parties and the Conservatives. The heated emotions that had been generated by the Agadir crisis of 1911 were brought still nearer the boil by journalists and military writers such as Friedrich von Bernhardi. The Army League that was formed in 1912 began, under the leadership of General von Keim, to subject the government's military policy to quite open and withering criticism. The League not only demanded further expansion of the German army but made a scarcely disguised call for a preventive war. In this atmosphere public opinion became increasingly receptive to extreme nationalist views. From 1912 onwards all of the political parties were being swept along, with the exception of the Social Democrats.

We can now return to our earlier question: namely, how this steadily accelerating process of radicalization is to be explained. Older generations of historians tended to take the view that popular nationalism had relatively little bearing on the conduct of foreign policy in Germany before 1914. By contrast, more recent writers, notably including Fritz Fischer, have stressed the enormous importance that the nationalist movement assumed in the years immediately before the outbreak of war. It is clear, however, that the new nationalism cannot be seen merely as the product of a manipulative strategy on the part of the Wilhelmine governing elites, in the sweeping sense in which Wehler, Stegmann, Puhle and others have sometimes been tempted to argue the case. The differences between the various currents of imperialist opinion were very wide and cannot be adequately explained in terms of a restrictive monocausal model of this sort. It was, rather, the relative powerlessness of the traditional elites, and not any masterful manipulation of public opinion, that led to the escalation in popularity of imperialist sentiment.

In the final analysis, the reason why German imperialism was so particularly aggressive was that the political system had not properly adapted to the rapid changes in social and political conditions that had been caused by the processes of modernization and industrialization. The huge growth of the German economy in the decades before 1914 had given the rising middle classes a powerful new injection of self-confidence, and this self-confidence had found particular expression in the conception of a strong nation state. By contrast, the Conservatives were becoming haunted by the nightmare of inexorable decline. Nevertheless, for the time being their influence within the machinery of state, especially the army and the bureaucracy, remained formidable. The three-class system of suffrage meant that the Social Democrats and the Progressive party had only nominal representation in the Prussian Chamber of Deputies, while the National Liberals enjoyed a relatively secure position only on condition that they were prepared to co-operate with the Conservatives. This strengthened the Conservatives in their desire to shore themselves up within 'Fortress' Prussia. The result was that the differences between the rising middle classes and the agrarian conservatives were never properly aired or resolved. The fact that the middle classes in their turn felt threatened by the rise of Social Democracy also made them prepared, at least on occasion, to make common cause with the Conservatives despite the fact that their political outlooks differed on many counts. Campaigning for nationalist and imperialist goals seemed a very tempting way of trying to head off the Social Democrats' continuing advance.

The government, too, did everything in its power to play up anti-socialist prejudices among the middle and upper classes. The charge that a refractory political party was merely playing into the hands of the socialists remained a highly effective means of enforcing loyalty to the regime. In a sense, indeed, we can see this tactic as a special variant of social imperialism. The increasingly critical nature of the domestic political situation, however, was displayed by the fact that these techniques were ceasing to be sufficient to ensure the stability of the system. Appeals to national and imperialist ideals were no longer capable of rallying the bourgeois and Conservative parties solidly behind the government. Indeed, the Social Democrats were beginning to find that they had a growing number of opportunities for co-operating with other parties on an *ad hoc* basis. It soon became clear to the other parties that it was possible to work with the Social Democrats on matters that were vital to the national interest, despite the fact that the Social Democrats were firmly committed to the principle of internationalism.

There were all sorts of signs that a new political coalition between the National Liberals, the Centre party and the moderate left might be in the offing: a coalition that would be backed, or at least tolerated, by the Social Democrats. If such an alliance were to come into being, then the Conservatives really would be driven into isolation. This prospect prompted the Conservatives to pay court more strongly to the nationalist organizations, in the hope of winning over the new right that had emerged since the turn of the century. Adopting nationalist slogans was an obvious gambit in the circumstances. By 1911 the Conservatives had realized that with the help of a campaign of extreme nationalism they had a good chance not only of halting their electoral decline but of winning new voters, both among the old middle class and also, to some extent, among the new middle class, especially in the western parts of Germany. They also hoped that by identifying themselves with the imperialist ethos they would be able to resist the mounting pressures for parliamentary democracy. It was no accident, moreover, that their vitriol was directed primarily against Great Britain, since the British parliamentary system was regarded by many German liberals as the model that Germany ought to follow, not least because it would finally make possible an effective imperialist policy. The

Conservatives' strategy, however, was only partially successful. In the wake of the 'defence levy' of 1913 and of the Zabern affair, they found themselves politically isolated and in danger of eventually forfeiting all influence over day-to-day events in Parliament. This prospect, understandably, caused them deep anxiety and strengthened their readiness to woo the nationalist pressure groups and their supporters, regardless of the cost. In Conservative eyes, the reunification of the old and the new right, under the banner of undisguised nationalism, seemed vital if they were to remain a political force in the long term.

The National Liberals faced similar problems. They had lost the support of many of their voters in the countryside and were threatened with long-term electoral decline. Bassermann, Stresemann and others came to the conclusion that the only way in which they could regain their pivotal position in Parliament was to win over the groups that had been recruited by the nationalist organizations. They therefore began systematically calling for an efficient, nationalist brand of imperialism, while arguing that it needed to be accompanied by the modernization of the political and social institutions of the German Empire. They saw this tactic as the best way of recapturing the backing of those sections of the old middle class that had deserted them during the previous twenty years, as well as of attracting those members of the lower middle class and the hitherto non-political intelligentsia who were gravitating towards the new right, as yet without its own separate parliamentary representation. Sooner or later, they believed, the combination of a policy of imperialism with a programme of cautious political modernization (though not of wholesale parliamentary democracy) would end the dominant role of the aristocracy in society and the state, and the National Liberals would once again become the 'natural' governing party in the country. There were also some grounds for supposing that some modest modernization of the social and political system was the only way of checking the continuing growth of Social Democracy.

Seen from this point of view, imperialism was a strategy of emancipation on the rising middle classes' part: the social and political status quo would be preserved, but on the condition that the bureaucracy and society were subjected to a moderate degree of anti-conservative reform. Removing inefficiencies and outmoded aristocratic privileges in the diplomatic service and the military was seen as essential if a political order were to be created that would permit the pursuit of an effective imperialist policy.

As a long-term strategy, the National Liberals' programme might have worked. In the short run, however, it gave an opening to the nationalist pressure groups, enabling them to drum up simplistic support for militant imperialist policies among significant sections of German society that had not yet been properly integrated into a political system which failed in many respects to reflect the needs of an age of mass politics. There had been, certainly, something of an 'imperceptible transition towards parliamentary government'; but the established parties proved to be incapable of locking the forces of extra-parliamentarism into the system.

This was in part due to the parliamentary situation that had been produced by the elections of 1912. The Social Democrats' sweeping gains partially immobilized the parliamentary process, preventing the formation of
either a national–conservative or a progressive majority coalition in the
Reichstag. The scope for the parties to take positive initiatives on policies,
as against practising purely negative oppositional politics, was still limited
in any case, but parliamentary stalemate ensured that none of the various
party groupings could act in a constructive fashion. The Imperial government had not been strengthened either, despite being able to continue to
rule in its previous authoritarian style. It no longer enjoyed solid party
backing, and hence became more dependent than ever on the Emperor and
his entourage and on the traditional pillars of the Hohenzollern throne (the
officer corps and the government bureaucracy). Bethmann Hollweg did not
dare to pursue an openly right-wing policy, for fear of alienating the electorate even further; but he did not dare, either – not that he would have
wanted – to opt firmly for reform.

Under these circumstances, the new right, which operated mainly outside
the parliamentary framework, had no difficulty in mounting effective agitation. The Army League took the lead, calling for a forward policy regardless of the risks and pressing Friedrich von Bernhardi's argument that a
world war was inevitable in any case if Germany were not to renounce her
imperial goals in perpetuity. The new right did not even shrink from attacking the political system head on, lambasting it for its supposed ineffectual-
ity and its inability to safeguard the inalienable interests of the German
Empire. In early 1913 the Pan-German League went so far as to try to drive
Bethmann Hollweg from office and replace him with Tirpitz. This projected
coup, which had the Crown Prince among its backers, misfired completely,
but the Chancellor's reputation suffered further damage as a result.

The government was in a desperate quandary. The Conservatives had
largely conceded the field to radical agitators of middle-class origin,
notably the leaders of the Farmers' Alliance (Bund der Landwirte). The
National Liberals, for their part, could see themselves being steadily outflanked on the right and found it increasingly difficult to stick to the programme of realistic, circumspect imperialism that they hoped would pose
an alternative to the militant nationalism of the new right. Government
ministers, however, did not even dare to deflate the public's faith in the fea-
sibility of imperialist policies, for fear of being accused of defeatism or of
pacifism. Since they did not enjoy strong political support in the Reichstag,
and had seen their control over the traditional bases of power in the Empire
(notably, the officer corps, court society and the Prussian bureaucracy)
gradually ebb away, they were totally lacking in effective political means of
stemming the rising tide of nationalist sentiment. With misgiving, they
watched events run their course. The result, however, was that the gulf
between public expectations and the real world grew wider by the day. An

irreversible process was set in train, carrying the leading groups within German society ever further away from a recognition of the constraints within which an effective foreign policy had to be conducted.

In consequence, the Imperial government steadily lost the initiative on matters of national policy. The Chancellor himself had long realized that Conservative policies would inevitably lead to growing alienation on the part of the mass of the population. Circumstances dictated that the government was increasingly dependent on the political parties of the right; these, however, were in turn feeling increasingly vulnerable to the pressure that was coming from the new nationalist right-wing propaganda organizations outside Parliament. Instead of giving a lead to public opinion, the government went more and more on to the defensive. Bethmann Hollweg and Jagow were well aware that the sort of foreign policy that would have assuaged the febrile demands of large sections of the middle classes – and, now, of Conservatives too – was not a practicable option in the current international situation; but they felt unable to offer an alternative. The government was gradually pushed into abandoning the more moderate form of imperialism that would at least have remained compatible with the constraints imposed by the international system.

In view of these various factors, it is not surprising that when, in July 1914, the German government had to deal with the European crisis that followed the assassination in Sarajevo on 28 June, it decided (contrary to its own real convictions) to make what Bethmann Hollweg himself admitted was tantamount to a 'leap in the dark'. The outbreak of the First World War was the inevitable result. The government was under considerable pressure from the military establishment, which was worried about the deterioration in Germany's strategic position and had concluded that if a European war was on the way, then it was better to fight it sooner rather than later. But the government was mindful, too, of the likely reaction of the parties of the right, particularly the Conservatives and the National Liberals, and also, if less acutely, of that of the Centre party, which on ideological grounds was demanding resolute support for Austria-Hungary.

The extreme right had been saying for several years that war was 'inevitable'. And yet if there had been greater self-restraint, and a greater willingness to negotiate, the First World War could have been avoided, albeit at the possible cost of some loss of prestige on the part of the Imperial government. With its position already weakened, however, both with regard to its opponents within the ruling elites and *vis-à-vis* the political parties and public opinion, the government did not have the nerve to follow the more prudent course.

Overnight, the outbreak of the First World War brought about a dramatic change in the domestic political climate in Germany. The old and the new right joined forces in proclaiming far-reaching war aims that would, for the most part, have been considered unthinkable before 1914. Although the government at first made some attempt, if not to suppress the clamour over war aims (which had taken all leave of reality) then at least to prevent its hands from becoming tied, in the end it gave way. This forestalled any chance there might have been later on of bringing the war to an acceptable end through negotiation.

The huge and rapid bidding-up of war aims that took place, both within the governing circles of the Reich and outside, marked the high point of the imperialist movement. And despite the fact that the movement had long since lost its grip on the real world, it continued to exert a substantial influence on German policy throughout the First World War. This made the eventual collapse of the German political system inevitable. Yet even after Germany's defeat, nationalist extremism remained a potent force. Nationalism did not immediately repossess the centre ground of politics in 1918, but with the rise of National Socialism it re-emerged in a new and more radical form, even further divorced from reality than middle-class nationalism had been before 1914.

6

Economy, society and the state in the German Empire, 1870–1918

Fischer's far-reaching claims concerning the aggressive nature of German foreign policy before 1914 stirred up great controversy when they were made in the 1960s. In the longer run, however, they helped bring about a fundamental break with earlier interpretations of German Imperial history. Scholars in the Federal Republic began to turn their attention, on a scale that had not been seen before, to questions of economic and social change within the Empire. This, it was now felt, was the only way of explaining why it was that such a great surplus of militant nationalist energy had built up in Germany, in comparison with other European states, and why this energy had then found its discharge in war in 1914. Analysing the sequence of diplomatic events that led to war, which had been the main concern of earlier historians, no longer seemed adequate, even to writers who remained unmoved by the preoccupations of Marxist theory. Questions of economic and social change ceased to be the exclusive preserve of economic historians, even though much of the work that was now done by the social historians rested on foundations that had previously been laid by political economists – the pioneering studies of Walter G. Hoffmann being a notable instance.

More recently still, there has been a fresh bout of interest in economic and social developments within the German Empire, but for quite different reasons. It is now recognized that there is a greater degree of long-term historical continuity in the economic and social spheres than there is in the political field. This newer concern with the economic, social and cultural aspects of the Empire is exemplified by Thomas Nipperdey's argument that historians should employ a number of varying time-scales, rather than a single scale designed to culminate in – say – the year 1933 or 1945. Several different sorts of trends, in fact, that originated during the Empire still exert their influence today: without passing judgement on them from a political point of view, we can say that some of these trends may be termed 'progressive', and some 'conservative', in character. It is also important to acknowledge, however, that many of the questions that are of particular relevance in this connection still find us groping in the dark. For example, despite the work of Jeck, Kaelble, Volkmann and others,[1] we still have much to learn concerning the degree of social mobility that existed in the Empire. Similarly, questions concerning the educational system – to what extent it was open, and to what extent exclusive – are also far from resolved.

The economic and social changes that took place in Germany between 1850 and 1914 are usually said to have effected a transition from an agrarian to an industrial state. There is no question that this period of seventy years witnessed an extraordinary transformation in German society. In 1850 Prussia, and Germany as a whole, were barely on the threshold of industrialization; by 1913 the German Empire had become a member of the leading group of industrial nations. Germany had unquestionably overtaken Great Britain in industrial production, though general living standards still lagged significantly behind. The German economy had become an integral part of the evolving system of multilateral world trade, and German exports represented one-fifth of national output.

Even contemporaries realized that the economic advances that had been made since 1850 represented a visible and indisputable success story by international standards, despite the fact that there had been some substantial setbacks. This perception of progress generated a strong sense of self-assurance on the part of the middle classes: a characteristic expression of this confidence can be found in the book *Deutschlands Volkswohlstand 1888–1913* (Germany's National Wealth, 1888–1913),[2] published in 1913 by Karl Helfferich, then the head of the Deutsche Bank, to mark Wilhelm II's Silver Jubilee.

Economic and social historians in the Federal Republic have tended to take a somewhat critical view of the economic and social changes that occurred during the Empire, notwithstanding the fact that the overall economic achievements were so considerable. According to what has become the standard interpretation (though it has lately come under fire from some quarters, as we shall see) there was a basic mismatch between economic change on the one hand and developments in the political sphere on the other. On this analysis, whereas the economy and the legal framework regulating the social order underwent a far-reaching process of modernization, the process stopped short when it came to the political system. As the industrial sector of the economy expanded, so the conflict between the Empire's political culture and its economic system grew ever more pronounced. The result was a series of gross failures of judgement on the political front – in particular, an expansionist foreign policy, pursued to the clamorous accompaniment of nationalistic slogans, which culminated in the outbreak of the First World War and cast a long shadow over the fragile new democracy established in 1918.

While this general paradigm has been largely undisputed, there have, of course, been differences of emphasis and perception concerning the nature of economic change under the Empire and the effects of economic change on politics and society. Periodization itself has not been uncontentious, and there has been considerable disagreement over the political consequences of the fluctuations in economic growth that occurred. And opinions are much more varied still with regard to the structural changes in the economy that resulted from rapid industrialization. In particular, did these changes also give rise to changes in social structures and within the political culture that slowed down, or even blocked, the gradual introduction of democratic forms of political decision-making?

As far as economic development is concerned, we can divide the overall period 1850–1913 into three main phases:

1. A phase of 'take-off into sustained growth' from 1850 to 1873.
2. The period of the 'Great Depression' between 1873 and 1896, ushered in by the so-called 'Gründerkrise', the crisis that brought the *Gründerjahre* to an end.
3. A phase of accelerating economic expansion between 1896 and 1913, sometimes labelled a 'second industrial revolution' in view of the important part that was played during these years by leading new sectors of the economy such as the electrical and chemical industries.

It is generally agreed that during the years 1850–73 the role of the Prussian state was a crucial one. In a major study (though one that some-times devotes rather too much space to detailed accounts of the individual political actors) Böhme has described how Prussia adhered consistently to a policy of free trade from the early 1850s onwards and succeeded in secur-ing the economic leadership of the German-speaking world at the expense of her less advanced neighbour and rival Austria, gradually transforming the Zollverein (Customs Union) into a Prussian-dominated institution.[3] Prussia's position of hegemony within the Zollverein, reinforced by free-trade agreements with other powers, foreshadowed the dominant political role she was later to assume within the German Empire.

The extent to which economic development directly helped pave the way to Imperial unification remains, of course, a matter of some dispute among scholars. Zorn has shown that the economic regulations that played so important a part in bringing about subsequent growth would also have been feasible, in a purely economic sense, within the framework of the reconstituted Zollverein.[4] Nevertheless, there is a substantial body of evi-dence (backed up, notably, by the wealth of detailed analysis provided by Hamerow)[5] to show that the political self-assurance of the middle classes, which had faltered somewhat after 1849, was significantly strengthened by the expansion of the economy. A situation had been created in which even the forces of conservatism could no longer simply ignore the economic and social interests of the rising middle class, which now possessed effective means of promoting these interests in the form both of the Nationalverein (National Association) and of numerous special organizations such as the Congress of German Economists. This, essentially, was the reason for the compromise that lay at the heart of the German Imperial constitution, which, though owing its existence to a 'revolution from above', nevertheless also made so many concessions to the demands of the middle class that the forces of Old Conservatism at first came out in bitter opposition to the new dispensation.[6]

In fact, however, the agricultural sector – and in particular, the East Elbian region of large estates – was still in the midst of a relatively prosperous phase. With some justice, Abel has described the years between 1830 and 1870 as the 'golden decades' of agriculture. Farmers still enjoyed fairly favourable conditions of production and continued to be able to export a considerable proportion of their grain; the impact of foreign competition did not become noticeable until the mid-1870s, though thereafter the effects were increasingly evident. The economic position of the big landowners was not, admittedly, absolutely secure during the period in question. For social reasons the prices of estates were steadily moving above the level that would have been warranted on a market-based reckoning of the highest attainable net yields: in other words, the relatively high social status that went with owning a manorial estate was driving the price of agricultural property considerably above its real commercial value. The process of social readjustment that Hans Rosenberg, somewhat polemically and misleadingly, has dubbed the 'pseudo-democratization' of the *Junker* class was well under way.[7] Nevertheless, in the short run this process actually served to stabilize the position of the landowning aristocracy, even though the proportion of middle-class landowners was sharply on the increase. For the time being the economic position of the large farmers remained a strong one, and this fact had indirect political consequences that should not be underestimated. On the other hand, it is no less true that in the newly-created Reich the initiative on questions of economic and social policy passed increasingly, though not entirely, to the upper echelons of the middle class, represented particularly by the National Liberal party, and to the Imperial and Prussian higher civil service with which the middle class had many links.

The divisions of opinion among social historians on the political system that was created in 1867 and 1871 remain very wide. Wehler, Berghahn and Engelberg, in particular (the latter writing from a Marxist perspective), have stressed the authoritarian and repressive character of the new system, seeing it as a device for ensuring the continuing dominance of the traditional ruling elites. The present author, among others, has argued the need to recognize the fact that the system was a compromise on the social and political fronts, while Gall has strongly emphasized the sense in which the system was appropriate to the 'spirit of the age'.[8] By contrast, however, Geoff Eley has recently claimed that the political order established by Bismarck should be seen as Germany's variant of 'bourgeois society', since although various features of the feudal framework survived, the middle class was given a very free rein in the areas that really counted, that is on economic and social questions.[9] Eley's account poses a direct challenge to the view that has been widely prevalent among historians in recent years, both in Germany and abroad: namely, that what was distinctive about German society in the Imperial era was the continuing presence of political and social forces that were specifically pre-modern (i.e. feudal) in origin. Essentially, Eley argues, the middle class was able to determine the economic and social conditions within which it wished to operate, and this was the primary reason why the German Empire's economic achievements were so considerable. In particular, the militant nationalism of the new right was a middle-class creation or, to put it more forcefully, a creation of the capitalist system itself, and not of the system's aristocratic adversaries and their followers. We shall return to Eley's thesis later.

This has already taken us on to the period 1873–96. Here Hans-Ulrich Wehler and Hans Rosenberg, in particular, have maintained (the latter in some ways even more forcefully) that there is a direct connection between the fluctuations in economic activity and the changes in political and social structures that took place after 1873. They see the 'Great Depression' as a period of social and political crisis. Reduced growth and severe recurrent economic setbacks during this period gave rise, they argue, to an ideological consensus among the dominant classes in society, the middle class included, that the consequent danger of social breakdown had to be averted by a policy of economic expansion overseas. If necessary, such expansion would have to include the acquisition of colonies. Wehler shows how such social-imperialist attitudes became increasingly common from the mid-1870s onwards and claims that they played a crucial part in prompting Bismarck to adopt a colonial policy. He has gone on to apply a generalized form of the social-imperialist model to the political and social structures of the German Empire in its entirety.[10]

Few economic historians have concurred with this relatively 'pessimistic' account of the years 1873–96. Taking their cue from S.B. Saul's study *The Myth of the Great Depression*,[11] most scholars have concluded that the ups and downs in the business cycle that occurred during this period, in particular the fluctuations during 1882–84 and 1891–94, were not especially serious. Knut Borchardt, for example, and, more recently, Karl Erich Born have pronounced favourable verdicts on the economic trends of the period and have emphasized the factors that combined to make for longer-term expansion.[12] On the other hand, it has to be said that the statistics of economic growth for the period are very general and do not reveal the dislocations that occurred in many individual areas of the economy as an extreme excess of supply and falls in prices coincided with the growing integration of the German economy into the international economic system. These dislocations occurred even in the areas of the economy that can be regarded as having been at the forefront of growth, such as the metal-producing and metal-working industry. Borchardt has shown that although the use of the older charcoal-burning technology in the production of iron and steel was rapidly becoming hopelessly outmoded in the 1860s, output based on this method was nevertheless reaching its peak at this time. Schomerus's study of the Esslingen engineering works, which was highly successful during the early phase of industrialization, paints a similar picture of industrial progress being achieved only at the price of severe problems of adaptation and economic and human hardship.[13] In textiles, too, the introduction of the new techniques was hesitant and badly phased; moreover, the result was not a general switch to factory production but, for a period at least, a marked rise in the amount of domestic working and 'putting-out'. As Hartmut Kaelble has recently pointed out, the growth of German industry was by no means as rapid in international terms as the aggregate data, taken in isolation, seem to suggest. Altogether, taking the period as a whole, we have to bear in mind that a small number of highly successful firms existed side by side with a large number of firms that remained technologically fairly backward, and that even though overall economic expansion brought marked benefits, it was also accompanied by severe problems, which were perceived as symptoms of crisis by those who were affected by them. In addition, of course, fiercer competition in the market place and sharp falls in prices meant that self-financing through price, which had been the main way of raising capital during the early phase of industrialization, was becoming increasingly difficult, and that the rapid amortization of invested capital was also less feasible than it had been in the preceding period. Furthermore, although real national income per capita rose markedly between 1873 and 1896 (except during the years of stagnation after 1873), this was mainly because of falls in prices rather than because of any rise in earnings.

It is fitting that social historians, in particular, should ask what happens to the losers, as well as to the gainers, from long-term processes of economic change; all too often, historians tend to write the history of the latter to the exclusion of the former. As far as this period is concerned, German scholars have paid particular attention for some considerable time to workers in the small craft trades (*Handwerk*) – a social group whose roots largely go back to the pre-industrial era. Nevertheless, although nineteenth-century statistical data do not differentiate between industry and the craft trades, so that a reliable picture covering the country as a whole is not easy to produce, it is clear that to claim that the craft trades died out, as Marxist analyses predicted they would – and, for that matter, as was widely feared by small craftsmen themselves – is not, in general correct. Indeed, in the take-off phase of industrialization the number of small craftsmen rose substantially, and it continued to increase as a proportion of the overall population during the later stages of industrial growth. Wolfram Fischer, who admittedly tends to take an 'optimistic' view of the period, concludes that altogether the craft trades grew 'roughly in line with the economy as a whole, although not quite as much as the secondary sector'.[14]

On the other hand, it has to be said that while such an assessment is doubtless correct in global terms, it does not address the great shifts of balance that took place within the craft-trade sector and that gave rise to much bitter hardship and misery. During the take-off phase of industrialization, until the 1870s, we find a large increase in the number of master craftsmen and a lesser rise in the number of journeymen; we also find that the living standards of the two groups were gradually becoming more similar. Although small craftsmen in general, with some exceptions, were becoming relatively poorer (their poverty being reflected, for example, in grindingly harsh living conditions) it is clear that by and large the traditional social barrier between the craft trades and the industrial working class remained intact (as Friedrich Lenger has demonstrated in the case of Düsseldorf, for example).[15] The new industrial enterprises recruited most of their labour, not from the local or regional craft trades, but from the stream of people who were leaving the land in search of work. As industrial change proceeded, however, sizeable shifts of balance among the different craft trades took place, even though small craftsmen retained their traditional sense of identity as a social group. The food trades profited directly from the spread of industry and the rise in national living standards, and the building trades actually became a leading and highly important sector as construction expanded with the rapid growth of towns from the 1880s onwards; similarly, other trades maintained their position by moving from the production to the service sector. Many other trades, however, such as shoemaking and tailoring, steadily lost ground in the face of competition, not only from industrial firms but from retailers, who began to offer their own repair services instead of passing on the work to craftsmen. This latter trend gave rise to bitter disputes among small businessmen and retailers and led to attempts to settle the problem by legislation, though the attempts were not successful. All told, we should not underestimate the adverse consequences of industrialization for the craft trades in the period between 1873 and 1896, despite the fact that the global statistics show that the craft sector fared well and, indeed, to some extent strengthened its position from the late 1890s onwards.

Of greater bearing on the changing social and political order was the fact that there was a crisis in agriculture from the 1870s onwards, although it was not to reach a climax until 1894. The introduction of protective tariffs in 1879 (which were then increased in 1885) mitigated the effects of overseas competition on agricultural markets but could not nullify them altogether. At the same time, however, the predicament of the farmers should not, in my view, be exaggerated. Farming productivity in fact went on to rise significantly, if not as rapidly as productivity in industry and the craft trades; and, more important, the number of people employed in agriculture also increased slightly. Generally speaking, the agricultural sector remained comparatively strong up to 1914, despite the fact that it had long since ceased to be big enough to feed the nation unaided. It is certainly true that industry and the craft trades had conclusively overtaken agriculture,

forestry and fisheries in terms of net production by the turn of the century
(by about 1885, if mining is also taken into account). Likewise, it was
industry, the craft trades, commerce and the service sector that absorbed
almost all of the large number of new recruits to the labour market.
Nevertheless, in comparison with, say, Great Britain, agriculture remained
very much the force it had previously been, albeit thanks in part to direct
and indirect support from government by means of economic and fiscal
policy. For this reason, the common formulation that Germany changed
from being an agrarian to an industrial society – or, in Hentschel's words,
from being a 'predominantly agrarian state' to being a 'predominantly
industrial state'[16] – seems to me to be misleading. Until 1914 the German
Empire was both an agrarian *and* an industrial state, and the two sectors
existed in relative isolation from one another, with social and political consequences that will concern us later. In addition to the large landowners,
who, though few in numbers, cultivated roughly 22 per cent of the agricultural land (it is reckoned that in 1880 there were about 17,500 *Gutsbezirke*
or estate districts) there was a highly ramified community of peasant farmers who were rather less directly affected by variations in grain prices. The
peasantry did profit, indirectly and in part, from the growth of industry,
but it also constituted a pool of anti-industrial and conservative sentiment
in the state and society, the importance of which should not be neglected.

We come now to the period of expansion between 1896 and 1913. All
told, these were years of dramatic advance, although there was a sharp
recession between 1901 and 1904 that had some of the features of a second
'Gründerkrise', and the period ended with a phase of stagnation, the effects
of which were neutralized only by the artificial armament-led boom of the
First World War. In 1913 Karl Helfferich claimed with some pride that
Germany's output had increased threefold since 1888, and in many respects
this period can, indeed, be compared with the West German 'economic mir-
acle' of the 1950s. Certainly, leading figures in industry and commerce were
infused with a remarkable sense of self-assurance and an optimism about
future economic prospects that had not been widespread among the previous generation.

Historians in the Federal Republic have offered very varied assessments
of the period. In the 1970s Hans-Ulrich Wehler, Jürgen Kocka and Heinrich
August Winkler proposed an analysis combining a model of 'organized capitalism', by which they meant a socio-economic formation conforming to
the classic, essentially market-based formation of individualistic capitalism,
with an emphasis on the emergence of the modern 'interventionist state'.[17]
This analysis was a fusion of two distinct approaches. On the one hand, it
took up ideas that had been put forward in the 1920s by socialists such as
Rudolf Hilferding, who had tried to explain why the series of steadily esca-
lating economic crises predicted by Marx had not come to pass. At the
same time, it incorporated a refined and more systematic account of features which Alexander Gerschenkron has regarded as characteristic of those

economies that did not undergo intensive industrialization until a second phase of development. In particular, it stressed the special role played by banks in paving the way for industrial amalgamation, both vertical and horizontal, and in aiding the drive for technological innovation, for example by facilitating the transfer of already matured technologies to comparatively larger, and hence more efficient, production units, where optimal use could be made of the 'advantages of backwardness'. According to Wehler, in fact, increasing capital concentration and the linked phenomenon of cartel formation and the creation of combines of all kinds are the defining features of the 'organized capitalism' phase. Certainly, there were widespread moves to form cartels and syndicates in Germany before 1914, particularly in primary industries – the Rheinisch-Westphälisches Kohlensyndikat of 1893 being the best known – and to that extent, at least, Wehler is justified in viewing this period in terms of a combination of 'organized capitalism' and the 'interventionist state'.

It is debatable, however, whether 'organized capitalism' was really capable of exerting a moderating, let alone an equilibrating, influence on fluctuations in the economic cycle. Likewise, there is little sign before 1914 of the sort of economically powerful 'interventionist state' that emerged after the Second World War in, say, Great Britain. The concept of state economic management was still unborn at this time, and the strategy of redistributing the national wealth by means of a progressive tax system was in its infancy at best. There has been some strong criticism of the model along these lines since it was first proposed. Moreover, even among advocates of the model there were differences from the outset concerning the question of when this phase of economic development should be seen as having started. Wehler argued that 'organized capitalism' was already under way in 1873, while Winkler – though he has subsequently altered his stance – maintained that the model should be applied only to the Wilhelmine period. Volker Hentschel in turn, has tried to demonstrate that the 'organized capitalism' model is inherently unsound, for the Wilhelmine period at any rate, though his study tacitly concedes that the attempt to provide a systematic overall account of the confusing changes of the period after 1896 by using idealtype models of this sort can actually be very fruitful.[18] If the 'organized capitalism' model does have one clear weakness, it is that it does not take account of problems of external trade and, in particular, of the process of imperialist expansion, since it deals only with the domestic economy.

There can be no dispute, however, that the period after 1896 saw the emergence – though their origins lay earlier – of economic structures which, despite all the political upheavals that followed, have in many respects remained intact up to the present day. The role of the large banks is especially important here, even if we do not subscribe to the formula, current at the time, of the dominance of 'finance capital' (a formula which was also of some importance, of course, in Lenin's account of imperialism as the highest stage of capitalism). In particular, the banks played a vital role in financing industrial enterprises in the new sectors of the economy such as the electrical and chemical industries. They also smoothed the path for German exporters by agreeing to cover export risks, which were often considerable, and by providing backing for large industrial enterprises that were seeking to establish subsidiaries elsewhere in Europe or overseas. In effect, a considerable number of multinational companies were being formed before 1914, although the term itself had not yet been invented. Admittedly, it is not clear whether or not the banks, as a general rule, actually played the dominant role as industry expanded after the turn of the century, and as horizontal and vertical integration became increasingly widespread, even extending across national boundaries. What seems to have happened is that even though the banks worked closely with industry in many ways, there were also clear demarcation lines. The banks adhered fairly strictly to the principles of economic liberalism and were reluctant for the most part to go along with anything more than an 'informal' brand of imperialism. Heavy industry, on the other hand, and to an extent also the electrical industry, were much more sympathetic to notions of imperialist expansion, and were also much more closely allied to the political right, from obvious motives, both because they saw such an alliance as in their immediate interest and because they shared the right's (anti-socialist) vision of society.

Historians have also shown considerable interest in the growth of organized economic interest groups, which had begun to spring up during the Bismarck era but became especially plentiful in the Wilhelmine Empire. It is certainly the case that interest groups tried more vigorously than ever during this period to influence events and political decision-making. How successful their activities actually were, however, remains a matter of dispute. Indeed, industrialists repeatedly voiced their irritation at the relatively small amount of leverage they exerted over legislation, even though Bismarck himself and, to a lesser extent, his successors were quite willing to cultivate close contacts with interested parties on economic questions. In the course of time, industry itself came to recognize that it had to try to play a direct part in decision-making in Parliament, and after the turn of the century the right wing of the National Liberal party, in particular, became something of a mouthpiece for industrial interests, though its effectiveness was rather limited. Altogether, the case of Germany fully bears out Max Weber's claim that it became harder, rather than easier, to implement the principles of liberalism and democracy under the conditions of advanced capitalism.

The achievements of the industrial sector during the last two and a half decades of the Empire, and the associated growth of large enterprises – particularly in primary industries, though also in the electrical and chemicals industries and in machine tools – tend to obscure the fact that there were very great discrepancies between different parts of the German economy in the Wilhelmine period. The big firms dominated the market in both economic and technological terms, but it would be wrong to exaggerate their role within the economy as a whole. Statistics relating to the size of firms in the German Empire certainly show that there was a long-term trend towards larger units, with the proportion of firms employing more than 50 people – huge enterprises by the criteria of the time – rising from 22.8 per cent in 1882 to 33.5 per cent in 1895 and 42.4 per cent in 1907. But enterprises that were large by modern standards (that is, employing over 1,000 people) constituted only 1.9 per cent of all firms in 1882 and 4.7 per cent in 1907, while the proportion of firms employing only between 1 and 5 people, despite falling by one-half, still accounted for 31.2 per cent of the total (cf. the figure of 16.2 per cent for the Federal Republic). In addition, very large firms were concentrated in a few sectors of the economy, notably primary industries, and were also confined to a very small number of parts of the country: mainly, in fact, to Rhineland-Westphalia. When looking at society as a whole, therefore, we should not overstate the importance of the typical large enterprise, with its usually paternalistic internal structure. (As Weber said: 'These gentlemen are really like the police'.)[19]

Indeed, the distinguishing feature of the Wilhelmine economy was the fact that it was segmented into a relatively large number of different sectors and interest groups: the banks, heavy industry, the consumer-goods industry, to say nothing of agriculture, with its own distinctive situation – each of these various spheres of activity constituted a separate social and political camp. It is also noteworthy that the craft trades, despite the far-reaching structural changes to which they were subjected in the course of industrialization, not only maintained their distinctive sense of social identity but gained enhanced status after 1897 as a result of state legislation that had the effect of reinstating compulsory guilds and certificates of qualification.

Let us now turn to the social effects that were caused by industrial growth from the middle of the nineteenth century onwards. In an essay of the present length it is difficult to avoid falling into commonplaces on this question, and we must certainly say straight away that the living standards of *all* sections of the population rose markedly during the period as a whole, even though – and on this point there has been much recent debate – the rise was very far from equally distributed. It is clear not only that emigration was eventually brought to a virtual standstill but that in the course of time the great majority of those who left the rural areas of the country managed to find employment in the new sectors of industry, the craft trades, commerce and services. Moreover, these developments took place despite a marked rise in population growth. This was the result, in the final part of the period, not of a rising birth rate but of falling mortality, and is a reasonably reliable indication that the economic circumstances of the broad mass of the population tangibly improved, along with standards of medical care. It should also be mentioned in this context that internal migration and the phenomenon of transnational migratory movements were probably important sources of economic dynamism,[20] even though they also gave rise to considerable problems of dislocation. In comparison with Great Britain, the great process of urbanization – which was sometimes quite spectacularly rapid after the 1890s – unfolded fairly smoothly and did not lead to widespread deprivation.

At the same time, of course, this broadly 'optimistic' picture of social relations under the Empire needs to be qualified in a number of ways. Compared with the lowly conditions under which most people had lived before industrialization – particularly in the countryside, though also in the towns – significant progress was indeed made. Germany was also largely spared the sort of harsh mass poverty and deprivation in the industrial conurbations that had accompanied the industrial surge in Britain during the 'hungry forties' – which does not mean that there were not serious problems of housing in Germany's western industrial cities and in Berlin as growth took off in those regions after the turn of the century. But we should not forget that the lower social classes continued to live under extremely straitened circumstances.

The position of industrial workers in the narrower sense seems to have improved rather more than that of other groups at the bottom of the social scale. The statistical foundations on which the varying assessments of the growth of workers' real wages that have been made by Kuczynski, Bry, Desai and others are far from wholly reliable, but real wages undoubtedly rose significantly (according to Desai, by about 57 per cent): at first mainly indirectly, because of falling prices, later (between 1870 and 1913) in their own right. On the other hand, wage levels, despite gradually catching up, probably remained about 30 per cent behind those of British industrial workers. Moreover, the growth of real wages does not of itself tell us a great deal about the actual conditions in which the working class lived. What is needed, as Heilwig Schomerus has shown, following British studies, is an analysis of the life-cycle of the average factory worker and his family, including the typical phases of acute hardship that coincided with various stages of familial development, especially old age. Unemployment is a further factor whose social consequences during this period of change in German society have not been widely studied. That said, it seems fair to assume that the result of the introduction of social insurance, the gradual raising of levels of benefits and the extension of the numbers of groups of workers covered was to make the effects of the typical cycle of relative deprivation somewhat less acute, particularly as far as provision for old age and compensation for industrial accidents were concerned. In addition, the unusually high degree of labour mobility that was a by-product of the massive migratory movements within and across Germany's borders probably helped to expand opportunities on the labour market. Many groups of workers undoubtedly availed themselves of these opportunities, despite the constraints that had been placed on trade-union activities and the numerous indirect methods whereby employers could keep workers yoked to firms and restrict their freedom of movement.

Comparable data for other groups of workers, particularly agricultural labourers, rural domestic servants and the like, are not yet available. In general, however, it is certain that there were great variations in income between individuals and between regions. That includes those employed in industry and the craft trades, but it applies especially to other lower-class groups. Industrial workers probably constituted a relatively privileged group among the lower social classes, notwithstanding the repressive measures, both administrative and political, that prevented them from effectively defending their interests against their employers. A close analysis of the considerable differences in income that existed within the industrial working class would be instructive, especially one involving a comparison with British conditions, but that is not possible here. What is unquestionable is that the economic situation of the great bulk of domestic workers, farm labourers and rural domestic servants, as well as many of those employed in small-scale industry, was far harder than that of the great majority of skilled industrial workers. Hentschel's verdict on the living standards of the great mass of the population is incontestable: 'On the eve of the world war, about 30 per cent of all family households in the German Empire still lived in "straitened" circumstances, and the living conditions of a further one-third were little more than "adequate".'[21]

This conclusion is based on an analysis of statistics of incomes in Prussia and Saxony, which have also been used by other scholars, such as Albert Jeck and Wolfram Fischer,[22] for calculating income levels and shifts in income distribution in the German Empire. It must be emphasized, admittedly, that any attempt to construct a model of social stratification in Germany on the basis of income data is subject to serious methodological difficulties. Moreover, tax statistics are intrinsically liable to error, and there is only a partial correlation between tax levels and actual social status, viewed over the longer term. Broadly speaking, though, the pattern of social stratification in the German Empire resembled an extremely steep-sided pyramid, and this pattern seems to have remained essentially unaltered from 1850 to 1914. If there were any long-term changes, they had the effect of turning the upper layers of the system into something more of a plutocracy, while the lower and very lowest income groups simultaneously became considerably broader and the upper-middle stratum strengthened its position somewhat. Industrial growth, in other words, did not lead to a fundamental redistribution of income in Germany before 1913. The overall income range was merely extended: a greater differentiation of incomes developed as the widening and slight raising of the base of the pyramid was countered by the gains made by those at the top (and by the substantial gains made by the originally tiny group at the very pinnacle). Although the number of people in Prussia with incomes in the lowest income-tax category (900 to 1,650 marks) rose by 2 million between 1895 and 1912, this rise was offset by a substantial simultaneous increase in the number of people who were not asessed for tax because their means were too modest. It is not possible, therefore, to say without qualification that the incomes of the broad mass of the population improved; at the same time, however, the statistics leave wide scope for 'optimistic' as well as 'pessimistic' interpretations.

These statistics enable us to draw some cautious conclusions about the social order in the German Empire and to propose certain hypotheses about the political consequences that flowed from it. In the process we can also return to the question whether Germany under the Empire became a 'bourgeois' society or whether, as most historians have argued, it was a society distorted by the survival of aristocratic features. Certainly, it cannot be denied that the Prusso-German aristocracy – in numerical terms, a small group consisting of at most 15,000–17,000 families – occupied a leading position within the social structure. But the economic foundations that underlay the aristocracy's traditional dominance in society and the state had long since begun to be eroded, and even though there was a sizeable influx into the nobility from the middle class, both through intermarriage and (as Hans Rosenberg has shown) through the transmutation of leading members of the propertied middle class into landowning aristocrats, this long-term process of erosion was not halted. Preferential treatment for the higher aristocracy in the officer corps and the Prussian civil service, and to some extent in the higher administrative echelons of the other states of the Empire, was, as we can see today, slowly on the wane, and did little to compensate for the dramatic trimming of the aristocracy's power base in rural local government that took place in the 1870s (to be followed by its complete disappearance after 1891). In contrast with the situation in, say, Great Britain, there was never a real fusion of the upper ranks of the rising middle classes with the landowning nobility: a new 'upper class', in other words, did not emerge, despite the steps that were taken in that direction. Indeed, the fact that a symbiotic link between the old and the newly risen upper strata was not formed was perhaps one of the key social phenomena of the Empire. At most, the alliance between 'manorial estate and blast furnace' carried some comparable surrogate social and political significance.

The evolution of the middle classes is a more complex matter. The *Mittelstand* has long been an object of close historical study, the more so since it is recognized as having been one of the principal sources from which National Socialism drew its electoral support. The statistical data indicate that the overall economic situation of the middle classes underwent a moderate improvement during the period, but that at the same time (as one would indeed expect) there was growing variation within this general picture. Whether the statistics underpin the view, which the political history of the period suggests, that the classical middle class with its attachment to liberal political ideas was gradually breaking up is not immediately clear. Particular attention has been paid in recent research to white-collar workers, as a group that was becoming emancipated from the working class, and to the lower middle class more generally.[23] Instead of merging into the liberal camp (as contemporaries would have thought natural) the lower middle class seems steadily to have turned away from it, becoming instead a hotbed for political movements that were predominantly hostile to modernization and industrial growth and that wished to stem the accelerating pace of change in society.

Sections of the rising lower middle classes, and with them a significant proportion of the 'intellegentsia', became recruits for the new right. This movement dissociated itself from the purely defensive policies of the conservatives, which were designed solely to protect the interests of agriculture, but nevertheless tended to come down on the side of the established authorities, partly out of bitter anti-socialist sentiments that can readily be attributed to the particular position within society of the movement's members. Identifying with a powerful nation state was particularly important for these groups, since it helped them in their drive for emancipation within the traditional social and party-political system: by equating their personal destiny with that of the nation as a whole, they could strongly bolster their sense of their own identity and worth. It was no accident that the core of support for the extra-parliamentary nationalist propaganda organizations that sprang up from the 1890s onwards lay in these areas of society, although there was also no shortage of recruits from higher up the social scale.[24]

Within the Catholic community, by contrast, the equivalent groups became politically active through the Centre party. The Centre increasingly found itself having to act as the mouthpiece for a range of conservative social attitudes that were difficult to reconcile with one another, as David Blackbourn has recently shown in the case of Württemberg.[25] This applied particularly to the members of the 'older' *Mittelstand*, craftsmen and small traders of all kinds who felt that industrialization offered them few benefits, and brought them many disadvantages, in the short run. In addition, the onward march of industry and the modernizing measures that followed in its train began to undermine the Catholic social milieu, with its wide range of social and political organizations. The Centre party thus became something of a focal point for a variety of efforts by social conservatives to resist the spread of industrialization and its associated secular values.

All of these factors help to explain why the liberal parties in the Empire were unable, after the fairly brief period between 1867 and 1879, to exploit the position of indubitable strength that they had originally occupied, and why they never achieved political hegemony. The reason is not just that they faced resistance from the conservative flank and from the largely conservative-minded higher civil service, but that wider social forces hostile to a thorough-going liberalization of society and the state (which was, or was held to be, a precondition of long-term economic growth) remained extremely well entrenched. This hostility, moreover, became more widespread after the turn of the century. The impact of industrialization on society in Imperial Germany differed greatly from one region to another and from one sector of the economy to another: in a sense the centres of industrial growth – the Ruhr, the Rhineland and all the areas of concentration along the Rhine railway, Greater Berlin, Hamburg and Saxony (though the latter had already begun to lose ground again after the turn of the century) – were only islands within a larger sea that was still, on the whole, a traditional society. Responses to industrialization were accordingly highly variable. By the same token, however, the forces of opposition to economic change, although not of a piece, were quite powerful in their combined impact, and became more powerful still from the late 1880s onwards. We hardly need reiterate the importance of agriculture as an almost natural breeding-ground of conservative politics and anti-industrial ideology. Even during the First World War, the debate within the industrial associations on Germany's war aims was strongly coloured by a concern that any territorial annexations that might be made should not disturb the delicate balance between the industrial and agrarian sectors – one is tempted to say, between the culture of industry and commerce on the one hand and that of the rural peasantry and the large farmers of the other. Thus, if regions that were mainly industrial, such as Belgium, were annexed, then, it was argued, there should be compensating annexations of agricultural regions in the east.

Nevertheless, it would also be wrong to underestimate the importance of the middle classes in Imperial Germany: in particular, the industrial and commercial class, with its new-found prosperity and self-assurance, and the educated middle class, in many ways closely linked to it, from which the professions and the civil service at national, regional and local level were increasingly being recruited as the proportion of aristocratic officials declined. Securely protected by the three-class system of suffrage, these groups dominated the towns and cities. They virtually monopolized public opinion through the press, and exerted a considerable further indirect influence over opinion through the educational system, which was largely under their control. Within the institutions of the Empire and the federated states, the liberals lost much of their political influence once the fairly brief 'liberal era' between 1867 and 1879 had come to an end. But in town and city government they preserved their position, by and large, until the First World War, even if this was mainly because the electoral system created an in-built bias against the Social Democrats. The effect of rapid urbanization was to transfer the centre of gravity in society to the urban centres, both old and new, and within this newly emergent urban culture the educated and propertied middle class set the pace, while the influence of the aristocracy went sharply into decline or even came close to extinction altogether. In this realm of society, in other words, a specifically midddle-class culture was indeed taking root, despite the fact that the semi-constitutional structure of the Empire guaranteed the continuing dominance of the traditional elites. Moreover, the representatives of this culture were fully aware of the opposition between it and the culture of the aristocracy and its offshoots. In this sense, at any rate, German society before 1914 can be said to have been a bourgeois society, and though it was a society that also contained certain feudal distortions, these latter features were more limited in their influence than has commonly, and rather uncritically, been assumed.

This middle-class culture had its economic base in the rapidly expanding industrial system, and in the service sector associated with it. At the same time, it was an explicitly nationalistic culture, in latent, and sometimes overt, opposition to the political tenets of the agrarian conservatives, until the latter decided after 1911 that they had no option but to jump on to the nationalist bandwagon. In this respect nationalism functioned as an ideology of emancipation on the middle class's part, a vehicle whereby it could free itself from aristocratic tutelage – though it was also an effective weapon that could be turned against the putative internationalism of the Social Democrats. Even when the middle classes gave their firm backing to Germany's bid to establish herself as a leading world power, they did not do so, primarily, on grounds of immediate material interest, but from political and social motives: they believed that an energetic imperialist policy would lead to a reduction of domestic tensions. When it came to providing finance for imperialist ventures, the same groups responded very warily, apart from the individual firms that were directly involved.

On the surface at least, the Empire was a distinctly authoritarian society. It was burdened by the heritage of the Prussian military state and by bureaucratic traditions that dated from the era of enlightened despotism and the subsequent age of reform. In the course of industrialization these bureaucratic features became further entrenched, partly at the expense of the aristocracy's political influence. This bureaucratic tendency was significantly reinforced by the fact that the system was comparatively late (in Gerschenkron's terms) in becoming industrialized. Any potential challenge to the bureaucratic elites from below was warded off by the policy of repressing working-class political movements and impeding the growth of trade unions. An open state, in which the broad mass of the population had an opportunity to participate in politics, was thought not to be proof against the 'red peril'. Strict social stratification also played an important part in entrenching the authoritarian features of the state.

On the other hand, this selfsame society exhibited an unusual degree of economic dynamism and, in due course, of social dynamism as well. From the turn of the century, if not earlier, opportunities for people to improve their circumstances within the system steadily increased – and not only for people with high incomes, but for the great bulk of the population. The educational system seems to have played a significant role here, since, although still extremely elitist in character, it was somewhat more open than those of comparable western societies such as Great Britain and France.[26] That again suggests that the German Empire, for all its reactionary political structure, had become a more middle-class society.[27] All told, although Imperial Germany remained an authoritarian society before 1914, we can discern within it the early stages of a process of upward mobility that was to lead the way towards an 'open society' of a modern type. And yet it also remains the case that the opposing forces around which the society of the Empire was founded – the aristocracy and the middle class; authoritarianism and liberalism – remained unreconciled; and it was these tensions, reflected in the competition between the power of the agricultural sector and the process of industrialization, that were to lead to the decline and, eventually, the fall of the system.

7

Culture and politics in the German Empire

Max Weber once observed, with something akin to alarm, that the political centre in Germany had not been a source of pure art or literature of a distinctively German character. This phenomenon was at odds with the view he held, as a sociologist, that national identity is 'generally anchored in the superiority, or at any rate, the irreplaceability of the "cultural goods" whose distinctive character is being preserved and cultivated (by the cultural elites)'.[1] Friedrich Nietzsche, writing about the effect of the establishment of the Empire on cultural development in Germany, pronounced a far severer verdict:[2]

> Within the history of European culture, the arrival of the 'Empire' on the scene means one thing above all: a shift of emphasis. It is common knowledge that on the question that matters most – which is still the question of culture – the Germans no longer count.

These judgements may be harsh and overstated, but it is undeniably the case that those at the centre of power in the German Empire stayed largely aloof from the pioneering developments in the visual arts, literature and music that took place during the Empire's lifetime. Indeed, from the first there was a perceptible tension between those who were responsible for official government policy on matters of art, culture, music and scholarship and those who were active in these fields in the proper sense, that is the artists, writers, composers and scholars themselves, together with their sympathizers and patrons in society.

Be that as it may, the fact that the variegated pattern of German states that had existed in the eighteenth and early nineteenth centuries survived, albeit in weakened form, within the federal structure of the Empire was highly beneficial for the evolution of art, literature and learning in Germany. Many quite different cultural centres were able to flourish, most of them originally the seats of princely courts, though a good number had also sustained a quite independent artistic and cultural life of their own: Mannheim and Düsseldorf, and former *Reichsstädte* such as Hamburg and

Cologne, were notable examples.[3] By contrast with the situation in France, the main impetus to the growth of literature, art and music in Germany came, broadly speaking, not from the largest city (Berlin) but from the various competing regional capitals; the one important sphere for which this did not hold true was modern scholarship and science. We may say, therefore, that those social groups that underpinned developments in literature, scholarship and the arts also stood at a clear remove from the ruling political elites. This fact inescapably prompts the question what political dimensions culture possessed under the German Empire – indeed, what political role it may have played.[4]

We can distinguish four cultural milieux within the German Empire. The traditional culture of the *aristocracy and the princely courts* had declined from its eighteenth-century peak, and in any case had become increasingly receptive to middle-class cultural ideals and achievements from the era of the Enlightenment and the aristocratic salon onwards. By now, however, the status of this milieu was unmistakably on the wane. Theodor Fontane, who provided an enduring memorial of the old Prussian aristocracy in his writings, notably in his *Wanderungen durch die Mark Brandenburg*, accused the aristocrats of his own era of having abandoned the cultivated standards they had once upheld and of having become narrow-minded guardians of self-interest: they had forfeited their former right to social and political leadership. The ossified life-style of the Prussian nobility, trapped by social convention and outmoded class arrogance, was one of the principal themes of Fontane's novels, especially *Der Stechlin* and the tragedy *Effi Briest*. Fontane can by no means be classed as an enemy of the aristocratic way of life, but he was forced to conclude that 'we shall have to disregard the nobility'.[5] It would be a mistake to underestimate the glamorous appeal that the life and cultural ideals of the aristocracy still had for other groups, especially the rising middle classes. Nor should we ignore the patronage that continued to flow from the German princely courts and, especially, from the court of the Emperor himself, even in an age when support for culture and the arts was increasingly being taken over by the state, by civic corporations and, notably, by private patronage. It soon became clear, however, that princely patrons who wished to be at the forefront of contemporary artistic and cultural movements would have to fall in with the cultural values of the middle class and the commercial practices of the middle-class art world. The days when King Ludwig I of Bavaria could declare, '*I am art*'[6] had gone, even though certain echoes of this absolutist conception of art could still be heard coming from Wilhelm II after the turn of the century.

The dominant cultural milieu during the Empire was undoubtedly *middle-class and Protestant* in character. The inexorable rise of the middle class as the dominant social group, in the cultural as well as the economic sphere, went back to the late eighteenth century. During the earlier part of the nineteenth century there had been close ties between the educated and the propertied sections of the middle class, partly because the process of industrialization came comparatively late to Germany. By the mid-1880s, if not before, these ties had begun to loosen, but they continued to be a crucial influence within middle-class Protestant culture.[7] The middle-class milieu rested firmly on a fairly advanced educational system, in which expressly religious influences had been supplanted by a partially secularized Protestant outlook, and on the rapid advance of rationalist modern science, with its associated faith in social and economic progress. Max Weber's famous account of the emergence of the modern capitalist system of markets and the division of labour from the 'spirit of capitalism' contains the classic description of the dominant characteristics of this new middle-class consciousness: life should be regulated by strict rationality, in the sense of 'inner-worldly' asceticism, and self-fulfilment was to be obtained through success in one's business or profession, in sharp contrast with the traditionalist conception of a life-style based on comfort and on conformance with status and the ideal of respectability. The middle-class ethos that prevailed in German society, however, differed from the basic puritan model of Weber's analysis in one important respect: it was not, by and large, hostile to artistic endeavour. On the contrary, for the German middle classes the principle of economic rationality almost always went hand in hand with the ideals of the new humanism. The central pillars of this outlook were Goethe and Schiller, Winckelmann's idealized version of Greek antiquity, and the Romantics' glorified vision of the German Middle Ages.

The close interconnections between the educated middle class, with its predominantly academic background, and the higher state civil service, and the continuing link between the middle class and the business class in the stricter sense – the 'liberal professions' forming a bridge between them – gave middle-class groups a dominant economic and social role during the take-off period of industrialization. Before the founding of the Empire, middle-class identity had been intimately bound up with political nationalism, principally expressed in the call for a unified state and the demand for constitutional government. Constitutional change, the middle classes believed, would give them (the true core of the nation) the central role in political decision-making that they deserved. Correspondingly, the middle-class culture that was evolving in the German states had a markedly nationalist colouring: bourgeois cultural attitudes and support for the strongly nationalist demands of constitutional liberalism were two sides of the same coin. The Schiller centenary celebrations of 1859 were a particularly graphic example of this phenomenon, combining veneration of the great writer with professions of faith in a nationalist form of liberal order. This modern liberal individualist culture, closely associated with education and scholarship, was one of the chief weapons in the hands of the liberal middle classes as they sought both to attack princely despotism and aristocratic tutelage and to defend their own position of political and social superiority over the forces of democracy and labour that were stirring lower down the social scale. In 1868 Friedrich Hecker voiced a widely shared middle-class conviction when he said: 'Industry and commerce, and art and science, render any form of absolutism unworkable in the long run.'[8]

Bismarck's policy of 'revolution from above' was a bitter disappointment for the liberal middle class. The longed-for nation state might now have come into being, but the middle classes were eventually to find that they had not been given access to the commanding heights of the political system, even if they were at first allowed a fairly free hand in shaping the new nation's economic and social policy. Nevertheless, although the semi-constitutional state fell a long way short of the aspirations of middle-class liberalism, the middle class laid 'claim to moral leadership [...] in the nation state, with its commitment to progress'.[9] The liberals were motivated by genuine conviction when they contested the privileges that the Catholic church had inherited within the modern secular state: the *Kulturkampf* was not a mere tactical exercise. They believed that the future lay with an individualistic, rationalist culture and that implementing the basic principles of this culture was in the general public interest. To be sure, the era of middle-class liberal dominance proved short-lived, both at the level of the German Empire and in the larger of its federated states. At a more local political level, however, and notably within the city corporations, the middle classes retained their position of hegemony virtually until the end of the Empire. This was due in large part to the continuance of the three-class electoral system, with its in-built bias in favour of owners of property, but the principal ground on which the middle classes defended the local system of suffrage and its almost total exclusion of the lower social classes was, precisely, that 'the question [was] one of fulfilling cultural functions that [were] appropriately carried out, in both material and intellectual terms, by the productive, mature and educated middle class'.[10] Indeed, by the middle of the nineteenth century the cities had taken over the role formerly played by the princely courts: municipal corporations, the members of which usually included a considerable number of prominent middle-class figures, had become the principal agencies in the transmission of middle-class cultural values. Working closely in tandem with private sources of patronage, the cities rapidly established a great array of theatres, museums of art and industry, concert halls, zoological gardens, scientific collections of all kinds, as well as academic and research institutions and, in some cases, fully-fledged schools of commerce. These institutions formed the foundation on which the rich multiplicity of middle-class cultural activity was able to flourish.

Unlike the middle-class Protestant cultural milieu, which continued to expand as the economy grew by leaps and bounds, the *Catholic cultural milieu*, which recruited most of its members from the Catholic lower middle class and was largely sustained by the Catholic clergy, had difficulty in holding its own. The Catholic section of the population was, of course, grossly under-represented in the cultural and educational institutions of the Empire, and this disadvantage was reinforced by official government policies, which gave Catholics very little opportunity of filling posts of major political and social importance, whether within the state or in society at large. It was not until the end of the century, and the founding of the People's Asssociation for Catholic Germany, that this situation began to be rectified. By now there were occasions on which Catholic interests coincided with those of the conservatives: over the Prussian Education Bill of 1892 and the Subversion Bill of 1895, for example, and indeed over specific disputes in the cultural sphere, such as that which occurred when Gerhart Hauptmann's play *Die Weber* was banned. On the other hand, episodes of this sort always provoked a strong wave of protest from the liberals, and governments generally lacked the courage to face down such protests when it came to the point.

Working-class culture was a more complex phenomenon. It evolved in isolation from the culture of the middle class, particularly during the period of the Socialist Law, and its institutional basis lay in an intricate network of proletarian organizations of all kinds. Among skilled workers, many of whom came from a background in the craft trades, the traditions of the liberal workers' educational associations (which held out to workers the possibility of escaping from straitened circumstances by means of a middle-class education, including commercial skills) had never entirely died out. August Bebel himself looked back with considerable pride on the liberal workers' education association to which he had belonged as a young man. Later, both while the Socialist Law was in force and thereafter, these older traditions were overlaid by the powerful and inspirational ideology of Marxism, most commonly in the evolutionist version propounded by Engels, in which the victory of socialism was cast as virtually a law of nature akin to Darwin's principle of natural selection. Below this grand surface, however, were cultural ideals that remained entirely middle-class in origin, above all a highly bourgeois belief in progress and an almost slavish faith in the blessings of modern science. A close analysis of the content of working-class culture during the Empire, in fact, shows that it was largely a sub-stratum of the dominant culture of the middle class, though it placed greated emphasis on rationalistic and emancipatory ideals. Indeed, when it came to a choice between conventional middle-class cultural values and explicitly modern art and literature, the champions of the cause of working-class culture, such as Franz Mehring with his Neue Freie Volksbühne in Berlin, came down in favour of the former rather than the latter. Having been an enthusiast for Naturalism during the public controversy over Hauptmann's *Die Weber*, Mehring concluded that the movement was actually a reversion to feudal Romanticism,[11] and after the turn of the century he concentrated on providing the Berlin workers with productions of bourgeois classics by Lessing and Schiller.[12] In the Social Democrats' debate on Naturalism at the Gotha conference of 1896, voices were even heard identifying the movement with the anarchism of the group known as 'Die Jungen', who had been expelled from the party a few years earlier.[13] Despite its use of the vocabulary of radicalism, then, the working class basically stayed loyal to orthodox middle-class cultural values, even though those very values were in the process of being overtaken by the modern movement in literature and the arts. On the other hand, the representatives of the dominant middle-class culture of the Empire had no cause to be triumphalist on this score, since the cultural sub-system that shaped the thinking of the working class actually showed far fewer signs of acculturation than might have occurred under conditions of greater freedom – as a comparison with the position in Great Britain during the same period, for example, would show.

In what follows we shall, inevitably, look most closely at middle-class culture and its relation to the state, since it was this milieu, with its foundations in the propertied and educated classes and its links with modern science and learning, that occupied a position of hegemony within the German Empire. Although the culture of the middle class had originally evolved in very close partnership with constitutional liberalism, particularly in the rapidly growing cities, it nevertheless soon found a comfortable home for itself within the new Empire. Strong nationalist sentiment, focused principally on the Imperial throne as the symbol of the new nation, formed a bridge connecting the spheres of culture and the state. Artists, musicians and writers were not slow to produce works that idealized the triumph of Prussian arms over the French. Theodor Fontane recorded the events of the Franco-Prussian war in lovingly crafted reports for the *Vossische Zeitung*. In January 1871 Richard Wagner wrote a poem dedicated 'To the German Army Before Paris', and not long afterwards he composed a *Kaisermarsch* (Imperial March) in honour of Germany's defeat of France. Even Johannes Brahms wrote a *Triumphlied* (Song of Triumph) commemorating Germany's victory, while Gustav Freytag hailed the founding of the Reich as the start of a new era in Germany's cultural as well as in her political life. Anton von Werner's gigantic historical canvases, recording almost all of the major political images of the period, such as Moltke on the battlefield of Sedan and the Imperial proclamation ceremony in the Hall of Mirrors at Versailles (scenes portrayed in painstaking detail, right down to the minutiae of the military uniforms) were prime examples of the historicist school of painting and of the belief that the supreme task of the artist was to glorify the climactic episodes of Germany's national history.[14]

Anton von Werner, indeed, was soon promoted to become the director of the Royal Institute for the Fine Arts in Berlin and the most powerful man in the world of the visual arts in Germany. The art academies, though they had been freeing themselves in the preceding decades from the narrow constraints of courtly taste, were increasingly becoming centres of the conventional historicist style and of the penchant for subjects drawn from antiquity and the Middle Ages as well as from the German past. The historicists regarded themselves as champions of an official style, in which the highly realistic use of detail was combined with monumentalist, grandiose and theatrical overall design. This idealizing approach, heavy on iconography as well as on historical, religious and classical themes, became for many years the preferred mode not just in the academies but also among independent artists, thanks in no small measure to the flood of commissions that was now coming in from local government and the state. Cycles of historical paintings began to adorn the large public rooms of the new town halls of many German cities, depicting scenes from local civic history as well as major events in the history of the German nation. Favoured subjects included the great mediaeval emperors, commemorated not only as forebears of the Hohenzollern monarchy but as guarantors of civic liberties; and the emperors were often, though by no means always, flanked by likenesses of Wilhelm I and (less frequently) of Wilhelm II.[15]

There was, however, a contrast between middle-class art on the one hand and official or semi-official art on the other, though this contrast was not fully manifest at the outset. The two branches of art did, to be sure, have certain basic features in common: in addition to the taste for historical subjects there was a widespread adherence to the stylistic precepts of neoclassicism, regarded as enduringly valid, and a belief that art ought to portray 'the noble, the beautiful and the true'. Wilhelm von Kaulbach, one of the leading representatives of the monumentalist school of the period, attributed the artistic resurgence that accompanied the founding of the Empire to the 'cultivation of art for its own sake, for beauty's sake'; 'only if [art] gives shape to the Ideal can it serve as a model for life [...]'.[16] Similarly, the theatricality exemplified by the work of Anton von Werner, at once realistic and profoundly untruthful, was entirely consistent with the middle-class taste of the time. On the other hand, we can also trace clear differences of emphasis between the artistic movements that enjoyed the favour of the official authorities and the art that originated within the heartlands of middle-class society itself. The contrast was particularly evident in architecture. The architectural style of the many town halls that were built in the second half of the nineteenth century and in the years before 1914 was quite distinct, not only from the florid baroque of the buildings that had been erected in princely capitals in the eighteenth century, but from the neo-baroque that was adopted for many public buildings such as law courts. The use of stylistic features borrowed from the Gothic era or from the German Renaissance (or what were taken to be such features) had a highly symbolic significance, certainly in the early days of the Empire; likewise the dominating towers and large gables borrowed from the Middle Ages. These buildings were intended to provide a fitting image of the status and importance of the civic corporations, and to serve as a declaration of political independence, while at the same time, of course, implying a profession of loyalty to the Imperial throne as the symbol of national unity. Only gradually did these very consciously conveyed ideas lose their force, as civic administration and cultural life became increasingly professionalized.

Nevertheless, despite these differences of emphasis, bourgeois art in the last thirty years of the nineteenth century was scarcely less affirmative than the state-influenced art of the academies. The realist paintings of Menzel and the neo-romantic works of Trübner and Leibl did not breach what most middle-class people regarded as the norms of artistic taste. Although Menzel was also one of the first artists to paint scenes from the modern world of industry, he handled these subjects in a very detached manner, playing down their darker aspects, and the results were not seen as provocative. Leibl's genre paintings depicted the everyday life of the common people in a new and impressive way, but it was no accident that they consistently evoked a solemn atmosphere, with figures clad in their Sunday best. A highly characteristic artistic style of the 1870s and 1880s was that associated with the name of Hans Makart, who wholly eclipsed his contemporaries in the virtuoso use of historicist techniques, producing works of showy display and formal abundance. This sort of painting is generally seen as particularly closely attuned to the spirit of the *Gründerzeit*, when huge fortunes were amassed overnight and the *nouveaux riches* demanded 'works of enduring significance' that would enable them to feel that they had truly joined the ranks of bourgeois society.[17] Significantly, too, portraiture became a particularly popular genre, since a work's value could be enhanced by the social status of the person portrayed. Leading portrait painters such as Franz von Lenbach, and sculptors such as Reinhold Begas, suddenly found themselves doing big business. The most graphic example, however, of the eclectic historicism of the *Gründerzeit* came in the form of the grand showpiece buildings that were erected in the new metropolitan centres. The Kurfürstendamm in Berlin, the Maximilianstraße in Munich and the Ringstraße in Vienna were lined with works of architecture that were prime symbols of the self-assurance of the upper middle class and its new-found wealth and social influence. The villa that Ernst Bassermann, later the long-standing leader of the National Liberal party, built on a prime site on the Marktplatz in Mannheim in 1886 had little in common with the strictly neo-classical lines of his grandfather's house: it too was a highly characteristic example of the early *Gründerzeit* spirit.[18] Generally speaking, the wealthy middle class plumped for the styles of the Italian Renaissance – a period whose ethos resembled the achievement-orientated individualism of their own era (or so, at any rate, Jacob Burckhardt had described it in *Die Kultur der Renaissance in Italien*, a book then gaining wide currency). The neo-Baroque or neo-Rococo manner was less favoured. In common with the academic artistic trends that were more heavily subject to official public influence, the middle class's taste for an eclectic mixture of different historical styles sprang from a desire to lend dignity and adornment to sober, functional buildings and a modest form of life through the use of techniques that came with a prior seal of aesthetic approval.

A similar phenomenon is evident in other paintings of the period. The examples that are most striking in aesthetic terms are overtly theatrical: they represent an attempt to realize (in Hamann's words) 'the ideal of nobility', but also show a particular preoccupation with the powerful personality or with heroic and mythic figures. Arnold Böcklin and Hans von Marées sought to depict solemn, ideal worlds that had nothing whatever in common with the everyday reality of accelerating industrialization. Their themes were largely confined to antiquity and mythology, though they were interfused with Romantic elements and given highly varied, dramatic settings. The works of Anselm Feuerbach were a particularly notable example of the cult of the elevated and the dignified, with subjects and stylistic features from the Italian Renaissance playing an especially prominent role.

Contemporary developments in the world of music are much less easy to categorize. Music was an important ingredient in the process of middle-class emancipation from princely tutelage that took place during the nineteenth century. A middle-class musical culture, independent of the church and the princely courts, had been evolving from early in the century. As Fellerer says in an outstanding study, the 'music festival and the concert were the social framework within which the major forms of musical life of the culturally conscious middle class evolved.'[19] Music festivals were often also public festivals, and thus occasions for general social interaction; not uncommonly they had political side-effects. In addition, middle-class musical culture was in many ways historically minded and can be credited, for example, with the rediscovery of great oratorios from the past. Classical and Romantic works by German composers were the principal fare, with choral music playing a substantial role by modern standards: newly composed oratorios, often devoted to historical or patriotic subjects, were also popular.

In several respects the work of Richard Wagner constituted a challenge to the musical tradition in Germany.[20] Wagner's pessimistic philosophy, influenced by Schopenhauer, was at odds with the liberal faith in progress that lay at the heart of the middle-class culture of the time; his music made a revolutionary impact on prevailing musical conventions, which he also attacked in a stream of books and pamphlets. Wagner was profoundly convinced that it was his destiny to compose works that would give expression to the true Germany. The establishment of a musical shrine at Bayreuth was intended to counteract what he saw as the superficial and trivial versions of Germanness that the Bismarckian state had created. His aim, which in a sense was highly political as well as musical, was to provide an alternative to the kind of art that German nationalist culture had thrown up: products of a state wrapped in military pomp and a capitalist system dedicated to the pursuit of material gain. By invoking in music the historic archetypes of German national consciousness, as embodied in the epic poems of the Middle Ages and the world of the Mastersingers of early-modern

Nuremberg, Wagner hoped to give new life to the 'essence of the German spirit', which 'builds from within'.

Friedrich Nietzsche, writing in 1884, said that Richard Wagner, 'if appraised for his value to Germany and German culture, [is] a great question-mark, a German fate, a fate in any event'. He immediately added that 'the German spirit,' which 'today [is] subject to the intense pressure of Fatherlandism and self-admiration', was incapable of coping with the 'Wagner problem'. The Wagner problem is, indeed, primarily one of reception. Wagner was canonized through the founding of the Bayreuth Festival, which was later run by Cosima Wagner in strict accordance with the presumed intentions of the 'Master', and he was also appropriated in a highly possessive way by the Wagner societies that sprang up throughout Germany in the 1870s. His work duly became the emblem of a Romantic, mystical outlook opposed to the rationalist *Weltanschauung* of the middle class. This counter-philosophy was echoed by the verbose Julius Langbehn, who argued that German culture needed to be regenerated through a return to indigenous styles of living and radically individualistic aesthetic principles, and by the Nietzsche cult of the 1890s, which was boosted by the posthumous publication of a misleading version of Nietzsche's *Will to Power*.[21]

The very success of Wagner's works – works 'out of season' in the sense that they actually sprang from a defunct era of neo-Romanticism and cultural pessimism – indicated that the time was more than ripe in the 1880s for a break with the predominantly backward-looking and affirmative attitudes that were prevalent in literature and the arts. By about 1880, in contrast with the situation in France (though also with that in Great Britain) German culture had become stalled. There was not even an approximate equivalent to the Naturalism of Zola in literature or the Realism and Impressionism of Courbet and Manet in painting. The loss of dynamism in the social sphere that had resulted from the creation of the semi-constitutional German Empire was closely mirrored in the cultural realm, music perhaps being the exception.[22]

From the mid-1880s a process of innovation began to get under way, both in literature and in the visual arts. Although the novels of Conrad Ferdinand Meyer continued to paint an idealized picture of the world based on historical exemplars, the works of Gustav Freytag, notably the highly influential *Soll und Haben*, celebrated the victory of the commercial middle class over the declining rural aristocracy. Theodor Fontane, using a technique akin to the closely-researched methods of a social historian, produced a highly refined portrait of a society in transition.[23] For Fontane, the decline of the aristocracy, hidebound by its adherence to morally untenable double standards, was as inevitable as the triumph of the *nouveau riche* middle class was loathsome; ultimately, he came to regard the world of the working class as 'more genuine, more true and more full of life' than that of the bourgeoisie.[24] But though Fontane's writings showed great insight into the workings of German society, and constituted a sensitive if carefully disguised critique,[25] he deliberately refused to go further than this, despite the fact that his letters are full of bitter observations on contemporary life. On the other hand, he responded with enthusiasm when he encountered Gerhart Haputmann's play *Vor Sonnenaufgang*, which painted a highly powerful, yet not partisan, portrait of the social conditions in which a working-class family was compelled to live. This was the first, pioneering work of German Naturalism.

As Richard Hamann argues, Naturalism was a revolt against the superficial and pseudo-idealistic salon culture of the *Gründerzeit*: it was the first attempt to treat the harshest rigours of social reality as the subject of literature. The movement had been gathering pace for some time. Arno Holz, Max Halbe, Paul Ernst and the brothers Julius and Heinrich Hart played a pivotal role, and the literary club Durch, founded in 1886, was one of the earliest of the mulitplicity of literary and artistic groups that eventually went to make up the artistic avant-garde. The first performance of *Vor Sonnenaufgang*, given by the Freie Bühne of Berlin in 1889 – before an invited audience, in order to evade the theatre censors, still active in Prussia – was something of a clarion call. Public reaction, not surprisingly, was at first very hostile. Wilhelm II was later to speak of the art of 'the gutter',[26] and this phrase sums up graphically the attitude that was almost universal in middle-class circles at the outset.

The climax of the Naturalist controversy came in the spring of 1892, when a ban was imposed on public performances in Berlin of Hauptmann's *Die Weber*, a dramatized account of the revolt of the Silesian weavers in 1844. The authorities had been powerless to prevent the many private performances of the play that had already been given by the Freie Bühne, and then by the Neue Freie Volksbühne (which had close links with the Social Democratic movement), but the Deutsches Theater, which was headed by Otto Brahm, decided all the same to contest the ban at the Prussian High Administrative Court. The court ruled that the play could be performed, subject to certain provisos, in particular that ticket prices were set fairly high; this would have the effect that workers would be unable to gain admission. After the court case there was a debate in the Prussian Chamber of Deputies on 21 February 1895, provoked by the action of the Prussian Minister of the Interior, von Köller, in publicly rebuking the court for its verdict. Von Köller voiced the views not only of the authorities but also of a broad section of the middle class and of the Catholic community when he declared: '... during the past decades the theatres should have been an educative institution – promoting historical remembrance; promoting, in short, everything that is good and noble – but in this task they have long since failed.'[27] The liberal deputy Heinrich Rickert responded by defending the principle of artistic freedom in the modern theatre against despotic control and high-handed behaviour on the part of the authorities.

This incident exposed divisions of attitude not only within public opinion but among the Prussian governing authorities, who were trying in somewhat schizoid fashion to execute orders emanating from the Imperial court on the question of acceptable and unacceptable literature, while at the same time not being entirely convinced of their value. In the course of the controversy Wilhelm II ostentatiously gave up his box at the Deutsches Theater, an action which cost the theatre a loss of annual income of 4,000 marks. The Emperor's gesture, however, did not prevent *Die Weber* from being a popular success; nor did further bans in the provinces. The German theatrical landscape was sufficiently diversified to frustrate the authorities' attempts to influence the theatres' repertoire and thus, indirectly, the shape of contemporary literature. After Naturalist drama, a whole range of avant-garde writing, German and foreign, now began to reach the German stage: plays by Ibsen and Strindberg – authors still regarded as particular *bêtes noires* – and by Wedekind, Sternheim and Schnitzler. The pace of change suddenly quickened. Indeed, for an Expressionist like Max Halbe, Naturalist drama soon became the prosaic product of a convention-bound society.

The debate in the Prussian Chamber of Deputies about Hauptmann's *Die Weber* and about the practice of state theatre censorship – the legal basis for which went back to 1851 and the era of the reactionary Interior Minister, von Hinckeldey – was itself overshadowed by a bitter controversy in the Reichstag over the so-called 'Zuchthausvorlage', the 'prison' (or 'forced labour') bill. This projected measure was aimed primarily against the Social Democrats, but the Centre, as well as many Conservatives, also wished to exploit it as a vehicle for combating all modernizing and liberalizing trends that posed a threat to religion and state authority alike. There was a passionate outburst of public protest, however, against what was seen as, or presumed to be, a curtailment of academic and artistic freedom, and the measure eventually came to grief.[28]

All told, the treatment of literature and drama by the Prussian state cannot be said to have done more than put a brake on change, while in the other states of the Empire official pressure was less effective still. It is true that in Bavaria a good number of obstacles, including criminal prosecutions, were put in the way of authors who did not meet with official approval – including Ludwig Thoma, for example, the editor of *Simplicissimus* – but on the whole the legal authorities tended to let events run their course, particularly where lay judges were involved.[29] In general, the federal structure of the Empire had a liberalizing effect. What was strictly taboo in Berlin might well be acceptable in the provinces: particularly in the southern German states, which rather prided themselves on being more open-minded about artistic innovation. Thus, while the political climate in Imperial Germany did not exactly encourage the growth of a modern and highly variegated literary culture, it was not fully capable of holding back the process either.

The position with regard to the visual arts was similar. But it has to be said that the influence of traditional attitudes was particularly strong here, owing to the central role that continued to be played by the art academies in the training of young artists and by academy teachers and their support- ers in the Deutsche Künstlergenossenschaft (German Fellowship of Artists), the body that staged the big annual exhibitions on which budding artists largely depended when trying to establish a reputation. The same was true of the acquisitions policies of the state collections – particularly the Berlin museums, where the Prussian National Commission for the Arts had been given a substantial formal say in decisions.[30] Within this system, which served, simultaneously, the ends of official policy and the interests of the majority of artists, who adhered to conventional principles and tended to be conservative in their general outlook, Anton von Werner was again a pivotal figure, particularly since it was widely known that he enjoyed the personal confidence of the Emperor. Alfred Lichtwark, who was receptive to the new movements in art and was keen to see the public become gradu- ally more receptive too, vented his sarcasm on the 'tenured geniuses of the academies, the arts and crafts schools – a priestly caste with priestly tastes, interests, intrigues and ambitions, and, above all, a priestly thirst for power'. The artistic establishment, he said, claimed the right to decree what was art and what was not: 'A group that sets itself up as a caste will, and must, dominate.'[31] More important than this, however, was the fact that the teaching staff at the art academies had the support of the public author- ities and received substantial commissions for public buildings and monu- ments from the state and from local government. Not least, they enjoyed the supreme patronage of the Emperor himself, who had hit upon state pro- motion of the arts and sciences as an area in which he could exert his 'per- sonal rule' in a way that contemporary jurists found constitutionally acceptable. Certainly in Prussia at least, official art remained largely gov- erned by authoritarian canons of taste during the 1890s, and the historical paintings of Anton von Werner were a perfect exemplification of these prin- ciples.[32]

It was not, therefore, a simple task for new artistic movements to chal- lenge the dominant affirmative view of art, with its commitment to 'the noble, the beautiful and the true', and its 'elevated' subject-matter, taken mainly from the historical past, classical mythology and mediaeval legend. Not surprisingly, change came as much from outlying parts of the Empire as from the metropolitan centres.[33] In Worpswede Paula Modersohn-Becker and Heinrich Vogeler laid the foundations for their new style of nature painting, which borrowed Romantic features but was also strongly influ- enced by French Impressionism. In Munich there had been a Secessionist group since 1892, attempting to promote artistic activity outside the official art nexus. In Berlin in the same year Liebermann and Leistikow set up the 'Group of Eleven', with the aim of staging their own exhibitions indepen- dently of the annual official salon held by the Verein Berliner Künstler (Association of Berlin Artists), whose exhibition rooms the dissidents irreverently dubbed 'the catacombs'; private art galleries made their premises available to the new body. The first exhibition held by the 'Eleven' was, to be sure, fiercely attacked by the critics as a display of 'bleak, wild Naturalism' and a gross example of 'Poor People and Misery art'.[34] In the same year a show of works by Edvard Munch in Berlin caused a public furore and was closed down prematurely at the insistence of the Verein Berliner Künstler. Again, characteristically, a private gallery in Düsseldorf immediately volunteered to take over the exhibition instead. Matters finally came to a head in 1898, when Walter Leistikow's painting 'The Grunewaldsee' was refused entry to the annual exhibition of the Verein. A group of artists – including Max Liebermann, Max Slevogt, Lovis Corinth, Walter Leistikow, Heinrich Zille and Käthe Kollwitz – who represented very different artistic approaches but were united in their opposition to the official art world, set up the Berlin Secession. The very first, somewhat improvised, exhibition held by the Secession, in 1899, was a huge success. The Berlin public, which until now had largely rejected the artistic avant-garde, flocked to see the Secessionists' work, signalling a new responsiveness towards modernism. In point of fact, the Secessionists – possibly excepting Käthe Kollwitz, with her radical political philosophy – were somewhat tame representatives of the modern movement: on the European scale, they were little more than a 'late pendant to French Impressionism'.[35] Nevertheless, within metropolitan Berlin they now called the tune, and they remained the dominant force until shortly before the outbreak of the First World War. Meanwhile, in the 'provinces', and particularly in southern Germany, newer and yet more radical avant-garde groups had already begun to form.

The Secession, however, remained a thorn in the flesh of those in charge of official art policy: particularly of Wilhelm II, who saw himself as the nation's supreme arbiter on artistic matters. The Emperor indulged in a heated outburst on the subject of the new movements in art on the occasion of the opening in 1901 of the Siegesallee (Victory Avenue) in Berlin, itself regarded by many contemporaries as a prime instance of misconceived public art. He said:[36]

> Sculpture, has remained, in large part, unsullied by the so-called modern trends and tendencies, and still holds the commanding heights. Preserve it thus! [...] Art that disregards the laws and limits I have described is no longer art: it is factory work, trade [...] Whoever [...] departs from the laws of beauty, and from the feeling for aesthetic harmony that each man senses within his breast [...] is sinning against the original wellsprings of art [...] If, as so often happens nowadays, art merely makes misery look more loathsome than it already is, then it is sinning against the German people. The nurture of the highest ideals is also the highest form of cultural endeavour [...].'

The Emperor's attempts to induce German artists to keep to the true path of traditional aesthetic values were, however, of no avail. In the freer atmosphere of southern Germany, in particular, and also in the Rhineland, it was becoming increasingly difficult to keep the modernist movement on leading-strings. An important reason for this was the fundamental change in the material conditions of artistic production that had come about with the emergence of the modern market-based industrial system. The artistic community was becoming less and less dependent on the support, direct or indirect, of state and local authorities, and the artists' associations that had previously played a pivotal role in the liberal middle-class art world were also becoming steadily less significant. Instead, an art market was expanding rapidly, and taking on international dimensions, and with it a new class of promoters of art was coming to the fore: dealers such as Cassirer, publishers such as Diederichs and Piper, and patrons from the worlds of commerce and big business.

Denunciations of modern art from official quarters accordingly began to find a less ready echo from the general public. Wilhelm II's desire that art should stay true to the 'laws of beauty and [to] the feeling for aesthetic harmony that each man senses within his breast' was no longer so widely shared.[37] Growing unease about official Prussian attitudes towards art reached a climax in late 1903, when it emerged that the Prussian authorities had tried, at the Emperor's instigation, to discriminate against the Secessionists while preparations were under way for an exhibition of contemporary German art that was to be held as part of the World's Fair in St Louis.[38] There was a storm of indignant protest, and in Weimar on 17 December 1903, despite Prussian representations to the Grand Duke of Saxony-Weimar, Count Harry Kessler set up the Deutsche Künstlerbund (German Alliance of Artists) as a rival organization to the officially sponsored Genossenschaft (the parent body of the Verein Berliner Künstler) in which Anton von Werner exerted a leading influence.[39] It was widely believed that the Emperor had had a hand in the whole affair. In February 1904 the matter was raised in the Reichstag. Spokesmen for the government, which had first declared in the Budget Commission that the Genossenschaft, and not the Secession, was the appropriate body for raising artistic standards, had the worst of the debate. Members of Parliament were unanimous in deprecating the bias shown by the state authorities in artistic matters and the favoured treatment that the traditionalist Genossenschaft received under the aegis of the Emperor's 'personal rule'. It was not that there was any more unanimity in the Reichstag than elsewhere concerning the merits of modern art as such. The Centre party deputy, Spahn, spoke very coolly about the new artistic movements, calling them the malformed products of an age of licence. The Conservative member, von Henning, described modern art as 'depressing and ugly' and bemoaned the 'artistic nihilism' that had become current among artists: 'Altogether, in the world of literature and the arts, just as in the world of politics, the drive for freedom has given rise to a widespread and alarming loss of restraint, excessive individualism and a cult of the superhuman.'[40] Nevertheless, the politicans were almost entirely at one in attacking the authorities' recent actions with regard to international art exhibitions and condemning the autocratic attitudes that lay behind them, particularly as differences had become apparent between the behaviour of the Prussian state government and the approach adopted by the governments of the south German states. Although the Social Democrat deputy, Singer, was rebuked by the President of the Reichstag for declaring, '[. . .] We gratefully decline to have a republic of the arts with Wilhelm II at its head',[41] his words undoubtedly reflected the mood of the great majority of members of Parliament. There was general disenchantment with Prussian attitudes towards art, and a widespread desire that the state should respect the principle of free individual artistic self-expression and that artistic questions should be dealt with in a strictly impartial fashion.[42]

The effects of this first major debate in the Reichstag on art and politics are difficult to assess. Almost certainly, however, the controversy led indirectly to a weakening of the influence of the Emperor and his entourage over the acquisitions policy of Prussia's art galleries. The growing professionalization of the museums, together with the rise of private patrons, had already created something of a new situation in any case. Among the directors of the public art collections, von Tschudi, the director of the Nationalgalerie (himself weary of the 'dreary showpiece painting' that was so esteemed at court) had begun to buy works of modern art, even though this meant bypassing the highly conservative and conventional official committees that decided on new acquisitions, and enlisting the support of private patrons. There was eventually a serious dispute between von Tschudi and Wilhelm II, which led to von Tschudi's resignation and the nomination of a rather more accommodating successor. None other than Anton von Werner, the Emperor's protégé, was chosen to serve as interim director, and was clearly in line to head the Nationalgalerie on a permanent basis. This plan, however, came to nothing in the aftermath of the furore generated by the *Daily Telegraph* affair.[43] Significantly, von Tschudi immediately took charge at the Gemäldegalerie in Munich, the federal structure of the Empire once again serving to aid the cause of liberalization in the arts.

In this connection it is worth mentioning the extent to which the dynastic princes in southern Germany, accurately sensing the new spirit of the times, became committed champions of the modern movement in the visual arts, sometimes in overt opposition to the notions of Wilhelm II. The role played by the Grand Duke of Weimar in the controversy over the Prusso-German handling of the exhibition for the St Louis Fair in 1903–4 was part and parcel of a wider effort to revive Weimar as a centre of German culture. A new art school was founded in Weimar, with Henry van de Velde as its pivotal figure, though it was closed only a few years later, after disagreements between the staff and the Weimar state government. Of particular importance was the effort by the Grand Duke of Hesse to encourage the spread of *Jugendstil* (art nouveau), which had blazed a trail across Europe in the 1890s, notably in Vienna and Paris, but had at first made less impact in Germany, except in Munich.[44] The Grand Duke brought a number of leading architects, including Joseph Maria Olbrich and Peter Behrens, to Darmstadt, where a colony of *Jugendstil* buildings was created on the Mathildenhöhe – a landmark in the evolution of modern architecture in Germany.

Like its analogues in other countries, however, *Jugendstil*, with its penchant for the purely ornamental, soon proved to be a late variant of classical historicism. Subsequent developments pointed the way ahead towards the 'neue Sachlichkeit' or 'new objectivity'. Olbrich's Tietz department store building, Behrens's office building for the Mannesmann brothers in Düsseldorf, Walter Gropius's Fagus factory in Alfeld and Hans Poelzig's exhibition pavilion in Posen were significant steps along the road to a new style of architecture that remains very much alive today. Under the Empire these innovative developments were championed, in particular, by the Deutscher Werkbund, which was founded in Munich in October 1907 in conjunction with the third German Applied Art Exhibition in Dresden. Its leading participants were Hermann Muthesius and Fritz Schumacher, and among its members were almost all of the most prominent architects working in Germany at the time, including Behrens, van de Velde, Poelzig and Gropius. Its aims were ambitious: to bring 'spirit' (*Geist*) and artistic design to craft and industrial production, and, in so doing, to bridge the dangerously wide gulf that had opened up between the visual arts and the modern world of industry.[45] Art and architecture, the Deutscher Werkbund believed, should not exist merely to satisfy the demands for luxury of the upper classes, but, by 'ennobling' work and the products of work, should permeate society as a whole and help to create more satisfying lives for the broad mass of working people. Fritz Schumacher summed up their aspirations in these words: 'We see the next task that Germany has to fulfil, after a century of technology and thinking, as the recapturing of a harmonious culture.'[46] There was a further, linked ambition: that German art and architecture would now achieve a leading position in the western world, and that this in turn would help strengthen the economic standing of the German Empire.

The decade before 1914 saw a wide variety of new artistic movements come to the fore, as artists were fired by the examples of Edvard Munch and the new painting in France, and old notions of what was aesthetically acceptable were overturned. Die Brücke in Dresden, with Erich Heckel, Ernst Rudolf Kirchner and Karl Schmidt-Rottluff; the Neue Künstlervereinigung in Munich, with Wassily Kandinsky and Franz Marc, a little later re-named Der Blaue Reiter; the Neue Sezession in Berlin, with Emil Nolde a prominent member, which after a fierce dispute broke away from the original Secession, itself now highly respectable and the dominant force on the Berlin artistic scene; the Sonderbund of Düsseldorf, whose shows in Düsseldorf and Cologne finally marked the breakthrough of modern art in Germany – together, these diverse groups constituted a force that burst the established conventions of the middle-class art world asunder. It must also be conceded, however, that the rise of the avant-garde did not come about without challenge from the general public; in particular, there were strong objections from nationalist quarters. Similar controversies arose in literature, although there is not space to describe these here.

One of the vital ingredients in the victory of the artistic avant-garde over the traditionalists, and notably over the schools that were especially favoured and actively sponsored in court circles, was the emergence of a modern art market. Change would not have taken place if it had not been positively promoted by the rapidly expanding number of art dealers and publishers of art journals, by the growing quantity of published reproductions, often of very high quality, and by the increasing professionalization of art as an academic and scholarly discipline. In addition, a new group of powerful patrons and purchasers was coming on to the scene, particularly from industry and commerce: individuals who were willing to spend what were already substantial sums of money in order to buy works of modern art.[47] Correspondingly, the role of public patronage declined somewhat, though it still remained significant.

The triumphal progress of modernism signalled the final collapse of official policy towards the arts in Imperial Germany. It is true that Wilhelm II's emotional outbursts against modern art found an echo with the great bulk of the middle class: in that sense, they were not merely an expression of courtly and aristocratic taste in artistic matters but a clear attempt to pander to prevailing attitudes. Moreover, official art left its mark throughout Germany, particularly in Prussia, in the form of numerous public buildings and, above all, of a great number of monuments. The statues in honour of Wilhelm der Große that were intended to adorn all corners of the country, and the monument in Leipzig commemorating the Battle of the Nations, were prime expressions of Wilhelmine megalomania; we might also mention the monstrous monument at the Porta Westfalica and the memorial to Wilhelm I at the Deutsches Eck in Koblenz, now destroyed (though at the time of writing its reconstruction is being urged on grounds of historical nostalgia). Nevertheless, all of this public display represented, in Eric Hobsbawm's words, 'a dying, and after 1918, clearly a dead past'.[48] Furthermore, official art was a heavy drain on artistic resources over a long period and diverted the energies of a large number of artists and architects into creative backwaters. In this context, at any rate, Nietzsche's mordant judgement that 'the Germans, procrastinators *par excellence*, are today the most backward cultured nation in Europe'[49] holds true. On the other hand, it should also be reiterated that the individual states of the Empire pursued quite independent policies on artistic matters, often strongly divergent from those of Prussia, and that they refused to be budged from them when the Emperor tried to intervene. Indeed, the upper ranks of the nobility produced a considerable number of individuals (such as Count Harry Kessler) who made a point of supporting contemporary developments in the arts, rightly believing that the only way in which the aristocracy could hope to justify its continuing role at the head of Imperial society was to sponsor innovation and creativity rather than cling rigidly to outmoded conventions.

Is it possible to make a more favourable case for the state of the arts in Imperial Germany by taking into account the changing social character of the middle class? Thomas Nipperdey has argued that the rise of the artistic avant-garde in the decade before 1914 demonstrates that the German middle class had come to terms with modernity: 'Modern art prevailed, not despite the middle class, but in conjunction with it.'[50] This is true to the extent that those who were actually responsible for the great and bewildering variety of new developments in the arts during these years, which left Naturalism and Impressionism far behind and redefined the task of art as the projection of highly individualized experience, were members of 'the younger generation of the *haute bourgeoisie*'. In most other respects, however, it would be quite wrong to postulate any inherent connection between the various avant-garde movements – Expressionism, Cubism, Futurism, Constructivism, abstract painting and the rest – and the ideals that governed middle-class life. Avant-garde art retained the middle class's unrestrained individualism, but it also represented a questioning of all 'objective cultural values', of the sort that Rickert was still trying to re-assert as the bulwark of an epistemology of 'cultural science' despite the fact that Nietzsche's doctrine of the 'revaluation of all values' had now blocked off such a route. With his characteristic acuity, Max Weber spelled out at the time the significance of this change for the notion of culture in a post-bourgeois world: '"Culture",' he wrote, 'is a finite excerpt from the meaningless infinity of events in the world, endowed with meaning by human beings', which is available only to those 'who are people of culture, with the capacity and the will deliberately to adopt an *attitude* towards the world and to bestow *meaning* upon it'.[51] Subjective value judgement within a disenchanted world, and the subjective seeking of self-assurance in the work of art, were supplanting the old belief in cultural values objectified by the historical process. As yet, such attitudes were held only by a small minority, but they pointed the way ahead to a post-bourgeois society of the future, based on the principle of an unlimited variety of possible ways of living and an ever-growing diversification of the social structure.

It is misleading, therefore, to see the emergence of modernism in Germany (which, in any case, happened significantly later than it did elsewhere in Europe) simply as a late flowering of middle-class consciousness. Rather, the avant-garde revolution in the arts (and the corresponding revolution in the academic and scientific sphere caused by the spread of relativism with regard to all knowledge) was a symptom of the crisis of the middle-class liberal society of the nineteenth century, which, in one way or another, was in the process of destroying the bases of its existence, the systems of value, convention and iellectual understanding which structured and ordered it.[52] The artistic revolution of the late nineteenth and early twentieth centuries, and the profound challenge that had been mounted to the nineteenth century's belief in progress and science, were part and parcel of the fragmentation of the middle class as a unified social group possessing its own distinctive ethos and life-style. The artistic avant-garde was peopled by members of the new educated class who positively prided themselves on not being the prisoners of middle-class cultural values – indeed, who laid claim to being authentic representatives of a post-bourgeois culture precisely by virtue of their opposition to advanced capitalism, with its mechanisms of exploitation, its bureaucratic structures of authority and its achievement-orientated work ethic. (This did not, admittedly, deter the representatives of the new and dynamic large-scale industries, and the new breed of patrons who were closely involved in the rapidly expanding art market, from giving active backing to the new artistic trends.) No one described the supersession of traditional middle-class values by avant-garde culture during the Empire more perspicuously than Thomas Mann, reflecting in 1919 on his own upbringing in the Hanseatic city of Lübeck: 'I am very clearly aware that the cultivation of a way of life achieved over centuries of struggle is in the process of dying out.'[53]

The example of Thomas Mann illustrates a related aspect of the avant-garde culture that came to the fore in the last decade of the Empire: the estrangement of artists and writers from the middle-class liberal political outlook that had remained unquestioned until the end of the nineteenth century. Thomas Mann acknowledged in his *Betrachtungen eines Unpolitischen* (Reflections of a Non-Political Man),[54]

> Yes, I am a *Bürger*, and in Germany that is a term whose meaning has as much to do with thought and art as it has with dignity, solidity and contentment [...] If I am a 'liberal', then I am liberal in the sense of 'liberality', not of 'liberalism': I am [...] national-minded but unpolitical, like the German of middle-class culture.

These words show that the close links that had traditionally existed between middle-class cultural attitudes and liberal political values had been broken: there had been a retreat from day-to-day political concerns. Politics, particularly party politics, began to be seen as part of the functionalist shell of modern industrial civilization, from which the artistic avant-garde wished to break free in pursuit of the untrammelled development of the self and its expressive realization in art. Such thinking, while making it harder for the ruling class or mass political movements to exploit art and literature for political purposes, also gave rise to a considerable degree of depoliticization within some branches of Wilhelmine society. Paradoxically, this contributed to the stabilization of the prevailing order in the short run, even though that had certainly not been the intention of those directly involved.

The spreading professionalization of all aspects of cultural life, from music to the visual arts and the museums, had a similar effect. Culture increasingly became a distinctive sub-system within society, administered and controlled by a class of professional specialists, while the influence that the general public exerted over cultural matters steadily declined. The growth of specialization in cultural activity led to a rise in standards in a technical sense, particularly on the stage and in the concert hall. At the same time, however, the theatre gravitated more towards the spectacular, offering a world that was an alternative to everyday life; Max Reinhardt's dazzling productions at the Deutsches Theater in Berlin were a notable example. To a certain extent the same was true of the music of Richard Strauss and Gustav Mahler. The path-breaking twelve-note music of Arnold Schoenberg and Alban Berg, on the other hand, had little appeal to a wider public.

On the surface at least, little attention was paid in the visual and performing arts to the political dimension of culture, either in a favourable or a hostile sense. The same was true of much of the writing of the period, in which a withdrawal into introversion was regarded as the profoundest response to the challenge posed by modern industrial civilization. Stefan George cultivated a prophetic vision accessible only to a select circle of disciples who had detached themselves from the trivialities of bourgeois life. Rainer Maria Rilke saw the poet's calling as a retreat 'into the chasms of his soul, which he will never plumb but which affect him unutterably more' than does the outside world.[55]

Georg Simmel gave a brilliant description and analysis of this process of disjunction between an objective culture, in which art, custom, science and learning, religion, law, technology and other practices are seen as concrete, externalized expressions of the human mind, and the new subjectivity, in which culture takes the form of a radically individualistic mode of life.[56] The 'inwardness' (*Innerlichkeit*) that characterized the latter became increasingly detached from any sense of social commitment and fostered instead a new, restless instability, an unfocused sense of urgency and, eventually, an empty desire for action for its own sake.[57]

As culture partly degenerated into spectacle, and partly broke up into a multiplicity of expressions of 'inwardness' lacking any kind of political or social commitment, so the resulting vacuum began to be filled, from the 1890s onwards, by a new and growing irrationalism. One example was the Nietzsche cult, which declared the core of Nietzsche's philosophical message to be the opposition between the self and the 'many too many' and called for the cultivation of an aristocratic form of individualism. There was also a great rash of sectarian movements of a pseudo-religious nature, of which the Monism of Ernst Haeckel was the most popular.[58] Perhaps the most important phenomenon in this connection, however, was the spread of various overblown kinds of mystical nationalism, inspired particularly by the writings of Paul de Lagarde and by Julius Langbehn's *Rembrandt als*

Erzieher.[59] In 1913 Eugen Diederichs set up a national shrine at his publishing house dedicated exclusively to de Lagarde's works and thought. Although the specific effects of this newer brand of nationalism are difficult to assess, it undoubtedly strengthened the predisposition towards imperialism and war that was already present within the political system in Imperial Germany. The loose symbiotic relationship between cultural and nationalist attitudes, and the simultaneous decline in substantive political content, that had together become the dominant features of the middle class's outlook in the Wilhelmine era helped prepare the ground for a particularly aggressive form of cultural imperialism. The new mentality was typified by Friedrich von Bernhardi's book *Deutschland und der nächste Krieg* (Germany and the Next War), published in 1912, which argued that a preventive war against the western powers was the only way to save German culture from being overwhelmed by France, Britain and Russia as the new system of world empires emerged. In this sense, the depoliticization of culture during the Wilhelmine period played its part in causing the German Empire to embark on the First World War and, eventually, to perish as a result.

8

The latent crisis of the Wilhelmine Empire: the state and society in Germany, 1890–1914

For earlier generations of scholars, the shortcomings of the Wilhelmine age – a period normally seen as coinciding with the reign of the Emperor Wilhelm II, from 1889 to 1918 – lay mainly in the field of foreign policy. The fateful events of the era were generally seen as the German government's abandonment of Bismarck's diplomatic strategy, with the severing of the link with St Petersburg, and, even more especially, its adoption of a strident, assertive 'Weltpolitik', or 'world policy', not tempered by an awareness of the constraints on German power. In particular, the blame for the manifest failures of German diplomacy was attributed to Wilhelm II himself and his so-called 'personal rule' (*persönliches Regiment*), that is, to the Emperor's unconstitutional interference in the shaping of Germany's foreign policy. By contrast, verdicts on domestic policy during Wilhelm II's reign were by and large more favourable, although the failings and weaknesses of the system were certainly recognized. It was held that as Bismarck's technique of ruthlessly playing off the parties against one another was gradually discarded, and as the attempt to combat Social Democracy by means of discriminatory legislation was dropped, so political antagonisms were slowly resolved. Tacit constitutional changes, it was argued, brought Germany significantly closer to a parliamentary system by 1914; the period of the 'Bülow Bloc' marked an important step towards parliamentarism; and government policies towards the Social Democrats, in particular, became steadily more realistic, cautiously setting in train the process of the integration of the working class into the state.

Theodor Schieder, however, has drawn attention to the deep internal fault lines that cut across the political system of the German Empire and has shown that it was a considerable while before the integrative force of the idea of the nation came fully into its own.[1] At the time when the Imperial proclamation ceremony took place in the Hall of Mirrors at

Versailles on 18 January 1871, the German Empire lacked many of the features of a nation state, a fact that was graphically evidenced by a dearth of symbols of state power. Only gradually did Germany develop into a modern nation state broadly attuned to the realities of government. That process of development, on the other hand, was an important factor in helping to mitigate domestic conflict before the First World War.[2] Indeed, a conception of nationhood centred around the Bismarckian state proved to be a powerful political binding agent, eventually extending to include even the working class and finding its clearest expression in the vote in favour of the war credits on 4 August 1914.

None the less, even this interpretation of the Wilhelmine era goes too far in seeing a harmony of interests where in reality there was social conflict. We also need to pay heed to the argument, frequently advanced in the more recent literature, that the German Empire was quite incapable of evolutionary change. On this view, the system remained intact solely because those in power exploited a whole range of strategies of 'secondary integration' and because potentially liberalizing energies were displaced on to external or internal adversaries,[3] with individual groups within the population – first the Centre party, and then, more and more exclusively, the Social Democrats – being demonized as *Reichsfeinde*, or 'enemies of the Reich'.[4] Particular emphasis is placed, in this approach, on Bismarck's 'imperialism'; on the 'Sammlungspolitik', or policy of 'gathering together' those elements that 'supported the state', that was called for after 1893; on the 'Weltpolitik' that was adopted in 1897; and, especially, on the fleet-building programme that was inaugurated by Grand Admiral von Tirpitz.[5] The historian who has developed this line of argument most fully is, of course, Hans-Ulrich Wehler, who describes the Bismarckian system as one of neo-absolutist dictatorship by Chancellor, upheld only by dint of the skilful use, at home and abroad, of a policy of social imperialism designed to counter the forces that had been set in motion by a society being rapidly transformed by industrialization. In Wehler's words, the Bismarckian system was a 'Bonapartist dictatorship: that is, an unstable, traditional framework of authority, threatened by powerful forces of social and political change, which [was protected by] the diversion of concern from the constitution on to the economy, from emancipation at home on to successes abroad, as well as by undisguised repression, tempered with limited concessions, on the domestic front'.[6]

This broad approach, exemplifying (in Eckart Kehr's terms) the 'primacy of domestic policy', has been adopted by Sauer, Groh, Stürmer and others as well as by Wehler. It has the merit of reducing the variety of conflicts that were present within the political and social systems of the German Empire to a determinate set of basic social processes. On the other hand, it has the drawback of tending to imply that the dominant classes and ruling groups in German society had the capacity and opportunity to manipulate political events and social changes to an extent that was, in reality, feasible only

under exceptional circumstances. Contrary to the intentions of its proponents, this approach casts Bismarck as the evil genius who held the fate of
Germany in his hands.

What is needed is a close examination of the main component features of
the Imperial system. These, I argue, can be explained in terms of the partial
disjunction between the political and social structures within Germany.
Two facts here stand out clearly at once. The first is that the system
Bismarck created was comparatively immobile and inflexible and was not
well equipped to adapt to the rapid social changes that were taking place
(partly, though not entirely, because powerful conservative forces were
resistant to any such response). The second is that the social landscape was
being fundamentally re-shaped as a result of the rapid spread of industrialization. The middle class was becoming split into an ill-defined collection of
separate groups, each with its own very different economic interests and, in
due course, political aims; the working class was emerging as an independent political force of growing strength; and, not least, the economic base
that had made possible the dominance of the old conservative agrarian
elites was increasingly coming under threat, notably in Prussia.

In the account that follows our principal point of reference will be the
constitutional system: its mode of functioning, and the shifts of balance
that took place within it even though its formal framework remained unaltered. As Lassalle pointed out, there is always a disparity between principles and practice on constitutional matters, and this is particularly true in
the case of Wilhelmine Germany. At the same time, however, a constitutional framework also plays a considerable part in defining the parameters
of existing and newly arising conflicts and the ways in which conflict is
fought out and resolved. We must begin, therefore, by considering briefly
the Bismarckian constitutional system itself.

This system has been under fire from historians for a long time. When
Sauer, speaking of the 'improper combination of contradictory principles
within the constitution', claims that the Bismarckian, and not just the
Wilhelmine, Empire was prone to 'chronic in-built bias',[7] he is echoing,
albeit quite unconsciously, arguments used by Carl Schmitt in 1934 in an
attempt to discredit the Bismarckian system of 'skirted decisions' and promote a fascist brand of soldierly state based on the leadership principle.[8]
Stürmer takes Sauer's thesis a significant stage further, maintaining that the
non-constitutional option of a coup was always on stand-by during the
Bismarckian era and that the pseudo-constitutional system that had been
established therefore never represented the true consitutional position.[9]
While such criticisms, however, may seem fair in the light of the liberal and
democratic attitudes of the present day, they ignore the fact that the constitution that emerged from Bismarck's negotiations with the liberals between
1867 and 1871 was not a mere diktat imposed by the ruling Prusso-
German elite but was, to a large degree, a compromise conditioned by the
social and political circumstances of the moment. Eugene N. Anderson's

study of the extent of popular support for reformist liberal ideas before 1867 shows clearly that in a society that was still essentially a pre-industrial one, middle-class liberalism had only a limited power base. The sole reason why the liberals enjoyed such prominence was the existence of the three-class system of suffrage in Prussia, which at that time worked heavily in their favour.[10] Similarly, during the period of domestic consolidation of the Empire between 1871 and 1878, the National Liberals, who are too readily criticized for having capitulated to Bismarck, were in fact almost painfully aware that they could not afford to oppose him head-on, since in any renewed conflict over the constitution the mass of the population might well side with the Chancellor and not with them. Altogether, during the first years after the establishment of the Empire there was no need of 'diversionary strategies', so much discussed in the recent literature, to keep the forces of progressivism in check. The system did not undergo a real crisis until the end of the 1870s, or, more exactly, the beginning of the 1880s, when it became apparent, first, that the rise of new mass parties – the Centre and, most significantly, the Social Democrats – was not going to be halted by means of state power and, second, that the strength of the Reichstag within the Empire's complex pluralistic system of division of powers was not only considerably greater than had originally been envisaged by Bismarck and, with him, by a large section of the conservative Prussian ruling class, but was continuing to grow.

It is easy to demonstrate that the Imperial constitution of 1867–71 fell far short of the ideals of liberal parliamentary democracy. There is no need today, however, to remain wedded to the liberal myth that liberal principles had gained the upper hand in Germany by the late 1860s and that it was only Bismarck's intervention that prevented them from coming fully into their own. The compromise of 1867 probably reflected the interests of the various groups within German society, including the Catholic community, better than is generally allowed. Nor was it simply and solely owing to Bismarck and the manipulative stratagems of the conservative ruling elite that no truly effective liberal democratic movement developed in Germany and that plebiscitary methods of governing *à la* Napoleon III and Disraeli were at first fairly successful.

What was of decisive importance was the relative immobility of the highly complex pluralistic system that Bismarck created. Power was dispersed among a whole range of competing individuals and institutions: the Emperor, and the Chancellor who was dependent upon him; the Bundesrat (Federal Council), and the individual state governments that were represented within it; the state of Prussia (which accounted for two-thirds of the territory of the Empire), represented by Prussian ministers with 'immediate' powers, even the Prussian Minister President being merely *primus inter pares*; the Reichstag; the two houses of the Prussian parliament; and, perhaps less significant, the parliaments of the other individual states. Effective government was possible only if the Chancellor could mobilize the full power that the Prussian state government possessed within the system as a counterweight to the other institutions of the Reich. This was essentially what happened under Bismarck, who was able to exploit the huge personal prestige he enjoyed among the general population in order to get the other institutions in the Empire to fall into line; it did not happen thereafter. The complex federal structure devised for the German Empire in 1867 blocked the way to genuine parliamentary government, as Max Weber pointed out. But the division of executive authority between Imperial institutions and the Prussian ministries was more important, though this did not become fully apparent until after Bismarck's fall. Bismarck's original intention in refusing to grant the Imperial Chancellor an independent administrative base had been to restrict the scope for parliamentary control over the executive by the Reichstag (a restriction that was maintained in the case of military affairs until 1917). But even he was unable to prevent the political parties from steadily strengthening their position within the system, partly because the Reichstag's opportunities for exerting political influence and taking action expanded as the role of the state within society increased.

By the end of the 1870s Bismarck already found himself forced to undertake a partial re-laying of the foundations of the Empire, when he shifted to a policy of protectionism. This 'second, or true, founding of the Empire', as Böhme has called it,[11] which marked the 'close of the era of unification', was intended to bring about, under the aegis of the new tariffs, a joining of forces between the old Prussian aristocratic ruling class and the 'new German' elite of industrialists and the upper middle class. The move, however, was much less successful than is often claimed. It did not generate genuinely stable and solid co-operation among what Bismarck called the 'productive classes'. Nor did it reduce the pressure for further shifts in the balance of power within the constitutional structure, as the fate of the 'Cartel of parties loyal to the Empire', forged with such difficulty in 1887, testifies. It is, incidentally, a distortion produced by hindsight to see a fear of Social Democracy as the primary motive force at work here. It was precisely over the question whether Social Democracy should continue to be countered by extreme repressive measures, or whether purely constitutional means should be employed, that the 'Cartel' broke up in 1890, making Bismarck's fall inevitable.

The only reason why Bismarck was able, during his time in office, to exert some restraint on the centrifugal forces within the political system was that he could draw on the enormous popular prestige that he had built up during his career as a whole. The potency of his reputation is indicated by the extraordinary number of occasions on which he used the threat of resignation as a political weapon. Nevertheless, it was an asset that began steadily to dwindle from the mid-1880s onwards, despite the recourse to the policies of social imperialism that Wehler and others have described in such detail (though their significance has surely been exaggerated). 'Nothing goes right any longer,' *Germania* proclaimed triumphantly in

1889, and although the newspaper was referring specifically to the failure of a foreign venture that Bismarck had been hoping to exploit for domestic political purposes, the phrase is an apt comment on the internal political situation generally. Bismarck's fall in 1890 was not the result of arbitrary intervention on the part of Wilhlem II, as a superficial analysis of events would suggest, but came about simply because the Chancellor's power base within domestic politics had collapsed. It was a pivotal moment only in the sense that it finally exposed to view the structural defects that were latent in the Prusso-German political system.

Since the early 1870s the process of government within the Geman Empire had undergone important changes that added to the difficulties in its functioning – changes that had taken place even though the constitutional structure had remained, in formal terms, virtually unaltered. (It should be mentioned, however, that Imperial government departments were established and the Deputization Statute was passed; in addition, decisions on military matters and the powers of the War Ministry were in practice largely exempted from parliamentary control.) At the same time – and this was of even greater significance – the social foundations on which the system of government had originally been built had also been transformed.

The process of industrialization, which had in part coincided with a severe crisis in agriculture, had enormously deepened the social fault lines within the German state, and these had been further magnified by Bismarck's domestic policies. The working class was more implacably opposed to the system than ever, since government policies of social welfare – while progressive as far as they went – applied only to workers who were ill, old or unable to work. The liberal middle class had ceased to be a unified social entity, partly owing to the political blows it had received at Bismarck's hands, but mainly as a result of industrial change – which, having started comparatively late, had then taken off at a hectic pace – and of sizeable cyclical swings in the economy: it was now fragmented into a multiplicity of rival groups, widely engaged in a battle of mutual political attrition. The agrarian conservatives and their supporters in the lower middle class were also under economic pressure, despite the high tariff walls, and were anxious to squeeze whatever they could from the state by way of further protection. The combined impact of these social changes, quite apart from any form of anti-socialist 'Sammlungspolitik', was to strengthen opinion on both the right and the left and to weaken, and to some extent neutralize, groups in the centre. The result in political terms was the emergence of right- and left-wing as well as centrist groupings, of roughly equal strength, that largely cancelled one another out. At the same time, however, it became significantly harder for the government to assemble comfortable majorities on individual questions and play off one party against another.

This shift of political balance impeded constructive policy-making. As the role of the state expanded, and as a sense of German national identity gradually deepened, so the institutions at Imperial level – not just the

Reichstag, but the position of Chancellor and the Imperial departments – had gained enormously in significance. The effect, however, far from increasing the functional efficiency of the system, was to reduce it. The dualistic division between the Empire and Prussia, in particular, which had originally been a device for limiting the power of the Reichstag, now gave rise to mounting political problems. Imperial–Prussian tensions became both the expression and the cause of a widening gulf between powerful social forces which a policy of 'gathering together the parties supporting the state' could not bridge in anything more than temporary fashion. Whereas it had previously been a source of strength for the Imperial Chancellor in his dealings with the Reichstag to be anchored in a highly conservative Prussian Ministry of State, with limited authority to instruct ministers and a limited say in making appointments to the key posts in the Prussian state civil service, this relationship now worked to the Chancellor's disadvantage. The system had the structural weakness that the potential existed for a sustainable secondary government to emerge in Prussia, alongside the Imperial Chancellor, and that such a government might seek to pursue quite different political goals.

The Imperial Chancellors who succeeded Bismarck were forced to govern with both the democratic Reichstag and the Prussian Chamber of Deputies, which became increasingly reactionary as differences in wealth widened – differences which in turn were powerfully reinforced by the three-class system of suffrage in Prussia. To a greater or lesser degree, a Chancellor's credibility was constantly on the line. The actions of the Chancellor were further hampered by the fact that it was not always easy to persuade the other federal governments, particular those in southern Germany, to fall in behind Prussian policy on domestic questions.

It is not, therefore, unreasonable to say that the German Empire had already become, in principle, an almost ungovernable entity by the early 1890s, given the potential roles that its different institutions had been allotted in the constitution. The only reason why the Empire did not become ungovernable in practice was that no reformist party majority was assembled before 1914. This, admittedly, was partly the work of the governments themselves, which did everything they could to prevent such an outcome, using a range of diversionary strategies, notably policies of imperialism and the naval programme.[12] As Lepsius has shown, the parties too were trapped in traditional patterns of political behaviour that considerably impaired their political effectiveness and their ability to co-operate during an era of transition.[13] The crucial factor, however, was that the division of power between the different social and political groups in Germany that had been, to a large extent, enshrined in the constitution of 1867–71 acted as a brake on truly progressive political change.

The structural weakness at the heart of the German political system already became vividly apparent during the short-lived term of office of the Caprivi government. The purpose of Caprivi's 'new course' was to scale down over-ambitious commitments and lessen tensions, both at home and abroad. At the Imperial level the new Chancellor sought to work closely with the bourgeois parties – particularly the Centre, which occupied a piv-otal position in the Reichstag – while resisting any diminution of the Imperial government's prerogatives. Within Prussia he made cautious attempts to prune some of the more extreme features of conservative ascen-dancy. He failed, however, to restrain Prussia effectively and soon decided to concede the Prussian ministers a free hand, no longer assuming responsi-bility for their policies himself. The dominant figure in Prussia was Miquel, who imparted an unambiguously social-conservative thrust to Caprivi's call for a more co-operative approach. Miquel's 'Sammlungspolitik', which was a continuation of the line adopted by Bismarck after 1879, was not so much liberal-conservative as downright reactionary. In a letter written to the Grand Duke of Baden in 1890 Miquel said[14] that the great challenge of the time was, 'without being prejudiced or biased by the struggles of the past, to gather together all elements that support the state and prepare our-selves for what may be an unavoidable struggle against the Social Democratic movement, the significance of which is often misunderstood and almost always underestimated'. From 1893 Miquel called formally for a policy of 'Sammlung' of all the 'productive classes', based on co-opera-tion between large-scale industry and the feudal aristocracy. The purpose of the policy was not so much to preserve the existing political and social sys-tem as to put the clock back: in particular, to reverse the trend towards democracy and social reform.

Whereas Caprivi hoped, by dint of his economic and social policies, to introduce modest liberalizing changes within the Empire and improve rela-tions between the Imperial government and the parties, Prussia was increas-ingly becoming a bastion of social conservatism and a source of obstruction and resistance. Caprivi tried to decouple Prussia and put her on the same footing as the other federal states, renouncing the Imperial Chancellor's right to determine Prussia's votes in the Bundesrat and even relinquishing the post of Minister President in favour of the arch-conservative politician Botho von Eulenburg. But this attempt to leave Prussia to stew in her own juice, as it were, proved a grave mistake. Given the nature of the constitu-tional relationships we have discussed above, it was simply not possible to govern without taking Prussia into account.

The situation was exacerbated by Caprivi's policy of trade agreements, which raise a basic choice of priorities: whether Germany should become a modern industrial state, or should remain a protectionist agrarian state with both feudal and industrial elements. The debate on this issue was con-ducted against the background of an international crisis in agriculture and a severe concurrent economic recession, and feelings ran high from the start. Caprivi himself had determined on the policy primarily for pragmatic reasons, but the arguments for and against the trade agreements became caught up in the wider question whether the German Empire should evolve into a moderate liberal society or whether the supremacy of the old elites should be maintained, even at the cost of persistent social deprivation among large sections of the population. Caprivi himself regarded the system of long-term trade agreements as a lever for increasing exports and stimulating the economy and thus as an indirect means of addressing the country's social ills. Significantly, however, his policy – which, from a long-term economic point of view, was unquestionably the only proper course for Germany to follow and was later implemented in its essentials, despite considerable resistance – was blocked in the short term by the dominant political and social groups. Part of the reason for this was that by his social policies Caprivi had alienated the big industrialists (or some of them, at any rate) and driven them into the conservative camp.

The trade-agreement policy, of course, posed a threat, indirectly at any rate, to the economic supremacy of the owners of the large agricultural estates. Within a very brief time the agrarians, through the Farmers' Alliance (Bund der Landwirte), had mounted a protest campaign that had a powerful impact. The Caprivi government could offer little in the way of resistance. The significance of Caprivi's failure was far-reaching. It showed that a programme of moderate conservative reform designed to adapt the political system to the rapidly changing state of society was highly difficult to implement, if not downright unworkable. In the first place, the pluralistic system of division of power tended to create immobility, by giving both the Prussian conservatives and the Reichstag (and also, of course, the Bundesrat) a blocking function that could be exercised at any time. Secondly, there was a sharpening of class tensions, caused not only by conflicts of economic interest but by traditionalist attitudes: in particular, resistance to any fundamental changes in the social and political spheres. Thirdly, the quite foolish fear of Social Democracy that was prevalent among the middle classes was a fertile soil for the propagation of a whole host of 'Sammlung' ideologies, all of which had at their root an insistence on the maintenance of a bureaucratic authoritarian regime, whatever the cost and however outmoded such a form of government might be.

Essentially, there were three different possible ways of attempting to overcome this structural crisis:

1. More or less openly repressing, or even crushing, the Social Democrats, and significantly restricting the power of the Reichstag within the political system, if necessary by recourse to a coup. The inevitable centrepiece of such a policy would necessarily be the abolition of universal, equal, direct and secret suffrage in Reichstag elections: the conflict between Prussia and the Empire would be resolved by the restoration of the hegemony of the Prussian aristocratic ruling class.
2. Stemming the pressure for parliamentary government by staging a policy of popular imperialism. The Emperor Wilhelm II, through his 'personal rule', would serve as a symbol of the 'new German' nationalism of

the sort urged by Friedrich Naumann and others[15] and would usher the German Empire on to the world stage as a great power. There was no shortage of people prepared to offer their services in the cause of this strategy. Bülow himself declared his willingness to be an 'executive instrument of His Majesty': to be, in a sense, the Emperor's 'political chief of staff'.[16]

3. If, however, these options proved impracticable, or had no lasting effect, the only alternative was to keep muddling through with the existing system, while trying as far as possible to patch up the cracks and weaknesses within the governing elite. The government might be riven with conflict, but a public show of unity had to preserved. The aim here was to play for time, granting concessions while trying to mobilize the bourgeois and Conservative parties behind a policy of moderate conservative reform and hostility to Social Democracy. In this way, it was hoped, a solid platform for more ambitious policies might be re-established in the longer run.

After 1894 each of these three approaches was tried in turn, though not with equal commitment and consistency. The underlying flaws in the German constitutional order, however, remained unrectified.

Caprivi resigned in 1894 because he refused to have anything to do with the plans for a new Socialist Law that were being hatched by Botho von Eulenburg and his circle: the only practical purpose of the new legislation would have been to prepare the ground for a full-dress coup. Between 1893 and 1897 those close to Wilhelm II repeatedly toyed with the idea of a coup, and in 1898 Count Waldersee, the head of the General Staff, actually advocated a military offensive against the socialists. But all that materialized were some rather feeble initiatives such as the Subversion Bill and the Prussian Law on Associations of 1898. Thanks mainly to Hohenlohe's resistance to a policy of confrontation, Wilhelm II and his arch-conservative advisers shrank from taking the ultimate step.

The ascent to power of Bernhard von Bülow and Admiral (later Grand Admiral) von Tirpitz saw the adoption of a more modern and more flexible approach. Bülow's aim, at least at the outset, was to make a reality of the Emperor's 'personal rule [...] in a good sense' to which he had referred when telling Eulenburg (on 23 July 1896) of his readiness to serve as an 'executive instrument' in the capacity of Imperial Chancellor.[17] By giving prominence to the Emperor as an individual and emphasizing his role as an European leader, which he did at every available opportunity, Bülow was not merely employing psychological tactics in order to win the Emperor over personally: he was pursuing a carefully meditated strategy (which in many ways was brilliantly executed, although the concrete results were few and far between) borrowed from Disraeli's 'Imperialism' of the 1870s. There was undoubtedly a great appetite for this sort of thing among a broad section of the middle class, as was shown by the huge success of

Friedrich Naumann's book *Demokratie und Kaisertum* (Democracy and Empire), first published in 1900. Naumann grandiloquently hailed Wilhelm II's adoption of Napoleonic methods of rule: 'As King of Prussia, he has assumed the legacy of the old tradition; as Emperor, he is the imperator of the nation, the embodiment of the collective will, the personal leader who will conduct the nation from the old era into the new.'[18] The thinking behind the German 'Weltpolitik' that Bülow launched with great bombast was the same: the policy was primarily a political device, the purpose of which was to stabilize the system. Bülow himself indicated as much on a number of occasions: 'I am putting the main emphasis on foreign policy,' he said: 'Only a successful foreign policy can help to reconcile, pacify, rally, unite.'[19] His hope was that a 'world policy' of grand gestures and overblown phrases, with Wilhelm II playing the role of the nation's leader on the international stage, would appeal to the bourgeois parties, severely disenchanted with the government as they had become, and win back their support.

Even more successful in this respect was the naval building programme that Tirpitz inaugurated at the urging of the Emperor. Volker Berghahn has convincingly demonstrated that the aim of the naval policy was, again, to stabilize the system and that its effect was to undermine Parliament. Tirpitz pulled off the trick of building up a great battle fleet despite the fact that for years politicians had counselled that the government could not attempt such an undertaking without coming into serious conflict with the Reichstag and making substantial concessions to the parties. Within a short time the idea of the fleet had become so popular in Germany that it could be exploited as a principal means of 'secondary integration'.

This period of ostentatious imperialism, manifestly indebted to Napoleon III as well as Disraeli, at first brought an astonishing new degree of stability to the domestic scene, especially since the government could afford to break with the extreme conservatives when import duties were raised through new regulations in 1901 and 1902. The leaders of the Conservative party were publicly branded *personae non gratae* by Wilhelm II as a result of their behaviour over the renewed rejection of the bill to build the Mittelland Canal in 1901, and conservative officials who voted against the bill were reprimanded. The middle class construed these actions as a sign that the Imperial government was now firm in its resolve to abandon the reactionary approach of the preceding years.

The policy of social imperialism, however, which had not been exempt from considerable domestic criticism at the time of the Boer War, lost much of its effectiveness after the fiasco of the first Moroccan crisis of 1905. The public contributions of Wilhelm II, the 'new-German imperator' (to quote Naumann), began to generate less pride and enthusiasm, indeed positively to attract harsh fire on to the Emperor's *persönliches Regiment*. The Emperor was directly blamed for the failures of German foreign policy, although Bülow's fine phrases and the Foreign Office's tactics actually bore a far greater responsibility than did the Emperor himself. Indeed, it was poetic justice that the débâcle over the *Daily Telegraph* affair of 1908 signalled the beginning of the end of the political career of Bülow the brilliant gambler. Though Bülow might not in a strict sense have been culpable in the *Daily Telegraph* incident, it was he who had nurtured the technique of bringing the Emperor to the fore on matters of foreign policy and had regarded it as a legitimate way of securing political authority. It was quite understandable that Wilhelm should have seen the Chancellor's speech in the Reichstag, in which Bülow turned a blind eye to his earlier ideas and delivered up the Emperor to a barrage of criticism from both left and right, as a despicable act of betrayal.

To return to 1905–6, however: it was now that both foreign policy and the naval programme began to lose some of their previous appeal as techniques of 'secondary integration' and domestic stabilization. Indeed, despite the anglophobia that was rife in Germany, there was an anxiety not to botch the chance of better relations with Great Britain by pursuing too assertive a foreign policy. Tirpitz himself was ultimately able to preserve his popularity only by taking the drastic step of presenting himself to Parliament, contrary to the truth, as a statesman basically committed to seeking rapprochement with Britain.[20] Slowly but surely the army began to regain the priority of esteem in the eyes of government and public that it had taken for granted before 1895, and the centre of gravity in domestic politics started to shift once again in favour of the conservatives.

For some considerable time Bülow had been casting about for an alternative political strategy in order to deal with mounting political opposition at home. An opportunity presented itself in 1907, when snap Reichstag elections were called after the Centre had fiercely criticized the Empire's colonial policy. Bülow took the bold though only apparently progressive step of formally creating a majority parliamentary coalition, the so-called 'Bülow Bloc', of conservative and liberal parties, and pledging that henceforth he would govern with it. Scholarly verdicts on the period of the Bülow Bloc differ enormously. Was this a first, genuine step in the direction of parliamentary government, as Friedrich Naumann believed at the time and as Theodor Eschenburg argued in 1926 in his widely discussed book *Das Kaiserreich am Scheidewege*? Or was it merely a new and ingenious manoeuvre of Bülow's, a trap into which the left liberals fell because they had not completely discarded their *Kulturkampf* attitudes? There are grounds for doubting whether the Chancellor sincerely intended to implement, without delay, the domestic reforms that he promised the liberal parties when forming the Bloc. On the other hand, he did not intend simply to betray the liberals: the Conservatives, in collaboration with the Centre, later brought him down precisely because it had been rumoured that he was planning significant concessions to the middle-class left on the question of electoral reform in Prussia. In fact, the goal that Bülow had in view when forming the coalition was clear enough from the first: he wanted to attract the bourgeois parties back to a position of moderation and support for the system, exploiting anti-Catholic *Kulturkampf* sentiments in the German middle class while making as few concessions in a liberal direction as possible. And in this he was initially successful, as the outcome of the argument over the *Daily Telegraph* affair, for example, demonstrates.

Given these circumstances, the break-up of the Bülow Bloc over Imperial financial reform in 1909, and the consequent fall of Bülow himself, represented an acute threat to the stability of the whole political system. The extraordinarily deep-seated antagonism that existed between the Conservative agrarians and the bourgeois liberal parties was scarcely promising. There were fears in government circles, with good reason, that the left (principally the Social Democrats, but also the left liberals) might seek to exploit the situation. The devices that had previously been employed to stave off the latent crisis of the Wilhelmine system had largely lost their efficacy. It was very difficult to know what should be done.

The very considerations surrounding the choice of a new Chancellor indicated that the crisis of the Wilhelmine Empire had entered a more dangerous phase. What sort of person should be appointed to the post? An ultra-reactionary trouble-maker (von Eulenburg)? A general (von der Goltz)? A moderate progressive who would be able to deal with the political parties (von Marschall)? Or a bureaucrat well versed in domestic policy (von Bethmann Hollweg)? After some hesitation the Emperor, on Bülow's advice, plumped for Theobald von Bethmann Hollweg, although Wilhelm's first reaction is said to have been: 'I'm not having a liberalizing parliamentarian like *that*.'[21] What is clear is that the new Chancellor was expected first and foremost to put the Reichstag vigorously in its place. On matters of foreign policy, by contrast, the Emperor seems originally to have wanted to exert a stronger personal influence over events; at any rate, he was reluctant, primarily on personal grounds, to agree to Bethmann Hollweg's request that Kiderlen-Wächter, a seasoned career diplomat, be made Secretary of State for Foreign Affairs.

Bethmann Hollweg's policy of remaining 'above party' was designed from the outset as a way of buying time. Minor palliative measures were applied to the problems of the immediate moment, in the hope that the breach between the Conservatives and the Liberals, which had been aggravated by the formation of the very powerful Hanse Union, might eventually be repaired. The government immediately abandoned the tactic of seeking political support in the Reichstag from a specific combination of parties in the way that Bülow had done, and reverted instead to the old Bismarckian technique of seeking majorities for its own parliamentary bills on a case-by-case basis. Its overriding concern was to minimize the influence of the parties over legislation and, as Bethmann Hollweg put it in 1911, to prevent, as far as possible, the 'disturbing descent into parliamentarism that was threatening to become a habit'.[22]

It was deemed vital at all costs to retain control over the Reichstag on matters of domestic policy. The first concrete manifestation of this principle came with the Prussian electoral reform bill of 1910. After months of discussion in both chambers of the Prussian parliament the government withdrew its suffrage proposals, already meagre enough in the first place, when the Conservatives, in alliance with the Centre, inserted crucial changes in the bill. Bethmann Hollweg defended this unusual step on the grounds that if the government were to maintain its authority, it could not bend to the will of any group of parties, whatever their political complexion.

For the rest, the Bethmann Hollweg government sought to pursue a form of parliamentary 'Sammlungspolitik': in other words, bringing the Conservative and Liberal parties gradually back together in support of a compromise line of moderate conservatism. In view of Conservative intransigence, however, this at first meant 'protecting the Conservatives from themselves' – in other words, refraining from introducing any bill into the Reichstag that would be likely to drive them into isolation. The domestic policies of the Bethmann Hollweg government after 1909 were dictated entirely by the concern to avoid undertaking any legislation for which the agreement of the Conservatives could not ensured in advance. If this principle were not followed, those in the Chancellor's circle feared, there was a renewed risk of the emergence of a coalition stretching 'from Bassermann to Bebel'. The whole thrust of the government's domestic tactics between 1909 and 1911 was to forestall the creation of such an alliance.

The government's thinking can be seen at its clearest in the economic and financial policies that were pursued in the years in question.[23] Bethmann Hollweg opposed the introduction of Imperial death duties, even though such a tax was virtually unavoidable on financial and fiscal grounds, because it was bound to reopen conflict between the bourgeois and Conservative parties. He opted instead to live within existing resources and to restrict the level of government expenditure; even the naval estimates, which hitherto had been sacrosanct, were cut back. But all legislative initiatives were subordinated to the goal of 'gathering together' the bourgeois parties, the government simultaneously working actively to maintain the political isolation of the Social Democrats. This does not mean that Bethmann Hollweg's policies were downright reactionary. Accusations from the left, particularly the Social Democrats, that the government was in thrall to the Conservatives are not borne out by the facts, even though the Chancellor certainly took careful account of Conservative opinion. Bethmann Hollweg was not seeking to pursue a 'Sammlungspolitik' on the Miquel model, with the intention of creating the political basis for retrogressive amendments to the constitution and the franchise: his strategy rested on, and acknowledged the legitimacy of, the existing political system.[24] Nevertheless, circumstances dictated an almost quietist approach in the short run, even though such a policy had the effect of endearing him to none of the different political camps.

This explains why from 1911 onwards the militant 'Sammlungspolitiker' associated with the Farmers' Alliance and the Central Association of German Industrialists (Centralverband deutscher Industrieller, or CVdI) became ever more vehemently opposed to the government. The reactionary 'Sammlungspolitik' advocated by the Conservatives and their associates in heavy industry and the old *Mittelstand* not only constituted an attack on the prevailing semi-parliamentary system *per se*, with a call for new and harsh discriminatory measures against the Social Democrats, but was increasingly directed against Bethmann Hollweg's moderate conservatism and its commitment to upholding the status quo. The Chancellor's cautiously reformist stance was an attempt to remedy certain very obvious shortcomings in the system, precisely in order to make the system itself more stable; yet all it succeeded in doing was to incur the Conservatives' hostility and resentment.

The pace of events in the domestic sphere was both disrupted and dramatically intensified in the summer of 1911 by Kiderlen-Wächter's Moroccan initiative, an ambitious venture and one that was highly Machiavellian in its strategic conception. One of the prime reasons for the despatch of the gunboat *Panther* to Agadir (the so-called 'Panthersprung' or '*Panther*'s leap') was to provide the government with an impressive nationalist propaganda coup before the forthcoming Reichstag elections, which were causing general anxiety within the conservative camp; the Chancellor himself estimated that the Social Democrats would win between 110 and 120 seats. Kiderlen-Wächter's action, however, not only helped to bring Europe to the brink of war but led to an enormous heightening of tensions within the German political system. The results of the Moroccan incident, disappointing when set against the public expectations that Kiderlen-Wächter himself had stoked up at the beginning of the crisis, provoked a surge of nationalist emotion which, while later receding again somewhat, nevertheless did much to strengthen the readiness for war among the German middle classes. From now onwards almost all of the bourgeois parties wanted the government to pursue an assertive foreign policy and not shrink from the risk of a European war if due recognition of Germany's international interests were not to be obtained by other means.

And yet while wide sections of the middle class might harbour imperialist longings, the domestic political situation was less propitious for them than ever. The elections of 1912, in which the government did not even dare to campaign, produced the big swing to the left that everyone had predicted. The results showed how greatly the people had lost confidence in the semi-constitutional system of government and bureaucracy. The Social Democrats became the largest party; if the constituency boundaries had been drawn fairly, the scale of their electoral victory would have been even more dramatic. The left liberals, who had reunited with the Progressive party in 1911, were badly under-represented in the Reichstag, despite having done well in the first ballot. Yet even if the electoral system had been fairer and the parties of the left had been less disadvantaged, the results would not have produced a majority in the Reichstag either for a progressive or for a Conservative coalition. As it was, the outcome was complete stalemate. Each of the separate political groupings – the Conservatives on the right, the National Liberals and the Centre in the middle of the spectrum, and the left liberals and Social Democrats on the left – was able to thwart the others and make all genuine political advance impossible.

The fact that neither a pro- nor an anti-government majority could be assembled enabled Bethmann Hollweg to continue in office as though nothing had happened. But although he acknowledged that the Empire could 'be governed neither in a reactionary nor in a radical way' if 'the best elements among the people [were] not to be excluded from making their contribution',[25] it soon became apparent that the situation was not such as to allow a genuine middle course to be pursued. Instead, the government was forced more than ever to play for time, while doing what little it could to paper over the cracks in the Imperial fabric that were becoming steadily more visible. The Zabern crisis of the autumn of 1913 was a particularly telling moment. Although Bethmann Hollweg himself, answerable as Chancellor, disapproved of the way the military had over-reached itself, he did not dare to associate himself publicly with the view of the matter taken by the great majority of party politicians. He felt it was his duty to give the army his formal backing in the Reichstag: 'The uniform of the King and Emperor must be respected under all circumstances.'[26] The Imperial Governor, von Wedel, was prevented from making known the findings of his report, on the grounds – as von Valentini, the Chief of the Emperor's Civil Cabinet, put it – that 'failings in our constitutional structure [should] not be acknowledged before a hostile public'.[27]

In the short run this tactic was in fact effective. The realities of political power were such that the Chancellor was able simply to disregard a huge no-confidence vote in the Reichstag: he had little difficulty in calling the bourgeois parties to heel by pointing out to them how their anti-government stance had played into the hands of the Social Democrats. The only concrete result of the Zabern crisis was the announcement of a new legal framework governing the relationship between the civilian and military authorities, which conceded, albeit belatedly, many of the constitutional arguments put forward by the bourgeois parties.

Likewise, the government's tactic of ignoring the Social Democrats, even though they were now the largest party in the Reichstag, was largely successful. On exceptional occasions during this period the Social Democrats were able to turn their political strength to concrete legislative account. But their overall achievements were decidedly meagre. Paradoxically, indeed, the real political influence of the Social Democrats was in a sense inversely proportional to their numerical strength: the very fact that they were so heavily represented in the Reichstag induced the other parties to side with the government at critical moments. As a result, from 1913 onwards the Social Democratic movement became embroiled in another fierce argument

over the party leadership's commitment to parliamentarism.[28] The controversy was further fuelled by the fact that for the first time the movement
was showing signs of stagnation: 1913 was the first year in which the number of party members had not increased.

All the same, in the eyes of the Conservative party and its allies – notably
the Imperial German Middle-Class Association and the Farmers' Alliance,
not to mention the CVdI and the ultra-conservative spokesmen for heavy
industry who were closely associated with it – the government's tactics of
playing for time and systematically isolating the Social Democrats were not
nearly reactionary enough. The officer corps, too, was becoming increasingly critical of the government, accusing it of not properly safeguarding
the army's rights when the Reichstag debated the military budget in 1913.
The military perceived the Reichstag's interference with the organization of
the army (in particular, the abolition of a string of privileges traditionally
enjoyed by the senior officer corps) as evidence of a concerted plan to
undermine the direct relationship between the army and the Crown, and
they made little secret of their distaste for what they saw as the government's feebleness. Bethmann Hollweg's standing with the Emperor was
affected. In the summer of 1913 Bethmann Hollweg himself doubted
whether he would remain Chancellor much longer. In 1914 the attitudes of
these groups found yet more militant expression, with the formation of the
Prussian Alliance (Preußenbund), a body that sought to combat the
advance of the democratic era by reactivating old Prussian traditions. The
Prussian Alliance's plan was first to build up a firm following in Prussia, the
stronghold of conservatism, and then launch a full-dress assault on the
democratizing ambitions of the Reichstag.

Altogether, in part as a result of the state of party-political paralysis
within the Reichstag, the centre of gravity of the political debate was shifting towards the extra-parliamentary arena. Much of the political running
was now being made by non-parliamentary propaganda organizations. The
most important of these groups were the Pan-German League (Alldeutscher
Verband), the Army League (Wehrverein, founded in 1912) and the Navy
League (Flottenverein), although the latter, while it retained an enormous
membership, had lost some of its former glory. The economic interest
groups we have just mentioned were also forced to follow the path of trying
to shape opinion through the use of publicity, since their influence over the
government was much slighter than they would have liked and their
attempts to gain a foothold within the political parties had not been especially successful.

The element in the situation that had a crucial bearing on the course of
subsequent events was the fact that the Bethmann Hollweg government –
lacking any firm political support, under fire from almost all of the parties
in the Reichstag, at best merely surviving on sufferance – was more closely
dependent than any preceding Imperial government had been on the good
will of those groups within the Wilhelmine Empire that were responsible

for the functioning of the state in the narrower sense, as well as on the Hohenzollern monarchy itself. The government would have been quite unable to hold out without the backing of the conservative higher civil service and, more broadly, of the highest echelons of society. Bethmann Hollweg's appeal for a politics 'above party' did enjoy some success with those sections of the German middle class that had no direct party-political commitments, particularly on the question of the 'defence levy' of 1913; the extent of this support is difficult to quantify, which does not mean that it was insignificant. Nevertheless, the government was unable to halt the accelerating shift in favour of the forces of extreme conservatism that was taking place within the governmental system itself. Devoid of any reliable support in the country, and possessing no other real power base, the 'civilians' lost ground steadily from 1913 onwards.

Those around Wilhelm II saw the Imperial Chancellor's principal task in the domestic sphere as keeping the Reichstag and its ambitions in check, not as pursuing a positive and far-sighted programme of reform (although no such programme was actually practicable). And yet Bethmann Hollweg did have one important source of power in the years before the war: this was his responsibility for the German Empire's foreign policy. Here, the Chancellor's reputation outside Germany deterred the Emperor from giving way to the growing number of voices in conservative and Pan-German circles that were calling for his dismissal on grounds of weak leadership. The Emperor himself, explaining his main motive for holding on to Bethmann Hollweg, at least in the short run, said: 'If I have a man who is trusted by foreigners for the honesty of his policy, and who follows my lead here, then I have to put up with many of the weaknesses of his domestic policies.'[29] The upshot of this, however, was that the Bethmann Hollweg government was under severe pressure to succeed in foreign policy. Any serious setback on the international front was bound to have fatal consequences for the position of the Chancellor at home. The heavier the domestic pressure bearing down on the government, the less the government could afford to betray any real or perceived weakness abroad.

Accordingly, the mood of readiness for war that was clearly spreading among significant sections of the German ruling class took on considerable importance. The fact that so many people were beginning to assume, almost fatalistically, that a major European war was likely, either sooner or later, added fuel to the militarist tendencies that were already present in German society. There was a widespread feeling that war would be a kind of cold-water cure for the nation, shocking it out of its lethargic complacency and endowing it with new energy and vitality. Mixed with this feeling was the notion, particularly popular in conservative circles, that war would provide the ideal opportunity for crushing Social Democracy and putting back the clock on the home front. There were plans, indeed, for arresting the entire Social Democratic leadership in the event of war, and it was thought possible that the mass of the working class might be split from its political leaders amidst the surge of patriotic sentiment that would accompany the declaration of hostilities. Even more important than such thinking (certainly more common) was the view that while the German Empire should not contrive to bring about a war, it should certainly not shy away from the prospect of war either, if Germany's specific international aims could not be achieved by any other means.

Many people also believed that a preventive war would be the best way of resolving Germany's military and strategic problems. This belief was particularly prevalent in senior military circles, such as the General Staff, and was held by Moltke himself. Russia's rapidly accelerating drive to build up her armaments made it likely that the Schlieffen Plan, which assumed that Russia would be slow to mobilize, would cease to be relevant in a few years' time. Fears among the German military concerning Russian warreadiness had hardened into the assumption that when the current armament programme in Russia had been completed, in 1916 or 1917, a military collision between the two powers was inevitable. Moltke had taken the view since 1912 – and held to it more firmly from late 1913 onwards – that if it were not German policy actually to bring about a European war, then at least nothing should be done to avoid one if the occasion were to arise. Swayed in the main by strictly technical military arguments, Moltke was convinced that the German Empire could be sure of winning if a European war were to take place immediately, but not if there were a delay of a few years.

Bethmann Hollweg and the Secretary of State at the Foreign Office, von Jagow, were opposed to a preventive war, though they did not rule one out, on principle, as a possible tool of policy. From the spring of 1914 onwards, however, as can be inferred indirectly from the sources, they came under mounting pressure (particularly from the military and intermittently, it would seem, from the Emperor as well) at least to consider a preventive war as a serious option. On 4 June 1914 Bethmann Hollweg and Lerchenfeld, the Bavarian delegate to the Bundesrat, discussed the fact that so many members of the military were calling for a preventive war. Lerchenfeld made a note of the Chancellor's response:[30]

> [Bethmann Hollweg said that] the Emperor had never waged a preventive war, nor would he do so. There were some in the Empire, however, who believed that a war would have a healthy effect on domestic conditions in Germany, and would help the conservative cause. He, the Imperial Chancellor, on the other hand, thought that a war, with its quite unforeseeable consequences, might enormously increase the strength of Social Democracy, which preached peace, and might topple a number of thrones.

This evidence contradicts Arno Mayer's thesis that the policy of the German government in July 1914, which resulted in the outbreak of war, was a calculated attempt on the part of the political leadership to resolve

Germany's domestic political problems by displacing them externally. On the other hand, it is clear that the fateful decision that was taken by the German government at the beginning of July 1914 – to change its previous line on Balkan policy and promise Austria-Hungary unconditional support for her action against Serbia, even if the result were a general European war, as was certainly considered possible – was crucially influenced by domestic political circumstances within Germany. Taking into account all of the factors that induced the German government to encourage Austria-Hungary to resort to force over the Serbian problem, we may conclude that the German decision was not the culmination of a cold-blooded imperialist drive for power but sprang from a domestic crisis of leadership, which in turn was ultimately a symptom of the wider, long-standing latent crisis of the system of government itself.

Although the evidence from sources remains patchy, it is possible today to give a fairly reliable outline of the basic attitudes of the most important groups that made up the inmost ruling elite in Germany in the early summer of 1914. The military, together with a significant number of conservatives, favoured a hard line on foreign policy, and were increasingly swinging towards the idea of a preventive war which could, of course, be presented as defensive in purpose. There was consensus within this group that if a European war were in the offing, then Germany should certainly not feebly seek to evade it by not deigning to play her trump cards. These attitudes, as we have seen, not only reflected the greater readiness for war that had been prompted by domestic political factors but also sprang from anxieties about the growing strength of Russia. Since the revolution of 1905, Russia had regained the status of a formidable European power, but her general political orientation could scarcely be called pro-German, certainly not since the Liman von Sanders crisis.

The political leadership, by contrast, took a much more pragmatic view. They were sure that a European war could be avoided, in the short run at least. The main official aim of the German government's policy was to defuse the immediate crisis among the great powers by seeking a rapprochement with Great Britain and, in the longer term, to use British support in order to make overseas territorial acquisitions. There was certainly also some anxiety within the political leadership about the supposed increase in hostile sentiment in Russia, but Bethmann Hollweg was convinced that improved relations with Britain would enable Germany to weather the difficult period in foreign policy that was looming as a consequence of Austria-Hungary's weakness and Italy's uncertain stance. Official hopes that significant imperialist acquisitions might eventually be obtainable, in Africa and, especially, in the Near East, were not entirely unreasonable.

The secret intelligence reports of Anglo-Russian naval conversations, however, that reached Berlin at the end of May 1914 dealt a severe blow to the pro-British assumptions that had underpinned Bethmann Hollweg's foreign policy, and thus to the central pillar of the Chancellor's relatively opti-mistic view of the international situation.[31] The encirclement of the Central Powers seemed to be happening after all, despite his hopeful predictions. Given the nature of the situation as we have described it, this made for a serious weakening of Bethmann Hollweg's position. In a sense, what now happened was a repetition of what had happened in early December 1912: the influence of the military over the Emperor increased sharply, while the 'civilians' were forced to take a back seat, and Moltke's notion of a preven-tive war gained yet more currency among the most senior leaders of the Reich.

With tensions already high, the explosive news of the assassination at Sarajevo then arrived, forcing the German government to produce a practi-cal response to the question that had previously been debated in a purely theoretical fashion: namely, whether to go to war, or to procrastinate, or unequivocally to avoid war, even at the cost of jeopardizing the postion of the government and its allies. After some days of hesitation, the Chancellor elected for a compromise course, which in a sense exactly mirrored the ten-sions that were present within the Imperial ruling elite. The leadership's decisions (which would seem, in essentials, already to have been taken by 5 July, when Austria enquired whether German support would be forthcom-ing in the event of action against Serbia) owed more to this internal clash of views than to the international situation itself, although the likely reactions of the other great powers were also soberly assessed, and indeed, as can now be seen in retrospect, accurately predicted.

This last point applies, among other things, to the government's view of the attitude of Great Britain. Contrary to what has commonly been claimed, notably by Luigi Albertini and later by Fritz Fischer, hopes that Britain might remain neutral played a negligible role. While the German government did think it not impossible that Britain might adopt a neutral stance during the opening phase of European hostilities, it assumed from the outset that she would not tolerate the crushing of France; Britain was therefore regarded as an inevitable enemy in the event of all-out war. In no sense did the German government count on British neutrality. On the other hand, it did believe, for that very reason, that pressure might be brought to bear on Russia and France.

Germany's strategy was to force Russia, over the Serbian question, to decide whether she wanted war or not. This was desirable not only from a domestic political standpoint, but also on the grounds that there was a good prospect, in Berlin's view, that if Russia were abandoned, or sup-ported only very reluctantly, by Britain and France, then she would eventu-ally pull back from the brink; this would give Germany a reasonable chance of breaching the Entente's encirclement and creating a new pattern of European alliances (perhaps even a Russo-German alliance) at the cost of a partial sacrifice of the interests of Austria-Hungary. If, on the other hand, Russia were to hit out immediately, without waiting for the results of possible negotiations among the great powers, that would effectively confirm the military's view that she wanted war at any price. In that case, though, with war inevitable, the political leadership likewise believed that it was better to fight sooner rather than later.

The German government was pursuing a high-risk strategy: Bethmann Hollweg spoke of a 'leap in the dark and this most onerous duty'.[32] The Chancellor, however, was no longer powerful enough to persuade the ruling elite of the German Empire to fall in with any alternative plan. It was not the proximate aim of German policy to unleash a major European war, even though the government was fully aware of the great gamble implicit in giving unconditional support to the Habsburg monarchy. By lending its support, the government was doing enough to satisfy the demand of the military that the German Empire should, at any rate, do nothing to prevent a European war, were that prospect to present itself. That did not mean, however, that it preferred war to a diplomatic solution. Bethmann Hollweg and Jagow seem to have believed that there was a good chance not only of isolating any possible Austro-Serbian conflict but of turning it to diplomatic account. Such an outcome would also have the useful by-product of demonstrating that the German General Staff's deep-seated fears concerning Russia's warlike intentions were unfounded.

In objective terms, Germany's policy during the July crisis of 1914 bears a considerable share of responsibility for the outbreak of the First World War. The policy, however, was not the product of an unbridled German drive for world power so much as a symptom of weakness and confusion within the highest leadership circles of the German Empire. The tensions and divisions within the ruling elite found their expression in the tortuous diplomatic calculations that left Germany's decisions dependent, to a remarkably high degree, on the decisions of other powers, notably Russia and Austria-Hungary. Only in this sense were Bethmann Hollweg's words to the Prussian Ministry of State on 29 July 1914 appropriate:

We have lost control, and the ball has been set rolling.

In fact, in the short run the extraordinary skill with which the outbreak of the war was stage-managed – creating a remarkable sense of national unanimity that Germany was engaged in a war of self-defence forced on it by Russia and the western powers – actually served to conceal the crisis of leadership that afflicted the German political system. Nevertheless, the reality gradually emerged more starkly as the hardships of the war itself began to make themselves felt. Walther Rathenau understood this from the very first. He wrote to his friend Fanny Künstler in November 1914:[33]

Something about this war rings false. It is not 1815, or 1866, or 1870. It did not have to happen in the way that it has happened this time.

9

Domestic factors in German foreign policy before 1914 [*]

Gordon Craig has recently lamented the fact that political history, particularly diplomatic history, no longer attracts the attention of historians or of the general public in the way it once did. There are no compelling grounds, in his view, why this should be so: international relations and diplomacy are of great importance and constitute, up to a certain point at least, a distinct field of historical research in their own right.[1] There are powerful reasons, however, why diplomatic history is in something of a crisis at the present time and why growing numbers of historians are coming to feel that the study of diplomatic documents, and of the actions and motives of the groups of individuals who monopolize the process of decision-making in international relations, is ultimately unsatisfying, however meticulously it is done. Most modern historians would probably now accept that it is necessary to study international relations, not just in terms of diplomatic decision-making at the official level, but with reference to the wider social and economic factors that affect the making of foreign policy.

As far as German historiography is concerned, for over a century the principle of the 'primacy of foreign policy' was generally accepted by professional historians and the educated general reader alike. Ranke's famous dictum, that the internal structure of a state is a function of its external relations, attracted little opposition, and the case of Bismarck seemed to put the matter beyond dispute.[2] There has always been a liberal historiographical tradition in Germany, however, and historians of this school have been reluctant to give unqualified support to the principle of the 'primacy of foreign policy'. Notable dissenters have included Droysen, Eyck, Ziekursch and Valentin, while even Meinecke, the theorist of *raison d'état*, was not a full-hearted adherent. It was Eckart Kehr, however, who first seriously challenged the validity of the principle, portraying it as a central ele-

[*] Revised and enlarged version of a paper read to the conference of the Anglo-German Group of Historians at the Institute of Historical Studies in London on 13 November 1971. For helpful criticism as well as many suggestions I am indebted to Volker Berghahn, Paul Kennedy, Anthony Nicholls, Hartmut Pogge von Strandmann and John C. G. Röhl.

ment of the conservative tradition in German historiography, first in his study of the social background to Germany's naval policy of the late 1890s, and then, in more detail, in his essay 'Englandhaß und Weltpolitik' of 1928. This essay should be seen, in part, as a critical response to Friedrich Meinecke's *Geschichte des deutsch-englischen Bündnisproblems*, published only a year earlier. Kehr claimed bluntly that Ranke's thesis of the primacy of foreign policy had become a vital part of 'the official and semi-official philosophy of power and the political theory of the German Empire': it had been a useful device for winning the middle classes on to the side of the ruling elites, so that the two groups could then jointly suppress the working class.[3] Kehr went on to argue that hostile German public attitudes towards Great Britain, and the deliberate abandonment of negotiations over an Anglo-German alliance in 1898 and 1901, had to be explained in social and economic terms. He concluded by proclaiming the 'primacy of domestic policy', at any rate as far as Germany's relations with Britain and Russia were concerned.[4]

Kehr's thesis went largely unnoticed in the late 1920s, and the rise of National Socialism then put a stop to all serious research in contemporary history. It was not until the 1950s that the debate was resumed, partly prompted, indeed, by the recognition that any attempt to explain National Socialist foreign policy solely in the traditional terms of diplomatic history was manifestly inadequate. Although Kehr's own work was not rediscovered until the 1960s, for various reasons that cannot be gone into here, his thesis that foreign policy is determined primarily by social and economic structures (in particular by the social and political interests of ruling elites) is now supported, with varying emphases and to varying degrees, by the great majority of historians.

This is true, especially, of scholars who have worked in recent years on the politics of Wilhelmine Germany. Accordingly, in the first part of this essay I shall compare and contrast some of the varying approaches that rest on the assumption that international relations in general, and German imperialism in particular, should be analysed by reference to domestic political processes rather than in terms of the complex web of actions and counter-actions that make up the process of diplomacy. Broadly speaking, five such approaches can be distinguished.

Of these, the Marxist–Leninist model is a special case. According to Marxist–Leninist doctrine, all political activity is determined, in the final analysis at least, by the economic system: more precisely, it is a specific manifestation of the class struggle, at any rate under the conditions of bourgeois capitalism. Under imperialist capitalism, the state is the tool, direct or indirect, of the bourgeois class, and its policies necessarily serve two main purposes: first, the suppression of the working class, to the advantage of the capitalists; and secondly, the protection and – if appropriate – the enhancement, by force, of the economic interests of the owners of capital, to the detriment of capitalist rivals beyond the state's borders. It has been a further crucial tenet of Marxism–Leninism since Hilferding and Lenin himself that the more advanced (that is, the more monopolistic) a capitalist system is, the more aggressive its behaviour becomes.

It is important to emphasize that the Marxist–Leninist model embraces both domestic politics and international relations: indeed, the model does not admit of a strict separation between domestic and external policies. Within the Marxist framework, therefore, neither sphere of policy can have 'primacy' over the other: the suppression of the working class at home and the exploitation of subjugated peoples abroad are simply two sides of the same coin. Militarism is at once a symptom of the growing exploitation and pauperization of the working class and the by-product of a highly aggressive foreign policy.

At first sight this explanatory scheme may seem coherent, indeed compelling. The argument that monopoly capitalism, on the one hand, is intrinsically associated with aggressive foreign policies, imperialist ventures and warmongering tendencies and, on the other hand, inevitably entails the ever-greater suppression of the working class, is a staple of the Marxist–Leninist literature.[5] Repetition, however, does not make it any more true to the facts. It is clear that capitalist systems do not all have an equal propensity to resort to a strategy of repression at home or aggressive expansion abroad. They behave in a wide range of different ways, and even orthodox Marxists are much more dubious nowadays about attributing the aggressive tendencies of capitalist systems to the capitalist mode of production as such. Only a minority of Marxists still clings to the doctrine that the law of diminishing profits forces capitalists to adopt imperialist policies for the sake of survival. A theory needs to incorporate a more sophisticated pattern of causal relationships if it is not to be glaringly at odds with the latter-day evolution of capitalist systems. Marxist–Leninist historians, indeed, have become adept at marshalling ancillary arguments in this way – exhibiting just the same eclecticism, incidentally, that they themselves regard as a typical characteristic of bourgeois historiography.

Lenin himself maintained that capitalism necessarily leads to imperialist wars, not so much because of the greed of capitalists and their unrestrained drive for expansion, as because capitalist economies evolve at unequal rates, with the result that huge disparities of economic, and hence political, strength among the various rival capitalist powers are created.[6] Similar arguments, however, are not uncommon among modern non-Marxist economists: W.W. Rostow is a case in point.[7] Moreover, disparities of economic growth are also a standing source of conflict within the socialist world and do not appear to be the exclusive property of capitalist systems. Recent claims by Marxist–Leninist writers that imperialist policies were a convenient device used by the bourgeoisie to provoke, split or even bribe the working class, do not, therefore, carry a great deal of conviction. Once we accept the notion that there is not simply one single version of capitalism *tout court*, but a wide spectrum of different social systems, each possessing the structural features of a capitalist market economy, and that within these social systems the actual political influence of capitalists themselves may be either considerable or quite small, then it becomes apparent that the explanatory force of the Marxist–Leninist framework is doomed to remain limited unless its underlying assumptions are substantially refined.

As yet, however, there has been little sign of a real change of theoretical approach in Marxist–Leninist historiography. We may take, as an illustration, the study entitled *Deutschland im Ersten Weltkrieg* (Germany in the First World War), jointly published in the late 1960s by a group of historians from the German Democratic Republic under the chairmanship of Fritz Klein.[8] This is an important and instructive work, but, aside from various recurrent professions of loyalty that at best are very loosely linked to the matter in hand, it contains precious little thinking that can be said to be genuinely Marxist in character. The authors certainly do nothing to bridge the yawning gap between the general postulates of Marxism–Leninism and the actual narrative content of the events they discuss. They bring out very strongly the repressive and reactionary quality of the Wilhelmine system and the aggressive nature of Germany's foreign policy, and they pay keen attention to the monopolistic structures of the German economy, but they fail to provide rigorous proof that the government was at the mercy of the capitalists, though this surely what one might have expected. By contrast, there is detailed discussion of the role of the working class, in particular the left wing of the Social Democratic movement, and of the peace movement – reasonably enough, in view of the neglect of the latter by traditional historians. In its general approach, however, this book does not ultimately differ in any fundamental way from the positivist accounts of the same period that have appeared in the West. Its ritual obeisances to official Marxist–Leninist doctrine sometimes obscure this fact, but if we analyse closely the book's methodology and theoretical framework we find that the devotional references generally have little connection with the main body of the text. Indeed, anyone hoping to find here a coherent and definitive Marxist–Leninist analysis of the Wilhelmine era will be disappointed. This is not, ultimately, the fault of the authors themselves so much as of the Marxist–Leninist model *per se*, which is simply too general and far too rigid, even though Marxist ideas can certainly provide rewarding insights within the context of a more sophisticated explanatory framework.

We need, then, to look at other approaches to the study of Wilhelmine Germany that have been followed by Western historians: approaches that are less eye-catching, perhaps, but also less grand in their ambitions. Four clearly distinct contemporary schools of thought can, I believe, be identified:

1. A quasi-Marxist approach, emphasizing the role of specific interest
   groups that were calling for imperialist policies of which they themselves

were likely to be beneficiaries. The best-known exponent of this approach has been G.W. Hallgarten.[9]

2. A 'moral attitudes' approach, resting primarily on a critical analysis of the ideological values (in particular, the anti-democratic beliefs) that were prevalent in Germany.[10]

3. The approach adopted by Kehr's followers, which tends to explain changes in the political system in terms of the defensive strategies used by the ruling elites to counter what may be called the process of democratization. At times this model takes on strong Marxist overtones.[11]

4. A structural-functional approach, concerned primarily with the functions and dysfunctions of the constitutional and governmental systems as they responded to the various social forces that were unleashed, in particular, by industrialization and by the emergence of a modern mass culture – in other words, by the process of modernization.[12] In this model the defensive strategies employed by the ruling elites are seen merely as one ingredient in the overall situation. The main emphasis is on the disparities between the social and political systems, which led, it is argued, to increasingly open conflict and seriously undermined the governing process. The decision to go to war is portrayed, in some accounts, as little more than a last, desperate throw of the dice.

It should be stressed, of course, that a taxonomy of this sort is inevitably somewhat over-schematic and that most historians tend to adopt a combination of these approaches, the exact pattern of emphasis varying in each individual case.

Of the four approaches, the one most easily dealt with is that associated with Hallgarten. Hallgarten was one of the first scholars to attempt to describe pre-1914 German politics in socio-economic terms, and he also characterized the First World War itself as the logical outcome of imperialism. At first sight, then, there would seem to be close affinities between such an analysis and the Marxist–Leninist approach. On closer inspection, however, Hallgarten's concept of imperialism can be seen to boil down to a recital of sinister political practices on the part of specific business interests and pressure groups that sought to further their private commercial ends by inducing political leaders to pursue a policy of imperialist aggression.

Hallgarten's writings are a personalized version of the Marxist theory of history: he sees imperialism as essentially the product, not of the social structures of capitalism as such, but of the parasitical intrigues of particular individuals and groups. It is therefore no surprise that Hallgarten explicitly dissociates himself from Lenin's concept of imperialism, which, as he rightly says, applies in the final analysis to any country that is capitalist in character, 'irrespective of whether the particular nation in question is expanding or not'.[13]

Hallgarten prefers to deal with cases in which it is possible to demonstrate a close intertwining of business interests and public administration.

He pays particular attention to individuals who occupied key positions in the governing apparatus (and therefore exerted significant influence over political decision-making) and who also acted to the advantage of specific economic interest groups with which they were directly or indirectly connected (often through kinship rather than on financial grounds). For Hallgarten, the real villains of the piece are the heads of the armament industries, who constituted a 'new International' that was 'ten times more powerful than the Marxist Internationals'.[14] He goes very thoroughly into the relationship, certainly a close one, between Wilhelm II and Friedrich Krupp. Similarly, he brings out the central importance of the role of heavy industry in supporting Tirpitz's naval policy, and argues that the personal ties that existed between the Young Turks and leading figures on the German side were crucial for the course of diplomatic relations between Germany and the Ottoman Empire.

As far as the analysis of German foreign policy before 1914 is concerned, however, some scepticism concerning this approach is in order. To take merely one example, Hallgarten's assertion that the world of high finance was responsible for luring Kiderlen-Wächter into his rather risky Moroccan policy in 1911 is simply incorrect. The roles in this episode were in fact reversed: German commercial interests served merely as the pretext for a diplomatic gambit, the aim of which was to force France to cede the French Congo to the German Empire. In general, any attempt to explain German policy in the decade before 1914 solely as a response to pressure from specific interest groups does not take us very far. It is not the case, for example, that particular economic pressure groups directly influenced the decisions taken by the German government on the eve of the First World War, or that the members of the government even paid any great attention to concrete economic problems at this time. If there were any attempts by German businessmen to exert political pressure during June and July 1914, these efforts would seem, if anything, to have been directed towards preventing war rather than encouraging it. Financiers were becoming increasingly uneasy about the course that events were taking, and the mood among industrialists – inasmuch as it found public expression, at any rate – also appears to have been far from bellicose. The *Westfälische Zeitung*, usually regarded as the mouthpiece of heavy industry, was one of the few newspapers that vigorously opposed the official policy of support for Austria-Hungary against Serbia until late in July 1914.

Fritz Fischer's approach, by comparison, is undoubtedly much more significant and enlightening. Whatever the rights and wrongs of the specific claims he makes, Fischer indisputably deserves credit for having re-opened the debate about a central body of problems that German historians had mistakenly believed to have been settled for once and for all. On the other hand, it is by no means obvious that his findings can be taken as the last word on German policy before 1914.

Fischer maintains that Germany's foreign policy was, in the final analysis, the inevitable product of a brand of aggressive nationalism that permeated German society and that was particularly virulent within the ruling elite. In 1961, in *Griff nach der Weltmacht*, Fischer argued that during the July crisis of 1914 Germany was deliberately seeking an imperialist war in order to establish herself as a world power. Subsequently he has adopted a yet more radical view, claiming that either as early as 1911, or at the latest by 8 December 1912, Germany had taken the firm decision to go to war in order to break out of the political impasse into which all her previous attempts to acquire colonial possessions and greater overseas influence had led her. He has also argued that the German war aims that took shape after 1914 similarly originated well before the outbreak of war. The claim to Longwy-Briey was a prime example, he maintains, but the same applied to the scheme to establish economic hegemony over the European continent, possibly including the Balkans, by means of a German-led European economic association. In *Krieg der Illusionen* Fischer presents an almost overwhelming quantity of source material (some of it stemming from Klaus Wernecke's study of German public opinion before 1914) in support of this thesis.[15]

It is not possible in the present essay to offer detailed criticisms of Fischer's interpretation of German policy between 1911 and 1915, but it is surely the case that he has allowed himself to be carried away as far as his central notion of Germany's 'will to power' is concerned. We should note, for example, that he never really states explicitly which sections or groups within German society actually opted for war as a way of cutting the Gordian knot of German imperialism. Was it the government, the Emperor, the military, the conservatives or industry? Was it only one of these groups, or more than one, or the nation as a whole? Fischer constantly equivocates on this point, attributing warlike intentions first to one group and then to another, while never actually asserting that the specific groups and individuals he examines were jointly committed, firmly and throughout, to war. Thus, although the reader gains important new insights on many matters, the overall thrust of Fischer's argument remains obscure.[16] To cite just one example: Fischer ascribes the highest importance to the informal 'war council' that Wilhelm II, in a bout of panic, convened on 8 December 1912, and he claims that from this time onwards the German Empire was bent on unleashing a general European war at the earliest possible opportunity. He maintains, moreover, that there was now a systematic drive to prepare German public opinion for such a war. This view has also been advanced, though in qualified terms, by J.C.G. Röhl, who is likewise inclined to take literally Tirpitz's statement at the 'war council' of 8 December 1912 that the German fleet would be ready for war by June 1914.[17] It is debatable, however, whether the decisions that were taken on this occasion were actually as significant as Fischer and Röhl (and also I. Geiss) have maintained. There is absolutely no evidence that any steps were taken to implement the Emperor's frantic order that the country should be prepared for war through an official press campaign. Nor can it be proved that the German government was deliberately steering towards war from this time onwards. The Chancellor was not told about the conference of 8 December until eight days after it had taken place, and even then only unofficially.[18] If the 'war council' had really reached a decision that the German Empire should embark on a war in eighteen months' time, and that a supporting press campaign should be launched, then it would have been astonishing, to say the least, if both the head of the government and the Wilhelmstraße had been left in the dark on the matter for over a week. Two hard facts emerge from the conference of 8 December 1912. First, the military leadership gave serious consideration to the possibility of attempting to solve the problems of Germany's foreign policy by means of a preventive war; Moltke, indeed, urged an early decision in favour of war, on the grounds that Germany's military position was deteriorating rapidly. Secondly, it was agreed that work on the new Army Bill, which was already in hand, should be speeded up. Beyond this, however, the immediate results of the gathering were fairly slight. Bethmann Hollweg managed to block a plan to introduce another navy bill, and he also worked discreetly but effectively to prevent the implementation of the Emperor's order 'to go to the press with a vengeance', though it is dubious whether the directive was ever taken seriously in the first place.[19] There is no doubt that the militarist tendency was gaining ground both within the government and outside, but that in no sense warrants the conclusion that the German government was firmly committed to war from 1912 onwards.

Similarly, it is by no means clear that German imperialism had really reached an impasse by 1914, as Fischer repeatedly and sombrely insists. Germany's economic stake in the Ottoman Empire had been consolidated, albeit at the cost of certain concessions to French and British interests. At the very least, despite the chronic scarcity of capital for 'political' investment, German influence in the region had held its own.[20]

It is evident that the nature of his methodology prevents Fischer from giving due weight to the forces of moderation within the political spectrum. He bases his conclusions on verbal testimony rather than on actual political events, and this makes him prone to see the aggressively nationalistic outbursts of his *dramatis personae* as the whole story. In his second book, admittedly, he makes a serious attempt to provide an account that goes beyond the predominantly ideological, even if the results are somewhat mixed. Nevertheless, it is fair to say that the main reason why Fischer's conclusions are too sweeping is that he tends to divorce quotations of an imperialist or nationalist cast from their context and to use them as the basis of his interpretation, instead of placing them within the framework of a consistent overall analysis of political and social structures.

There is a further point. The main premiss of Fischer's account of Wilhelmine policy, that aggressive nationalism was the root cause of events, leads him to characterize the behaviour of the other great powers as a mere reaction to diplomatic initiatives taken by Germany. This, however, is hardly an adequate way of explaining French nationalism or the rise of militarism in Russia. A comparative analysis would show that the steady growth of popular participation in the political process went hand in hand with a strengthening of nationalist sentiment in all of the countries of Europe.

The approach adopted by those historians who have followed in the footsteps of Eckart Kehr is more illuminating in this respect, since it takes much greater account of universal factors such as the process of industrialization, though it still tends to be too narrowly restricted to German trends alone. This approach, however, is able to provide something of an answer to the question why imperialist ideas were particularly powerful in Germany even though significant sections of the German population (notably the working class) would have nothing to do with them.

According to this model, German imperialism was first and foremost a defensive strategy employed by the upper and middle classes against Social Democracy and, more widely, against the democratic currents of the age. Within this broad explanatory framework there have been marked differences of emphasis. Hans-Ulrich Wehler, for example, has maintained that German imperialism was the product of the belief, widespread among the upper classes, that the prevailing social order could be upheld only by dint of permanent economic expansion: economic growth and the acquisition of colonies were seen as vital at least as much from socio-psychological motives as on economic grounds.[21] This thesis, however, which is an extension of Wehler's account of what he calls 'Bismarck's imperialism', is not particularly plausible for the period under discussion here, since the two decades after 1894 were years of unparalleled and virtually uninterrupted economic growth.[22] A socio-political version of Wehler's argument, on the other hand, to the effect that imperialism was an instrument for preserving the privileged position of the upper classes and suppressing Social Democracy, carries much greater conviction. This view has been put forward by Dirk Stegmann, Volker Berghahn and Helmut Böhme, among others. They claim that the 'agrarian-industrial complex' was the most important social force in Wilhemine Germany and that German foreign policy was shaped more or less directly in response to pressure from this quarter. On this analysis, imperialist ventures and the construction of a colossal battle fleet were primarily devices for welding together the conservative and middle-class sections of German society against the common enemy, Social Democracy. Kehr had already advanced a similar theory in 1928: 'Miquel's "Sammlungspolitik" [the policy of 'gathering together' those elements that 'supported the state'],' he wrote, 'was the ultimate source of the foreign policy of the German Empire, which led to war.'[23] Stegmann's book *Die Erben Bismarcks* is, in effect, an attempt to confirm this thesis on the basis of an impressive wealth of empirical data. Stegmann also closely echoes the Fischer view, inasmuch as he places an insistent stress on continuity, detecting a seamless progression from the 'Sammlungspolitik' inaugurated by Bismarck in 1879, and put on a more formal basis by Miquel in 1899, to the crisis of 1933: the earlier policies, he argues, were an important contributory cause of the rise of National Socialism. Helmut Böhme, in his study of German imperialism, takes a broadly similar line but does not go so far as to pin all the blame on the industrialists for the course of subsequent events.[24] Volker Berghahn, in his work on Germany's naval programme, is rather more cautious, confining himself to maintaining that Tirpitz's policies not only had an anti-parliamentary thrust but functioned specifically as a form of social imperialism.[25]

It is still questionable, however, how well these Kehr-inspired accounts actually help explain Germany's foreign policy before 1914. One central problem can be dealt with straight away. It is surely the case that both Stegmann and Böhme considerably overstate the impact of the 'Sammlungspolitik' on German foreign policy. In particular, Stegmann's ambitious attempt to demonstrate (despite the clash between conservatives and industry over Imperial financial reform in 1909) that from the 1890s onwards there was continuous co-operation between the Central Association of German Industrialists (Centralverband deutscher Industrieller, or CVdI) and the Farmers' Alliance (Bund der Landwirte) is not wholly persuasive. Even if we grant that there was co-operation between agriculture and heavy industry on the scale that Stegmann claims, it still needs to be explained why this alliance of convenience actually produced such meagre results. Can the temporary halting of welfare legislation in 1914 really be regarded as a major victory? Is it really possible to argue that combined pressure from agricultural and industrial interests was the only, or even the most important, reason why constitutional reforms were blocked? It is plain that the CVdI, supposedly so powerful, in fact failed even to exert decisive influence over the leadership of the National Liberal party. Although the National Liberals became increasingly willing to work closely with the Conservatives after 1912, many of them remained very dubious about the openly reactionary policies that the Conservatives and the CVdI advocated.

This example shows that we need a much more sophisticated model than that provided by Kehr's followers if we are to do justice to the complex set of problems that German imperialism poses. Contrary to Kehr's thesis, there was not an unbroken progression from Miquel's 'Sammlungspolitik' of the 1890s to the policies of 1913.

Indeed, there was a marked difference between Miquel's blatantly reactionary call for a 'Sammlung' of the 'productive classes' and the form of 'Sammlungspolitik' that was pursued, first, by Bülow and Tirpitz and then, in a more concerted manner, by Bethmann Hollweg.[26] Miquel had unambiguously anti-parliamentary aims and was particularly eager to combat the growing influence of the Reichstag. He not only proposed that the franchise for Reichstag elections be 'adjusted' to match the Prussian model but also favoured outright measures of repression against the Social Democrats. After 1898, however, this strategy was abandoned for a much more flexible approach, permitting an accommodation within the existing constitutional framework and enabling the government to create a workable relationship with the Reichstag, or at any rate with the bourgeois parties; there was no new round of specifically anti-socialist legislation. Rather than making constitutional concessions to the Reichstag, however, Bülow and Tirpitz inaugurated a policy of popular imperialism, including the building of a 'bourgeois' fleet, in the hope that this would put relations between the government and the parties of the centre on a new footing under the aegis of a plebiscitary Caesarism.

This strategy did not rule out some degree of modernization of the political system, even at the risk that the Conservatives might temporarily be affronted.[27] By playing the imperialist card, Bülow managed, in the short run at least, to stabilize the political system and hold down the growing power of Parliament. As an international strategy, however, the new 'Weltpolitik', or 'world policy', was pursued only rather half-heartedly and in an unplanned way. Bülow saw the policy as a device for diverting public attention away from domestic political and social tensions and on to overseas concerns: what he was interested in was glamorous short-term successes that would boost the government's popularity, not the acquisition of overseas territories for their own sake. Imperialist expansion was not an aim in itself but, primarily, a way of helping to revive the fortunes of the Emperor and of the political system as a whole, which had dipped badly since 1892. It was little accident, therefore, that the Bülow government was never able to make up its mind where to concentrate its activities. It consistently held back, moreover, from acting assertively on colonial questions if there was a risk that Germany's supposed position of independence betwen the 'British lion' and the 'Russian bear' might be affected. On the other hand, Bülow's special brand of 'mock imperialism' was well adapted to the time-scale of Tirpitz's naval policy, since the latter required a spell of relative calm on the international front in order that its planning stages could be safely completed without the danger of conflict with the British fleet. After the failure of the attempt to split the Entente Cordiale, however, Bülow became increasingly concerned about the deterioration in Anglo-German relations, and in 1908 he took issue with Tirpitz over the question whether a submarine force might not be better suited to German's strategic interests than a battle fleet.[28]

In the first decade of the twentieth century, German imperialism underwent a profound functional change. Whereas hitherto it had been, first and foremost, a contrivance for restoring public respect for a government that was far from popular, it now became the overriding preoccupation of the middle classes. This was not merely because the middle classes were afraid of the Social Democrats. Imperialism now became associated with social modernization and industrial advance, and it took on a distinctly anti-conservative tinge. Imperialist ideology helped to integrate the middle classes into the prevailing political framework; it also enhanced their political standing, at the expense of the conservative aristocracy. It is not at all surprising, therefore, that the Reichstag elections of 1907, called early owing to a colonial dispute, resulted in a conservative-liberal coalition, requiring concessions on both sides. The coalition, however, was fated not to last long: as soon as domestic questions returned to the forefront, the fragility of the 'Bülow Bloc' became all too apparent. The Conservatives were not willing to keep to their side of the bargain, and with the help of the Centre party they brought down Bülow on the issue of Imperial financial reform.[29]

As far as the evolution of German foreign policy after 1909 is concerned, the label of 'social imperialism' that has now become so common is surely particularly unhelpful, since it can hardly be argued that it was the most reactionary groups within German society that were clamouring most loudly for the acquisition of territories overseas. By and large, the strongest supporters of an ambitious, indeed aggressive, 'Weltpolitik' were the upper middle classes (represented by the National Liberal party), intellectuals, who formed a strikingly high proportion of the membership of the Pan-German League (Alldeutscher Verband) and the Navy League (Flottenverein), and sections of the lower middle class. By contrast, it was not until 1911 that the Conservatives came round to giving unreserved backing to a fully fledged imperialist policy, and even then their misgivings about industrialization, which they saw as the twin brother of imperialism, were far from stilled.[30] The Conservatives' conversion to the imperialist cause sprang, in any case, from highly opportunist motives: it was an attempt to revive their waning electoral fortunes at a time when mounting participation in the political process by those groups in the population that had previously been apathetic or neutral posed a particularly disturbing threat to the old bastions of Conservative power, and when the rapid spread of industrialization was destroying the last safe havens of the traditional social order where the writ of the *Junker* on social and political questions had once run virtually unchallenged.

Repeated attempts by the Conservatives and by reactionary groups within German industry (notably the dominant right wing of the CVdI) to launch a new 'Sammlung' of the 'productive classes' and unite the upper middle classes on a common political platform did not, in the end, get very far. The National Liberals were chary of such an alliance, principally because they felt that coming out in favour of a manifestly repressive policy on social and constitutional questions would be tantamount to committing electoral suicide. They chose instead to consolidate their position as champions of what they called a sound and efficient form of imperialism, combined with a policy of piecemeal modernization on domestic and constitutional questions. The Bethmann Hollweg government likewise refused to be stampeded into repressive measures, although it declared its willingness to seek accommodation with the Conservatives wherever that seemed possible. It was no accident, therefore, that it was the supporters of an uncompromising version of social imperialism who became the government's fiercest and most visible critics, on domestic as well as on foreign policy.

As events after 1909 showed, the reason why Bethmann Hollweg became the target of attacks from the conservative and upper-middle-class camps was precisely that he refused to embark on a policy of headlong imperialism, combined with a ruthless clampdown on the Social Democrats and other progressive groups at home. The summer of 1909 had seen, in addition to overt questioning of what had hitherto been the basic thrust of Germany's foreign policy, a serious domestic political crisis. It was the first time that a coalition of two parties had brought down, albeit indirectly, an Imperial Chancellor. The situation was particularly grave for the ruling elites since the Conservatives had not only taken on the government openly but had also, simultaneously, incurred the overt hostility of significant sections of the middle class and the business community. The débâcle led a good number of people to conclude, correctly, that the Social Democrats would make huge gains at the next elections, not least because the lion's share of the new taxes had been passed on to lower-income groups.

Whereas Bülow had succeeded, at the turn of the century, in averting open conflict with the Reichstag by playing the imperialist card, Bethmann Hollweg had grave doubts about the wisdom of applying this risky strategy once again – except on one occasion, to which we shall turn shortly. He believed that the political situation that followed the crisis of 1909 was highly unsuitable for an adventurous foreign policy and that the priority was to create calm at home. The main theme of his foreign policy during the years 1909–11 was the consolidation of Germany's position *vis-à-vis* the other European powers. Germany drew back from the rather odd stance over Morocco that she had adopted at Algeciras, even though the Mannesmann brothers strove energetically to torpedo this move. The government also attempted to lessen tensions with Russia, an enterprise that at first seemed to go well. At the same time, Bethmann Hollweg placed high hopes on an improvement of relations with Great Britain, even after a half-hearted attempt to negotiate a neutrality agreement in exchange for a modest reduction in naval construction had failed.[31] The principal reason why the Chancellor regarded a rapprochment with Britain as a priority was that he wished to avert the risk that Germany might be drawn, at any moment, into a European war as a result of the smouldering rivalry between Austria and Russia in the Balkans.[32] He also believed, however, that stabilizing the German Empire's position on the continent would help it to achieve its colonial objectives. The chief aim of the Bethmann Hollweg government was the creation of a cohesive German colonial empire in central Africa through the acquisition of the Portuguese, Belgian and French territories in the Congo region. The government was also anxious to secure, and if possible increase, Germany's economic stake in the Ottoman Empire. Bethmann

Hollweg reckoned that this policy of cautious expansion would win British support. He was well aware, however, that rapprochement with Britain would not be easy to achieve, not least because of the formidable degree of popular hostility towards Britain that existed within Germany. His hope was that German public opinion could gradually be won round to a more realisitic view of Germany's options in foreign policy, as he saw them. It is questionable, though, how realistic his own vision was, since neither the Emperor nor the middle class was willing to contemplate any substantial reduction in the naval programme, which was a precondition of closer co-operation with Britain. And in any case, the quite disastrous impact of Kiderlen-Wächter's Machiavellian initiative on Morocco in 1911 practically nullifed any remaining chances of success.

In many ways the Agadir crisis of 1911 marked a watershed in German policy before 1914. Kiderlen-Wächter's over-ingenious calculations completely misfired. The Secretary of State had made the optimistic assumption that a final settlement of the Moroccan question would clear the way for an Anglo-German rapprochement.[33] In fact, however, the arrival of the gunboat *Panther* off Agadir on 1 July 1911 not only led to a significant worsening of relations with Great Britain but aroused angry anti-British feeling within Germany, where it was now felt that Britain always intervened just when Germany was on the point of pulling off a coup in colonial policy.

The move against France over Morocco did not come about as a result of pressure from economic interest groups. Indeed, the Mannesmann brothers, who had a financial stake in southern Morocco, had deliberately been kept out of the plot. At the request of the German Foreign Office, a Hamburg banking group was used to provide cover for German intervention, but was kept completely in the dark about the government's true intentions.[34] The same applied to the press and even to the Pan-German League, which were officially encouraged to take an uncompromising line on the Moroccan question in order to soften up the French and induce them to cede their territory in the Congo.[35]

It is clear that not the least of the reasons why the whole affair was launched was the approach of the Reichstag elections.[36] Bethmann Hollweg's hesitant attempts to make the maintenance of the existing system of economic treaties an official election issue had found little echo with the electorate, and a handsome success in foreign policy would have been highly welcome. The modest results of Kiderlen-Wächter's diplomacy, however, fell far short of popular expectations, deliberately inflamed as these had been by the government's manipulation of the press. The domestic political situation ran completely out of control, and the government found itself being vehemently attacked from almost all political quarters for what was seen as its feebleness. In particular, the Conservatives and National Liberals now swung into line behind an openly imperialist policy, while at the height of the crisis heavy industry also called loudly for a forward strategy. Military leaders, too, were plainly dissatisfied with the turn that events had taken, Moltke letting it be known that he would have preferred a war to what he saw as a shameful betrayal of German interests,[37] and Tirpitz seizing the moment to request a new navy bill.

The Chancellor was deeply disturbed by the thirst for war that was evident among wide sections of German society. He spoke out firmly against it, but to little avail.[38] Although there was no obvious consensus about what the specific aims of German foreign policy should be, conservatives and the middle classes were united in the view that in future the German Empire should act more vigorously whenever the opportunity to acquire overseas possessions arose – if necessary, at the risk of a major conflict. As a result, by 1912 the political situation had come to foreshadow the internal divisions that were to characterize the first years of the war. On the one side was the government, which, while not hostile to an expansionist policy, was trying to keep to an essentially moderate approach; on the other side were significant sections of the upper middle class, enjoying considerable support from the political parties, who were calling for an energetic foreign policy and were quite prepared to accept war as the *ultima ratio*. Not only was the 'civilian' government unable to make its views prevail, but it was forced to give ground, step by painful step.

To understand the logic of this situation we need to look more closely at the distinctive features of the German political system on the eve of the First World War. Far-reaching structural shifts had taken place in Wilhelmine society since the turn of the century, and the system of government had become less appropriate than ever to the new social structures that were being created by accelerating industrialization. The social base of traditional conservatism was being steadily eroded. The shift from a social order based primarily on agriculture to an urban industrial society was increasingly driving conservatives on to the defensive, and the rising level of social mobility, in combination with the widening of differences of income, was affecting sections of the population that hitherto had been loyal to broadly traditional values. In social and economic terms, the upper middle class was now becoming the dominant group in Germany, and it was only because of the rapid rise of the labour movement that the conservatives were able to hold their own in the struggle for political leadership. At the same time, however, we should not exaggerate the pace of social change. The advance of industrialization certainly alarmed the traditional sections of German society, but the pace of change was not headlong enough actually to destroy their inherited social position or assets. Germany in 1910 was, to use W.W. Rostow's term, a 'mature industrial economy',[39] but that does not mean that it was a fully developed industrial society. In statistical terms, the agricultural and lower-middle-class strata of society were in the majority: this is clearly indicated by the figures for average sizes of business enterprises before 1914, which were astonishingly low. These social groups could be counted on to support conservative policies and were the constituency to which the pseudo-constitutional governments headed by Bülow and Bethmann Hollweg appealed.

Traditionalist forces within German society, then, remained extremely powerful, but were no longer powerful enough to sustain full-fledged conservative policies. On the other hand, a move in the opposite direction was not possible either. The Social Democrats, the Progressives, a section of the National Liberal party and – to an extent – the left wing of the Centre party together represented a rising political force, but they did not yet command a majority. In the medium term the fortunes of this potential coalition seemed likely to prosper, but even as late as 1912 parties could not afford to be too progressive in outlook. Despite making impressive gains in the 1912 elections, the Social Democrats were still far from able to exert any real role in shaping legislation. Indeed, if anything their political influence was inversely proportional to their numerical strength, since the government took pains to avoid introducing bills that could not be passed without Social Democratic support. Moreover, whenever the bourgeois parties contemplated collaborating with the Social Democrats on a specific question, the government consistently succeeded in bringing them to heel by invoking the national interest. The National Liberals could not, in any case, ignore the fact that most of the people who voted for them were fairly traditionalist in their attitudes, and any alliance with the left would have created the risk of a split in the party. The Social Democrats, however, would also have been wary about a coalition 'from Bassermann to Bebel' had such an alliance actually been within their grasp. Both parties, in other words, were committed to values and atitudes that made political compromise virtually impossible to achieve.

The impasse was worsened, in turn, by the economic situation, which had been causing considerably sharper social polarization since 1909. Employers tried to halt the rise of the trade unions by forming powerful organizations of their own and doing all they could to mobilize public opinion against any extensions in social policy. Real wages, after a period of almost uninterrupted increase, had begun to stagnate, primarily because of a rise in food prices. Campaigners for social reform such as Lujo Brentano and Max Weber began to voice concern that the unions had lost any realistic hope of prevailing against the employers. In 1912 Weber complained that social policy had gone out of fashion, and he tried in vain to make it popular again by setting up a pressure group to publicize the cause.[40]

The state of near-deadlock in parliamentary politics was in no small part the result of hostility between the Social Democrats and the liberal parties, but was ultimately a reflection of the deep-seated social antagonisms in German society that had been magnified by the dramatic surge in economic growth. None of the main political groupings – neither the Conservatives, nor the bourgeois parties, nor the Social Democrats – had the capacity to end the paralysis. The Conservatives, backed by the right wing of the

Prussian National Liberals, were able to sustain a strong rearguard action, thanks to the overwhelming majority they enjoyed in both houses of the Prussian Landtag. The Centre and the National Liberals were increasingly dubious about collaborating with the Conservatives, but did not have the numbers to mount a programme of moderate reform while simultaneously keeping the Social Democrats at bay. The Social Democrats, in turn, were almost totally excluded from any real role in political decision-making, and their leaders were also rightly alarmed by signs that the number of potential Social Democrat voters had reached its peak.

It was only because of this situation of political stalemate that the semi-authoritarian government of Bethmannn Hollweg was able to remain in power, despite the manifest hostility it aroused in all political quarters. Or to put it more positively, the paralysis of the party system was the main source of Bethmann Hollweg's relative strength. In addition, the Chancellor was able to count on the loyalty of those middle-class groups that continued to regard party politics as a 'dirty business'. Sometimes he specifically sought the support of these sections of society by appealing to them to distance themselves from the 'futile wrangling of the parties'.[41] From the same motives, he kept himself as aloof from the parties and their leaders as he could and tried to minimize their influence on political decision-making. The only result, however, of his attempt to maintain a stance of politics 'above party' was an exacerbation of the inevitable side-effects of authoritarian rule. Official government policy-making and party politics proceeded along separate, parallel tracks, and the breakdown in communication had fateful consequences, notably in foreign policy. By tradition the Reichstag had had no say on matters of foreign policy, and the Chancellor accordingly saw no reason for keeping the party leaders properly informed about the real difficulties that Germany faced; superficial consultations, together with appeals for national solidarity, were still thought to be enough. This gave the party leaders the opportunity to indulge in highly irresponsible nationalist agitation, a temptation that was all the stronger because they were finding themselves having to compete with extra-parliamentary organizations like the Pan-German League and the Army League (Wehrverein). The lack of any regular flow of information between the government and the country's other political institutions inevitably created a growing gulf between short-sighted fashionable ideology and political realities.

Political stalemate not only fostered sterile propagandist agitation but also made any significant constitutional change impossible. This, however, did nothing to strengthen the position of the government. On the contrary, since the government had to function without firm support from even one of the parties in the Reichstag, it became increasingly dependent on the bureaucracy, the officer corps and the aristocratic Prusso-German ruling elite in general. Without them it would have had no hope of surviving the Reichstag's repeated onslaughts, nor could it have held out against the militancy of the Pan-German League and similar extra-parliamentary bodies or against the less direct pressure that came from the CVdI.

The higher bureaucracy and the officer corps, however, were becoming increasingly worried by the spread of democratic ideas within German society. The military was highly sensitive on this score and reacted very vehemently to any interference in its traditional domain by the Reichstag or by public opinion. Bethmann Hollweg had his work cut out, for example, defending himself against charges emanating from the army and court circles that he had been half-hearted in his defence of the army's rights during the debates on the military budget in the Budget Committee of the Reichstag in 1913.[42] Since Wilhelm II regarded the 'Kommandogewalt', or 'royal power of command', as the central surviving core of the royal prerogative, Bethmann Hollweg found it impossible to prevent the scope of this prerogative from being interpreted ever more widely, in practice if not in constitutional law, despite the Reichstag's strong objections.[43]

In the eyes of the Emperor and the military establishment, the supreme task of any Imperial Chancellor was to keep the Reichstag in check. Even under the comparatively favourable conditions of the Wilhelmine system, however, this task was becoming increasingly hard to carry out. The long-term trend towards more popular-based, if not necessarily more democratic, forms of government was as evident in German society as it was elsewhere, and one of its main symptoms was the mounting self-confidence of the Reichstag, the demands of which could no longer simply be rejected *in toto.* This in turn made conservatives and their supporters increasingly anxious, many of them now concluding that they had their backs to the wall and were going to have to fight. The room for compromise on social and political questions was thus very limited. The Imperial government's response to this dilemma was to opt for what it believed was a neutral course. Bethmann Hollweg did not dare look for political support from the left, and even if he had seriously considered the possibility – though we can safely conclude that he did not – the continuing intransigence of the Social Democrats would have made it highly unlikely that any such overtures would have succeeded. On the other hand, he also had no desire to ally himself with the right and institute a policy of all-out repression against the labour movement and the forces of democracy, even though significant sections of the bureaucracy expected him to do so and the Conservative party and influential interest groups such as the CVdI wanted to push the government in this direction. Bethmann Hollweg did yield to this latter pressure on some points, but he remained basically opposed to such a course, and it is not hard to see why, since it would have made the divisions between the political parties even deeper and the chances of achieving a realignment among the Conservative and bourgeois parties – which he believed was the only way out of the impasse – even slimmer. In this sense, Bethmann Hollweg's 'diagonal' policy, which pleased no one, can be termed a genuinely conservative strategy.

Hostility to this approach within the ruling elite was bound to have its effect on foreign policy. In certain respects Bethmann Hollweg was very mistrustful of the role of public opinion in foreign-policy matters. His attitude, however, would have paid dividends only if all branches of the government had preserved a united public front, at least on controversial questions. This, though, the Chancellor became increasingly unable to achieve.

Bethmann Hollweg believed that foreign policy ought to be conducted by means of secret diplomacy, and that the general public and even party leaders should be provided only with very rudimentary information on the subject. He was well aware that this way of proceeding was sure to bring down fierce condemnation on his head from both conservatives and extreme nationalists, since on the surface his policy would inevitably look irresolute and inconsistent. Nevertheless, he refused to spell out a programme and give the country a general idea of the goals of his foreign policy, as Rathenau[44] had urged him. In the Chancellor's view, any publicity would have jeopardized the success of his efforts. Riezler similarly noted at the time, with a touch of complacency, that the only way to achieve lasting results in foreign policy was to shun public applause and instant, superficial triumphs.[45] The reverse, however, was actually the case. It was because Bethmann Hollweg never made a serious attempt to fight for his policy at the bar of public opinion that he placed himself at the mercy of the various factions within the ruling elites.

In the short run Bethmann Hollweg's ideas had the backing of the Emperor and were accepted, though with considerable misgivings, by the military establishment and the conservative bureaucracy – particularly since he gave in, reluctantly, to the pressure from the navy and the General Staff for increases in armaments in 1912 and obtained parliamentary approval for a further substantial expansion of the army in 1913. A strong army was compatible, up to a point, with his own overall political strategy, since he regarded it as vital that Germany's position on the European continent should be unassailable if she were to be able to pursue an expansionist policy overseas.[46] On the other hand, as we have said earlier, the Chancellor also believed that a lessening of tensions between Germany and Great Britain was the key to an improvement in Germany's tangled international relations, on two counts. First, the risk of a European war would be reduced, which would enable the German Empire – partnered by an ally, in Austria, who was shaken by crises and confronted by a possible enemy, in Russia, who was rapidly arming – to follow a more steady and consistent foreign policy. Secondly, there was reason to think that with British support, Germany might be able to attain at least some of her colonial goals – particularly in central Africa, though also in the Near East and perhaps even in China.[47]

Bethmann Hollweg could count on a certain measure of support for these plans from the National Liberals and the Centre, although the anglophobia that was prevalent in both parties was not easy to overcome. He was also able to establish close contacts with some of the major banks and induce them, up to a point, to invest in spheres of interest on the African continent and elsewhere which the government was trying to stake out in the course of intricate diplomatic negotiations – this even though there was a general scarcity of capital in the German economy and the prospective returns on this sort of investment were very poor.[48] The Chancellor's relations with heavy industry, on the other hand, were far from satisfactory, and for many industrialists the idea of a German Central Africa held no appeal whatsoever; if any region did arouse their interest, it was the Near East.[49] A number, including Walther Rathenau, believed that it was preferable for Germany to concentrate her economic activities on the European continent rather than strike out overseas.[50] Bethmann Hollweg did everything he could to foster the political conditions that would allow Germany's economic penetration of the Ottoman Empire to continue, although he was careful to leave British interests ample room for manoeuvre. It was only under the pressure of war that he joined the ranks of those who were calling for a European economic association dominated by Germany on the grounds that territorial imperialism was now obsolete.[51]

It is quite clear that until May or June 1914 the Bethmann Hollweg government did not seriously contemplate achieving these objectives by means of war, with one exception: it would not have stood idly by if the Ottoman Empire had broken up without appropriate account being taken of Germany's interests.[52] Bethmann Hollweg was confident that war could be avoided, though from the end of 1913 onwards he was increasingly anxious about the deterioration of Germany's position within the system of European powers. One of the main reasons why he wanted to adhere to a policy of peace was that he was convinced that the existing political order would not survive if war broke out.[53] Fritz Fischer has steadfastly held to the view that Bethmann Hollweg's repeated attempts to reach a neutrality agreement with Great Britain were part and parcel of a strategy of military expansion. On Fischer's argument, Britain had to be manoeuvred into a position of neutrality so that the way would be clear for Germany to crush France and Russia: this aim, he maintains, lay at the core of German calculations.[54] The sources do not, however, bear out such a thesis.[55] What is true is that hopes for a neutrality agreement, or something akin to one, played a symbolic role, as it were, in the internal struggle between Tirpitz and Wilhelm II on the one hand and Bethmann Hollweg and the German Foreign Office on the other. This dispute was at work behind the scenes during and after the Haldane mission of February 1912. The committed proponents of a hard line were not prepared to make substantial concessions on naval construction unless Britain were to reciprocate by radically amending what was alleged to be her hostile attitude towards Germany. The key to the ambivalence in the German Foreign Office's stance during February and March 1912 on the question of the extent of the concessions that should be demanded from Britain in exchange for a naval agreement is the power struggle that was going on in Berlin.

In 1912 Bethmann Hollweg was unable to get what he wanted, but the collapse of the Anglo-German negotiations did not make him lose heart. He still believed that it was possible to achieve an improvement in relations with Great Britain, together with colonial concessions. Not surprisingly, therefore, the Chancellor came to be considered within the ruling elites as essentially a pro-British statesman, and from now onwards his political fortunes were indissolubly linked to the vicissitudes of Anglo-German relations. Thus when Sir Edward Grey gave the German government an unequivocal warning in December 1912 that Britain would side with France and Russia in the event of a European war ignited by the Balkan crisis, Wilhelm II's circle immediately took this as conclusive proof that Bethmann Hollweg's hopes for a gradual improvement in relations with Britain were unfounded – an inference that was, in fact, quite invalid. As has been described earlier, the Emperor went behind the backs of the 'civilians' and consulted Tirpitz and the General Staff on the best way of preparing the nation for the war that he believed was now imminent.[56] The Chancellor's prestige had taken some damaging blows. Although he was soon able to regain his footing, he could no longer ignore how weak his position had become.

It is clear, in fact, that after 1912 Bethmann Hollweg's moderate line met with mounting resistance from the ruling elites, particularly the General Staff, whose political influence, as we have said, had grown considerably. The leaders of the military had become very disturbed by the re-emergence of Russia as a top-rank military power and (as has been established beyond doubt) were harbouring thoughts of a preventive war against Russia and France, especially since the Schlieffen Plan seemed likely to become inapplicable in the not too distant future. As far as we can ascertain from the scattered sources, Moltke became increasingly irritated with the diplomats, who kept insisting that the current period of danger could be weathered in view of the improvement in Germany's relations with Great Britain.[57] It is not impossible that an article by an Oberleutnant Ulrich which appeared in the *Kölnische Zeitung* in March 1914, and which set off a feud between German and Russian newpapers, was instigated by individuals close to the General Staff. There is no conclusive proof of this supposition, but the fact that the article closely reflects the fears and anxieties that were prevalent in German military circles certainly provides circumstantial evidence.[58]

We should not, of course, neglect the role that public opinion played at this time. Relations among the military establishment, the court and the Conservatives were undoubtedly very close, and there was a widespread belief among Conservatives, as well as in the Pan-German League, that a war would clear the air and have a healthy effect on the German national character; war was also seen as a sure way of resolving domestic tensions. But the belief that the diplomatic situation had deteriorated alarmingly in the previous few years, and that a European war was therefore likely, had spread to a considerable proportion of the middle classes too. Friedrich Bernhardi's *Deutschland und der nächste Krieg* (Germany and the Next War), written in a style drawing equally on bourgeois cultural tradition and the newer militant nationalism, made a particularly strong impact on the German intelligentsia. On the other hand, the pressures that were bearing down on the government from wide sections of society in favour of the adoption of a tough line in foreign policy were not sufficient in themselves to give rise to the sequence of events that finally caused war to break out. The popularity of imperialist policies helps significantly to explain what happened, but there are no compelling grounds for concluding that such factors played a specific, or ultimately decisive, role in the government's deliberations on the eve of war. Rather, it was the structural weakness of the system of government as such that led those in positions of power to resort to a strategy of aggression.

We have pointed out already that the Bethmann Hollweg government did not enjoy the support of a majority in the country or of a majority grouping in the Reichstag. This meant that the Chancellor was more dependent than any of his predecessors since Bismarck had been on the goodwill of the conservative establishment, and particularly on those surrounding the Emperor, who were closely interlocked with the establishment through a multiplicity of social connections. From 1913 onwards the conservatives launched a whole series of fierce onslaughts on the Chancellor and sought to convince the Emperor that Bethmann Hollweg was weak in his dealings with the Social Democrats and the Reichstag. The Pan-German League also hoped to exploit the situation to its own advantage, and in October 1913 Class set about trying to oust the Chancellor from office: with conservative help, a detailed memorandum by General von Gebsattel was brought to the Emperor's notice, in which Bethmann Hollweg was ferociously attacked for the feebleness of his foreign policy.[59] Although Wilhelm II could not bring himself to dismiss his Chancellor, Bethmann Hollweg's position was now gravely at risk and the charge that he was pliant and ineffectual in his conduct of foreign policy was henceforth to be a constant danger to him.

The threat that came to Bethmann Hollweg's policy from the General Staff, however, was the most serious. The leaders of the military were becoming alarmed by the likelihood that the main assumption underlying the Schlieffen Plan – namely, that Russia would be slow to mobilize, so that the German army would have time to crush France before Russia could pose a serious threat – was going to prove false as the Russian Empire built up its armaments and extended its western railway network. These fears were strongly reinforced by the decidedly ambiguous official Russian response to allegations in the press that the Tsarist Empire was preparing to go to war with Germany. Accordingly, in May or June 1914 Moltke proposed that since war was bound to break out, the government should ensure that it took place while there was still a realistic chance that

Germany would win.[60] The idea of a preventive war was plainly becoming more and more attractive in military circles. Even the Emperor – who, for all his show of pompous militarism, was genuinely in favour of peace – was wondering whether Germany should not resort to arms before Russia's armament programme was completed, as he confided in a conversation with Warburg in July 1914.[61]

Beyond the inner circle of government, other considerations also came into play. Heydebrand, for example, believed that a war would provide the perfect opportunity for destroying the Social Democrats.[62] Bethmann Hollweg was greatly angered by such 'nonsense',[63] probably because he could see the likely consequences for his own position if the Emperor were to adopt a similar point of view. The Chancellor argued strongly that it was an illusion to believe that a European war would lead to a strengthening of 'patriarchal order and mentality': on the contrary, Social Democracy would be likely to be the beneficiary, and it was by no means impossible that some monarchs would even lose their thrones.[64] Although the sources are rather sparse on the matter, it is apparent that Bethmann Hollweg and Jagow had their hands full trying to counteract this sort of thinking. They were anxious to make it clear that they were not opposed under all circumstances to the idea of a preventive war – if they had failed to do so, they would have been exposed to the charge of weakness – but, equally, they took exception to the notion that a preventive war offered a way out of Germany's diplomatic difficulties. Their prime concern was to show that an improvement in relations with Great Britain would make such a strategy quite inappropriate.[65]

The power that the Chancellor wielded within the complex German system of government was contingent to a high degree on his position as the chief architect of foreign policy. Wilhelm II was averse to the notion of changing chancellors because of the possible consequences for Germany's diplomatic relations, and one of the main factors that weighed with him was the very favourable image that Bethmann Hollweg enjoyed in Britain. Inevitably, therefore, it was a disastrous blow to the Chancellor's domestic position when news of Anglo-Russian naval conversations reached Berlin in May 1914 through a spy in the British embassy in St Petersburg. Bethmann Hollweg's chief argument against a preventive war (the hope that Britain would help restrain Russia) had now collapsed overnight. Worse, Britain seemed prepared at last to accede to an alliance with Russia and France. This played right into the hands of those who argued that the worsening of the German military position made it unquestionably better for Germany to trigger the 'inevitable' war as soon as possible. Bethmann Hollweg's note to Lichnowsky in London, incidentally, sent on 16 June 1914, spells out the position clearly enough.[66]

Bethmann Hollweg's essentially pro-British stance was well known, and the failure of his hopes for an Anglo-German rapprochement was a gift to his domestic political opponents. For this reason, in particular, the

Chancellor did not openly set forth his own assessment of Britain's likely response in the event of a European war. It must be emphasized, however, that Bethmann Hollweg was not counting on British neutrality in the case of a major European conflict (even though several of his contemporaries believed that he was, and many historians have argued as much since). He believed that closer relations between the German Empire and Great Britain would help stabilize Germany's position on the continent and reduce the risk that a full-scale European war would flow from a new Balkan crisis. A rapprochement would also make it significantly easier for Germany to undertake economic and political expansion overseas. But Bethmann Hollweg was very well aware in 1914 that Britain would never stand aside and allow Germany to crush the French. At most, he thought, Britain might remain neutral in the initial phase of a European war and try to bring about a diplomatic solution. He hoped that the British would back the attempt to prevent a war, but he did not bank on long-term British neutrality in the event of a major conflict – indeed, all the available information indicated the contrary.[67] Altogether, the assumption that Britain would stay neutral did not play a key role in German calculations on the eve of the First World War, although hopes to this effect were – rightly, in fact – not entirely abandoned. Indeed, if anything it was the dismaying news that Britain was apparently about to commit herself to the enemy camp that finally, in Bethmann Hollweg's phrase, 'set the ball rolling'. This move reinforced the conviction of the Chancellor's domestic opponents that a preventive war should be launched at the next available opportunity, to head off the formation of a more definite Entente and the adoption of warlike measures by Russia that that would encourage.[68]

We can see this from the events that followed, culminating in Germany's decision to let the Danube monarchy have its punitive war against Serbia whatever the outcome, even though the German government was well aware that an Austro-Serbian war was very likely to escalate into a general European conflict. Until this stage German diplomacy had if anything leaned towards the Serbs, more than once restraining Vienna from intervening in the Balkans with force. To the Austrians' intense annoyance, Berchtold had had to listen to a series of German warnings that it would be much better if a peaceful settlement with the Serbs were reached. In the days immediately following the assassination of the Austrian heir to the throne, the Wilhelmstraße seems to have continued to take this line, as Tschirschky's counselling of caution implies (though the Emperor quickly took vehement exception to it). The decision to give the Danube monarchy a blank cheque over Serbia was a crucial shift in German foreign policy. Bethmann Hollweg acted 'only after initial hesitation',[69] though the decision had already been taken, essentially, before the arrival in Berlin of the Austrian special envoy Count Hoyos on 5 July (probably on 2 or 3 July).[70] It was in effect a compromise between the policy that the Chancellor and the Foreign Office had hitherto pursued and the aims of the General Staff, who had argued that the German Empire should not strive to maintain the peace if there was a prospect of the main trial of strength with Russia and France. As he later admitted,[71] Bethmann Hollweg conceded that it would be better (provided that the General Staff were correct in their assessment of the position of the Central Powers and of Russia's hostile intentions) to have the war 'now rather than later'. The Chancellor, in other words, now adopted a 'diagonal' course on the foreign-policy front too: the Habsburg monarchy would play the role of *agent provocateur*, turning the Serbian conflict into a test to establish whether Russia were bent on a European war or not.[72] In this way Bethmann Hollweg could satisfy the military's demand that Germany should do nothing to avoid a possible war, while not actually endorsing the strategy of preventive war himself. For his part, he still assumed that Russia was not ready for war and that there was therefore a realistic chance that Germany could break up the encirclement imposed by the Entente without sparking off a European conflict. Although everyone involved in the decision-making process was aware that Austrian action against Serbia might lead to a European war – if that were to happen, the Chancellor expected that Russia's declaration would follow within days[73] – Bethmann Hollweg and the Foreign Office, at least, believed that Russia would ultimately hold back, particularly since France and Britain had obvious reservations about going to war over Serbia.[74] Incidentally, an unambiguous declaration by the British government that it would not remain neutral in the event of war would not have altered the outcome in the slightest. On the contrary, such a statement would merely have given extra ammunition to Moltke, reinforcing his belief that in view of the deterioration in Germany's military position it would be better to wage war now, when victory was still attainable within months, than to wait till some later date.

The policy decision taken by the German government, then, was a very risky gamble played for extremely high stakes. Bethmann Hollweg described it as a 'leap in the dark', and yet also as the 'most onerous duty'.[75] The Chancellor's position, however, was no longer strong enough for him to be able to persuade the ruling elite to accept an alternative course of action. His policy was the resultant of the conflicting pressures that existed within the government. It was a compromise between two rival strategies: it remained an attempt to resolve the crisis by diplomatic means rather than directly by war, but it also went some way towards meeting the wishes of the military, inasmuch as it proposed no way of actually averting the outbreak of war once Russia had come out firmly on Serbia's side. The attempt to manoeuvre Russia into a position where she would effectively have to make the final decision for war or for peace was dictated partly by the belief that this was the only way of persuading the Social Democrats to rally behind the government; it was partly the result of a calculation that this was the only way of exploiting the crisis in diplomatic terms; and it sprang, in addition, from an ulterior motive that this would be a means of rebutting the fears of the General Staff – always provided, of course, that the Russians actually shrank from taking the final step.

Bethmann Hollweg, in other words, determined on this policy, not from a desire to dominate the world stage, but from weakness and confusion. The contradictions in the German government's thinking during the July crisis were a faithful reflection of the fierce antagonisms that prevailed at the highest levels of power. It should be emphasized again, however, that this situation had come about only because the social groups that made up the ruling elites – notably the leading ranks of the bureaucracy, the General Staff (backed by the officer corps) and the arch-conservative Imperial court – enjoyed a degree of influence over political decision-making that was grossly out of proportion to their actual significance within German society as a whole. This was due in no small part to the fact that stalemate in Parliament had enabled the government to pursue its tactic of politics 'above party' as though nothing within the domestic political situation had changed. It is worth noting that during the July crisis the Imperial government contrived to ignore the views of the party leaders completely.[76] There is absolutely no evidence that any of the party leaders was given a chance to help influence the government's decisions. The Chancellor, admittedly, seems to have been confident that the bourgeois parties at least, with the possible exception of the Progressives, would support the government's gamble and would be reluctant to let the opportunity of Sarajevo pass without coming to the aid of Austria-Hungary and turning the crisis to the Central Powers' advantage.[77] It is doubtful whether Bethmann Hollweg, even if he had consulted the party leaders, would have obtained whole-hearted support from the bourgeois parties against the advocates of a preventive war. The party leaders, however, would surely have rejected a strategy that was designed to satisfy militants and moderates alike and that was therefore bound to fail. These are, of course, very much matters of speculation. What is certain is that it was the desperate attempt by the Bethmann Hollweg government, faced with a more or less hostile majority in Parliament, to shy away from any serious moves towards constitutional reform that left it critically dependent on the goodwill of those groups within the ruling elites that held unswervingly to a policy of intransigence, both at home and abroad.

The causes of the First World War, then, lay not only in the failures and miscalculations of the governments concerned but in the fact that the very system of government in the German Empire, as in Austria-Hungary and in Russia, had ceased to be appropriate to an age of rapid social change and to the new conditions that had been created by a modern mass society.

10

Public opinion and foreign policy in Wilhelmine Germany, 1897-1914

Mass-market journalism was a product of the heyday of imperialism. The emergence of the popular press was a symptom of the expansion of what may be called the 'political nation' – that is, of those groups within society that were actively interested in politics, as against the great and still largely unpoliticized majority of the population. Until the 1890s politics had been conducted mainly by *Honoratioren*, to use the term employed by Max Weber: people who were prominent in the local or regional community. By the turn of the century, however, this older form of politics was being supplanted in most western societies, and, in parallel, the terms 'public' and 'public opinion' were gradually ceasing to denote the educated or governing sections of society and their views.

The case of Wilhelmine Germany, however, was somewhat distinctive. There, progress towards constitutional democracy was kept in check and mass politics still lay in the distant future, despite the fact that the gradual strengthening of the political role of the electorate – in practice if not in constitutional principle – had begun to pose new problems for the ruling elites. Likewise, there was not yet a popular press of the sort that had begun to take shape in Great Britain. 'Public opinion', in its published manifestations, was still directed towards a fairly restricted audience, made up of the middle and upper-middle echelons of society as well as the traditional governing class. Governments had enormous scope for moulding public political attitudes, although direct manipulation by a handful of hireling journalists was becoming increasingly difficult, if not impossible.

A Social Democratic press had sprung up in Germany, and with it something that can be seen as a distinctive working-class body of opinion. This latter differed somewhat from middle-class 'public opinion' (indeed defined itself through its opposition to bourgeois attitudes) while in a curious sense also imitating it: its political rhetoric was heavily influenced by orthodox Marxism, and yet it shared the middle class's faith in science and progress and in law and order. In the present context, however, we can largely ignore working-class opinion, since it had little bearing on foreign policy during

the Wilhelmine era, at any rate before 1914. Indeed, if anything the powerful streak of pacificism and anti-imperialism that ran through the Social
Democratic press (though there was a nationalist streak too) indirectly
helped to reinforce the nationalist and imperialist tendencies that were present in 'public opinion', particularly among the ruling groups within
Wilhelmine society. On the whole, however, the Social Democratic press
played very little immediate part in the interaction between government
press policy and 'public opinion' that so strongly influenced the formation
of German foreign policy.

The subject of this study is a government's handling of its public relations under conditions of semi-constitutional rule. For all its authoritarian
features, the Wilhelmine system of government never really found a satisfactory way of coping with the problem of public opinion. During the earlier years of the Empire the government had been very successful in
influencing, and even directly manipulating, public opinion through the
skilful use of the press. During the 1860s and 1870s Bismarck and others
had wielded this weapon as one means of getting their own way, notably
though not only in the matter of German unification.[1] When Bülow became
Imperial Chancellor, however, and the government began systematically to
employ a press policy for the purpose of building support for its foreign
policy at home and abroad, its efforts eventually ended in disaster. On frequent occasions, especially on questions of foreign policy, the government
firmly convinced itself that it could influence the 'respectable' press to take
its side, only to find that public opinion had asserted its independence and
that the state was being assailed with new and highly radical demands. This
was the case, in particular, with the ambitious 'Weltpolitik', or 'world policy', that Bülow proclaimed as the centrepiece of his new programme in
1897, after a decade of wrangling at home and failure abroad.

A study of the sort we are conducting here faces serious methodological
problems. It is very difficult, if not impossible, to establish precisely what
the dominant currents within public opinion were, and it is an equally
daunting task, even if we confine ourselves to foreign policy, to assess how
successful the government was in its attempts to influence or manipulate
public opinion.[2] On the other hand, we can certainly document with some
accuracy the relevant measures that the government actually undertook,
and in a few cases – when matters reached crisis point – we can trace
clearly, if not beyond all doubt, the effect that state propaganda had on
contemporary attitudes. Our task is made somewhat easier, moreover, by
the fact that public opinion, to the extent that policy-makers did actually
pay attention to it, on the whole found expression in publications that
would nowadays be called 'national' newspapers, for example, the *Berliner
Tageblatt*, the *Vossische Zeitung*, the *Kölnische Zeitung*, the *Tägliche
Rundschau*, the *Post*, the 'Kreuzzeitung' (i.e. the *Neue Preußische Zeitung*)
and *Germania*, as well as, perhaps, the *National-Zeitung* and the
Münchner Neueste Nachrichten.

Particular attention needs to be paid to the nationalist propaganda organizations that sprang up during this period. These bodies, notably the Pan-German League (Alldeutscher Verband), the Navy League (Flottenverein) and later the Army League (Wehrverein), developed new forms of propagandist agitation and sought mainly to enrol support from sections of the population that had previously been on the margins of politics. Their ideas were slow to percolate into the serious daily press, but their influence over public opinion steadily increased. They mounted quasi-democratic campaigns, employing deliberately populist techniques and posing a vigorous challenge to the existing political system.[3] This forced the parties of the right to follow suit and to take up some, at any rate, of their demands, even though they abhorred the political style of these upstart extra-parliamentary rivals.

From the early 1890s there was growing popular enthusiasm for a policy of imperialist expansion overseas, after the lull in the late 1880s that had followed the collapse of Bismarck's colonial policy based on indirect control. By and large, however, the politicians and diplomats who were responsible for German foreign policy during the 1890s assumed that they would be able either to keep these imperialist ambitions in check or, if need be, turn them to their advantage. In the early 1890s there were very few convinced imperialists at senior – or, indeed, lower – levels of government. As in other countries, the 'official mind' was fairly wary on the subject of overseas colonial acquisitions; diplomats thought primarily in terms of the European continent. There was an awareness in Germany, however, that the new imperialist mood could, and perhaps should, be exploited as a way of restoring faith in the country's system of government, seeing that there had been a serious erosion of confidence in the system since the fall of Bismarck and, more especially, since the resignation of Caprivi in 1894, both events the result of ill-advised policies arising from Wilhelm II's 'personal rule'.

In 1895 Count Monts claimed that the only way in which particularism and local prejudice could be slowly uprooted was through the idea of Emperorship, successes in foreign policy and stability at home.[4] Holstein was more explicit. Similarly maintaining that the Emperor's government needed a significant success abroad, which would then have a beneficial effect at home, he reasoned that the success in question might come either as the result of a European war – a risky policy, with world-wide repercussions – or by means of territorial acquisitions outside Europe;[5] a policy of colonial expansion was therefore preferable, although possessing colonies was not of genuine value in itself.

Admiral Caprivi steadfastly refused to pursue a colonial policy on any substantial scale. His aim was to consolidate Germany's position on the European continent and to disentangle Bismarck's over-complicated system of alliances. Rather than stage an aggressive drive for colonies, he reached an agreement with Great Britain whereby Heligoland would be returned to the Reich in exchange for the dropping of a contentious claim to Zanzibar. Likewise, he was reluctant to press German claims to Samoa and thereby run the risk of a serious conflict with the other powers involved. This provoked a dispute with Wilhelm II, who was one of the first to see that an imperialist policy would have popular appeal.

The Pan-German League had come out vociferously for a vigorous imperialist policy from the start, and had evoked a positive response from the German public. For the time being, however, the Reichstag parties were loth to support any new colonial ventures, particularly since they did not trust the intentions of the Imperial government under the new Chancellor, Prince Hohenlohe. Nevertheless, imperialism gradually became fashionable, especially among the upper middle class and the intelligentsia. Max Weber gave perhaps the most striking expression of this new trend, in his inaugural lecture of 1895: 'We must appreciate that the unification of Germany was a youthful prank which the nation perpetrated in its old age – an extravagant gesture which would have been better left undone if it was to be the conclusion, rather than the beginning, of a German policy of world power.'[6]

The Emperor Wilhelm II himself was always highly susceptible to new fashions in public opinion, in particular among the upper middle class and the academic world. He was fascinated by the new doctrine of expansionism, even though it clearly ran counter to traditional conservative values, since imperialist expansion was commonly invoked in the same breath as modernization and industrial development. With the appointment of Bülow and Tirpitz to key positions in the Imperial government in 1897, the Emperor found two 'political lieutenants' who were ready to comply with his wishes and adopt an ambitious imperialist policy. The principal objective of the policy was to build a powerful battle fleet, although the government could be sure that if it tried to do this it would meet with a hostile response from a majority of the parties in the Reichstag, principally in view of the considerable costs involved.

Bülow had let it be known among the members of Wilhelm's entourage that he was ready to act as what he called the Emperor's 'political chief of staff' in order to implement the monarch's 'personal rule'.[7] But Bülow was far from being a docile instrument of the Emperor's. From the start he skilfully exploited Wilhelm's prestige to enhance the government's standing with public opinion and thus win himself room for political manoeuvre *vis-à-vis* a largely hostile Reichstag. His 'new imperialism' was in a sense a copy of the Tory Imperialism that Disraeli had pursued a generation earlier: Bülow hoped to win over the Reichstag parties by systematically building up the Emperor as the figurehead of a grandiose 'Weltpolitik', while simultaneously keeping Wilhelm happy through flattery.[8]

The government made great efforts to mobilize public opinion behind its new policy; in this respect the Bülow era marked a break with what had gone before. The government's aim was to create a populist base of support right across the traditional party spectrum (though not, of course, including the Social Democrats); the technique was to arouse a new, emotional form of nationalism among the German people. Bülow even saw this as his *arcanum imperii*. Representatives of the government, as well as the Emperor himself – relishing his role as the mouthpiece of the 'new German' imperialism – made public speeches extolling the notions of national pride and national greatness. Bülow not only regarded it as the government's task to try to turn these newly awakened feelings to account but was convinced that the population could be persuaded to rally behind the 'national idea'. He was sure, indeed, that public attitudes would be fairly easy to manipulate. He wrote in his notebook: 'What is "the people"? What is public opinion? It is a point of view which has been reached by 80 or 90 intelligent and influential minds – usually in the face of the ideas of the vast majority – and which they then gradually broadcast until they make it the *communis opinio*.'[9]

Government propaganda, in fact, seems to have played a substantial role in the revival of 'patriotic feelings' among the political parties and the general public that took place in the late 1890s and that Bülow saw it as his task to 'awaken, stimulate and preserve [. . .] spontaneously and without prejudice'.[10] To enlist public support for his and the government's goals, Bülow ordered a thorough overhaul of all official press propaganda machinery. By the time of Bismarck's last years as Chancellor, the government's handling of the press had become largely discredited. Bismarck had increasingly confined himself to relying on personal contacts with individual journalists; a large part of the elaborate apparatus for directly influencing public opinion had been dismantled, in favour of indirect methods that the Chancellor could control himself. Most of the official press organs had been closed down, and even the *Norddeutsche Allgemeine Zeitung* had lost much of its official status as the mouthpiece of government. Bülow's changes were sweeping, although Bismarck's conclusion that it was best to influence public opinion indirectly was still borne in mind. Within the Foreign Office, elaborate institutional mechanisms were set up with a view to giving the public suitable 'guidance' and ensuring that the government's ideas would receive full and sympathetic coverage in the press. Similar press bureaux were created in other ministries. In the Imperial Naval Office a highly successful press department developed a variety of modern techniques for rallying support among all sections of German society for the idea of a German battle fleet: as well as influencing what appeared in the daily press, it distributed leaflets, published relevant books, and collaborated, at least at first, with the newly founded Navy League. On top of all this, relations with the official and semi-official press were put on a new footing, newspapers that were close to the government (notably the *Norddeutsche Allgemeine Zeitung)* being used to transmit the government's point of view.

The government had at its disposal various highly useful outlets for its publicity. First, as well as promoting official views through the *Norddeutsche Allgemeine Zeitung*, it exerted great influence over the international news issued by the Wolff Telegraph Bureau, even though the agency was affiliated to Reuters and Agence Havas. It was also able to make use of a number of regional press agencies, an important consideration, since most national, regional and local newspapers were highly dependent on the information that these agencies provided. Secondly, however, the government was also clear from the outset that the publication of news based on obvious official sources was bound to be fairly ineffective, and it therefore built up a network of informal contacts with a variety of newspapers. Papers that were willing to support the government's line on foreign policy and to publish articles written by government officials (sometimes even by the Foreign Secretary himself) were rewarded by being given inside information. The key figure in this arrangement was Otto Hammann, who soon became a close confidant of the Chancellor on all policy matters.[11] During these years the *Kölnische Zeitung* and the *Berliner Lokal-Anzeiger* were, in effect, officially inspired newspapers. They were not, admittedly, always loyal partners. The *Kölnische Zeitung*, for example, fell foul of the Foreign Office as a result of its reports on Russia, and when the editor was summoned to Berlin in 1913 to be reprimanded for his hostile stance, he flatly said that he would not take any more orders from the government in future. The system was based on informal give-and-take, and none of the newspapers could really be relied on if their editors disagreed with particular government decisions.[12] The third and, in a sense, even more indirect method used by the government was to arrange for independent journalists or public figures to write articles in praise or defence of specific aspects of government policy. Here there was no shortage of writers and academics who were prepared, in a given instance, to be recruited, including people such as Hans Delbrück and Otto Hoetzsch and, occasionally, even Friedrich Meinecke and Karl Lamprecht.

This whole system depended very much on voluntary co-operation: it could not work through compulsion. This, though, had the consequence that the government's ability to exert effective influence over the press became increasingly circumscribed by public opinion itself. In the early phase of Bülow's period of office, Hammann, at the head of the Foreign Office press department, was largely successful in getting the press to report favourably on the government's foreign policy. As time went on, however, this became steadily harder to achieve. The government increasingly had to confine itself to fending off public criticism of particular aspects of its policy by giving appropriate instructions to those newspapers that were 'available': it was able to operate tactically, but no longer strategically. The reason for this retreat was simple enough: official, or government-inspired, statements, if recognizable as such, were liable to be attacked by other publications, both of the left and, increasingly, of the right. During his later years in office, indeed, Bülow ceased to believe that it was possible to 'make' public opinion, and the government's press policy amounted mainly to an attempt to obtain a favourable presentation of official views and measures in the uncommitted press. Imperial governments had never been able, in any event, to get their views accepted without reserve by the big liberal organs such as the *Frankfurter Zeitung*, the *Berliner Tageblatt* and the *Vossische Zeitung*. But now they could not entirely count, either, on the newspapers of the right – such as the 'Kreuzzeitung', the *Post*, the *Tägliche Rundschau* or the *Rheinisch-Westfälische Nachrichten* – to keep strictly to the official line when reporting on important aspects of government policy. On the contrary, in the course of time the right-wing press became ever more vocal in its criticism of the government's foreign policy, despite the fact that this was a field in which the government would normally have expected the backing of national newspapers regardless of their party affiliation.

Co-operation with the nationalist propaganda organizations – bodies which Bülow and Tirpitz at first had effusively welcomed and indirectly supported – was even more problematical. Although campaigning by the Navy League, in particular, played a significant part in helping to win public backing for the fleet-building programme, Bülow and Tirpitz soon realized that these pressure groups were always liable to outbid the government and attack its policies from an ultra-nationalist standpoint. Official relations with the Navy League became very strained almost from the first, as the League's leadership, to Tirpitz's irritation, ignored any advice the government had to offer. Bülow likewise found himself unable to pursue a consistent political line in tandem with the Pan-Germans: he complained in 1901 that these 'armchair politicians' were impossible to work with.[13]

The nationalist sentiments that Bülow had sought to exploit as the basis for his new integrative 'Weltpolitik' soon took on an uncontrollable momentum of their own.[14] During the Boer War, to Bülow's dismay, there was a mass outbreak of anglophobia in many newspapers and among the public at large. The government itself preserved an attitude of benevolent neutrality towards Great Britain, since there was a vague prospect, arising out of the Angolan agreement of 1898, that Germany might be able to acquire a share of the Portuguese colonial empire, which seemed to be on the brink of collapse. The half-hearted attempts by Hammann's press department, however, to induce the press to back the government and counteract the violent anti-British shift in public opinion had little effect.[15] To mounting annoyance in government circles, it became clear that official action was not going to curb the surge of nationalist feeling. This was partly because German foreign policy had got itself into an awkward corner as a result of the secret Anglo-German agreement of 1898 and the German commitment to benevolent neutrality towards Great Britain; partly because German public opinion was overwhelmingly sympathetic towards the Boers. The government tried in vain to persuade the press to tone down its anti-British agitation. Bülow made a personal appeal to Class, the leader of the Pan-German League, but his appeal fell on deaf ears. The nationalistic excesses of this period did much to pave the way for the even greater excesses that were to come a few years later.

In general, it can be said that the wave of imperialist and nationalist sentiment that had begun to sweep through the German middle and upper middle classes tended to leave the government lagging behind on virtually every important question of foreign policy. The government steadily lost the initiative in its attempts to influence public opinion. The result was that the official press became preoccupied with appeasing or cautiously seeking to modify public opinion on individual questions of foreign policy and tried to avoid doing anything that might cause nationalist feelings to run even higher. Increasingly it found itself on the defensive.

An important reason for this was, precisely, that the 'new imperialism' had no tangible successes to show for itself. Almost all of Bülow's imperialist ventures ended in failure. Not only did they weaken Germany's international position: they brought no benefits at home either. It is true that the bourgeois parties were brought back into the government camp in 1897 as a result of Bülow's exploitation of the new upsurge in nationalist sentiment, but by 1906 the pseudo-plebiscitary basis of Bülow's authority had collapsed, and his attempt to shore up his position by means of the so-called 'Bülow Bloc' also eventually came to grief.

Bethmann Hollweg, who succeeded Bülow as Chancellor in June 1909, hoped to repair the fragments of Bülow's semi-authoritarian system of rule by trying to govern 'above party' in the Bismarckian manner. This tactic, however, meant that all controversial questions had to be carefully skirted. In foreign policy Bethmann Hollweg sought to consolidate Germany's position in the short term, rather than pursue new territorial gains. The German Empire acknowledged France's rights over Morocco, thereby provisionally easing Franco-German relations. Similar overtures were made to Russia, though to negligible effect. The top priority was an attempt to achieve closer relations, perhaps even a neutrality agreement, with Great Britain, for the sake of which the government was prepared to slow down its fleet-building programme. These somewhat naive manoeuvres, however, produced few results.

When Kiderlen-Wächter took over at the Foreign Office in 1911 the 'Weltpolitik' of the Bülow era was vigorously revived, albeit in a radically revised form. Kiderlen-Wächter's most spectacular imperialist venture was the operation at Agadir, part of a grand design whereby France would be forced to cede the Congo in exchange for obtaining a free hand in Morocco. Kiderlen-Wächter tried to strengthen Germany's bargaining position by mobilizing public opinion behind the German cause, deliberately inflaming nationalist passions with all the means at his disposal. He had confidently assumed that the French advance to Fez, in the wake of the collapse of the Sultan's authority, created an ideal opportunity for re-opening the Moroccan question. On 1 July 1911 a German gunboat dropped anchor off Agadir, ostensibly to protect German interests, although there were precious few interests to protect. At the same time Kiderlen-Wächter allowed the idea to circulate in the German press that Germany would claim the southern part of Morocco in exchange for France's having a free hand in the rest of the country. Early in July 1911 the Foreign Office invited some fifty journalists to the Wilhelmstraße, and Kiderlen-Wächter, while not making his position explicit, did nothing to dispel their assumption that the government was hoping to acquire the Sous region. In September 1911 he talked at length with Class, the leader of the Pan-Germans, and gave his seal of approval to the latter's pamphlet *Westmarokko deutsch*, numerous copies of which were sold within a few weeks. (Kiderlen-Wächter did, admittedly, ask Class to delete some particularly aggressive passages demanding that the German acquisition of Burgundy be declared a war aim in the event of a Franco-German conflict.) As he later conceded before the Budget Committee of the Reichstag, Kiderlen-Wächter was convinced that strong public support for the annexation of southern Morocco would help to induce France to surrender the whole of the French Congo. His Moroccan policy, however, miscarried completely, securing merely some insignificant French territorial concessions.[16]

When the real facts became known in early November 1911, public dismay knew no bounds. For the first time, the government's handling of the press came in for severe criticism, both in the Budget Committee and in the Reichstag proper.[17] The government was accused of having deliberately misled the nation. Bassermann wound up the debate in the Budget Committee with a stinging indictment:[18]

> We have just seen that foreign policy cannot be pursued with complete disregard for popular feeling. That is what those in charge of our foreign policy have failed to understand, and that is the reason for the justifiable discord in the country.

The government had a hard time in the Reichstag defending its questionable manipulation of the press.[19] Kiderlen-Wächter gave Parliament an evasive, and yet revealing, account of his meeting with Class:

> I told him: the position is such-and-such, we want compensation, but we are not yet at the stage when we can say that matters are settled. It will be a good thing if there is a mood of patriotism at home, and if you make a case for it, that will certainly do no harm. It is not, I think, a criminal offence.

He denied, however, that he had 'ever said to anyone that we wanted to acquire parts of Morocco and that propaganda might be made on the matter'.[20] The main bourgeois parties were united in their condemnation of the government's use of the press. Count Hertling was particularly outspoken in his criticism:

In my judgement, the press in general, and the semi-official press in particular, has failed in its duties during recent months, and has been quite incapable of instructing public opinion properly and guiding it in accordance with the government's intentions.

He also complained that there was not just a single official press department, but three: in the Foreign Office, in the Imperial Naval Office and in the Imperial Colonial Office.[21]

These events throw the shortcomings of the government's information policy into sharp relief. Official propaganda was highly ambivalent and often used dubious methods. It was also arbitrary in the sense that certain journalists were supplied with information while others were denied it. Worst of all, the information policies of the different government bodies were mutually inconsistent and, apart from generating a diffuse mood of national acquisitiveness, did little but sow confusion.

Early in 1912, prompted by calls from the Reichstag parties, the government began to reform the machinery of official information policy. It made a brave effort to abolish the press departments of the different ministries and to centralize press policy under the jurisdiction of the Chancellor. The attempt, however, was a dismal failure, because the various ministries (in particular, the Imperial Naval Office) put up stubborn resistance and refused to surrender their separate press bureaux. The press departments of the Foreign Office and the Imperial Naval Office became involved in a running battle over the question whether the navy should be further expanded or whether Germany should proceed more cautiously.[22]

Bethmann Hollweg came to the conclusion that it was virtually impossible to influence public opinion. He decided not only that there were very strict limits to the government's ability to get its views to prevail by means of official information policies, but that such methods could often be positively damaging to the government's cause. Accordingly, there was now a sharp change in official attitudes towards the press. The failure of Kiderlen-Wächter's audacious attempt to manipulate public opinion brought about a return to the familiar authoritarian practices of the past. Once again, the government sought to conduct foreign policy as secretly as possible and pay minimal heed to the national mood; it virtually abandoned the effort to shape public attitudes. The only way in which the public was told about the broad goals of German foreign policy was through dry official articles in the *Norddeutsche Allgemeine Zeitung* and cautiously worded reports in the semi-official press, while every endeavour was made to inhibit discussion of specific questions. Ernst Bassermann, the leader of the National Liberals in the Reichstag, complained repeatedly, and with justification, that the government was failing to keep closely in touch with Parliament on matters of foreign policy, despite the fact that such questions were of vital importance to the German Empire. It was a disgrace, he said, 'to have to depend on the extremely meagre information provided by the *Norddeutsche Allgemeine Zeitung*'.[23]

The Chancellor plainly believed that playing down the role of foreign policy and steering clear of major controversies was the best way of retaining freedom of manouevre in a political situation that had become very heated, as the extremist campaigns of the nationalist pressure groups found a growing response among National Liberals and Conservatives, and as reserves of moderation and balanced judgement began rapidly to run out. It was far from easy, however, to stage a return to classical cabinet politics, even in a modified form. The Reichstag parties were no longer prepared to be ignored on matters of foreign policy and were calling for regular briefings from the government, either in the confidential meetings of the Budget Committee or in the Reichstag itself. In the main, the government acceded to their demands. In sessions of the Budget Committee, government representatives repeatedly spoke with surprising candour about the aims and objectives of German foreign policy and about the hopes and fears on which it rested. Foreign policy, indeed, became one of the main battlegrounds of parliamentary debate, as the government ceased to be able to take refuge in the constitutional principle that the conduct of foreign policy was an Imperial prerogative. The big armaments bills of 1912 and 1913 gave rise to intense debates on foreign policy in the Reichstag; so did the Balkan crisis that reached its climax in early December 1912, when it seemed that a general European war was about to break out, or was at least a very real possibility.

The crisis led the Bethmann Hollweg government to try to assemble a united front embracing the Reichstag parties and the general public in support of its policy, which was to give Austria-Hungary unconditional backing in the Balkans in order to induce Russia to abandon her rigid posture and allow Austria a free hand. On 1 December 1912 Bethmann Hollweg even approached the Social Democrats in an attempt to win their endorsement for the pro-Austrian statement he proposed to make in the Reichstag the following day, warning Russia of Germany's position.[24]

But Bethmann Hollweg's speech in the Reichstag on 2 December 1912 had an unexpected consequence. Sir Edward Grey informed the German government that Great Britain would be unable to remain neutral if the Balkan conflict were to lead to a European war and a military attack on France. When Wilhelm II heard of this response, he concluded that the great powers were on the brink of war and flew into a state of panic. He summoned his army and navy commanders to discuss the military situation, in a meeting that has become known as the 'war council' or 'crisis conference' of 8 December 1912.[25] There was serious discussion whether it might not be better, if war were imminent, for Germany to strike first rather than wait and allow the military balance to change to her disadvantage. Those present also debated whether, under the circumstances, the German people was really prepared for the possibility of war, bearing in mind that a modern war could not be waged without popular support.

The only concrete outcome, however, of this otherwise rather inconclusive gathering – it took place behind the backs of the Foreign Secretary and the Chancellor, and the latter was merely giving a cursory account of it after the event – was an instruction to Bethmann Hollweg that he should use the press to prepare the German public for the possibility of a major conflict. Admiral von Müller wrote to the Chancellor after the conference:[26]

> His Majesty the Emperor has issued an order from the Royal Palace today, on the occasion of a discussion of the military and political situation, that the people shall be informed through the press of the great national interests that would be at stake for Germany were a war to break out as a consequence of the Austro-Serbian conflict. The people, he said, should not be placed in the position of not being aware, until a great European war had broken out, of the interests for which Germany would be fighting. The idea of such a war should be made familiar to them beforehand. Since this is a purely political matter, I have the honour of respectfully informing Your Excellency of His Majesty's order and of leaving the rest to your discretion.

This order was evidence of the concern of Wilhelm II and his military advisers that no government could embark on the gamble of waging war without adequate popular support and a 'just' cause. At the same time, however, its purport was far from clear. It did not even spell out whether the public was to be prepared for a war in alliance with Austria-Hungary that might break out at any moment, or for a more general war that might take place either in the near or the more distant future.

The Foreign Office moved very quickly to allay the Emperor's fears. It pointed out that the public had already been informed (in a semi-official article published in the *Norddeutsche Allgemeine Zeitung* under the fairly colourless title 'For Durazzo') that a war in support of Austria-Hungary would be tantamount, in the prevailing international situation, to a war in defence of Germany's position in the world.[27] Kiderlen-Wächter also conceded that it was necessary to bring greater pressure to bear on the press over the matter. But in the end no specific measures were taken, at any rate of the sort envisaged by the Emperor (who had also told Tirpitz to put his publicity machine into action). Contrary to the argument that has been advanced, on very circumstantial evidence, by Röhl, the government made no concerted attempt to prepare public opinion for war; nor did it even try to generate popular enthusiasm for a policy that constantly hovered on the brink of conflict.[28] On the contrary, Bethmann Hollweg did all he could to play down the war-mongering tendencies in the country. He did so, admittedly, primarily for tactical reasons. He did not want a noisy press campaign to jeopardize a possible joint Anglo-German solution of the Balkan crisis, and he was anxious to get the new Army Bill through the Reichstag without stirring up undue commotion abroad. Instead, the government opted for indirect methods of winning public support for the Army Bill and the fiscal measures that were needed to finance it. Independent figures such as Karl Lamprecht and Hans Delbrück were asked to speak out in the bill's favour. The Chancellor was also highly conscious of the dangers that might arise if the government were to engage in open nationalist agitation, whether of the subtle Bismarckian variety or of the more flamboyant sort employed by Bülow (which would undoubtedly have been to the Emperor's liking).

These rather clumsy, hesitant attempts to encourage patriotic sentiment while avoiding any form of radically nationalist propaganda that would give further credibility to the Pan-German League and the Army League eventually proved a sorry failure. In a speech in the Reichstag on 21 April 1913 the Chancellor made a highly unfortunate reference to the likelihood of a future war between the Teutonic and Slavonic peoples. Although his intention was actually to dissociate the government from the talk to this effect that was current among ultra-nationalist groups, and even in sections of the quality press, his words sparked off a heated debate whether a war with Russia was imminent.[29] Friedrich von Bernhardi's extremist view, put forward in his influential book *Deutschland und der nächste Krieg* (Germany and the Next War), that a European war was not only inevitable but desirable, began to harden into an accepted doctrine – indeed, gradually took on the character of a self-fulfilling prophecy. Again, the government tried by indirect means to counteract such thinking. Richard von Kühlmann arranged for the jounalist Hans von Plehn to publish, under a pseudonym, a book entitled *Deutsche Weltpolitik und kein Krieg* (German World Policy and No War), presenting the case for a cautious but consistent brand of 'Weltpolitik' conducted in close co-operation with Great Britain. None the less, more and more people were coming round to the view that time was not on Germany's side, especially given that Russia was building up her weaponry at an alarming rate.

The conservative *Post*, like many other newspapers, argued that Germany ought to prepare for a major European war as rapidly as possible, since there was no point in continuing to hope for support from the British. The government tried to insist that such ideas were untenable and dangerous, but it made little headway, particularly since in other contexts it was itself playing a distinctly nationalist card as a way of combating and isolating the Social Democrats.[30] It faced mounting criticism not only from the new right, in the form of the nationalist propaganda organizations, but also from the National Liberals and Conservatives, who now came out strongly for a vigorous 'Weltpolitik', projecting themselves as champions of a businesslike drive on behalf of German interests. These tactics were, of course, designed to win votes in the short term, but they made a strong impact on public attitudes. Imperialist greed was becoming widespread, seizing hold not only of the middle class but of a number of radical liberals and Social Democrats. The government was now expected to come up with tangible imperialist successes. As well as the extreme nationalist groups, the right-of-centre parties in the Reichstag took up the cry with increasing intensity. In May 1914 Bassermann (a key figure in all debates on foreign policy in the Reichstag) complained rather sarcastically that while France, Italy, Great Britain and Russia had seen 'territorial growth' in recent years, 'we have been playing a very modest role'.[31]

In point of fact, the government could cite a number of rather promising projects that looked as though they might lead to acquisitions of territory or – perhaps more important – might create lucrative economic opportunities abroad. Negotiations with Britain over the future of Angola and Mozambique, based on the assumption that Portugal could be induced to surrender these territories in return for a financial settlement, were successfully concluded by late 1913. The German government, however, did not dare accede to the British demand that these agreements should be published. It believed, with some reason, that this might jeopardize the plans, but, more significantly, was concerned that the German public, now in the grip of anglophobia, would see them as yet another British 'trap'. The scheme therefore came to nothing at this stage. The government was simultaneously involved in secret negotiations over the possible acquisition of the Belgian Congo, while international agreements concerning the scope of Germany's economic spheres of influence in the Ottoman Empire had also yielded some tangible, if not wholly satisfactory, results: at any rate, the obstacles to the building of the Baghdad Railway had been removed, and Germany had also secured a modest stake in the exploitation of oil reserves in the Persian Gulf. Again, however, the government did not dare make these developments known publicly, partly because it did not want to put them at risk by revealing them prematurely, but also because it was afraid that in the prevailing climate of nationalism and grossly inflated expectations they would be seen as too paltry and too uncertain of success. Instead, it confined itself to making cautious statements in the Budget Committee of the Reichstag and refrained from generating publicity on its own behalf.

In the years immediately before the First World War, then, the German government's relationship with public opinion was reactive rather than active. The leadership tried to remain as aloof as possible from the public debate about imperialism; it also shied away from taking a clear stand against those who argued that sooner or later the German Empire would have to go to war in order to secure its long-term international position. It spoke in a timid voice, confining itself to details, having long since been outbid by far more extreme groups. Indeed, it had every reason to fear that any direct steps it might have taken against the ultra-imperialists would have backfired, exposing the Chancellor and his advisers to the charge of being weak, irresolute, for good measure perhaps even pacifist. This would have damaged its standing in the eyes of the Emperor, conservatives and the military establishment, who played a far more important role in the power structure of Wilhelmine Germany than any majority grouping of parties in Parliament.

By 1913 the Bethmann Hollweg government was under mounting pressure on at least three fronts. First, it was under fire from the 'staatstragende Parteien', the parties 'supporting the state' – the Conservatives, the Free Conservatives, the National Liberals and even, to a lesser extent, the conservative wing of the Centre party, which was moving rapidly towards a policy of nationalist identification with the established political system. Secondly, the extremist nationalist propaganda organizations had succeeded in winning over significant sections of the middle classes and the intelligentsia. Thirdly, the military and the Emperor's court were becoming increasingly panicky about the Reichstag's efforts to curtail their traditional privileges and overturn the special position that the army enjoyed under the Wilhelmine constitution. A fair number of people in these latter circles had become convinced that a war would be the easiest way out of their difficulties, since it would provide an opportunity of suppressing the Social Democrats and curbing the process of democratization or, as it has recently been termed, the 'imperceptible' transition towards parliamentary government.[32] The government's inability to withstand these pressures was demonstrated by the 'Zabern affair' of late 1913 and, more especially, by the events of March 1914, when the *Kölnische Zeitung* published an article by its correspondent in St Petersburg entitled 'Is War in Sight?' To the Foreign Office's dismay, the article set off a fierce Russo-German press war. The political atmosphere was inflamed by public outrage at Russia's supposedly aggressive intentions, and the Foreign Office's half-hearted attempts to face down the extremists were largely ineffective. The editor of the *Kölnische Zeitung* was summoned to the Foreign Office and told that articles on such sensitive matters should not be published without prior consultation with the government. The editor, however, flatly refused to let his newspaper be subjected to such censorship. The government's relations with the press bore little resemblance to what they had been in Bülow's day.

Increasingly, the 'Russian threat' was beginning to be accepted as a reality by the German public as well as by senior government figures and the General Staff. This in turn gave further fuel to nationalist sentiment. There was now a well-established pattern, as rival groups stirred up ever more extreme and grandiose expectations in order to prove their patriotic credentials: Conservatives competed for popular support with National Liberals; more broadly, the Old Right competed with the New. The process had already come very close to running out of control by 1912; certainly, since then the government had clearly been on the defensive. Even were the government to have tried to give a lead to public opinion, there would have been little chance that its views would have prevailed. With its standing weakened both in the nation at large and among the influential groups close to the Emperor, it was finding itself being hauled along in the wake of an imperialist ideology that had no specific goals or, in Joseph Schumpeter's words, 'definable limits'. The situation filled the leading statesmen with anxiety and foreboding – as well it might, since the government's willingness to be led on by nationalist public sentiment was bound to have serious consequences.

The nationalist attitudes that were prevalent in so many sections of German society were largely a matter of emotion. They sprang partly from a feeling of national pride, but also, and perhaps more significantly, from fear and from a deep-seated sense of insecurity. The rising tide of socialism seemed to be an almost unconquerable force, threatening to sweep away the very foundations of social order. Many businessmen were caught up by the nationalist and imperialist cause simply because it seemed to be the only political ideology that was capable of stemming the further spread of socialist doctrine: certainly, it offered them few prospects in purely economic terms. The same was true of most of the bourgeois parties, to say nothing of the Conservatives, who played the anti-socialist card at every opportunity now that the principles of their own political philosophy had lost much of their appeal. Perhaps an even more important influence on public attitudes, however, was the fact that the nationalist propaganda organizations had succeeded in mobilizing new sections of the population that had not previously been involved in politics at all, rallying them under the banner of an integrative nationalism that contrived to be both conservative and progressive at once. In the last analysis, their success was possible only because the semi-constitutional system of government in the German Empire had ceased to be appropriate to the demands of a modern industrialized society and of modern mass politics. In July 1914[33] the 'latent crisis' of the German political system spilled over on to the international stage, setting in train a world war that the 'civilians' at the head of the German government would really far sooner have avoided.

|11|

The spirit of 1914 and
the ideology of a
German 'Sonderweg'

The First World War marks the beginning of an era of European history that wrought unimaginable destruction and human suffering, on a scale perhaps comparable only with the misery created by the Thirty Years' War. And yet in August 1914, as the young men of the combatant nations readied themselves to fight what they believed was a war of self-defence, they were imbued with a fervent sense of national pride. Contrary to what has often been said, the upsurge of patriotic feeling that occurred in all of these countries – the 'spirit of 1914' – was not entirely unanimous, but there is no doubt that at first the war was a popular cause among very broad sections of society. In particular, a significant proportion of the ruling elites across Europe greeted the outbreak of hostilities, after a long period of suffocating international tensions and social crisis, as a moment of deliverance. A representative spokesman of his generation, the historian Karl Alexander von Müller, recalled in his memoirs that 'it was a conflagration in which all the enormous inward turmoil that had been piling up was engulfed in flames'.[1] Within the German ruling class, especially, the sense of national unity that was felt at the beginning of the war left an indelible impression:[2]

> For the first time in the nation's history the mass of the German people had united around a single point, fusing silently and with lightning speed into a single organism in a manner that had never been seen before – like an enormous piece of machinery, yet animated by self-sacrifice, heroism and the most scrupulous sense of responsibility. A people of seventy million had become a single host.

For these Germans, the 'spirit of 1914' – the sudden advent of which was in many respects akin to a religious awakening – found its purest and profoundest embodiment in the German conception of the state, in a way that did not hold in the other countries of Europe.

There were, of course, comparable sentiments in other countries. In France, the notion of an *union sacrée* rested on a widespread and passionate popular commitment to French national ideals; in Britain, national indignation at Germany's infringement of the basic rights of the Belgian people sprang from analogous convictions. But in the case of Germany, the upwelling of feeling that occurred in August 1914 was not merely a matter of straightforward patriotism: it also involved nationalistic beliefs, militaristic attitudes and, above all, a specific sense of mission. It is this sense of mission that lies at the heart of the ideology of a 'deutscher Sonderweg', that is to say, the notion of a 'special German path of development' that played such a prominent role in determining the shape of German history for over a century.

The concept of a distinctively German 'path', midway between the materialism and utilitarianism of the western democratic systems on the one hand and the autocracy of Tsarist Russia on the other, originates from the opposition between the political philosophies of the west and those of the central European powers. But the first systematic study to analyse the distinctive features of Germany's political culture in terms of a deficit of liberal institutions was Thorstein Veblen's *Imperial Germany and the Industrial Revolution*, published in 1915. In this work, together with Anglo-Saxon writings contemporary with it, we find numerous variants of the thesis that the German political system, by retaining a whole range of authoritarian characteristics, was not properly equipped to cope with the demands of a modern industrial society. In particular, it was claimed, there was no effective democratic control over the executive in Germany, and aristocratic and monarchical traditions hostile to the spirit of middle-class enterprise remained intact. The result was that Germany's response to the problems of the international arena took the form of aggression and 'militarism'.

The model of a German 'Sonderweg' diverging significantly from the route taken by western societies has gained wide currency in the modern historical and political literature and has come to form the foundation of a new, critical approach to German history. It is now common practice to regard the disparity between the processes of economic and political change in the German Empire as the ultimate cause of the sequence of events that culminated in the rise to power of the National Socialists and the subsequent German catastrophe. Germany's political institutions, it is argued, failed to adjust in response to the rapid economic and social changes that were taking place within the country. An antiquated political system was preserved, enabling a governing class that owed its position to pre-industrial conditions to hold on to power long after those conditions had disappeared. The failure of German society to liberalize led to the growth of an overweening, strident, aggressive, integrative brand of nationalism, with all its fateful consequences.

More recently, however, the 'Sonderweg' model has come under criticism, notably from the British historians Geoff Eley and David Blackbourn. These writers maintain that the model rests on a misplaced idealization of the change from an aristocratic oligarchy to a 'bourgeois' democratic state that took place in Great Britain. Social change in Britain, they point out, was in fact by no means free of conflict or even wholly peaceful, and older social formations showed a considerable capacity for survival. It is certainly the case that the explanatory model that has been favoured by modern German historians needs to be modified in important ways. In particular, it is false simply to assert without qualification that the backwardness of the German political system led to the feudalization of the middle class. In the socio-economic sphere, at any rate, the bourgeois order came, by and large, to prevail in Germany, even though the state was undoubtedly distorted by authoritarian features. What is needed is something more refined than a stark opposition between, on the one hand, a model of a German 'Sonderweg' and, on the other, a model based on the specifically British evolution towards a modern democratic industrial society. One possibility is to argue, as Thomas Nipperdey has done, that there have been many different 'Sonderwege' in European history, of which Germany's was only one instance. Other writers have contested the validity of the concept of a 'special path of development' altogether.

And yet it is also clear that the German 'Sonderweg' thesis is more than just a concoction on the part of left-wing intellectuals and that the process of change that took place in Germany *was* a distinctive one. In particular, it differed from that which took place in west European societies by virtue of the fact that in Germany the state, and the higher civil service that underpinned the state, were assigned special importance from the very first. On the one hand, Germany's bureaucratic regime, as Max Weber called it, was notable for the close links that existed between the higher civil service and the educated middle class; these served to mitigate certain of the authoritarian features of the political system. The bureaucracy, however, also functioned as something of a protective shield for the aristocracy and the royal court, and this had the result that potential constitutional reforms were generally stifled at birth because their effect, had they been implemented, would have been to lessen the power both of the traditional elites and of the bureaucracy itself. Ideologically speaking, the system rested primarily on a framework derived from German idealism, according to which the role of the state, and above all of the civil service (termed by Hegel, not coincidentally, the 'allgemeiner Stand' or 'universal estate') whose primary purpose was to serve the state, was expressly regarded as superior in importance to that of 'society'. In effect, from the time of Hegel onwards the supremacy of this 'universal estate', dedicated in theory or indeed in practice solely to the general good, was regarded as incompatible with the principle of parliamentary government: under a parliamentary system, it was believed, the material interests of society – in particular, those of the upper strata – would become identical with the goals of the state and would cease to be subject to restraint or modification. By and large, this view retained its importance within the German political tradition throughout the nineteenth century; indeed, as class differences became more pronounced, it even took on new force in certain respects.

The influence of this ideological framework within the political culture of Imperial Germany was virtually all-pervasive. Nowhere, however, did it find more graphic expression than in the debate about the 'spirit of 1914' – a spirit which, as we have said, the German ruling elites generally saw as expressing a specifically German conception of the state, fundamentally opposed to the view of the state that was prevalent in the western democracies. The unprecedented sense of national awakening that gripped the country in August 1914 was hailed as marking Germany's return to her true path, and the German intelligentsia (particularly the academic community) believed that its principal task was to harness this mood and the moral and political sentiments it encapsulated in order to bring about the lasting intellectual and ethical regeneration of the German people. This belief underlay the creation of an ideological syndrome which contemporaries – taking up formulations by Johann Plenge, Ernst Troeltsch and the Swedish political scientist Johann Rudolf Kjellén – dubbed the 'ideas of 1914'.[3]

As we have already indicated, the immediate impulse behind the articulation of the 'ideas of 1914' was the collective experience of 4 August 1914, which had surpassed anything that the German ruling elites had imagined possible. There was also a felt need to provide counter-arguments to the fierce criticisms of Germany's policies, of her conduct of the war and of her whole political system that had been voiced in the west very soon after the war had broken out. The best known, and also the most questionable, expression of this feeling was the so-called 'Appeal by the 93 to the world of culture', an attempt by leading academic figures, ranging from the right to the centre left, to confront what they called Germany's 'literary encirclement' by western journalism and scholarship.[4] Ultimately, however, the roots of all of these gestures lay deeper, in a conception of Germany's political identity and national history that was shaped by authoritarian thinking and that was fundamentally inimical to democracy.

The German journalists and academics who hastened to the 'literary front' at the outbreak of hostilities to do their bit for the national war effort were profoundly convinced that German culture was superior to the cultures of the other countries of Europe. They wanted not only to do everything they could to defend German culture but, if necessary, to impose its values on the rest of the continent by force. Such thinking was, as we shall see, a significant factor in ensuring that from the very beginning of the war there was no willingness, in Germany in particular (though the position was not dissimilar in the other combatant nations) to bring an end to the bloodshed through negotiations. Only victory would suffice. For the sake of this principle, millions of young people from a host of countries around the world perished on European battlefields in the course of the next four years, often as a result of military strategies that were guaranteed to cause losses in the hundreds of thousands: indeed, the carnage on the Western

Front, as repeated attempts were made to jolt the paralysed battle lines into motion through the ruthless sacrifice of human lives, was scarcely matched even in the battles of the Second World War.

As we shall indicate later, the 'ideas of 1914' also had a further, longer-term consequence. The collective emotion that inspired the Germans as they rallied to fight for their country, despite their deep-seated political and social differences, was to play a part in preparing the ground for the later rise of extremist nationalism and, eventually, of National Socialism in the years that followed Germany's defeat.

From the start, the First World War was more than just a struggle for power among the nations of Europe, and especially on the part of the German Empire: it was a struggle between political systems, and between the intellectual traditions that underlay those systems. In the western European countries – notwithstanding their alliance with the authoritarian Tsarist Empire, which had long subjected the nationalities of eastern central Europe to a process of Russification – there was a mounting conviction that the war was being fought primarily for the sake of the principle of national self-determination, which had been so grossly violated in the case of neutral Belgium. By contrast, leaders of opinion in the German Empire believed profoundly that the war was not merely about the defence of the German political order but about the preservation and strengthening of Germanic culture in the heart of Europe. Even Friedrich Meinecke, usually a voice of moderation, said at this time: [5]

> It may be, during these momentous days, that our entire culture is being impressed, directly and palpably, into the service of the state; but in the realm of the impalpable, our state, our power politics and our war are now at the service of the supreme values of our national culture.

It is also evident that a sense of inferiority *vis-à-vis* the relatively more advanced societies of western Europe, particularly Great Britain, came subliminally into play.

Here, arguably, we can see the mainspring for the launching, amid a blaze of publicity, of the 'ideas of 1914'. The exercise was designed as a comprehensive demonstration not merely that the German political order was in no way inferior to that of the west but that Germany's semi-constitutional system (in which the major share of political power resided in the state and the high officials who safeguarded the interests of the state, while Parliament and the parties were confined to a subsidiary role and were excluded from any real say in political decision-making) was immeasurably superior to that of the western democracies. Whereas the societies of the west largely looked back to the 'ideas of 1789', the German political system, with its balance between order and freedom, pointed the way to the future. In the new age that was dawning, the decisive factor would be Germany's special talent for organization, embodied in a state to which all citizens would voluntarily submit since it would guarantee the nation's collective political welfare; the western democracies would be subject to the all-powerful tyranny of individualism. This clash of philosophies, it was claimed, was the paramount reason why the war was being fought.

As well as idealist semantics, social considerations also played an important role in this thinking. There was a fundamental assumption that the prevailing semi-constitutional system in Germany, if stabilized and ideologically revitalized, was especially well fitted for dealing with the major problems of society and, in particular, that it would serve to keep the working class in its subordinate position within the social structure. Alois Riehl, for example, made no bones about the matter in an address delivered on 23 October 1914 on the theme '1813 – Fichte – 1914':[6]

> There will be political parties again, and so there should be: the health of the state demands diversity. But let us have an end to class conflicts! [...] We seek to defeat England, not follow England's example. The English example shows only too clearly what happens when a state is dedicated exclusively to the pursuit of commercial and industrial goals. We do not wish the state to be concerned solely with the acquisition and production of material goods. The motherland of social legislation must also remain the land of social advance and social reform.

Such arguments flowed, essentially, from revulsion at the profound effects that industrial change had had on society and from the belief that the role of the state was to mediate class conflicts (which in industrialized societies had primarily taken the form of a struggle for emancipation on the part of the working class) by means of bureaucratic intervention. Whereas in the western system the aim was for conflicts between different social classes and groups to be freely resolved within the framework of democracy, the German model of authoritarian constitutionalism created, it was claimed, an administrative form of conflict resolution from above. 'German freedom', so defined, was held up as the answer to the conception of a pluralistic industrial society of the sort that had evolved in the western democracies.

Max Weber regarded such ideas, however well-intentioned, as symptoms of a fatal general tendency to believe that bureaucracy was sufficient of itself to resolve the pressing political and social problems of the modern age: '[...] behind the so-called "German ideas of 1914",' Weber said, 'behind what the literati have euphemistically called the "socialism of the future", behind the catchwords "organization" and "a co-operative economy"', lay the 'sober fact of universal bureaucratization'. He added for good measure that this widespread enthusiasm for bureaucratization was quite incompatible with Germany's national interests.[7] In this respect, however, Weber – who said on more than one occasion that he had 'had quite enough of all the talk about the ideas of 1914'[8] – was a voice crying in the wilderness. The great majority of intellectuals, including Weber's brother Alfred, were swept along by the ideology of German distinctiveness. There was much public philosophizing about 'Germany's mission'. For Georg Simmel, the very outbreak of war was a form of liberation from the toils of intellectual nihilism in which German culture had been trapped during the preceding decades: the national awakening of August 1914 was a historic turning point, the start of Germany's renewal. In particular, the attitude of 'Mammonism' that had been dominant in modern times (the widespread devotion to purely material values, symbolized by the cult of money for its own sake) would now give way to a new sense of community. What was happening was the 'consummation of 1870', the re-creation of the German nation state on a more exalted plane: a process that would necessitate the cultivation of an ideal of a new man, who would not strive to achieve material goals first and foremost but would merge his identity into that of the nation as a whole.[9] More than many of the comparable declarations that were made during the first days and weeks of the war, Simmel's speech gave voice to a highly emotional and irrational faith that the war would resolve the problems of personal life in general and that the enthusiasm that had swept the nation would inevitably lead to a new and brighter future.

The 'ideas of 1914' – the attempt to make the heady nationalistic atmosphere of August permanent – were hailed as the expression of a new kind of revolution, a German revolution: resembling the French Revolution of 1789 in the sense that it would usher in a new era of human history, but the diametrical opposite of its predecessor in both intellectual and political terms. Whereas the ideas of 1789 – liberty, equality and fraternity – were in reality 'shopkeepers' ideals, pure and simple, which served solely to provide individuals with particular benefits',[10] the aim of the 'German revolution' of 1914 was to 'exert all the powers of the state in concerted oppostion to the revolution of destructive liberation of the eighteenth century'.[11] What this entailed in practice was an idealization of the traditional semi-authoritarian Imperial state. Such a state, it was argued, was far better suited for dealing with the problems of the future, through a corporatist form of 'national socialism', than were the democratic systems of the west, with their complete subservience to materialist principles.

The most forthright contemporary statement of this position was Werner Sombart's highly influential book *Händler und Helden. Patriotische Besinnungen*, which summed up the confrontation between the democratic societies of the west and the political culture of the German nation – with, as we would now recognize, its authoritarian cast – as a conflict between the mentality of the Shopkeeper and that of the Hero. The British, Sombart maintained, had long been a nation of petty tradesmen, in thrall to material possessions and obsessed with unmartial matters such as their creature comforts and their sports. In the German nation, on the other hand, the great primal warlike virtues remained intact; Germany's models were the great heroic figures of her history from the time of the Wars of Liberation onwards. Sombart hailed the First World War as nothing less than a supreme effort on the part of the entire German nation to bring about the regeneration of these heroic qualities: 'War is the consummation of the heroic outlook, and springs from it; it is necessary in order to prevent the the heroic outlook from falling prey to the forces of evil, to the narrow, abject spirit of commerce.'[12] He combined this affirmation with a fervent entreaty to his fellow countrymen to prosecute the war to a victorious conclusion, regardless of the cost in human lives and material goods, in order that the moral ideals embodied in the German nation might be preserved for posterity.

The 'spirit of 1914' also contained an unmistakably religious dimension. Many saw the outbreak of war as a blessing, saving the German people from a state of introspection, intellectual emptiness and hedonistic materialism and offering them a vision of lofty new communitarian ideals that would make life once more worth living. As harbingers of a new social order that would supersede the materialism and the hopeless, overweening individualism of western democracy, the 'ideas of 1914' were widely seen as the expression of a German mission. Werner Sombart went so far as to maintain that the German nation, by dint of its special moral and political qualities, had become the century's paramount representative of the 'idea of God on earth'. The Germans, he said, were the successors of the Greeks and the Jews: they were God's 'chosen people' of the contemporary era.[13] Despite the scorn and hatred that the other peoples of Europe had poured upon them, the Germans should conduct the war 'with pride, with heads held high, certain in the knowledge that they are the people of God'.[14] From countless pulpits, similar language was used to describe the First World War as a righteous cause in Christian terms.

Even among writers who were less ready to espouse such vague and emotive, yet widely popular, notions, there was a strong tendency to idealize the German political system and to see it as more forward-looking than western democracy. In 1915, for example, Ernst Troeltsch – though at this time he was beginning to try to reconcile the differences between the political and intellectual traditions of Germany and western Europe, both of which, as he properly pointed out, had sprung from the selfsame Christian and humanist roots – was still disposed to favour the notion of 'German political freedom', in the sense of rule by the 'central will of government' basically unfettered by Parliament: in other words, unregulated bureaucracy.[15] In 1917 Friedrich Naumann argued that 'this is, or is becoming, our national faith': the German people would be 'the first revolution-less great nation in the organized world', able to conquer the social and demographic problems of the second half of the twentieth century by virtue of their talent for organization and their discipline founded on the nation state.[16]

The 'ideas of 1914', however, were also the ideological soil that nourished the extremist nationalist sentiments that were to proliferate as the war went on. At the heart of these ideas, as they were worked and re-worked into a full-dress ideology by a host of professors, journalists and writers, there was not only a nationalist arrogance, a wholly uncritical belief in the superiority of the German nation and its intellectual and political traditions, but a readiness to impose those traditions on other peoples by force. For those who subscribed to this ideology, the 'defensive war' of 1914 almost inevitably became transmogrified into a 'war of conquest', the purpose of which was to create the conditions in which the new intellectual and political order could be established across Europe. Johann Plenge, for example, felt no compunction about making a direct comparison (at the cost of blatantly distorting the facts) between Wilhelm II and Napoleon I. Just as Napoleon had sought after 1797 to extend the domination of post-revolutionary France across the continent, so, 'for the second time, an Emperor traverses the world, the leader of a people possessed by the huge, world-shaking sense of strength that comes from its supreme unity'.[17] The notion – here expressed particularly starkly – that the world should 'find recuperation in the German spirit', and that the war was justifiable as a means to this end, gave ideological legitimacy to schemes of territorial annexation that quickly went far beyond the bounds of reality. Such thinking reached its peak with the campaign that was mounted by the German Fatherland party (Deutsche Vaterlandspartei) from early 1917 onwards, which called almost fanatically for victory at all costs and succeeded for a time in casting its spell over wide sections of German society.

In retrospect it is hard to understand how this assortment of half-digested and emotional arguments on behalf of the prevailing political order in Germany, appealing to a corporatist, organic conception of the state whose roots went back to Hegel, Fichte and Adam Müller, can have found so many adherents among the educated sections of Imperial German society. Those who were caught up in the excitement included not only the members of these groups who were receptive to right-wing ideologies in any case, but many who normally swam against the intellectual current and who favoured policies of conciliation and the modest expansion of opportunities for the lower classes – figures, as we have seen, such as Friedrich Meinecke and Ernst Troeltsch, for example, and even Friedrich Naumann. Max Weber, however, somewhat disdainfully described the 'ideas of 1914' as irresponsible literary chatter. 'Clever people,' he said in August 1916, in his address 'On the Threshold of the Third Year of War',[18]

clubbed together and invented the 'ideas of 1914', but no one knows in what these ideas actually consisted. They were grander, far grander than those of 1870, which were mere intoxication by comparison with the majestic way in which the German people arose to fight the present battle for its very existence. There is nothing unusual about uniting and organizing in war; it does not call for new ideas [...]. It is the ideas of 1917 that will count when peace comes.

What was vital, in Weber's view, was the introduction of domestic reforms that would give the 'returning warriors' equal rights as citizens, as happened in Great Britain in the spring of 1918 with the passage of the Representation of the People Act, which abolished the last remaining restrictions on the male franchise. Inevitably, however, the fact that the semi-constitutional state and its centralized bureaucratic power structure were so idealized in Germany played an important part in ensuring that reforms of this sort did not take place. It was part and parcel of the long history of the ideology of a German 'Sonderweg' that all attempts to bring the political order into line with the social structure were undercut by the desire to make a positive virtue out of the relative backwardness of the political system.

For the same reason, the few slender opportunities that arose for bringing the First World War to an acceptable conclusion through negotiation also came to nothing. The war became, as it was termed, a *guerre à outrance*, the only outcome of which would be outright defeat for one side or the other, principally at the expense of the starving mass of the population, including the working class. It must also be said, however, that on the western side too a reciprocal conviction gradually took hold that the only acceptable peace would be one that enabled the victors to impose sweeping terms on the German people, with the aim of eliminating the German Empire as a power in Europe and the world. National arrogance, in other words, was not confined to Germany. By the time the war came to an end, feelings in France and Great Britain were running very high, and these nationalist pressures prevented the statesmen who attended the Paris Peace Conference from bringing about the lasting European peace settlement that had been the subject of so much earlier debate. The common European home, severely damaged by the war, was laboriously rebuilt, but none of the nations of Europe was fully prepared to settle down within the refurbished structure. Even the states that had been brought into existence by the peace treaties immediately contracted nationalist and imperialist ambitions of their own and began to try to increase their power at the expense of others or to prevent their neighbours from regaining their footing. Those that had been on the losing side were filled with bitter resentment against the new democratic order, particularly as they were at first debarred from participating on equal terms in the new system through the League of Nations, which was meant to play a central role within the system. The rise of the Fascists in Italy, swept to power very soon after the end of the war on a wave of irredentist sentiment and brutal violence against the socialists, was a presage of even greater calamities to come.

Nevertheless, it was in Germany that the spirit of irreconcilability and national arrogance, which had found such clear expression in the 'ideas of 1914', remained most powerful. From the start there was a deep-seated reluctance to look facts in the face and to pursue policies of realism and moderation that took account of the new circumstances. The illusions that had been so dominant at the outbreak of war retained their hold. The new right, which had equipped itself with a highly effective organization during the war in the form of the Fatherland party, was anxious to cast a veil of retrospective propaganda over its own gross over-estimate of the political and military strength of the Reich. No sooner had the war ended than it launched the 'Dolchstoßlegende', the myth of the 'stab in the back' that the socialist labour movement had supposedly inflicted on the German army at the crucial moment when victory was in its grasp. This myth undoubtedly played an important part in undermining the political credibility of the newly established Weimar Republic.

The protracted campaign that the extreme right waged against the parties of the democratic centre and, in particular, against the Social Democrats, saddling them with the blame for Germany's defeat and the imposition of the Versailles settlement, had its roots in the authoritarian conception of 'German freedom' that had been prevalent under the Empire. It was sustained by the delusory belief that it was possible to establish a political order that would be free of conflict and would guarantee in perpetuity the privileges and authority of the traditional elites. Within this ideological atmosphere, the idea of a 'Volksgemeinschaft' or 'national community', likewise harking back to the propaganda of 1914 and purporting to offer an anti-modern alternative to the spectre of socialism, became increasingly attractive. The nationalists who promoted the idea of a 'Volksgemeinschaft' were to become ground down by their bitter struggle against the hated Weimar 'system'; but their successors were not. The ultimate beneficiaries of the ideological war that was waged against the new democratic republic, and against all the baleful values that the traditional right had attributed to the materialistic democracies of the west both before and after 1914, were the National Socialists.

On 21 March 1933, in a ceremony at the Garnisonskirche in Potsdam, Hitler and Hindenburg shook hands in public for the first time; before a shrine of Prussian tradition, the conservative elites and the National Socialist 'movement' made their peace. In his sermon the pastor of the church declared that the occasion was tantamount to the 'rebirth of the "spirit of 1914"'.[19] The ceremony at Potsdam marked the start of a new stage in the history of the German claim to uniqueness, in the demonization of those groups in society that refused to submit to the dictates of a racist myth, and in the glorification of war. It would be only a matter of time before Hitler unleashed the European conflict he had long been planning, not merely in order to provide the German people with *Lebensraum* in the east but, above all, to establish the permanent hegemony of the Germanic master race in Europe.

From now onwards, the very survival of a common European home would be in doubt; the extremist political forces that had first manifested themselves in such numbers in 1914 would assume a new and even more destructive character. War broke out little more than five years later, on 1

September 1939. Not only Hitler but many of his supporters from the former Wilhelmine elites believed that this second war – which would cost the 'united' German people immeasurably greater expenditure of effort than the first, and would be conducted with unprecedented brutality – would reverse the course of history and obliterate the memory of defeat. German history would return to its own 'special path' once again. The ideology of the German 'Sonderweg', having played a vital part in bringing the National Socialists to power, now also enabled them to extend their influence until they had infested every corner of Germany's political culture.

12

The social consequences
of World War I:
the case of Germany

The First World War was waged with the utmost expenditure of energy and effort on the part of the combatant nations. As the fighting wore on, without seeming to bring the end any closer, all available manpower and materials were eventually thrown into the struggle. The social consequences of such a colossal mobilization of resources are far from easy to assess. When the war finally came to a close, victors and vanquished alike had reached a state of total exhaustion; their economies were in disarray. Except in France and Belgium, destruction by enemy action was limited (by comparison, at any rate, with the devastation wrought by the Thirty Years' War or by World War II) but a return to life as it had been before 1914 was out of the question. In three of the countries of Europe (Tsarist Russia, Austria-Hungary and Imperial Germany) the system of government had broken down altogether. Reconstruction, if it was going to be possible at all, was certain to take many years.

The German revolution that broke out early in November 1918, a few days before the signing of the armistice, was directed primarily against the Imperial authorities. Its first aim was to end the war, at whatever price. Only at a later stage did it become a political and, in part, a social revolution, headed by the working-class parties, notably the Majority Social Democrats. After a bitter struggle the revolutionary movement was contained and a new democratic order was established. And yet from the start the Weimar Republic proved to be an unstable political entity. The ruling elites and, with a few exceptions, the members of the educated middle class were not willing to accept the new system but continued to hanker after the political dispensation of the Imperial era. They blamed the left for the distress and upheaval that had befallen the country, accusing it of stabbing the German army in the back and of being chiefly responsible for the oppressive terms of the Versailles settlement, especially the demand for reparations.

What most Germans did not recognize was that much of their suffering was the direct result of four years of warfare and of wartime economic policies that had bordered on the suicidal. The war economy had been entirely dedicated to maximizing military production, despite mounting scarcities of human and material resources of all kinds. By the end of the war the consequences of this ruinously wasteful strategy should have been only too plain to see: a grossly distorted economic structure, including a swollen heavy-industrial sector, and galloping inflation. It did not help that Germans also failed to understand that most of the other European states, including the victors, were little better off than they were.

The war had taken an enormous toll in human terms. Although the number of lives lost, as a proportion of the total population, was not as great as in France, nevertheless 2.7 million Germans had died: about 4 per cent of the total population of 1914. In addition, 4 million people had been wounded or disabled and now had to be supported at public expense. The proportion of the mobilized forces that had been either wounded or killed was 41 per cent – a very large fraction by any measure.[1] And these figures, of course, do not reflect the extent of the suffering and despair that had been caused to those whose quality of life had been permanently impaired or who had lost members of their family.

It goes without saying that the material costs of the war were also huge. It is difficult, if not impossible, to be precise on the matter, but there was a sharp decline in Germany's standard of living: it has been estimated that the fall in national wealth brought about, directly and indirectly, by the war was of the order of 35 per cent. To this was added the severe financial burden created by reparations, as well as the obligation to pay social benefits to war invalids and to the relatives of soldiers who had been killed.

The situation was made worse still by the fact that Germany had paid for the war, largely if not entirely, by means of wholly unsecured government loans and bonds. Only a small fraction of the cost had been met directly by increases in taxation. Most of the expenditure had been financed by the printing of money, backed by war loans, with the debt left to be shouldered by the next generation. Members of the public had been persuaded by nationalist propaganda to invest all of their savings into these war loans, assured that they would be repaid, in full and with handsome interest, when the war was won: the bill would be footed by Germany's defeated enemies. The result was a gigantic mountain of debt, which – if the public debt that had accumulated before 1914 is included – had reached 150.7 billion marks by the time the war was over.[2] At the end of the fiscal year 1918–19 Germany's debt had risen to 156.1 billion marks, 40 per cent of it in short-term loans. This rise was accompanied by a sharp increase in the money supply.

At first the inflationary impact was limited, thanks largely to the general scarcity of goods, and there was little public anxiety. Inflation certainly posed a serious longer-term threat to the entire social fabric: during the war, prices had risen by 250 per cent,[3] and this was only a taste of what was yet to come. On the other hand, inflation concealed the damage that the war economy had inflicted on German society: the German public was not yet aware how much harm had been done. As long as interest kept being paid on the war loans, albeit at the cost of a continued rise in public debt, few people realized that their war bonds had lost most of their value and that their savings had largely evaporated.

Wars are usually seen as periods of accelerated social change, or even as breeding-grounds for entirely new forms of social order. The First World War undoubtedly had far-reaching effects on the social fabric in Germany, even though in the final analysis the forces of continuity outweighed those of change. While the specific exigencies of war may not have brought about a complete socio-economic transformation, they significantly hastened various changes in the economy and society that had already been under way for some time, by removing certain brakes and constraints that had been in force during peacetime.

The war brought dramatic alterations to the overall structure of the German economy. Overnight, the economy ceased to be one based on exports. The Allied blockade robbed the German Empire of most of its overseas markets, and, with a few exceptions, also gradually cut it off from most of its supplies of raw materials. To a degree these shortfalls could be remedied by an increase in trade with neutral countries in Europe, notably Sweden and Norway; this in turn led to an increase in the production of goods that would generate the currency that was urgently required for raw-material imports. Nevertheless, a fundamental restructuring of the German economy was unavoidable. Industry, having previously been heavily export-orientated, had to be converted to war production; in certain cases, substitutes for particularly scarce raw materials (such as nitrogen) had to be developed. The details of this restructuring, which by and large was left to industry itself, need not concern us here. Suffice it to say that war industries underwent enormous expansion, while consumer-goods industries were drastically cut back as supplies of raw materials and energy fell; in a number of cases the authorities ordered firms to close (although owners were given generous compensation). The chief effect was a significant shift in favour of large-scale industry and away from smaller businesses. This happened in all areas of production, including even the craft trades (*Handwerk*), which had always prided themselves on their independence during the Imperial era and still made a significant contribution to the nation's wealth. The statistics in Table 12.1, though rather crude, show the extent of these changes. The shift in the industrial structure also led to a significant corresponding redistribution of employment.

Jürgen Kocka has drawn attention to the extent of the switch towards heavy industry, especially chemicals, and away from consumer-goods industries and the craft trades.[4] The German economy, of course, had already been notable for the strength of its heavy industry before 1914. In the decade before the war, however, the gap between the two sectors had begun to close; this trend was now reversed. Although the pressures of war do not

Table 12.1 The shifting industrial structure, 1914–18

Product	Percentage change
Chemicals	+ 170%
Mechanical engineering and electrical	+ 49%
Timber	+ 13%
Metal processing	+ 8%
Mining	+ 5%
Leather	− 17%
Paper	− 20%
Food	− 24%
Printing	− 31%
Clothing	− 32%
Construction	− 57%
Textiles	− 58%
Quarrying and clay	− 59%

seem to have created such acute difficulties in Germany as occurred in Italy, where excess capacity in heavy industry led to a serious post-war crisis, it is fair to say that excessive heavy-industrial capacity proved to be a severe burden for the Weimar Republic to bear. Overall, the effect of the war was to reinforce the long-term trend towards larger units of production at the expense of small firms, which had virtually no say in the War Raw Materials Corporations that played a large role in the management of the wartime economy. Agriculture also continued to lose ground *vis-à-vis* industry and commerce, although this was not immediately apparent during the war owing to dramatic rises in the prices of all agricultural products and to relatively high farm profits. Government attempts to regulate agricultural production – in particular, through controls over marketing – did little to alter the position, indeed merely made the rural population more angry about bureaucratic interference in their affairs.

It is not easy to assess the exact extent of the wartime restructuring of the German economy. We need to remember that the war effort affected different sectors of industry and commerce in very different ways. In many cases what counted was not so much the economic efficiency of a firm as whether its owner or managing director had, or had not, been able to obtain exemption from military service. As the war went on, the military authorities responsible for the allocation of raw materials took increasing care to place orders with smaller producers and craftsmen in order to head off the widespread complaint that the impact of state intervention in the economy had been inequitable. Nevertheless, although there was no explicit policy of favouring big producers, the general trend was in that direction, and big firms undoubtedly fared better during the war. Profits in the iron and steel industry, for example, were significantly above the average, as figures for dividends show in Table 12.2.

Table 12.2 Dividends in German industry, 1914–18
(values of shares (nominal value 1.00))

Period	Iron and steel	Chemicals	Average
1913–14	8.33	5.94	7.96
1914–15	5.69	5.43	5.00
1915–16	10.00	9.69	9.90
1916–17	14.58	11.81	6.52
1917–18	9.60	10.88	5.41

Not surprisingly, contemporaries complained bitterly about the new class of 'war profiteers' who seemed to be reaping enormous rewards from war production while the mass of the population had to put up with excessive working hours, under-nourishment and shortages of consumer goods of all kinds. There were somewhat belated attempts to impose a special tax on war profits, but it is questionable whether they were very effective. On the face of it, the war made a small number of owners of capital very much richer, while subjecting the great bulk of the population to mounting poverty. This is certainly the conclusion that Kocka reaches in *Facing Total War*: '... it would seem that, apart from the early adaptation crisis and the months of collapse in 1918, the War was not unprofitable for the large industrial enterprises generally.'[5]

In view of the general movement of prices, however, even this very judicious assessment may not be entirely correct. It should be noted that dividends, and probably also profits, lagged well behind prices during the war. If an index of 100 in 1913 is taken as a base, wholesale prices rose from 106 in 1914 to 415 in 1919: an increase of 300 per cent. There were certainly plenty of people who made big personal fortunes by skilfully exploiting the new economic opportunities the war had created (and by evading tax), but by and large all sections of the population, including the owners of capital, incurred sizeable financial losses. The question is how large these losses were, and which groups suffered more than others and which groups less. The precise extent to which different sections of society were affected by the general process of impoverishment that took place during the war remains a matter of considerable dispute.

Kocka argues that German society came significantly closer during the war to being a class society in the classic sense of the term. He maintains that the war exacerbated class divisions, citing as evidence the falling trend in real wages and the relatively high profits that were earned in the war industries: employers in these industries, he says – about 120,000 people, by his reckoning – saw a marked improvement in their economic position. It is certainly beyond doubt that the entrepreneurial class was among the gainers during the war, albeit only in relative terms. Equally, the working class, taken as a whole, was among the losers. Kocka also makes the important claim, however, that the war led to polarization within the middle class. The new middle class – made up particularly of white-collar workers – suffered a considerable fall in real income. Its social status, which previously had been perceptibly higher than that of the working class, was undermined: indeed, white-collar workers became proletarianized and politically radicalized. By contrast, Kocka maintains, the old *Mittelstand*, made up, in particular, of higher civil servants, small businessmen and rentiers, while also undergoing a loss of social status, continued to feel a much closer affinity to the industrialist camp than to the working-class masses, and its members turned their faces firmly against all forms of state socialism and state intervention in the economy. In Kocka's view, this split within the middle class reinforced the sharpening of divisions between entrepreneurs and the working class that was created by the war.

There is no doubt that the economics of war brought about important changes in social stratification and social attitudes in Germany. It is debatable, however, whether the schematic dichotomy between the propertied and working classes that Kocka invokes (albeit as a broad frame of reference rather than as part of a substantive theory) is a particularly suitable way of describing the complex processes of social change that took place during the war. This point applies particularly to the position of the working class within the wartime economy.

It is clear that money wages both of skilled and unskilled workers rose significantly (except during the first months of the war, when the economy was in a state of considerable upheaval). In addition, with the dramatic rise in female employment, as women in large numbers took over the jobs of their husbands or sons, wage differentials between male and female workers narrowed markedly. The same was true of differentials between skilled and unskilled workers (though the available aggregate data do not take account of the fact that many skilled jobs were taken over by less well qualified workers whose wages rose accordingly). For these various reasons, not surprisingly, the relative status of skilled workers, which previously had been higher than that of the great majority of workers in general, declined; by the same token, the economic interests of the working class became increasingly homogeneous. The result might have been to make the working class more cohesive and to strengthen its class consciousness, which in turn would tend to bear out Kocka's thesis of sharpening class divisions. The main reason, however, for the relative decline in socio-economic differentiation within the working class would appear to be the fact that workers switched jobs more rapidly as a result of wartime economic conditions. This, though, would not necessarily have produced a rise in class consciousness.

Although money wages increased steadily, workers' real wages fell sharply, at any rate until 1917. On the other hand, from the late autumn of 1917 onwards organized labour was successful in stemming any significant further decline in real wages. It should be borne in mind, admittedly, that the statistics ignore the fact that the real living standards of the great bulk of the population continued to deteriorate dramatically. Money could not buy sufficient quantities of consumer goods, and workers commonly had no option but to resort to the black market. The distress suffered by the working class is amply documented. Nevertheless, certain groups of skilled workers, such as those in the Berlin engineering industry, were able to earn exceptionally high wages, and from 1917 onwards it was common practice for skilled workers to play off one employer against another. With labour scarce, and production costs counting for little, employers were prepared to keep raising wages, secure in the knowledge that the authorities would buy their products regardless of price.

Altogether, it is not easy to reach a reliable assessment of the position of the working class. It seems probable, however, that despite the widespread and mounting hardship in the industrial centres, the income levels and general economic situation of organized industrial workers had more or less stabilized by the later stages of the war, at any rate in comparison with the situation of the population as a whole. We need to bear in mind, admittedly, that wage levels were highly conditional on location and industrial sector. In the coal mines of the Ruhr, face-workers and hauliers plainly failed to maintain their levels of real wages after 1917, and unskilled workers in key state factories comfortably overtook them. Printers, who had constituted one of the highest-paid groups of workers before the war, fared comparatively worse.[6] Although, as Bry argues, differentials between wages in vital war industries and those elsewhere became less marked after 1917, they were nevertheless significant over the period as a whole.[7] The cost of living also varied considerably from place to place, and even though the authorities tried to compensate for the relatively high living costs and severe supply shortages in the big cities by paying special bonuses, these differences were by no means eliminated. In view of the difficulties, therefore, in providing a reliable assessment of the movement of real wages, the global figures shown in Table 12.3 should be treated with great caution. All the same, they clearly demonstrate the general trend we have described.[8]

Table 12.3 Relative real wages in Germany and Great Britain, 1914–18 (1914 = 100)

Year	Germany	Great Britain
1915	96	86
1916	87	80
1917	79	75
1918	77	85

The relative easing-off of the fall in real wages from 1917 onwards, which was certainly significant in view of the dramatic deterioration in supplies of food and consumer goods, was broadly mirrored by events in the political sphere. In 1916, in response to strong pressure from the Supreme Command, the government introduced the so-called 'Hindenburg programme', under which the economic war effort would be stepped up as far as possible. The nation's human and material resources would be fully mobilized for war production, regardless of the ensuing economic and social costs. The aim was to maximize the production of war materials while at the same time calling up even more workers into the armed forces. Circumstances, however, had reached the point where was no prospect of achieving these goals without the co-operation of the trade unions. Accordingly, the Hindenburg programme now officially acknowledged the unions as equal partners. Although in practice the attitudes of employers and the military authorities towards trade unions did not change appreciably, and industrial relations were still coloured by the employers' longstanding misgivings about trade-union power, this was nevertheless a first step in the direction of a system of social partnership. From now on the trade unions were consulted on a regular basis and were able to exert a significant influence over legislation affecting wage and price policies. It is fair to conclude, moreover, that the effects on the material welfare of the working population were on the whole beneficial. The unions succeeded, for example, in excluding from the Hindenburg programme all provisions that would have restricted workers' freedom of choice of employment. Those sections of the workforce, in other words, that had been able to exploit the labour market by changing employers frequently, and so obtaining higher wages (as had become common practice in the engineering industries, for example) retained the ability to do so.

Such gains were perhaps limited in monetary terms, but they constituted a breakthrough none the less. The working class had proved itself to be a powerful bargaining group within the economy, at a time when almost all other sections of society were continuing to lose ground. This did not mean that Imperial German society had reached a state of outright polarization between organized labour, on the one hand, and the propertied classes, the professions, agriculture and non-unionized wage earners on the other; there was never a division into 'two nations' (the working class, and the rest of the population) of the sort that *The Times*, echoing Disraeli, claimed had come about in Great Britain as a result of the war.[9] The industrial working class, however, had plainly ceased to be the weakest group within the working population. Indeed, if we analyse the economic situation of other sections of German society, we can see that some them fared decidedly worse than industrial workers did.

One of the groups that suffered the greatest fall in real income was the higher civil service. Civil servants' money incomes remained more or less constant during the war: this was tantamount to a virtual halving of their income in real terms.[10] The only conceivable way in which this group was able to survive was by drawing on its accumulated savings. Since salary increases generally took the form of uniform cost-of-living allowances for all salary groups, rather than percentage rises, civil servants on middle and lower salary scales were somewhat less seriously affected, but they too did worse than industrial workers. Statistics published by the Imperial Statistical Office show that the salaries of civil servants on the lowest grades fell to about 70 per cent of their pre-war levels, probably more or less in line with the fall in national average earnings. Salaries of middle-rank civil servants, on the other hand, fell to about 55 per cent of pre-war levels, and of higher-rank civil servants to 47 per cent. In other words, the middle and topmost echelons of the public service – people who had generally received some form of higher education – lost the relatively comfortable social position they had previously enjoyed. The levelling-out in social status of the professional middle classes had been a general long-term trend, but the war served to accelerate it.

Another group to suffer a marked decline in social status as a result of wartime economic policies and galloping inflation was that comprising small businessmen and craftsmen, apart from those who worked in sectors immediately germane to the war effort or who owned a substantial amount of property. This group had always particularly prided itself on its independent status *vis-à-vis* both the working class and industrial employers. Those craftsmen who supplied goods or services that had a direct or indirect bearing on war production undoubtedly came off better than the great majority of their colleagues, but all occupations associated with retailing or services to the general consumer seem to have undergone a sharp drop in income. Publicans and small shopkeepers were hit particularly hard. As Kocka demonstrates, the actual number of small businesses did not fall appreciably during the war years, but the fall in income suffered by small retailers, publicans and people in consumer-based businesses was probably even greater than that experienced by industrial workers, at any rate if the position before the war is taken as a yardstick.

The situation in agriculture is difficult to establish. Both the peasantry and the big landowners did well during the war, thanks to the dramatic rise in the prices of all agricultural products and the limited effectiveness of the government's attempts to impose price restraint. In addition, inflation had the indirect effect of reducing significantly the burden of debt that was carried by the large landowners. On the other hand, even though agriculture enjoyed a favourable market position, it also faced a number of serious problems. Military recruitment affected the countryside more severely than the cities, exacerbating an already acute shortage of agricultural labour. This made it even harder for farmers to maintain agricultural production under wartime conditions, especially since fertilizers and agricultural machinery were also in limited supply so that in many areas the soil became exhausted. Only a limited proportion of the shortfall in labour could be made up by the use of prisoners of war. The amount of land in production was reduced, and there was a shift from grain to livestock production.

Moreover, the restructuring of the economy adversely affected the position of agriculture relative to other sectors, at any rate in the long run. Farm workers had begun to leave the land in large numbers well before the war, seeking more lucrative employment in the cities. What had already been a serious quandary for the large landowners became even more acute in wartime, as wages in war-related industries surged ahead of those on the land; agricultural wages had to rise in order not to lag too far behind. After the war was over, this trend proved impossible to reverse. The measure of prosperity that agriculture had enjoyed during the war, in other words, later worked to its disadvantage and played a part in accelerating its relative decline within the economy as a whole. In 1913 agriculture, forestry and fisheries had accounted for 23.2 per cent of Germany's national wealth; by 1925 this share had fallen to 15.7 per cent.[11] Since the agricultural sector continued to employ 30 per cent of the workforce, it is clear that agricultural incomes fell substantially. These figures indicate that the position of agriculture was not as rosy as might appear at first sight, despite the fact that huge windfall profits were made during the war as a result of desperate food shortages.

The war, then, did not lead to a profound economic transformation in Germany. (There was little support, incidentally, even among trade unions, for those like Wissell and Möllendorf who urged that the centralized direction of the war economy be retained in peacetime, in the form of state socialism.) On the other hand, the war did see some significant shifts of balance in the structure of the economy. Some of these shifts, admittedly, were merely the product of an acceleration of trends that had been under way long before the outbreak of war: the rise of large firms at the expense of small and middle-sized businesses, for example, and the decline of craft methods of production. But the very fact that so much change occurred within such a short space of time was itself a source of destabilization, and during the 1920s this placed an added strain on a social system that was in any case riven by other crises. We should remember that traditional social structures and patterns of behaviour had remained well entrenched in Imperial Germany, despite the spectacular rise of large-scale industry from the 1880s onwards. The process of adjustment to industrialization was therefore inevitably a painful one for many social groups, but the effects were particularly keenly felt by those for which the process was most rapid – small businesses and the craft trades being the most obvious cases in point. The particular circumstances of the war also created certain specific structural distortions in the economy that hampered growth during the post-war period. The iron and steel industry, for example, expanded disproportionately during the war; vital external trading links were lost, so that exporters had difficulties in re-establishing a foothold in overseas markets; German agriculture became increasingly uncompetitive within the international economy. All of these processes, again, had already been in train for some time, but the war speeded them up considerably. Finally, the war saw a growing acceptance of state intervention, in place of market forces, as a way of dealing with economic problems. Max Weber was one of those who argued that the most urgent priority was was to restore Germany's competitiveness, which had been badly damaged by the demands of war, though he recognized that this would be a difficult task and that the United States would inevitably come to dominate the world economy.

Let us now review the position in which the different sections of German society found themselves once the war was over.

The agricultural community had managed to preserve its privileged social position during the war, shielded by the state from the winds of economic change and overseas competition, though it had had to accept a great deal of government intervention in the process. At the end of the war, however, its traditionally privileged status as a protected sector collapsed overnight and it found itself without the substantial state subsidies it had received in the past.

The comparatively high status enjoyed by the upper middle classes before the war – in particular, by the higher civil service and the professions – had been a distinctive feature of German society. By 1919, however, they had badly lost out, partly owing to their relative impoverishment during the war and partly because they had invested such a large proportion of their savings in war bonds that now retained merely a fraction of their earlier value. Whether or not some of these groups were actually 'dispossessed' is a moot point; but they were certainly the main losers in socio-economic terms. The same applied, on a somewhat lesser scale, to those small businessmen and craft tradesmen who were involved in retailing and services, though it should be borne in mind that the sharp fall in their status was merely an acceleration of a trend that had already been under way for some time.

The position of the working class at the end of the war was by no means a happy one. Workers had undoubtedly been hardest hit by shortages of food and of virtually all kinds of consumer goods, and they had suffered most from the miserable economic and social conditions that had been prevalent during the war in nearly all of the industrial regions of the country. The dramatic rise in the number of strikes in 1917, to say nothing of the draconian counter-measures that were taken by the military authorities (a common sanction being to enlist strike leaders into the armed forces, even though as skilled workers they were usually exempt from military service) is clear evidence that conditions in the working-class districts of the big industrial centres had become intolerable. By the last year of the war, discontent among workers had become so widespread, usually with good reason, that trade-union leaders found it difficult to resist calls for strike action in the way they had during the previous three years. At the same time, however, we should note that these strikes were mainly directed against the war policies of the government rather than against employers, though they were often triggered by economic factors such as shortages of food or other goods.

The founding of the Independent Social Democratic Party (USPD) in 1917 came about largely as the result of deep-seated differences of opinion within the socialist camp, in particular over the question whether the strategy of benevolent tolerance of the Imperial government was still justified or not. Political considerations were uppermost in the argument. The labour movement had become increasingly impatient with the government's war-aims policy and with the procrastination of both the government and the conservative parties over reform of the three-class system of suffrage in Prussia. As Lademacher has pointed out, the radical Zimmerwalder group had very little support among the German working class at the end of the war, despite the growing distress of the great bulk of the population. Working-class protest was directed primarily against the government's policies and, in particular, against the Supreme Command, which was still staking its hopes on outright military victory and extensive annexations in both east and west. No serious assault on the prevailing social order was in prospect, even though there was undoubtedly a great deal of support for socialist ideas. It was no coincidence that there was a wave of strikes when it became obvious to all, with the collapse of negotiations at Brest-Litovsk, that the government and the military were still bent on outright victory regardless of the desperate misery on the home front. Revolutionary propaganda from Russia did play a part, but it is plain that its significance was limited. The dominant impulse was a desire for peace at any price and for an end to the sufferings of the people, regardless of the political consequences.

Discontent among the industrial working class continued to mount after January 1918, and the trade unions and the Social Democratic party leadership, which persisted in their policy of support for the war effort, found it increasingly difficult to keep the discontent within bounds. The working class, however, was in no sense intent at this stage on revolution in a socialist sense. The strikes and protests remained clearly directed against the system of government and the policies of the Imperial authorities, and, in particular, against the military leadership, which was deeply mistrusted by workers; they were not targeted against the economic system as such. The spreading working-class resentment was not caused only by increased hardship and disillusionment: it reflected an awareness that the strength of the working class within the system could no longer be ignored. Workers had become much more conscious of the fact that the functioning of the war machine was vitally dependent on their own willingness to supply their labour. Effectively confirming this, the authorities began to be more flexible in their response to strikes and protests and to desist from applying the usual harshly repressive methods, for fear of provoking yet further waves of protest that they would be unable to control (although indirect kinds of pressure, such as the enlistment of strike leaders and known representatives of the far left, continued to be widely used.)

Despite rising popular discontent and increasing shortages, the great bulk of the working class was still prepared to support the loyalist policies of the Social Democratic party leadership. Syndicalist and ultra-radical ideas had some currency on the fringes, but remained insignificant in purely numerical terms for the time being. Though it may seem paradoxical to say so, the working class did not count itself among the losers from the war. Certainly, the leaders of the trade unions and of the Majority Social Democrats were convinced that they had to stick to their policy, not only because it was in the national interest but because they believed that the full emancipation of the working class within the prevailing socio-economic system was at hand. All told, from 1917 onwards both the political and the economic bargaining position of the labour movement had steadily improved, and its leaders knew it.

This explains why the German revolution of 1918–19 was not a socialist revolution, even though political power fell overnight into the socialist parties' lap without the need for a struggle. It likewise explains why the revolution did not become socialist later on, for all that the middle classes saw that as a potent threat. What did take place was a huge surge of protest against the prevailing system, led by sections of the industrial working class which previously had not been politically organized and which favoured syndicalist tactics that promised immediate results. This protest movement got under way, somewhat belatedly, in January and February 1919 and was not really quelled until 1920, when the crisis in the Ruhr came to an end. These waves of protest, however, really had little connection with the official policies of the socialist parties, either of the Majority Social Democrats or of the Communists. They were inspired by a variety of vague syndicalist and socialist ideas, not by the very different tenets of scientific socialism as expounded by Marx, Kautsky or Bernstein. Part of the reason why the Majority Social Democrats, aided by the German Democratic party and the Centre party, finally succeeded in halting the campaign of mass strikes that dominated the first half of 1919 was that both government and employers chose to accede to most of the workers' economic demands in order to stave off any process of further radicalization. In many cases, demands for higher wages were met at once, with the effect that industrial workers not only made up much of the ground that they had lost during the war but did so significantly more rapidly than other social groups. (It should, of course, be added that most of these gains were then lost once more during the hyper-inflation of 1921–22.)

Recent research on the German inflation, incidentally, confirms that during the revolutionary period government and employers regarded full employment and a relatively high level of wages as indispensable political objectives. They were seen as more important than balancing the budget, despite their potential for accelerating the rate of inflation. Knut Borchardt, indeed, has argued that it was only by virtue of inflationary budgeting that the Weimar experiment in democracy was possible at all.[12] His studies of the Great Depression and of the economic policies of the Weimar Republic have provoked an impassioned debate on the question whether wage levels of German workers in the 1920s were too high to allow German industry to remain internationally competitive.[13] If that was indeed the case, it can plausibly be included among the socio-economic consequences of the First World War.

Leaving this specific controversy aside, however, it seems clear that the main factor that shaped the course of events in Germany after the war was not a process of polarization between an impoverished working class and upper-middle-class employers, but the decline of the traditional middle strata of society. It was the middle classes, pinning the blame for their misfortunes on the left, who unleashed a chain reaction that eventually undermined the Weimar political order. Trade-union leaders and entrepreneurs, by contrast, together decided in November 1918 that the moment was right for trying to stabilize socio-economic relations by establishing a system of social partnership between workers and employers. The unions believed that they were offered a unique opportunity for consolidating the influence over economic policy that they had acquired during the war years, joining 'Arbeitsgemeinschaft', or 'working association', that was instituted on 10 November 1918 was designed to give institutional form to their new role. Borchardt's claim that this agreement was really an attempt by the unions to forestall a radical revolution[14] is questionable: the unions saw it, first and foremost, as a way of securing their position on the commanding heights of the economy. (Admittedly, the unions' confident assumption that the November agreement would be honoured by the workers was not fulfilled. During the second phase of the revolution the workers opted to pursue their economic and political objectives by means of 'direct action', a tactic that included the demand for 'socialization'. What this meant, though, was not the conversion of the economy into a centrally directed system with a large bureaucractic apparatus , but the management of large enterprises by their workers.)

These events add weight to the argument that it was not the working class that had suffered the greatest loss in social and economic status during the war, as compared with its pre-war position, but the middle classes. The biggest losers of all were certain sections of the old *Mittelstand*: civil servants, white-collar workers and various groups of craftsmen who occupied a rather precarious position midway between business and the working class. These middle strata also suffered indirectly by having invested a high proportion of their savings in war loans that had now lost their value. The decline in the socio-economic status of these groups as a result of the First World War is not easy to quantify but is quite indisputable, though we must also recognize that their status had already begun to be gradually eroded as Germany became transformed into an advanced industrial society.

The rise in the number of wage-earners as a proportion of the overall population during and after the war is another important symptom of the same socio-economic trend. If it is perhaps too strong to say that the old *Mittelstand* was 'dispossessed', the war certainly accelerated the emergence of social structures characteristic of advanced industrial societies, at the expense of traditional patterns. However the great speed with which this restructuring took place made it particularly difficult for the groups concerned to adjust to these changes. Their response was one of deep resentment and political radicalization.

This helps to explain why the middle classes in Weimar Germany were far more susceptible to anti-Marxist propaganda than their counterparts in other European countries. The bitter arguments about the reasons for Germany's defeat and about the Versailles peace settlement were a direct product of the social and economic straits in which the middle classes now found themselves. It is scarcely surprising that the middle classes steadily moved towards the right and eventually gave their support to National Socialism. The fate of the Weimar Republic was, in a sense, sealed from the start. We should not antedate the origins of fascism, but it is clear that against this background the National Socialist pledge to liberate Germany both from Marxism and from the excesses of capitalism was likely to find a wide and receptive audience. The same applies to the hostility towards modernity that was a central part of National Socialist ideology (though not, in practice, of National Socialist policy), with its promise of a return to a society in which peasants, small businessmen, craftsmen and shopkeepers would be shielded against the relentless pressures of competition from big business.

We should also note that the war economy and the economic changes that had been caused by wartime market distortions served to exacerbate serious imbalances that had already been present in the structure of the Imperial economy. In heavy industry, considerable excess capacity had been built up during the war, and not enough attention had been paid to the problems of technological innovation and cost-effectiveness; competitiveness had suffered accordingly. In the chemical industry, which had also expanded during the war, the main hope was that problems would be solved by cartelization and the control of domestic prices; there was also talk of a cartel agreement covering the international market. The banks, which had fared reasonably well during the war, were willing to follow where industry led. Small firms, on the other hand, never recovered from the effects of wartime state intervention. In 1907 the self-employed accounted for 15.3 per cent of those active in industry and the craft trades; by 1925 the proportion had fallen to 10.7 per cent. In commerce and transport the decline in the proportion of the self-employed was even sharper, from 29.1 per cent in 1907 to 21.6 per cent in 1925.[16] Again, the war was not the sole cause of these changes, but it certainly seems to have accelerated them.

There is no doubt that the structural imbalances in the economy that resulted from the pressures of war significantly exacerbated the economic problems that the Weimar Republic had to face, even though these problems were not really to come to a head until after the period of relative expansion between 1924 and 1928, with the onset of the Great Depression. It is not surprising that employers took the view that the only way to solve these problems was to make drastic cuts in the welfare state so that labour costs could be reduced. When democratic governments proved unwilling, or unable, to follow this course, employers started to look towards authoritarian alternatives; or, at any rate, decided that such alternatives should not be resisted if they were proposed on other grounds.

A final word on agriculture between the wars. As we have noted, the war years were comparatively good ones for the agricultural sector. In the postwar period, however, agriculture suddenly found itself at the mercy of unrestricted international competition. Not surprisingly, the response of both the large landowners and the peasantry was to look back wistfully to the golden days when the state had protected them from overseas competitors and had granted them generous tax relief and other benefits, both direct and indirect. Of all social groups in Germany, they had most difficulty in adjusting to the new conditions. The peasants were among the earliest supporters of National Socialism, while the landed aristocracy played a crucial part in the forging of the coalition between the traditional right and the National Socialists that paved the way for Hitler's appointment as Chancellor. There are good reasons for saying that the seedbed for the growth of extremist nationalism and the eventual rise to power of the National Socialists was a set of social and economic factors and mental attitudes that had their origins in the First World War.

13

The German revolution, 1918-1920: political revolution and social protest

The revolutionary movements which marked the collapse of the German Empire at the end of the First World War, and which an earlier generation of scholars used to label, in very inaccurate shorthand, as 'the November revolution', have long been a favoured topic of historical research, not only in the Federal Republic and the German Democratic Republic but also among Anglo-Saxon scholars.[1] This is scarcely surprising, since the events of the revolution and its aftermath had a considerable bearing on later developments in German politics, while the eventual breakdown of the new, unstable Weimar system, and the rise to power of the National Socialists, in turn had a fateful impact on Europe and the world. As early as 1928, Arthur Rosenberg posed the question whether German democracy might not have taken firmer root if the revolution had followed a different course and ushered in more far-reaching changes in German society;[2] and recent studies of the years immediately after 1918 have repeatedly returned to the same question. The Majority Social Democrats, in particular, have been accused – on varying grounds, and at times with some severity – of failing to seize the opportunities of the moment. The charge has been that instead of pressing ahead with the revolution to the point at which the foundations of a truly democratic new order might have been laid, they set their faces against radical change and did all they could to halt it in its tracks. Correspondingly, most of these recent studies have been concerned, from their differing standpoints, to scour the events of the period for pointers to alternative positions which the leading participants in the revolution might have adopted and against which their actual attitudes and actions may be judged.

So long as it is openly acknowledged that the search for alternative outcomes belongs to the realm of the counter-factual, this way of proceeding is perfectly legitimate from an academic point of view. It has significantly extended our insight into the German revolution of 1918–20, and has led to the emergence of new criteria for assessing the revolution which, whether valid or not, certainly enable us to determine much more precisely the period's historical significance. At the same time, of course, it has to be said that the search for other, and perhaps more salutary, paths that the revolution might have taken has gone hand in hand with attempts to give legitimacy to political ideas that are at odds, to a greater or lesser degree, with those of western parliamentary democracy. Since the late 1960s, with the rise of the student movement and the 'New Left', both of which have subscribed to a romantic-utopian, anti-authoritarian version of Marxism, the German revolution of 1918–20 has become a veritable battlefield, as those campaigning for alternatives to parliamentary democracy have sought to invoke the revolution as historical evidence in favour of their case. In particular, there has been a great deal of interest in the system of *Räte* – the workers' and soldiers' councils, or soviets – which the socialist left fought bitterly to make permanent, especially from the end of 1918 onwards, though without making many converts to their cause among the Majority Social Democrats.

In point of fact, the pioneering studies of the *Räte* had already come out before the 1960s, partially anticipating the romantic neo-Marxist ideas that were later to obtain wide currency among the younger generation. We should mention, in particular, the work of Tormin, Kolb and von Oertzen, who were the first to describe the councils movement, in basically favourable terms, as an instance of spontaneous democratic action.[3] (Historians in the German Democratic Republic, incidentally, have always regarded the German revolution as part of the prehistory of the GDR alone; the Federal Republic has been cast as the belated offspring of the counter-revolutionary forces of 1918–19. And yet they have always been hard put to it to adopt a coherent attitude towards the diffuse phenomenon of the workers' and soldiers' councils. According to strict Marxist–Leninist historical doctrine, although the councils sometimes represented progressive attitudes – notably during the early stages of the revolution – they adopted a 'reactionary' posture at the critical moments of the revolutionary process.)[4] Subsequently there has been a wealth of work on the councils, and rather less on the activities and internal workings of the different parties and political groupings that played a leading role in the revolution. A large number of regional studies have also been published, which, though very variable in approach and quality, have enabled us to construct a precise analysis of the events of the revolution across the country as a whole, and not merely in the big cities. Altogether, the volume of information about the revolution has expanded enormously, and our understanding has correspondingly deepened, for all that the literature has embodied a wide range of attitudes and assumptions.

It goes without saying that earlier writing on the period had been equally influenced by contemporary preoccupations and criteria of evaluation, these in turn partially reflecting the basic political attitudes prevalent in German society at the time. This becomes readily apparent if we examine the historiographical record, which shows that the study of the revolution of 1918–20 has gone through a number of different phases since 1945. At first there was a strong emphasis on the positive achievements of the Majority Social Democrats, in reaction to the demagogic propaganda that had been produced after 1918 by the German right and then by the National Socialists, directed in particular against the 'November criminals'. It was argued that by adopting a realistic and responsible policy of moderation (postponing the realization of their own aims, and indeed making some heavy sacrifices) the Majority Social Democrats played a crucial part in bringing the democratic Weimar state into being and saving German society from sliding into communist dictatorship. According to Karl Dietrich Erdmann, the Majority Social Democrats were faced with a choice between the 'stark alternatives of social revolution in alliance with the forces that were pressing for the dictatorship of the proletariat, and a parliamentary republic in alliance with conservative elements such as the officer corps'.[5] This view was accompanied by the claim that the far-reaching compromises which the Social Democrats made with the forces of conservatism (that these compromises were disagreeable is hardly disputed) became necessary only as a result of the escalation of revolutionary activity that followed the infiltration of the German labour movement by small communist groups controlled from Russia.

In the course of the 1950s, however, the assumption – which had also been current at the time – that direct and indirect influence from Bolshevik Russia played a crucial part in the revolution was shown to be false. In 1954 Walter Tormin, in *Zwischen Rätediktatur und sozialer Demokratie*,[6] exploded the widespread myth that the councils movement had been Bolshevik in character. He demonstrated that while the movement had unquestionably derived inspiration from the Russian example, its central aim had been, not the 'dictatorship of the proletariat', but a new form of 'social democracy'. Further evidence that the goals of the councils movement were distinct from those of the communists came from studies by Anweiler, which showed that the soviets in Russia too had originally had nothing to do with Bolshevism and that it was only relatively late in the day that the Leninists took advantage of the soviet movement to further their own revolutionary ends.[7] Not until the workers' councils had been successfully infiltrated, shortly before the October revolution, did the Bolsheviks recognize them as suitable instruments in their political strategy, issuing the call 'All power to the soviets'. The emergence of similar workers' councils during the Hungarian uprising of 1956 also perhaps came as something of a revelation to those historians who had stubbornly stuck to the view that communism and the *Räte* movement were identical. More recent research, incidentally, has made it clear that the accusation that the councils were bent on a policy of Bolshevization was used by the the Majority Social Democrats at the time, partly indeed against their own better judgement, as a device for legitimizing their own, anti-revolutionary, policies.[8]

Starting with the studies by Kolb and von Oertzen, and also by Rürup, a steady stream of new work on the role of the workers' and soldiers' councils during the German revolution of 1918–20 now entirely overturned the earlier assumption that the councils movement had been a device for bringing about a communist revolution in Germany. It became clear that the councils had, in the main, emerged spontaneously as organs of provisional democratic self-government at a moment when the traditional institutions of authority in society had completely collapsed. As the established organs of authority abruptly forfeited their legitimacy in the eyes of the bulk of the population, leaving government in a state of breakdown or paralysis, so the workers' and soldiers' councils sprang up everywhere to fill the vacuum. Matthias had already stressed the spontaneous character of the movement, as it started with the soldiers and then spread to the workers; Kolb similarly maintained that the councils were an authentic expression of national revolt against a totally discredited *ancien régime*. Scholars still differed about the exact ideological make-up of the movement, but on one point there could no longer be scope for disagreement: the workers' and soldiers' councils were determined that German society should be reorganized on a democratic basis, and, in particular, that the traditional military authorities should be stripped of their power. On the other hand, the councils' views on socialization – whether or not it was desirable, and, if so, how it might be put into effect – were very diverse and, on the whole, fairly vague. It was not until the fighting in Berlin in January 1919, which marked the start of the second phase of the revolution, that the councils became both radicalized and broader-based. The Independent Social Democrats (USPD) and the Spartacus Union (Spartakusbund) now obtained majorities in many of the local council organizations and began to win backing for their own political aims, while in many cases the Majority Social Democrats withdrew. In the big cities, however, the left's attempts to gain political power with the help of the councils miscarried, usually in spectacular fashion.

Most historians would now maintain, on the basis of these findings, that the Majority Social Democrats failed to perceive the 'democratic potential of the workers' and soldiers' councils' and thereby missed a historic opportunity for carrying out, with the councils' support, a more far-reaching democratization of German society. On this view, instead of hastily committing themselves to an alliance with the officer corps and the rapidly reviving middle class, the Social Democrats ought to have pressed ahead with the revolution to the point at which it would have been possible to eradicate most of the surviving anti-democratic features of German society and build the solid foundations of a new democratic order.[9] One of the writers to have gone furthest in this direction is von Oertzen, who has argued that the establishment of 'proletarian democracy' based on the councils, or of a system combining the councils and Parliament, would have been a feasible alternative to the formal democracy of Weimar.[10] Rürup, too, in a series of publications, has claimed that the Social Democrats missed the opportunity of thoroughly dismantling the old authoritarian state and its social foundations, in alliance with the councils, and carrying out a 'far-reaching democratic reorganization of political, social and economic relations'. Such a reorganization, Rürup argues, would have provided a more stable basis for democracy than was created under Weimar, with its still highly traditional social structures. The revolution, he says, failed in its historic aim, which had been to 'liberate the great mass of the people from political and social subordination and to establish a constitution of freedom'. The history of the revolution was a 'history of continuous retreat'.[11]

Today, this general interpretation of the revolution – detailed emphases vary from one scholar to the next, Rürup being particularly outspoken – can be said to have become the standard view, even though older approaches can still be found, particularly in reference books and textbooks on the Weimar period. It rests on the premiss that democratic institutions will endure only if the principles of egalitarian democracy are enshrined within society itself, and not merely in the political system: to echo Lassalle, the real, and not merely the formal, constitution of a country must be democratic in structure if democracy is to be truly stable and proof against crises. The fact that Weimar democracy later failed to stand firm against the assaults that were made upon it, particularly by the right, has been a central pillar of this view. And yet there is surely something utopian about such thinking. Moreover, those who maintain that the momentum of the German revolution of 1918–20 should have been stepped up so that German society might have become truly democratized remain rather vague when it comes to specifying the actual policies that would have brought about such a result. The commonest argument is that primary and other key industries could have been nationalized, large estates expropriated, the machinery of the old civil service dismantled and the officer corps broken up. Nothing, however, is said about the concrete ways in which these measures might have been implemented, nor is it spelled out how far the process should have been taken or when it could have been regarded as completed. Above all, this whole approach stands or falls with the assumption that the workers' and soldiers' councils constituted a 'democratic potential' that would have been capable of underpinning a programme of substantive, and not merely formal, democratization in Germany if only the socialist revolutionary governments had recognized them as political partners – instead of, as was generally the case, first being obliged to tolerate them, while simultaneously trying as far as possible to manipulate them for their own purposes, and then, as soon as political circumstances permitted, either manoeuvring them to the political sidelines or doing away with them altogether.

A vast number of regional studies of the workers' and soldiers' councils have now been published, and the whole spectrum of the councils movement has been subjected to minute scrutiny. Kluge, for example, has closely examined the soldiers' councils that played a vital part in the first phase of the revolution in particular;[12] Muth has drawn attention to the peasants' councils, whose role was not confined solely to the Bavarian *Räterepubliken*, as had previously been assumed.[13] Only the middle-class councils that were also formed have not yet been properly investigated, since most of the surviving sources say nothing about them. All of this evidence undoubtedly establishes beyond question that the workers' and soldiers' councils – particularly during the first phase of the revolution, though in principle later too – constituted a political force that contributed to the establishment and upholding of democratic structures. That does not mean, however, that everything they did was in furtherance of the processes of revolution. Establishing democratic structures in the state and in society also entailed heading off left-wing insurrections and seeking to restrain huge strikes. Although most of the workers' and soldiers' councils moved perceptibly to the left after the spring of 1919, particularly at local level (a trend magnified by the fact that the representatives of the Majority Social Democrats withdrew from them) the councils as such, with rare exceptions, were not responsible for the attempted coups and strikes that shook German society first in the spring and early summmer of that year and then again in March and April 1920. Most councils either were clearly less militant than that or were merely swept along on the tide of these events. In few cases did the councils play a leading role from the start. The impetus for the second phase of the revolution came spontaneously from the workers themselves, not from the councils; not coincidentally, mines councils and factory councils now sprang up alongside the workers' and soldiers' councils. It was at this stage that control of many of the workers' councils passsed to Spartacist groups, supported by sections of the USPD.

In the first phase of the revolution, from November 1918 until the end of December, the councils, which had sprung up spontaneously as organs of self-government, were the true carriers of the banner of the revolutionary movement. Their activities, however, were directed primarily against the wielders of power in the old system. The old authorities having been overthrown at the first attempt, and power at national and *Land* level having fallen into the hands of the two Social Democratic parties without a struggle (indeed, in the main without effort on the Social Democrats' part) the workers' and soldiers' councils confined themselves to preventing the forces of reaction from fighting back. Only in a few instances did they embark on political initiatives that were directly at odds with the policy of the Council of People's Representatives (Rat der Volksbeauftragten). Indeed, by and large the Council of People's Representatives was able to count on the workers' and soldiers' councils as faithful allies in the struggle against the Spartacus Union and the extreme left, which had promptly set about transforming the rebellion against the *ancien régime* into a socialist revolution.

After the end of December 1918 and the January fighting in Berlin in 1919, the picture changed. Whereas the soldiers' councils had originally been a force for moderation within the *Räte* movement, they now began to play a more active role in resisting restorationist tendencies within the army. As the broad mass of the working class swung to the left, so left-wing representatives assumed a leading role in many of the local and regional councils, especially in those parts of the country where the left had already been strong; many representatives of the Majority Social Democrats stood down. It was only now that the socialist left's call, 'All power to the councils', and the notion that the councils system should become permanently institutionalized, began to pose a potential threat to the Majority Social Democrats. Nevertheless, the councils' swing to the left benefited the two rival socialist parties – the USPD and the Communist party (KPD, founded on 31 December 1918) – far less than has hitherto been assumed. The radicalization of the working class that took place at the start of 1919 cut right across the established pattern of party divisions within the labour movement. While the anarcho-utopian left made a whole string of attempts to set up local or regional *Räte* regimes, there was simultaneously a widespread spontaneous outbreak of social protest, largely bypassing the established workers' and soldiers' councils, which had as its direct target the workers' 'class enemies' in the shape of the big industrial employers. For the most part the workers' and soldiers' councils were left stranded by these rapid developments, and either had to adapt to the radical mood of the masses or made wary attempts to damp down the upsurge of strikes.

In the final phase of the revolution, which culminated in the 'Red Army' insurrection in the Ruhr that followed the Kapp putsch of 1920, the councils movement took on an entirely different character – in those parts of the country, that is, where it did not begin to falter completely, as happened in Munich after the collapse of the Second Republic. Most of the revolutionary activity now came from councils that were based on the workplace and that had little in common with the workers' and soldiers' councils of the earlier phases of the revolution. These councils were unambiguously committed to class warfare and, in the main, represented only the more radical elements within the industrial working class.

Bearing this broad pattern of events in mind, let us try to establish what sort of phenomenon the councils movement was. Were the councils really the vehicles of a spontaneous, revolutionary bid for power on the part of the broad mass of the population? Rürup maintains that the workers' and soldiers' councils 'emerged spontaneously [...] as the revolution's provisional instruments of struggle and authority'.[14] It is questionable, however, whether the councils can properly be described in such unqualified terms. In the first phase of the revolution, at least, the tactics of the workers' and soldiers' councils were largely defensive, not offensive. In Kiel the councils found themselves being driven virtually against their will to take what was effectively political action; their original intention had been solely to move against the military commanding authorities. And although the councils movement did then bring about the collapse of the old political order in

Germany, we should not forget that its objectives were limited. Its main targets were the traditional seats of political authority: in the first instance, in particular, the military. The councils were concerned to bolster the new regime against potential military counter-revolution and against any counter-revolutionary measures that might emanate from the bureaucracy; they did not propose to make permanent changes in the prevailing military command structure or the administrative hierarchy. This was the case even at the highest levels. The Central Council of the Workers' and Soldiers' Councils did lay claim to being the highest-ranking revolutionary organization, and hence the sovereign body of the revolution, but it made no attempt to translate this status into constitutional reality. It confined itself to asserting a right of control – the nature of which was never precisely defined and the scope of which was continually disputed – over the policies of the People's Representatives government. In practical terms, this right fell well short of the powers that the Imperial Reichstag had enjoyed.[15] With certain exceptions, the same pattern applied, in even more marked form, at regional and local level. By and large, during the first two phases of their existence, the workers' and soldiers' councils did no more than oversee the existing apparatus of government. Where they demanded a change in administrative organization, or a purge of personnel, this was usually to forestall any potential counter-revolutionary activity, not to create brand-new structures. By and large, apart from departmental heads, the only officials who were replaced at the councils' insistence were those responsible for the police. The councils certainly saw it as their responsibility to deal with matters that had a direct and significant bearing on the welfare of workers, such as food supplies or aspects of welfare policy, but on many of these questions they were acting with the approval or the connivance of the authorities.

The councils were not, admittedly, always as ready to co-operate with authority as they were in Cologne – where Sollmann informed 'our chief burgomaster Adenauer' that the revolution had taken place, whereupon the latter took a realistic view of the situation – or in Lübeck, where the workers' and soldiers' council announced on 7 November 1918: 'The provisional workers' and soldiers' council does not regard itself as a government, but presents demands to the authorities.'[16] But even in cases where particular council bodies temporarily succeeded, in response to pressure from left-wing socialist groups, in assuming power in a formal sense (as happened, for example, in Hamburg, Bremen, Düsseldorf and Braunschweig in November 1918) they nevertheless largely restricted themselves in practice to overseeing the apparatus of public administration. These council regimes remained façades. At most they exercised a form of dual authority on the model of the February revolution in Russia; never, however, proletarian dictatorship in the classical sense. Altogether, indeed, the most conspicuous feature of the German revolution was the fact that the 'overthrow of the system' went hand in hand with the full maintenance of 'public order' – a

fact to which the workers' and soldiers' councils themselves repeatedly referred with pride.

This account demonstrates that the workers' and soldiers' councils in no sense posed a threat of Bolshevik revolution in Germany. But it is also doubtful whether the *Räte* ever really aspired to make the system of government truly democratic – leaving aside the question whether they would actually have been capable of doing so, assuming that the Imperial government and the authorities had not stood in their way. There were, certainly, some calls for a programme of full-fledged democratization, but words were never really matched by deeds, even in the case of highly radical councils.[17] Moreover, in the rather few instances where a wholesale onslaught on the bureaucracy provoked strikes on the part of the groups of officials affected, the councils generally gave way at once.[18] The councils lacked not only the power, but also the will, to stage a full-scale confrontation with officialdom. They contented themselves with dismissing a small number of particularly disagreeable senior officials, usually on the grounds that the latter had been harbouring counter-revolutionary intentions. Nowhere, however, was there the sort of thorough-going reorganization of the bureaucracy that would have been an essential precondition for setting up a new democratic order on a firm basis.

We must conclude, therefore, that the claim that the councils were potential vehicles for a sweeping democratization of Germany's bureaucracy is overstated, given the absence of any clear-cut action by the councils to that end. There was only one sphere in regard to which the councils (contrary, indeed, to the views of the Council of People's Representatives) issued a very firm call for traditional structures of authority to be dismantled, and that was the army. Otherwise, however, the case for the 'democratic potential' of the workers' and soldiers' councils rests on fairly insecure foundations. Even Rürup admits that the councils served for the most part to stabilize, not undermine, the existing bureaucratic apparatus. All told, Bermbach is right when he says that 'the fact that the councils movement confined itself to having a say [...] and did not seek to exercise political leadership on its own [...] indicates the inherent limits to the effectiveness of the councils system', and that attempts to go further than this and descry a possible alternative form of constitutional structure involving the councils system cannot be sustained.[19]

With the withdrawal of the USPD members from the Council of People's Representatives at the end of December 1918, the revolution entered a new phase. The first spectacular high point of this second phase was the January uprising by the extreme left in Berlin; the climax came with a wave of huge strikes in the spring and early summer of 1919 in the Ruhr, Berlin and central Germany. The workers' and soldiers' councils now entirely lost the political initiative that they had held at the start of the revolution. The great bulk of the councils followed the lead of the Central Council, which formally transferred its powers to the National Assembly on 5 February 1919,

and acquiesced voluntarily in the efforts of the first parliamentary government of the Weimar Republic to bring the councils movement under control
and convert it into, at most, a vehicle representing purely economic interests. Those workers' and soldiers' councils that remained faithful to the
goal of a socialist version of democracy now mostly found themselves being
outflanked on the left by the spontaneous mass protest movement that had
sprung up within the working class.

This latter movement was fuelled by a mixture, not easy to separate, of
political motives and short-term economic grievances, of disappointment at
the meagre results of the revolution and immediate financial hardship. The
first signs of upheaval had been mass strikes by miners in Duisburg-
Hamborn in early December, called in explicit defiance of agreements
between the trade unions and the coal-owners' associations. The strikes
then spread in sporadic, unco-ordinated fashion to the whole of the coalfield of the eastern Ruhr. These outbreaks of industrial action, which the
'Alter Verband' (Old Federation), the official miners' union, described as
'wildcat strikes', had a decidedly syndicalist tinge. But although propaganda by the syndicalist Freie Vereinigung (Free Alliance) and similar organizations played some part in them, essentially they were spontaneous mass
outbursts, not inspired by any specific doctrine. They took the 'class enemy'
as their direct target and were powered by a deep mistrust of the established trade unions and the political organizations of the labour movement,
notably the Majority Social Democratic party.[20] Conventional economic
demands for shorter working hours and higher wages went hand in hand
with a call for the mining industry to be 'socialized'.

Earlier historians, following Spethmann's lead in particular, tended to see
the protest movement as the work of a small number of Spartacists, but this
was fundamentally to misunderstand its nature. It was a huge and powerful
groundswell, and it caught *all* sections of the political labour movement
unawares and unprepared. As recently as 23 November 1918 the Berlin
executive council of the workers' and soldiers' councils had affirmed the
principle that the socialization of private firms 'should be undertaken only
by the government, in systematic and organic fashion, taking all internal
and external matters into account'.[21] Now, however, the socialist parties
found themselves in head-on collision with a mass movement that wanted
to seize the mines at once, with the help of specially formed colliery councils. Ironically, the workers' belief – however misguided on political and
economic grounds – that their living and working conditions would auto-
matically improve as soon as the hated owners of capital had been ousted
was a direct consequence of years of socialist propaganda to the effect that
under the capitalist system the 'surplus value' produced by workers had
been unjustly appropriated by entrepreneurs and that under socialism the
workers would receive the full reward for their labour.

The broad mass of workers, including those who until now had given
their unconditional support to the policies of the Council of People's

Representatives, had also been growing increasingly angry that the revolution had achieved so little and that the People's Representatives had made far-reaching political concessions to the established powers within German society, the officer corps in particular. At this moment of apparently mounting mass working-class unrest, the fighting in Berlin erupted. The immediate cause was the dismissal on 5 January 1919 of Eichhorn, the Berlin chief of police and a member of the USPD, but the primary reason behind the outbreak was the fact that the newly founded KPD – or rather, its utopian left wing – believed that it was vitally important at such a juncture to establish power bases that would play a key role in any potential full-dress revolution. It was no accident that the Spartacists' main aim in the fighting was to gain control of the Berlin newspaper buildings, in particular that of *Vorwärts*, rather than to seize objectives of military importance. This goal was partly a symbolic one, having its roots in the change of line that had been forced on *Vorwärts* during the First World War, but the intention was also to acquire what was regarded as the best instrument for influencing the behaviour of the undirected mass movement of protest. The Spartacists wanted to silence, or cow, the bourgeois press too, but the first step towards the eventual victory of the revolutionary movement, they believed, was to end the powerful hold that the hated Majority Social Democrats still exerted over the masses, and capturing *Vorwärts* and changing its function therefore took priority.

The uprisings and attempted coups that took place in a whole series of German cities in the wake of the January fighting in Berlin – in Düsseldorf on 8–9 January, for example, and in Bremen a day later – were similarly inspired by the belief that it was essential, now that the working-class masses were really on the move at last, to exploit every political and propaganda opportunity to propel the revolution forward. In all cases, the amount of violence used was minimal. Contrary to widespread popular belief, there was never an intention to seize power by armed force, in defiance of the will of the broad mass of the working-class population. The Spartacists always confidently assumed that if the working class were kept properly informed – and, certainly, if the publicity organs of the Majority Social Democrats were silenced – then mass support would promptly be forthcoming. When it became clear that this was not the case, many of the Spartacist groups gave up of their own accord, often after only a few days. In Bremen, for example, the 'dictatorship of the proletariat' was quietly declared terminated on 14 January (just three days after it had been proclaimed) once it became apparent that the coup had no effective working-class backing. In most instances the use of Freikorps (free corps) and regular army units to depose these regimes was quite unnecessary. The German revolution of 1918–20 did not throw up a Lenin or a Trotsky, and the regimes would have collapsed anyway, from internal conflict as well as for lack of mass support, as indeed happened in the case of the first council dictatorship in Bavaria. By sending in Freikorps units ruthlessly to suppress

the left-wing socialist uprisings of the spring of 1919, the national government led by the Social Democrats made an historic error. In Austria, the
Social Democrats were faced with the selfsame problem, but chose to let
the radical left-wing movement run itself into the ground: there was no serious danger that a communist regime might be formed.[22]

The radicalization of the working-class masses that took place after
December 1918 caught all of the socialist parties more or less off guard: not
only the Majority Social Democrats and, to a lesser extent, the USPD,
which was hoping to swim with the revolutionary tide, but also the KPD.
The parties could not fully endorse the demands of the protest movement
while at the same time remaining faithful to their doctrinal principles.[23] For
the protestors, 'socialization' meant the transfer of the running of a firm to
its workforce – not, however, because this was a step towards a 'fundamental restructuring of social relations as a whole', but because they believed
that it would bring about an immediate improvement in their living conditions.[24]

This becomes clear if we look at the outcome of the movement for socialization that got under way in Essen in the course of the wave of mass
strikes of January 1919. On 9 January 1919 the Essen workers' and soldiers' council, which contained equal numbers of representatives of all
three socialist parties, resolved of its own accord to proclaim the socialization of the mining companies. Then, on 13 January, in direct response to
mass workers' demonstrations, a manifesto calling for the 'immediate
socialization of the coal mines' was issued by the Council of People's
Representatives and a nine-man commission was charged with the task of
drafting plans to bring this about. The immediate purpose of these actions
was to end the strikes in the Ruhr coalfield, which were having a catastrophic effect on the whole economy; whether the plan, however, with all
its provisions for effecting the transfer of direct control of collieries to their
workforces, might actually have been implemented at short notice, is highly
debatable.[25] The political nature of the manifesto is immediately apparent
from its emotional language:[26]

> Socialization is not a word that everyone understands. It means that
> the exploitation of the worker by the employer shall be brought to an
> end; that large firms shall be taken from the capitalist and become the
> property of the people. In future, no one shall be able to grow effort-
> lessly rich through the labour of others; all those who work shall ben-
> efit from the fruits of their own labour. We shall begin with the mines
> – with those mineral resources which, more than any others, belong
> by right to the people and not to a chosen few.

The miners were given an explicit assurance that socialization would be
combined with a workplace-based council system that would ensure 'joint
participation in decisions by workers on all questions, major and minor'.
Yet neither the socialist parties nor the Council of People's Representatives

contemplated keeping to these promises in full. The Council of People's Representatives was not in a position to do so, because it did not want to pre-empt any decisions by the Constituent Assembly. But the Majority Social Democrats were opposed to any real socialization measures in any case, because they regarded them as inappropriate and economically damaging at that stage. The Council accordingly confined itself – 'pending the statutory provision of comprehensive national control of the whole of the coal-mining industry, and pending the establishment of participation in its proceeds by the people as a whole, or socialization' – to appointing three national commissioners for the Rhineland-Westphalia coalfield. These were the mining director Röhrig, the industrialist Vögler and the trade-union leader Otto Hué: all of them men who could definitely be expected to thwart the socialization of the mines.[27]

Not surprisingly, the Freie Gewerkschaften (Free Trade Unions) were particularly indignant about the strike movement, which for the most part had come about against their wishes. At the start of the revolution the trade-union leaders had believed that they would be able to regulate production on a broad scale in tandem with the employers; but the strikes had left them completely out-manoeuvred. The only account Otto Hué could give of what had happened was that the strikes had mainly taken hold in areas 'where the socialist movement among the miners was least broad and deep'. He complained bitterly:[28]

> The very fact that all comradely representations of the urgent necessity for alleviating the great shortage of coal at the present time have made so little impression on the workers concerned is proof that we are not dealing with well-schooled, convinced socialists. The socialist will put the common interest first. [...] In these strike movements, however, which to those unacquainted with the circumstances may seem to be a demonstration in favour of the socialization of the mines, we have, on the contrary, actions that are inimical to the whole of organized labour – that is, syndicalist actions that will lead to anarchic excesses of the most anti-social nature.

Spokesmen for the Majority Social Democrats were equally incensed:[29]

> The great strike movement [...] continues to send tremors through our economy, and in view of the forms it has taken, there can be said to be only *one* truly dangerous enemy of the German revolution at the present time, and that is the German working class. The trade unions have long since lost hold of the reins: the union organizations have been flooded by a new generation of people who know nothing of the old discipline and who are not willing to submit to the properly appointed leadership. With these masses, the idea of socialism does not even go skin-deep: swayed by individualist needs, lacking political experience, and lacking also any overall view of the condition of

industry or any concern for the general interests of the revolution, they have made an assault on the German economy and are systematically bringing it to the point of disintegration.

For their part, however, the USPD and the KPD were not really able to derive much advantage from the mass protest movement. They promptly set themselves up as spokesmen for the miners and made more vocal demands than ever for the immediate socialization of the major industries, especially the mines; but the goals of the protest movement were very different from their own. The USPD was principally concerned to avoid losing touch with mass opinion as it became radicalized after mid-December 1918, but it had even fewer concrete proposals for the building of a socialist society than the Majority Social Democrats did. At a Congress of Councils held at the end of December 1918, Barth, an USPD People's Representative, called for socialism on primarily political grounds:[30] the working-class masses had to be offered something, if only rhetoric. The stance of the Spartacus Union and the KPD on these questions was more rigorous, but in practice their Marxist conception of a socialized economy was also quite different from what socialization as an idea, or more properly a symbol, meant to the miners and other workers.[31]

In the light of these considerations, then, it is highly questionable whether the 'Essen model' of socialization, whereby the ownership of enterprises would have been converted into a complex system of workplace and regional mines councils, could ever have succeeded, even if the national government had not opposed its implementation from the outset.[32] It is quite clear that the Essen resolutions calling for socialization had been adopted in direct response to the spontaneous upsurge of mass working-class protest and that their primary purpose, at any rate as far as the Essen workers and soldiers' council was concerned, was to bring the strikes to an immediate end. For the rest, the socialist parties were not in control of events, but were controlled by them. The most that can be said is that the Spartacists strove to stoke up popular feeling in favour of immediate socialization, but even they did not devote much thought to the actual ways in which socialization might be implemented.

The call for the socialization of the mines (which had been preceded by numerous 'wildcat' declarations of socialization, some more fanciful than others) did not represent a desire for the long-term transformation of Germany into a fully-fledged socialist society; it stood proxy for a number of much more concrete goals. These goals included, first and foremost, an immediate improvement in workers' living conditions, through the abolition of 'unearned' and 'exploitative' surplus value, and the establishment of self-determination in the workplace. Enterprises would simply operate on a self-managed basis; there would be no reorganization as such.[33] Such notions were 'naive' in the sense that they contained, at most, merely traces of a genuinely Marxist programme. They were an expression of spontaneous social protest, directed in the first instance against the immediate class enemy, and of a deep-seated mistrust of all of the socialist parties. In this situation the USPD stood to profit most, for the very reason that it did not have a clear-cut political identity but was simply following in the wake of the popular mood. The KPD, by and large, gained little, because its broad aims were perceived as too remote from people's specific grievances. The miners' call for socialization was not a demand for public ownership in the bureaucratic sense, a first step in the direction of a society based on an exclusively socialist mode of production, in accordance with the socialist parties' programme, but had clearly syndicalist overtones.

This was less true, admittedly, in the case of the big general strike that took place in Berlin on 2–6 March 1919 and of the mass strike movements in central Germany. Here the syndicalist element was much less in evidence, and the call for socialization was much more political in character (in the traditional sense), partly because by now the politicians were anxious to attune themselves to the popular mood. Thus in the Halle region, the focal point of the strikes in central Germany, a group of USPD politicians led by Wilhelm Koenen took control of the strike movement and attempted to give it an unambiguously political, anti-Berlin thrust.[34] But even in this instance the symbolic call for socialization went hand in hand with demands that were very much more concrete than historians have so far recognized. In particular, the workers wanted a greater say in the running of enterprises and an immediate improvement in wages and working conditions.[35] None of the different strands within the German political labour movement, though, had ever thought about socialization in such concrete terms: they had seen it simply as a magic doctrinal key that was guaranteed to open the door on to a new era of world history, either through revolutionary or through evolutionary means.

It is worth noting in this connection that most of the striking workers assumed that the three socialist parties would set aside their gaping differences over doctrine and strategy and would work together. Indeed, in some cases they even forced them to do so. What the workers wanted was immediate action, not long-term policies of social transformation. This was the reason – and the only reason – why the Essen movement for socialization appeared, on the surface, to be a common effort on the part of all the socialist parties.[36] It was not the parties that imposed this line, but the mass of protesting workers themselves, who did not understand the doctrinal disputes among the politicians and in any case viewed the parties with growing mistrust. The position was similar in the case of the general strike in Berlin in March 1919 to which we have just referred. Although the *Rote Fahne* tried, with partial success, to present itself as the prime mover here, the strike was essentially a spontaneous action by workers at the major factories in Berlin, where there had always been something of a syndicalist tradition. The strike committee, on which the different socialist parties had equal representation, ruled – to no avail, as it turned out – that all of the socialist party newspapers should suspend publication and that only the committee's own information sheets should be issued. This was a clear appeal for party differences to be set aside in the interests of working-class unity. Significantly, it was the two KPD representatives who then withdrew from the committee, on the grounds that they were not prepared to agree to suspension of publication of the *Rote Fahne*.[37]

What all of these mass strike movements had in common was the belief that socialization was a way of bringing about an immediate improvement in the economic situation of the working class: the strikers were not greatly exercised about the long-term objectives that went hand in hand with socialization in the theories of 'well-schooled' socialists. They also felt intensely, and increasingly, bitter about the government's recourse to military force, which had conjured up the spectre of counter-revolution and seemed likely to jeopardize the realization of the concrete short-term objectives that their call for socialization symbolized. The strikers may have been vague in their aims, but they were becoming steadily less willing to defer to the leadership of the established socialist parties.

We need to bear this point in mind when we consider the many coups and attempted coups that took place from early January 1919 onwards – for example, in Bremen, Braunschweig, Düsseldorf and then Munich. In each case, the Spartacists and their fellow-travellers in the USPD were mainly concerned to gain power bases for the next stage of the revolutionary process: in particular, to try to force the press into line and thereby exert some control over popular opinion. They scarcely ever attempted to bring about any really fundamental change in existing political relations, except to secure their own position, as best they could, against the forces of counter-revolution, which in many cases entailed dismissing local administrative heads. Apart from that, they simply waited for the influx of mass support that they were confident would come. This, however, was badly to misconstrue the actual aims of the striking workers. What the mass of protesting workers wanted was immediate action: this did not necessarily translate into political support for the putsch-based regimes. On the contrary, the great majority of workers disapproved of these attempts to seize power.[38]

For its part, the KPD was hesitant and uneasy about heading such attempts to wrest control; on doctrinal grounds, failure seemed inevitable. Within even its own ranks, however, the tide of mass opinion was bringing to the fore utopian elements that were convinced that the protest movement in the Rhineland, the Ruhr and central Germany would continue to gain momentum and could be steered in the direction the KPD wanted. As a result, the KPD became embroiled in a whole series of hopeless battles, in defiance of the express aims of its leadership (which, admittedly, had been weakened by the murders of Liebknecht and Rosa Luxemburg) until the crushing of the strike movement and the suppression of the experimental coup-based regimes inflicted a succession of defeats on the party that left it seriously weakened as a political force.

In the light of the foregoing analysis, then, it is clear that the standard latter-day interpretation of the revolution discussed at the beginning of this essay needs at least to be modified in certain respects. In particular, we must question the claim that the processes of revolution might have been taken somewhat further in view of the 'democratic potential' that was present in the workers' and soldiers' councils. It was entirely appropriate, under the prevailing circumstances, for the workers' and soldiers' councils to urge that greater heed of new political ideas be taken in the administration of government and in society, and that the principles of democracy be implemented more fully.[39] But it is debatable whether such a policy would greatly have altered the actual outcome of events in the spring of 1919 (except, possibly, with regard to the role of the military) since, when confronted with the elemental force of the mass strike movement, even the workers' and soldiers' councils proved largely unable to cope. Like the socialist parties, in particular the Majority Social Democrats, they were incapable of tapping the raw energy that fuelled the strikes and directing it along productive channels. For the most part, they found themselves at a loss, sometimes even on the defensive; in some cases they simply the vacated the field for small groups of Spartacist firebrands. The councils might, arguably, have been able to play a more positive role in response to the strikes if the Majority Social Democrats had treated them as real political partners, along the lines successfully followed by the Social Democratic party in Austria. On the other hand, perhaps too much should not be made of the Austrian example. Although the Austrian Social Democrats dealt with the workers' and soldiers' councils in a quite different way, the eventual outcome was more or less the same as it was in Germany.[40]

It is also highly questionable whether the instant socialization of large sections of primary industry, in conformance with the model of bureaucratic state ownership to which all European socialist parties then subscribed, would really have prevented the great mass of the working class from becoming radicalized. Socialization would have done nothing, in the short run at least, to redress the financial hardship from which the workers were suffering; indeed, we can see after the event that the Majority Social Democrats were right to believe that at first it would probably have made the workers' situation even worse. At most, a positive response to the idea of participation by workers in decision-making in the workplace might have helped to alleviate the general mood of disaffection and done something to reduce the potential for mass protest. Such a response, however, was ruled out by the doctrinal preconceptions of all of the socialist parties, whatever their precise political colouring.

Both the Majority Social Democrats and their rivals on the socialist left failed to come properly to terms with the radicalization of the mass of the working class that occurred in the spring of 1919. The KPD was induced, against its own better judgement and to its rapid regret, to launch a whole series of coups and attempted coups that would discredit the idea of communism for a long time to come. The USPD allowed events simply to take their course, mainly because in the short run it was able to reap the benefit of being a party of protest. The most it did of a positive nature was to look for ways of combining the *Räte* system with parliamentary government. The attempts by Däumig and his supporters to campaign for a pure councils system, dispensing with parties and trade unions altogether, were a mere sideshow and found few backers even within the USPD. As for the Majority Social Democrats, the only answer that they, in alliance with the bourgeois parties, could come up with to the wave of mass strikes that hit the Ruhr and central Germany in February 1919, Berlin in early March and the Ruhr again in April was suppressing them by force. They also made an honest though somewhat feeble attempt to incorporate the councils system into the Weimar constitution by means of the Works Councils Law, thereby going some small distance towards meeting workers' demands for a direct say in their own economic and social destiny. But their endeavours to address the call for socialization directly, if modestly, by moving towards the 'orderly' nationalization of some primary industries through bills in the National Assembly and the establishment of a new Socialization Commission, came to nothing.

The consequences of the Majority Social Democrats' policies were serious. Through its alliance with the Freikorps and other proto-fascist military bodies, the Majority SPD inevitably forfeited the goodwill of a great number of workers, even though the latter had no sympathy for the Communists' strategy of trying to seize power by coup. Disappointment with the achievements of the revolution was widespread and deep-seated. At the second Congress of Councils in April 1919, Max Cohen delivered a sharply critical review of the policies that had been pursued by all of the socialist parties, in particular by the Majority Social Democrats. The socialist parties, he said, had made dreadful errors, not only during the revolution but during the fifty years of their existence: 'We have issued our supporters with a promissory note, which they have now presented, and we cannot honour it [. . .]. It is perhaps our misfortune that on 9 November we found ourselves in a situation for which none of us was prepared.'[41]

In the eyes of the Majority Social Democrats and the parties of the Weimar coalition, the revolution (which they had not actually sought in any case) had been brought to a clear end by the opening of the National Constituent Assembly on 6 February 1919. The government was therefore bound to construe the strikes of February, March and April 1919 as acts of rebellion by workers who had been led astray by Spartacists and other radical elements. That is why it stuck to the policy of suppressing the strikes by force and paid little heed to the motives that lay behind such an enormous groundswell of protest. With goods in desperately short supply, the nation's paramount need was a rapid resumption of production, and the Majority

Social Democrats were disposed to regard the strikes, without further examination, as a betrayal of the true interests of the working class of which they were the chief representatives.

In many respects, earlier historians have echoed their verdict. To the impartial observer, however, it is evident that the formal convening of the Constituent Assembly and the passing of the Law Concerning Provisional Authority in the Reich on 10 February 1919 did not mean the end of the revolution. Nor was the revolution brought to a close by the crushing in May 1919 of the second Munich *Räterepublik* – the far left's last major attempt to seize power – even though peace now began to return temporarily to the working-class districts in the big industrial centres. Despite the restoration of law and order, the Weimar democratic system had by no means gained real legitimacy in the eyes of the bulk of the population. On the contrary, German society was becoming increasingly polarized in political terms, partly as a direct result of the way in which the Freikorps and civilian militias had 'pacified', and increasingly exacted revenge on, the working class; and this polarization was to pose a grave threat to the stability of the Weimar Republic. The far right was becoming steadily more self-confident and was beginning seriously to contemplate the possibility of counter-revolution and the overthrow of the Weimar regime; large sections of the working class were turning to the left. Now, indeed, there were the makings of a real potential for revolution, and there was a much greater readiness to support radical socialist slogans, even though popular sentiment still mainly took the form of acts of protest against the immediate class enemy and in this sense retained clear syndicalist features.

The USPD was quick to try to place itself at the political forefront of these trends. In early December 1919 it adopted a new action programme, which declared that its central goal was the 'attainment of socialist democracy' by means of the 'dictatorship of the proletariat', and called for the deployment of 'every political, parliamentary and economic weapon', in planned and systematic 'co-operation with the revolutionary trade unions and the proletarian council organizations'.[42] The most significant development, however, was the fact that large numbers of miners now flocked to join the syndicalist trade-union organizations, in particular the Allgemeine Bergarbeiterunion (General Miners' Union) and then, after this was crushed in April 1919, the Freie Vereinigung, while the 'Alter Verband' lost something approaching two-thirds of its members. This was especially remarkable because the German labour movement, unlike its counterparts in western Europe, had had no previous syndicalist tradition of any sort. Once more, admittedly, the phenomenon was mainly an emotional response to the slogans of these syndicalist bodies rather than a sign of intellectual commitment to their doctrines. It was an expression of protest against *all* of the political branches of the labour movement, the Freie Gewerkschaften in particular. A desire for 'direct action' against the class enemy, born of a sense of deep disenchantment, was combined with, and nourished by, a profound mistrust of the national government and its military arm, the Reichswehr, and the White volunteer units that supplemented it.

This steadily rising groundswell of opinion, which was particularly strong in the Ruhr (and which the USPD and the KPD did their best to channel to their own advantage, though without real success) reached a new climax in March 1920, with a general strike that was called to defeat the Kapp putsch. Suspicions about the attitudes of the Reichswehr units under General Watter, who adopted a highly ambivalent policy of wait-and-see during the putsch, played a crucial part in inducing sections of the working class in the Ruhr to engage in active military conflict with the Lichtschlag Freikorps in mid-March 1920, when the latter showed signs of making a move to suppress the strike movement in the eastern Ruhr.[43]

Overnight, the mass strike of Ruhr workers against Kapp and Lüttwitz was transformed into a movement of open insurrection, directed simultaneously against the counter-revolutionary activities of suspect Reichswehr units and the policies of the national government, and accompanied by somewhat ill-concerted 'wildcat' acts of socialization. The aims and make-up of this movement were not clearly defined, and none of the the parties of the socialist left succeeded in bringing it under political control. Nor did an integrated leadership apparatus emerge: instead, a host of local executive councils and similar groupings, only loosely connected with one another, sought to implant an organizational backbone into what was a spontaneous upsurge of popular feeling. Nevertheless, within days a force of over 80,000 men was assembled that succeeded in confronting the Reichswehr units, inflicting substantial initial casualties and compelling them to withdraw from the Ruhr. Faced with the stark spectacle of a great mass of workers spontaneously resorting to military force, the Majority Social Democrats and, especially, the Freie Gewerkschaften now had no option but to recognize the revolutionary nature of the movement and seek to deprive it of its momentum by accepting some of its demands, in the form of the Free Trade Unions' 'Eight Points'. After gruelling negotiations, led by Severing, sizeable numbers of workers were persuaded to lay down their arms and forsake their mainly syndicalist leaders.

Even though the insurgent workers had very vaguely defined aims, and were united only by their outrage at the reactionary machinations of the Reichswehr, the fact remains that this uprising was a mass movement of social protest on a remarkably powerful and broad scale, which grew directly out of the earlier strike movements in the same region and was inspired by deep misgivings about the policies that had emanated from Berlin since November 1918. Members of the USPD and the KPD may have played a prominent role in many aspects of the disputes and the fighting, but the movement was certainly not started, or even guided, either by the USPD or by the KPD or by both. These two parties merely attempted, each in its own way (and with precious little more success than the Majority

SPD) to preserve contact with the protesting masses. It was not until April 1920 that the protest movement was split (though it had never had a unified character), the remnants of the 'Red Army' were finally defeated and the Ruhr was 'pacified'. That was the true end of the German revolution, if we leave out of account a few belated episodes such as the uprising led by Max Hoelz in the central German industrial region in 1921. The political price paid by the government, however, was unquestionably high. The effects were felt, for instance, in the Reichstag elections of June 1920, in which the USPD made enormous gains, while the Weimar coalition lost its previously comfortable majority, never to regain it.[44]

Let us sum up our discussion. The German revolution of 1918–20 took place on two levels: it was a political revolution, which had actually begun merely as a revolt against the military authorities and against the monarchical establishment that gave the military its legitimacy, and which had had quite limited objectives; and, on top of this, it was a movement of powerful social protest on a substantial scale. Those who made up the protest movement generally subscribed to the political programme of the socialist parties, in particular the call for the socialization of the means of production, but they were not swayed by the doctrinal considerations that governed the thinking of the parties' leaders. They saw socialization, not primarily as a fundamental transformation of the conditions of production, but as a means of procuring an immediate improvement in their living conditions at a time of severe hardship. For their part, none of the competing parties of the socialist left properly gauged the nature of the protest movement. They established a parliamentary system, though this would probably have come about even without a revolution; otherwise, however, their actions either were confined to preserving the status quo in society, or petered out in a series of coups and attempted coups that were bound to fail because they lacked the mass backing on which those who staged them had confidently counted. The Majority Social Democrats fulfilled their promise to save Germany from Bolshevism, but the promise had been made on the basis of false assumptions, and the methods that were employed, and the political allies who were chosen, to carry it out proved to be quite unsuitable. The KPD was eventually forced to recognize that despite the massive scale of the workers' movement, German society was not ripe for a 'dictatorship of the proletariat' on the Russian model. The USPD, having let itself be borne along by events, at first profited from the wave of protest by attracting the discontented, but soon turned out to have made ephemeral gains.

The crucial fact is that the Majority Social Democrats – hidebound by traditional notions of socialist discipline, and quite unprepared for the radical shift in mood that had taken place among their own supporters – hit back at the protest movement with disproportionate force, when they ought to have tried to get to grips with the underlying reasons why the unrest had arisen in the first place. Their historic error was not that they failed to tap the 'democratic potential' inherent in the workers' and soldiers' councils, but that when confronted with protests from within their own camp – protests which the USPD and the KPD were quick to exploit to their own advantage – they rushed into an alliance with the traditional authorities in order to maintain their political position, instead of trying to steer the working-class protest movement into constructive channels. What occurred, in essence, was a leadership crisis of major proportions, which had been some time in the offing but which the Majority Social Democrats blamed only on agitation by the Spartacists or on shortcomings in the political education of sections of the working class. The Majority Social Democrats did succeed in speedily laying the foundations of the Weimar system of parliamentary democracy – in close association, it should be said, with the bulk of the workers' and soldiers' councils. But by remaining trapped in an over-formalist conception of democracy, they misread the scale of popular discontent, and were dismayed when the measures of 'pacification' taken by the military against the Sparticist minority regimes provoked mass strikes and acts of insurrection on the part of large sections of the working class. They simply failed to grasp why these protests were taking place.

By this stage, of course, the use of traditional military force to suppress the strikes was virtually inevitable. But though the Weimar system seemed to stabilize after the conflicts of the spring of 1919 and, more particularly, of March and April 1920, the price was a lasting political polarization within German society, not least within the working class itself. This polarization was to prove critically damaging to the social foundations of the new state during the battles that lay ahead.

Notes

The German Empire as a system of skirted decisions

1 Walter Bußmann, 'Wandel und Kontinuität der Bismarckwertung', *Welt als Geschichte* 15 (1955), p. 132; cf. also the same author's account, still essential, 'Das Zeitalter Bismarcks', in Otto Brandt, Arnold Meyer and Leo Just (eds.), *Handbuch der deutschen Geschichte* (Constance, 1956), p. 153, which emphasizes Bismarck's absolute determination to preserve the status quo and to 'subdue modern pressures for change'. See also Gustav Adolf Rein, *Die Revolution in der Politik Bismarcks* (Göttingen, 1957), *passim*, esp. pp. 332f.

2 Hans Rothfels, 'Bismarck und das 19. Jahrhundert', in W. Hubatsch (ed.), *Schicksalswege deutscher Vergangenheit* (Düsseldorf, 1950), esp. pp. 246f., reprinted in Rothfels's *Zeitgeschichtliche Betrachtungen* (Göttingen, 1959), pp. 60f.; see also Rothfels, *Bismarck. Vorträge und Abhandlungen* (Stuttgart, 1970); Theodor Schieder, *Das Reich unter der Führung Bismarcks* (Stuttgart, 1962); Schieder, 'Bismarck und Europa', in *Deutschland und Europa. Festschrift für Hans Rothfels* (Düsseldorf, 1957); Schieder, 'Das Problem der Revolution im 19. Jahrhundert', in *Staat und Gesellschaft im Wandel unserer Zeit* (Munich, 1968); also Schieder, 'Bismarck – gestern und heute', in Lothar Gall (ed.), *Das Bismarck-Problem in der Geschichtsschreibung nach 1945* (Cologne/Berlin, 1971), esp. pp. 364f.

3 Hans-Ulrich Wehler, *Das Deutsche Kaiserreich 1871-1918* (Göttingen, 1973), pp. 37f.

4 cf. the preface to the collection *Die großpreußisch-militaristische Reichsgründung 1871 – Voraussetzungen und Folgen*, ed. Ernst Engelberg and Horst Bartel (Berlin, 1971; 2 vols), vol. 1, p. VII and Bartel, 'Zur historischen Stellung der Reichsgründung', vol. 2, pp. 4ff.; see also Ernst Engelberg, *Deutschland von 1848–1871. Von der Niederlage der bürgerlich-demokratischen Revolution bis zur Reichsgründung* (Berlin, 1959), p. 242, in which Engelberg speaks of 'Bismarck's Bonapartist dictatorship in the interests of the *Junker* and the grande bourgeoisie, the most aggressive classes in German society'.

5 Theodor Schieder, 'Vom Deutschen Bund zum Deutschen Reich', in Bruno Gebhardt, *Handbuch der deutschen Geschichte* (1960), p. 70; Schieder, 'Grundfragen der neueren deutschen Geschichte', in Böhme, *Probleme der Reichsgründungszeit 1848-1879* (Cologne, 1968), pp. 24ff. and 'Die

Entfaltung des Nationalstaatenproblems', in Schieder, *Das deutsche Kaiserreich von 1871 als Nationalstaat* (Cologne, 1961).

6   Ivo N. Lambi, 'The Protectionist Interests of the German Iron and Steel Industry, 1873–1879', *Journal of Economic History* 22 (1962), pp. 59ff.; Lambi, 'The Agrarian-Industrial Front in Bismarckian Politics 1873–1879', *Journal of Central European Affairs* 20 (1961), pp. 395f.; Lambi, *Free Trade and Protection in Germany 1868–1879* (Wiesbaden, 1963).

7   Helmut Böhme, *Deutschlands Weg zur Großmacht* (Cologne, 1966); Böhme, 'Politik und Ökonomie in der Reichsgründungs- und späten Bismarckzeit', in Michael Stürmer (ed.), *Das kaiserliche Deutschland. Politik und Gesellschaft 1870–1918* (Düsseldorf, 1970), pp. 34–40.

8   Wolfgang Sauer, 'Das Problem des deutschen Nationalstaates', in Helmut Böhme (ed.), *Reichsgründungszeit*, pp. 466ff.

9   In the case of Wehler, this is particularly clear in *Bismarck und der Imperialismus* (Cologne, 1972). For Stürmer, see his 'Staatsstreichgedanken im Bismarckreich', *Historische Zeitschrift* 209 (1969); 'Bismarck in Perspective', *Central European History* 4 (1971); and, especially, *Regierung und Reichstag im Bismarckstaat 1871–1880* (Düsseldorf, 1974).

10 The term 'secondary integration' (derived from Günther Roth) is first used in Sauer, 'Das Problem des deutschen Nationalstaates', p. 468; the thesis of 'social imperialism' is first developed in detail by Hans-Ulrich Wehler in *Bismarck und der Imperialismus* (pp. 454ff.), along with the sharpened notion of a 'manipulated social imperialism'.

11 *Bismarck und der Imperialismus*, p. 137.

12 See Heinz Gollwitzer, 'Der Cäsarismus Napoleons III. im Widerhall der öffentlichen Meinung Deutschlands', *Historische Zeitschrift* 173 (1952), pp. 23ff.; Ernst Engelberg, 'Zur Entstehung und historischen Stellung des preußisch-deutschen Bonapartismus', in *Beiträge zum neuen Geschichtsbild. Festschrift für A. Menzel* (Berlin, 1956); also, more recently, Lothar Gall, 'Bismarck und der Bonapartismus', *Historische Zeitschrift* 223 (1976), pp. 618–637.

13 Bismarck, *Gesammelte Werke*, vol. 14/II, p. 752.

14 Not surprisingly, Böhme's study breaks off at the year 1881 and is thus not required to deal with this problem. We should note that even the so-called 'Cartel' majority of 1887, which was indeed assembled by means of various manipulative devices, notably the playing-up of external threats from France, did not provide Bismarck with a secure political base. It was no coincidence, in fact, that the conservative camp played a crucial part in initiating Bismarck's fall. See Wilhelm Mommsen, *Bismarcks Sturz und die Parteien* (Berlin, 1924), pp. 18f. and Heinrich Heffter, *Die Kreuzzeitungspartei und Bismarcks Kartellpolitik* (Leipzig, 1927), esp. pp. 137ff.

15 Wehler, *Kaiserreich*, pp. 63ff. Wehler admittedly speaks somewhat ambiguously about a 'desperate defensive struggle against the social and political consequences of industrialization' (p. 66) and portrays Bismarck as the saviour of the middle-class 'man of order' as well as of the traditional governing elites.

16 Stürmer speaks of a 'triangular relationship' involving the threat of a coup, the growing role of Parliament and the fear of revolution; he sees Bismarck's persistent threat to resort, if necessary, to non-constitutional means as the basis of his Caesarist political method, which elevated him into a 'power factor *sui generis*'. This, he argues, was the main reason why there was a 'process of destruction of, and self-exclusion by, the bourgeois parties, and of loss of power on the part of the Reichstag as an institution'. Certainly, we cannot say that the Bismarckian era saw a gradual move towards parliamentary government in the conventional sense. On the other hand, it cannot be denied that the

political balance underwent a shift in the Reichstag's favour, despite Bismarck's policies. The fact that the Reichstag parties exhibited so little in the way of democratic energy was by no means due solely to the constitutional situation and certainly not only to Bismarck's manipulatory policies, but was primarily a reflection of the structure of German society, which remained highly traditionalist even though modernizing measures had been successfully introduced in individual spheres. Stürmer's account, which – again, not by accident – effectively breaks off in 1880, with the bold but quite inappropriate assertion that nothing more needs to be said about the Reichstag thereafter, turns into an elaborate recital of the host of techniques for wielding power that Bismarck deployed in his perpetual battles with the parties and largely loses sight of the broad underlying structural and socio-historical situation.

17 This was the price that the liberals, to their great chagrin, had to pay in order to obtain an otherwise fairly progressive press law in 1874.

18 On this point, we are in accord with Heinrich August Winkler, *Preußischer Liberalismus und deutscher Nationalstaat. Studien zur Geschichte der Deutschen Fortschrittspartei 1861–1866* (Tübingen, 1964), pp. 23ff., rather than with more recent interpretations – such as, notably, that of Michael Gugel, *Industrieller Aufstieg und bürgerliche Herrschaft. Sozialökonomische Interessen und politische Ziele des liberalen Bürgertums in Preußen zur Zeit des Verfassungskonflikts 1857–1867* (Cologne, 1975) – which concentrate on the changed economic circumstances of the middle class and highlight the middle class's defensive social strategies *vis-à-vis* the rising lower classes. See also fn. 20 below.

19 cf. also Gustav Schmidt, 'Politischer Liberalismus. "Landed Interest" und organisierte Arbeiterschaft 1850–1880', in Hans-Ulrich Wehler (ed.), *Sozialgeschichte Heute. Festschrift für Hans Rosenberg* (Göttingen, 1974), pp. 269f. See also Heinrich August Winkler, 'Vom linken zum rechten Nationalismus. Der deutsche Liberalismus in der Krise von 1878/79', *Geschichte und Gesellschaft* 4 (1978), pp. 5–28. Gordon Mork, in 'Bismarck and the "Capitulation" of German Liberalism', *Journal of Modern History* 43 (1971), pp. 59ff. is wholly faithful to the prevalent view. Mork, admittedly, emphasizes that the liberals achieved their socio-political objectives in significant respects, but maintains that they always gave way to Bismarck when he opposed them directly. The question why this was so, however, is not posed.

20 Lothar Gall attempts to provide a new definition of the relationship between liberalism and industrial development in his article 'Liberalismus und "bürgerliche Gesellschaft". Zu Charakter und Entwicklung der liberalen Bewegung in Deutschland', *Historische Zeitschrift* 220 (1975), reprinted in Gall (ed.), *Liberalismus* (Cologne, 1976). The aim of liberalism, he argues, at any rate in Germany, was to bring about a 'classless civic society of heads of households'; liberalism was thus philosophically at odds with large-scale capital and the substantial disparities in income that accompanied industrialization. Viewed in these terms, liberal ideas gradually became a mere ideology from the 1850s onwards, masking real economic class interests of the propertied middle class. This account – itself by no means unproblematical as far as the relationship between early liberalism and its class foundations is concerned – has been used by Gugel as the basis of his attempt to demonstrate that the ideology of liberalism had already lost its original character as a doctrine of social emancipation by the 1850s, and that with the rapid rise of bourgeois capitalist enterprise the liberal programme acquired purely defensive social features and abandoned its political thrust. Henceforward 'the goal of strengthening the middle class' did not 'go hand in hand with all of the general emancipatory ambitions ... that had lent the middle class's demands their particular impact, and a broader mass

appeal, at the beginning of the century'. Instead, the 1850s saw the 'protection of a privileged position, essentially defined in terms of property interests' (Gugel, *Industrieller Aufstieg*, p. 205). Not only does this interpretation quite unwarrantedly idealize the liberalism of the *Vormärz* era, but, more important, it also completely overstates the degree of social change that had been brought about by industrialization in the 1850s. It assumes, without adequate support from the sources, that the liberals' dominant political preocccupation was to defend themselves against the proletarian strata of society, even though the latter did not represent a sizeable force at this time, and draws the contentious conclusion that the real interests of the middle class were identical with those of Bismarck's state. At most, this might be asserted of the industrial upper middle class, then still relatively small. It was scarcely true of the whole range of organized party-political groupings within German liberalism that existed during the Bismarck era. See also the present author's essay, 'Der deutsche Liberalismus zwischen "klassenloser Bürgergesellschaft" und "organisiertem Kapitalismus"', *Geschichte und Gesellschaft* 4 (1978), pp. 77–90.

21 'Das Problem der Revolution im 19. Jahrhundert', in *Staat und Gesellschaft in unserer Zeit* (Munich, 1958), pp. 11ff.

22 Wolfgang Zorn, 'Wirtschafts- und sozialgeschichtliche Zusammenhänge der deutschen Reichsgründungszeit (1850–1879)', in Böhme, *Reichsgründungszeit*, pp. 304f.; cf. also Zorn, 'Wirtschaft und Gesellschaft in Deutschland in der Zeit der Reichsgründung', in Theodor Schieder and Ernst Deuerlein (eds.), *Reichsgründung 1870/71. Tatsachen, Kontroversen, Interpretationen* (Stuttgart, 1970), pp. 197ff.; Zorn, 'Die wirtschaftliche Integration Kleindeutschlands in den 1860er Jahren und die Reichsgründung', *Historische Zeitung* 216 (1973), pp. 304ff.

23 Otto Becker, *Bismarcks Ringen um Deutschlands Gestaltung*, edited and completed by Alexander Scharff (Heidelberg, 1958), esp. pp. 388ff.

24 *Neue Freie Presse*, 1 January 1874, quoted in James F. Harris, 'Eduard Lasker and Compromise Liberalism', *Journal of Modern History* 42 (1970), p. 349.

25 *op. cit.*, p. 350.

26 It was only by dint of the three-class system of suffrage, with its strong multiplier effect – especially marked because of the lack of a developed party structure and the prevalence of a politics of prominent citizens – that the Progressive party and, more generally, the range of liberal groupings in their entirety obtained spectacular majorities in the Prussian Chamber of Deputies in the 1860s (in 1862, 314 liberals of all types, excluding the Old Liberals, as against 11 conservatives; in 1863, 247 liberals as against 35 conservatives). The liberals themselves were well aware how weak their standing was in society at large, and were never able to risk their position during the revolutionary struggle against the Prussian monarchy. As Winkler says (pp. 23f), the parliamentary strength of the middle class rested 'on unstable soil'; there was thus never any real challenge, from within the liberal camp, to the principle that the forces of reaction would have to be defeated with the help of the right rather than in head-on confrontation. For the social base of liberalism during the *Konfliktzeit*, see Eugene N. Anderson, *The Social and Political Conflict in Prussia 1858–1864* (Lincoln, Nebraska, 1954; reprinted, New York, 1958); also Anderson, *The Prussian Election Statistics 1862 and 1863* (Lincoln, Nebraska, 1954).

27 The data that follow are taken from Walter G. Hofmann, *Das Wachstum der deutschen Wirtschaft seit der Mitte des 19. Jahrhunderts* (Berlin, 1965) and from Gerd Hohorst, Jürgen Kocka and Gerhard A. Ritter, *Sozialgeschichtliches Arbeitsbuch. Materialien zur Statistik des Kaiserreiches 1870–1914* (Munich, 1975). See also Theodore S. Hamerow, *The Social*

Foundations of German Unification 1858–1871: Ideas and Institutions (Princeton, 1969), pp. 70ff.

28 For a section of the lower middle class, see the more recent study by Robert Gellately, *The Politics of Economic Despair: Shopkeepers and German Politics 1890–1914* (London, 1974); Gellately shows (pp. 13ff.) that the number of retailers grew significantly more rapidly than the population as a whole during the period of industrialization between 1871 and 1914. There is as yet no definitive study of the middle class during the Bismarckian era. See, however, Wolfram Fischer, 'Das deutsche Handwerk in der Frühphase der Industrialisierung', *Zeitschrift für die gesamte Staatswissenschaft* 120 (1964); Fischer, 'Die Rolle des Kleingewerbes im wirtschaftlichen Wachstumsprozeß in Deutschland 1850–1914', in Friedrich Lütge (ed.), *Wirtschaftliche und soziale Probleme der gewerblichen Entwicklung im 15. bis 16. und 19. Jahrhundert* (Stuttgart, 1968), pp. 131ff.; Jürgen Kocka, 'Vorindustrielle Faktoren in der deutschen Industrialisierung. Industriebürokratie und "neuer Mittelstand"', in Stürmer, *Das kaiserliche Deutschland*, pp. 265ff.

29 cf. Hamerow, *Social Foundations*, pp. 78f., who points out that the position of craftsmen at first remained strong in quantitative terms, though he does not dissociate himself from the standard view as far as the crisis of the lower middle class is concerned.

30 On the basis of the data available in Hoffmann, *Wachstum der deutschen Wirtschaft* and Hohorst, Kocka and Ritter, *Sozialgeschichtliches Arbeitsbuch*, we find the following global structural pattern of employment in the German Empire, classified by sector and by employment status (figures in millions):

Sector	Status	1867	1882	1895
Agricultural sector	Self-employed	?	2.3	2.5
	Agricultural workers and dependent employees	?	5.9	5.6
White-collar workers			0.062	0.067
Other sectors	Self-employed	2.3	2.8	3.0
	Professionals and civil servants	0.5	0.63	0.78
	White-collar workers	–	0.30	0.62
	Industrial workers	?	4.8	7.2

Many of the sources on which these data rest are inaccurate or misleading: thus the number of people employed in the agricultural sector, as a proportion of the population as a whole, probably exceeded that in industry and commerce; similarly, the figures for 'professionals and civil servants' unfortunately include barbers and hairdressers. Nevertheless, the data provide a basis on which actual changes in social stratification during the Empire can be assessed. Few dramatic changes resulting from industrialization can be discerned before 1882. In particular, the relative strength of the position of the self-employed – taking the agricultural and the industrial and commercial sectors together – is marked. In other words, the first big spurt of industrialization that began in the 1850s did not generate large-scale social-structural change. It was not until the second spurt of industrialization, beginning in the early 1880s, that a broad impact on social patterns began to be felt. Even then, however, the agricultural sector was not affected in absolute terms, and at first only slightly in relative terms.

31 Gustav Schmidt's thesis, that the National Liberals waged 'domestic preventive war', in the form of the *Kulturkampf*, in order to exclude from the outset a potential rival for the position of governing party, is surely questionable. In the first place, the Centre party could never have vied for political pre-eminence with the National Liberals in 1871, since it had too clearly voiced its opposition to Bismarck's drive to establish the Empire; moreover, the Conservatives were still much too disorganized in the early 1870s – and, incidentally, still much too hostile to Bismarck – to be able to act as the Centre's political allies. In the second place, the liberal movement as a whole, including the Progressive party – which had never entertained hopes of such a role – waged the *Kulturkampf* with conviction and passion because it regarded Catholicism and its party-political advance guard as a force profoundly hostile to progress and modernization. It was the political mobilization of broad sections of the population with almost exclusively social-conservative attitudes that the liberals had cause to fear. At a local level – as in Krefeld, for example – the *Kulturkampf* commonly degenerated into a kind of class struggle between the Catholic lower classes and the Protestant, industrial upper social strata.

32 As early as 1905 Max Weber issued a severe warning, with regard to Russia, that advancing industrialization should not be assumed to lead necessarily to social liberalization: 'If it were a question only of the "material" conditions, and of the patterns of interest "created" by them, sober reflection would prompt us to say: All of the economic weather signs point towards mounting "unfreedom". It is quite absurd to claim that modern high capitalism of the sort that is now being imported into Russia and that exists in America – the "inevitable" outcome of our economic development – has a special affinity with "democracy" or even with "freedom" (in whatever sense)' *Gesammelte Politische Schriften* (3rd edn., 1971), p. 64. See also Wolfgang J. Mommsen, *Max Weber und die deutsche Politik 1890–1920* (2nd edn., Tübingen, 1974), pp. 89f.

33 Regrettably, this aspect of the development of the German Empire has not been thoroughly investigated since the time of Gerhard Ritter's first book, *Die preußischen Konservativen und Bismarcks deutsche Politik 1858–1876* (Heidelberg, 1913) and Heinrich Heffter, *Die Kreuzzeitungspartei* (fn. 14 above).

34 Michael Stürmer, 'Konservativismus und Revolution in Bismarcks Politik', in Stürmer, *Das kaiserliche Deutschland*, p. 161.

35 Quoted in Hermann Onken, *Rudolf von Bennigsen. Ein deutscher liberaler Politiker*, vol. 2 (Leipzig, 1910), pp. 263f.

36 John C.G. Röhl, 'Staatsstreichplan oder Staatsstreichbereitschaft? Bismarcks Politik in der Entlassungskrise', *Historische Zeitschrift* 203 (1966), pp. 614ff.

37 cf. Carl Schmitt, *Staatsgefüge und Zusammenbruch des zweiten Reiches* (Hamburg, 1934), pp. 24f.

38 'Bismarck – gestern und heute', in Gall (ed.), *Das Bismarck-Problem*, p. 364. See also the systematic discussion of this question in Wolfgang J. Mommsen, 'Die latente Krise des Wilhelminischen Reiches' (translated in the present volume, pp. 141–162); also Peter Leibenguth, *Modernisierungskrisis des Kaiserreiches an der Schwelle zum Wilhelminischen Imperialismus. Politische Probleme der Ära Caprivi* (doctoral thesis, Cologne, 1975), pp. 54ff., though this study places undue weight on Bismarck's aim of blocking the emergence of parliamentary government.

39 On this, see Theodor Schieder, 'Die Krise des bürgerlichen Liberalismus', in *Staat und Gesellschaft im Wandel unserer Zeit* (Munich, 1958), p. 77 and Wolfgang J. Mommsen, 'Liberalismus und liberale Idee in Geschichte und Gegenwart', in Kurt Sontheimer (ed.), *Möglichkeiten und Grenzen liberaler*

Politik (Düsseldorf, 1975), pp. 28f.

40   cf. Bismarck's declaration in the Prussian Ministry of State on 6 October 1877 (quoted in Dietrich Sandberger, *Die Ministerkandidatur Bennigsens*, Berlin, 1929, p. 85):

I am governing with the constitution, with the National Liberal party; if Count Eulenburg withdraws, I shall propose to the King a member of that party as his successor, though of course I do not know whether I shall prevail. The National Liberals ought to have been represented [long ago] even in the Ministry, in order to bear joint responsibility for government and to see how different and how much harder it is than parliamentarians think.

Bennigsen's ministerial candidacy presents a problem for those who espouse the thesis that the introduction of protectionism ushered in a 'second founding of the Empire'; the problem is usually either simply ignored or hastily discounted as another manipulative strategy on Bismarck's part.

41   Quoted in Onken, *Bennigsen*, p. 513.
42   In his *Prolegomena zu einer Sozialgeschichte Deutschlands im 19. und 20. Jahrhundert*, Böhme admittedly modifies the interpretative framework he himself had introduced, pointing out that even after 1879 political and social tensions were 'resolved only in individual cases' (p. 89). For the view indicated above, cf. Dirk Stegmann, *Die Erben Bismarcks. Parteien und Verbände in der Spätphase des Wilhelminischen Deutschland* (Cologne, 1970), esp. pp. 59ff., and Wehler, *Kaiserreich*, pp. 100ff.
43   Sauer, 'Das Problem des deutschen Nationalstaates', pp. 450f.

A delaying compromise:
the Imperial Constitution of 1871

1   'Bismarck – gestern und heute', in Lothar Gall (ed.), *Das Bismarck-Problem in der Geschichtsschreibung nach 1945* (Cologne, 1971), p. 357.
2   David Blackbourn and Geoff Eley, *Mythen deutscher Geschichtsschreibung. Die gescheiterte bürgerliche Revolution von 1848* (Berlin, 1980), p. 29 (cf. also the subsequent English edition, *The Peculiarities of German History: Bourgeois Society and Politics in Nineteenth-Century Germany*, Oxford, 1984).
3   Lothar Gall, 'Bismarck und der Bonapartismus', *Historische Zeitschrift* 223 (1976), pp. 618ff.
4   Lothar Gall, *Bismarck. Der weiße Revolutionär* (Berlin, 1980), p. 383.
5   *op. cit.*, p. 382.
6   *op. cit.*, p. 381.
7   This view was first put forward by Johannes Ziekursch in his *Politische Geschichte des neuen deutschen Kaiserreichs*, 3 vols. (Frankfurt, 1925ff.), and then developed, in particular, by Erich Eyck. In more recent studies, notably Hans-Ulrich Wehler, *Bismarck und der Imperialismus* (4th edn., Cologne, 1974) and Wehler, *Das deutsche Kaiserreich 1871–1918* (Göttingen, 1973), this interpretation has been further sharpened.
8   Wolfgang J. Mommsen, 'Das deutsche Kaiserreich als System umgangener Entscheidungen', in Helmut Berding et al. (eds.), *Vom Staat des Ancien Régime zum modernen Parteienstaat. Festschrift für Theodor Schieder* (Munich, 1978), pp. 239ff. (translated in the present volume, pp. 1–19).
9   cf. fn. 2 above.

10 A notable exception is the essay by Gerhard A. Ritter, 'Entwicklungsprobleme des deutschen Parlamentarismus', in Ritter (ed.), *Gesellschaft, Parlament und Regierung. Zur Geschichte des Parlamentarismus in Deutschland* (Düsseldorf, 1974), pp. 11–54. Ritter emphasizes, in particular, the contrast with constitutional change in Great Britain.

11 In Helmut Böhme (ed.), *Probleme der Reichsgründungszeit 1848–1879* (Cologne/Berlin, 1968), pp. 450ff.

12 Hans Boldt, 'Deutscher Konstitutionalismus und Bismarckreich', in Michael Stürmer (ed.), *Das kaiserliche Deutschland. Politik und Gesellschaft 1870–1918* (Düsseldorf, 1970), p. 125.

13 Ernst Rudolf Huber, *Deutsche Verfassungsgeschichte seit 1789*, vol. III, *Bismarck und das Reich* (Stuttgart, 1963), pp. 654ff.; Huber, 'Die Bismarcksche Reichsverfassung im Zusammenhang der deutschen Verfassungsgeschichte', in Theodor Schieder and Ernst Deuerlein (eds.), *Reichsgründung 1870–71. Tatsachen, Kontroversen, Interpretationen* (Stuttgart, 1970), pp. 173, 190f.

14 'Der deutsche Typ der konstitutionellen Monarchie im 19. Jahrhundert', in Werner Conze (ed.), *Beiträge zur deutschen und belgischen Verfassungsgeschichte* (Stuttgart, 1967), pp. 70ff.

15 For evidence, see Theodor Schieder, *Das deutsche Kaiserreich von 1871 als Nationalstaat* (Cologne, 1961). See also Elisabeth Fehrenbach, *Wandlungen des deutschen Kaisergedankens 1871–1918* (Munich, 1969).

16 cf. Manfred Rauh, *Föderalismus und Parlamentarismus im Wilhelminischen Reich* (Düsseldorf, 1973) and Rauh, *Die Parlamentarisierung des Deutschen Reiches* (Düsseldorf, 1977). Rauh's argument in the first of these works, admittedly, is much more cautious than that in the second. Rauh's analysis concentrates exclusively on the relationship between the Bundesrat and the Reichstag, and ignores the fact that in the circumstances a growth in the power of the Reichstag did not, of itself, signify a move towards parliamentarism, even in an informal constitutional sense.

17 *Gesammelte Werke des Fürsten Bismarck* (hereafter *GW*), vol. 6, no. 615, p. 167.

18 Gall, *Bismarck. Der weiße Revolutionär*, p. 390.

19 On this, see the recent study by Wolfgang Schwentker, *Konservative Vereine und Revolution in Preußen 1848/49. Die Konstituierung des Konservativismus als Partei* (Düsseldorf, 1988), which furnishes proof of the the strength of the Volksverein movement in the later phases of the revolution.

20 cf., for example, the interesting comment in *Meyers Konversationslexikon* for 1874 (quoted in *Hundert zeitgenössische Biographien berühmter Personen des 19. Jahrhunderts*, Mannheim, 1981, p. 28):

The responsibility for the dangers that arise from completely unrestricted direct elections fall mainly on B[ismarck], for it was he who advocated this principle and who fought for it in the Constitutent Reichstag with a determination that intimidated and silenced many who were ready to voice their opposition [...] Though his statesmanly wisdom is to be admired, there is no denying that on this point he made an error that will be hard to rectify and that may cause great dangers for the Empire.

21 cf. *GW*, vol. 6, no. 659, p. 238.

22 Klaus Erich Pollmann, however, in 'Vom Verfassungskonflikt zum Verfassungskompromiß. Funktion und Selbstverständnis des verfassungsberatenden Reichstags des Norddeutschen Bundes', in Gerhard A. Ritter (ed.), *Gesellschaft, Parlament und Regierung*, pp, 189–204, emphasizes the weak-

ened position of the liberal parties in the North German Constituent Reichstag, the effect of which was to lower their expectations.

23 Johannes von Miquel, *Reden*, ed. Walther Schultze and Friedrich Thimme, vol. 1 (Halle, 1911), p. 198.

24 *Bismarcks Ringen um Deutschlands Gestaltung*, edited and completed by Alexander Scharff (Heldelberg, 1958).

25 'Die Bismarcksche Reichsverfassung' (fn. 13 above), p. 172.

26 Gall, *Bismarck. Der weiße Revolutionär*, p. 389.

27 Order to Redern, 5 April 1865, *GW*, vol. 5, pp. 154ff.

28 See, however, Miquel's remarkably precise statement, in *Reden*, vol. 1, p. 217:

> [...] the weakness of the draft [...] lies in the combined position of the Federal Council, inasmuch as it has [...] administrative powers encroaching on to the executive and, in part, legislative powers. If it were possible to clarify that relationship, so that the Federal Council and the Parliament had solely legislative powers, while the Presidency, the Prussian Crown, simply and exclusively possessed the executive authority, then the draft would certainly rest on a much clearer and firmer basis.

29 cf. Rauh, *Föderalismus*, pp. 54f.

30 For evidence, see *op. cit.*, pp. 110f.

31 Rauh too hastily concludes from this, his central thesis, that the collapse of the Bismarckian system of government meant the removal of the barriers in the way of an 'imperceptible' transition towards parliamentary government.

32 Horst Kohl, *Die politischen Reden des Fürsten Bismarck* (Stuttgart, 1892–1905), vol. 4, p. 186.

33 cf. Hans-Otto Binder, *Reich und Einzelstaaten während der Kanzlerschaft Bismarcks 1871–1890* (Tübingen, 1971), esp. pp. 53ff.; also Rauh, *Föderalismus*, pp. 91ff.

34 cf. Wolfgang J. Mommmsen, 'Die latente Krise des Wilhelminischen Reiches' (translated in the present volume, pp. 141–162), and Mommsen, 'Domestic Factors in German Foreign Policy before 1914' (re-translated in the present volume, pp. 163–188).

35 Miquel, *Reden*, vol. 1, pp. 226f.

36 Karl Erich Born, *Preußen im Kaiserreich* (Tübingen, 1967).

37 Kohl, *Die politischen Reden*, vol. 4, p. 192.

38 cf. *GW*, vol. 6c, no. 1, pp. 1f.

39 Constantin Frantz, *Bismarckismus und Friderizianismus* (Munich, 1873), p. 13.

40 cf. Bennigsen's statement (15 April 1867) (quoted in Hermann Onken, *Rudolf von Bennigsen. Ein deutscher liberaler Politiker*, 2 vols. (Leipzig, 1910), vol. 2, p. 59):

> I am convinced that Germany's whole position is so favourable that this constitutional enterprise will give rise to many, and great, benefits not only with regard to the powers of the German state but also as far as the internal development of the German nation is concerned. I hope that it will lead to large and important developments in the constitutional sphere in Germany.

41 For a more detailed discussion of this question, see Mommsen, 'Die latente Krise', pp. 145ff. below.

42 For documentation, see Wolfgang J. Mommsen, *Max Weber und die deutsche Politik 1890–1920* (2nd edn., Tübingen, 1974), pp. 187–189.

The Prussian conception of the state of the German idea of Empire

1 In its original form, this essay was to have been one of two lectures marking the conclusion of a series of discussions of Prussia's role in German history arranged jointly by the Fritz-Thyssen-Stiftung and the Stiftung preußischer Kulturbesitz. It was rejected, however, at the last minute. The lecture was to have been preceded by a lecture by Richard Koselleck on the topic 'Learning from the History of Prussia', which did not materialize. The other essays in the series are published in two volumes: *Preußen. Seine Wirkung auf die deutsche Geschichte*, vol. 1, containing contributions by Karl Dietrich Erdmann, Raymond Aron, Thomas Nipperdey and Lothar Gall (Stuttgart, 1982), and vol. 2 (Stuttgart, 1985), in which see the contributions by Theodor Schieder, 'Über den Beinamen "der Große" bei Friedrich II. von Preußen – Reflexionen über die historische Größe'; Hagen Schulze, 'Die Stein-Hardenbergschen Reformen und ihre Bedeutung für die deutsche Geschichte'; Clemens Menze, 'Bildungsstruktur und Bildungsorganisation. Wilhelm von Humboldts Grundlegung des Bildungswesens'; Wolfram Fischer, 'Industrialisierung und soziale Frage in Preußen'; Walter Bußmann, 'Das Scheitern der Revolution in Preußen 1848'; Karl-Dietrich Bracher, 'Das Ende Preußens'; Michael Howard, 'Prussia in European History'.
2 cf. Bracher's objections against deterministic interpretations of the history of the Weimar Republic, pp. 12f.
3 *op. cit.*, p. 15: '20 July 1932 – both the blow struck by the Papen government, and its acceptance by the Braun government – was Prussia's final hour ...'
4 'Bismarcks Preußen, das Reich und Europa' (cf. vol. 1, cited in fn. 1 above). I am very grateful to Gall for his comments on the present essay, which closely echo the themes of his own work at a number of points.
5 My remarks here are based on a number of studies, including Stig Förster, *Der doppelte Militarismus. Die deutsche Heeresrüstungspolitik zwischen status-quo-Sicherung und Aggression 1890–1913* (Wiesbaden, 1985). See also G. Eley, *Reshaping the German Right: Radical Nationalism and Political Change after Bismarck* (New Haven/London, 1980).
6 This assessment differs from that of Michael Howard, who sees Treitschke and Bernhardi as representatives of the Prussian tradition. My argument is that the distinction between Prussian and German nationalistic traditions needs to be kept quite clear.
7 'Preußen und die Universität' (cf. fn. 1 above), pp. 65ff.
8 cf. Hans Boldt, 'Die preußische Verfassung vom 31. Januar 1850. Probleme ihrer Interpretation', in Hans-Jürgen Puhle and Hans-Ulrich Wehler (eds.), *Preußen im Rückblick*, Sonderheft 6, *Geschichte und Gesellschaft* (1980), pp. 224f.
9 cf. Hanna Schissler, 'Die Junker. Zur Sozialgeschichte und historischen Bedeutung der agrarischen Elite in Preußen', in *op. cit.*, pp. 89ff.; also Wolfgang J. Mommsen, 'Preußen/Deutschland im frühen 19. Jahrhundert und Großbritannien in der viktorianischen Epoche', in Adolf M. Birke and Kurt Kluxen (eds.), *Viktorianisches England in deutscher Perspektive* (Munich, 1983), pp. 31ff.
10 cf. Nikolaus von Preradovich, *Die Führungsschichten in Österreich und Preußen (1804–1918)* (Wiesbaden, 1955), pp. 160ff.; see also studies by Hans Rosenberg.

11 It is not possible, on grounds of space, to elaborate this – here somewhat over-stated – claim in the present essay. Hagen Schulze is surely right to assert that it was the revolutionary situation and the examples set in France and in the states of the Confederation of the Rhine that first released the reforming energies of the bureaucracy. Nevertheless, the way in which these energies found practical expression was undoubtedly in keeping with the tradition of the Enlightenment state.

12 Speech in the Prussian Landtag, 27 January 1863, reprinted in Horst Kohl, *Die politischen Reden des Fürsten Bismarck*, vol. 2 (Stuttgart, 1903), p. 87.

13 'Entwicklungstendenzen in der Lage der ostelbischen Landarbeiter', *Preußische Jahrbücher* 77 (1894), p. 438.

14 *op. cit.*, p. 440.

15 Max Weber, *Gesammelte Politische Schriften* (3rd edn., Tübingen, 1971), p. 19.

16 cf. Fischer's essay cited in fn. 1 above, which rebuts the notion that the Prussian state played a decisive role in the process of industrialization during the 1850s and 1860s. It remains a matter of dispute, however, whether state initiatives operated predominantly as a brake on industrial growth, as Fischer argues, or whether they played – to a certain extent, at any rate – a triggering role.

17 These words were used by Bethmann Hollweg in his letter of resignation of 23 March 1912 when resisting irresponsible interference by Wilhelm II in the Anglo-German negotiations that had been taking place.

18 Weber, *Gesammelte Politische Schriften*, p. 335.

19 Gustav Schmoller, *Zwanzig Jahre deutscher Politik (1897–1917)* (Munich, 1920), p. 71.

20 cf. the study of Wilhelm II's 'personal rule' and its intellectual and social background by Isabel V. Hull, *The Entourage of Kaiser Wilhelm II 1888–1918* (Cambridge, 1982).

21 Theodor Schieder, in his essay cited above (fn. 1), shows that Friedrich II 'accepted in silence' the honorific title 'der Große' and that he viewed such tributes with some scepticism. Wilhelm II was a very different case, having no capacity for self-criticism whatever. Although he tried to secure the appellation 'der Große' for his grandfather Wilhelm I, he was anxious to go down in history himself as the great exponent of a glorious German 'Weltpolitik'.

22 cf. Raymond Aron, 'Clausewitz – Stratege und Patriot (cf. fn. 1 above), p. 42.

23 cf. Lerchenfeld's report to Hertling, 4 July 1914, in Pius Dirr (ed.), *Bayerische Dokumente zum Kriegsausbruch und zum Versailler Schuldspruch* (2nd edn., Munich, 1922), p. 113.

24 On this, see Walter Bußmann, 'Das Scheitern der Revolution in Preußen 1848' (cf. fn. 1 above); Bußmann gives a striking account of the reasons that prevented Friedrich Wilhelm IV from placing himself decisively at the head of the Prussian liberal movement, as the whole of middle-class Germany desperately hoped that he would. Despite making some verbal gestures in favour of the liberal *Zeitgeist* – notably, his pronouncement that 'Prussia is henceforth dissolved in Germany' and in his promise of a constitution – Friedrich Wilhelm IV, as Bußmann shows, adhered continuously to the Prussian 'military state tradition' (p. 22).

25 The concept of 'Caesarism' is taken from Max Weber. In the light, however, of recent studies of Bismarck's domestic policy – notably by Michael Stürmer and Lothar Gall – the most appropriate use of the term would appear to be as a way of distinguishing the specifically non-Prussian, yet authoritarian, style of government of Bismarck from the older traditions of Prussian rule.

Society and State in Europe, 1870–1890

1 John Stuart Mill, *On Liberty* (reprinted London/New York, 1972), p. 67.
2 Jacob Burckhardt, *Weltgeschichtliche Betrachtungen*, reprinted in *Gesammelte Werke*, vol. IV (Darmstadt, 1956), p. 70.
3 Charles Morazé, *Les Bourgeois conquérants: XIXme siècle* (Paris, 1957); Eric Hobsbawm, *The Age of Capital 1848–1875* (London, 1976).
4 David Blackbourn and Geoff Eley, *The Peculiarities of German History: Bourgeois Society and Politics in Nineteenth-Century Germany* (Oxford, 1984).
5 cf. Rosebery's speech at the Royal Colonial Institute in London, 1 March 1893, quoted in G. Bennett, *The Concept of Empire: Burke to Attlee, 1774–1947* (London, 1953), p. 310; see also Joseph Chamberlain, *Foreign and Colonial Speeches* (London, 1897), p. 114.

The causes and objectives of German Imperialism before 1914

1 Quoted in John C.G. Röhl, *Deutschland ohne Bismarck. Die Regierungskrise im Zweiten Kaiserreich 1890–1900* (Tübingen, 1969), p. 229 (cf. also the earlier English edition, *Germany without Bismarck: The Crisis of Government in the Second Reich, 1890–1900*, London, 1967).
2 Walther Rathenau, 'Deutsche Gefahren und neue Ziele', in Rathenau, *Gesammelte Schriften*, vol. 1 (Berlin, 1918), p. 278.
3 Quoted in Fritz Fischer, *Krieg der Illusionen. Die deutsche Politik von 1911–1914* (Düsseldorf, 1969), p. 340.
4 Reproduced in Wolfgang J. Mommsen, *Der Imperialismus. Seine geistigen, politischen und wirtschaftlichen Grundlagen. Ein Quellen-und Arbeitsbuch* (Hamburg, 1977), p. 145.

Economy, Society and the State

1 Albert Jeck, *Wachstum und Verteilung des Volkseinkommens. Untersuchungen und Materialien zur Entwicklung der Volkseinkommensverteilung in Deutschland, 1870–1913* (Tübingen, 1970); Hartmut Kaelble, 'Sozialer Aufstieg in Deutschland 1850–1914', *Vierteljahresschrift für Sozial-und Wirtschaftsgeschichte* 60 (1973), pp. 40–71; Kaelble, 'Social Stratification in Germany in the 19th and 20th Centuries: A Survey of Research since 1945', *The Journal of Social History* 10 (1976); Kaelble *et al.*, *Probleme der Modernisierung in Deutschland. Sozialhistorische Studien zum 19. und 20. Jahrhundert* (Opladen, 1978); Jürgen Kocka (ed.), *Soziale Schichtung und Mobilität in Deutschland im 19. und 20. Jahrhundert. Deutschland im internaionalen Vergleich* (Göttingen, 1983).
2 Berlin, 1913.

3 Helmut Böhme, *Deutschlands Weg zur Großmacht* (Cologne, 1966).

4 Wolfgang Zorn, 'Die wirtschaftliche Integration Kleindeutschlands in den 1860er Jahren und die Reichsgründung', *Historische Zeitschrift* 216 (1973), pp. 304–334; Zorn, 'Wirtschafts-und sozialgeschichtliche Zusammenhänge der Reichsgründungszeit (1850–1879)', *Historische Zeitschrift* 197 (1963), pp. 313–342.

5 Theodore S. Hamerow, *Restoration, Revolution, Reaction: Economics and Politics in Germany 1815–1871* (Princeton, 1958).

6 cf. Wolfgang J. Mommsen, 'Die Verfassung des Deutschen Reiches als dilatorischer Herrschaftskompromiß', in Otto Pflanze (ed.), *Innenpolitische Probleme des Bismarck-Reiches* (Munich, 1983), pp. 200f. (cf. translation in the present volume, pp. 11ff.).

7 Hans Rosenberg, 'Die Pseudodemokratisierung der Rittergutsbesitzerklasse', in Rosenberg, *Machteliten und Wirtschaftskonjunkturen* (Göttingen, 1978), pp. 83–101.

8 For details on the literature, see the author's essay cited in fn. 6 above.

9 David Blackbourn and Geoff Eley, *The Peculiarities of German History: Bourgeois Society and Politics in Nineteenth-Century Germany* (Oxford, 1984).

10 Hans-Ulrich Wehler, *Bismarck und der Imperialismus* (Munich, 1976); Wehler, *Das Deutsche Kaiserreich 1871–1918* (5th edn., Göttingen, 1983); Hans Rosenberg, 'Wirtschaftskonjunktur, Gesellschaft und Politik in Mitteleuropa, 1873–1918', in Rosenberg, *Machteliten*, pp. 173–197.

11 S.B. Saul, *The Myth of the Great Depression 1873–1896* (London, 1969).

12 Knut Borchardt, *Die industrielle Revolution in Deutschland* (Munich, 1972); Karl Erich Born, *Wirtschafts-und Sozialgeschichte des deutschen Kaiserreichs (1867/71–1914)* (Wiesbaden, 1982).

13 Heilwig Schomerus, *Die Arbeiter der Maschinenfabrik Esslingen. Forschungen zur Lage der Arbeiterschaft im 19. Jahrhundert* (Stuttgart, 1977).

14 Wolfram Fischer, in Hermann Aubin and Wolfgang Zorn (eds.), *Handbuch der deutschen Wirtschafts- und Sozialgeschichte*, vol. 2, 1800–1970 (Stuttgart, 1976), p. 408; see also Adolf Noll, *Sozio-ökonomischer Strukturwandel des Handwerks in der zweiten Phase der Industrialisierung, unter besonderer Berücksichtigung der Regierungsbezirke Arnsberg und Münster* (Göttingen, 1975).

15 Friedrich Lenger, *Zwischen Kleinbürgertum und Proletariat. Studien zur Sozialgeschichte der Düsseldorfer Handwerker 1816–1878* (Göttingen, 1987).

16 Volker Hentschel, *Wirtschaft und Wirtschaftspolitik im wilhelminischen Deutschland. Organisierter Kapitalismus und Interventionsstaat* (Stuttgart, 1978), p. 62.

17 Heinrich August Winkler (ed.), *Organisierter Kapitalismus. Voraussetzungen und Anfänge* (Göttingen, 1974).

18 Hentschel, *Wirtschaft und Wirtschaftspolitik*, p. 62.

19 Max Weber, *Gesammelte Aufsätze zur Soziologie und Sozialpolitik* (Tübingen, 1924), p. 396.

20 For an authoritative discussion, see Klaus J. Bade, *Vom Auswanderungsland zum Einwanderungsland? Deutschland 1880–1980* (Berlin, 1983).

21 Hentschel, *Wirtschaft und Wirtschaftspolitik*, p. 74.

22 cf. fn. 1 above and Fischer's contribution in Aubin and Zorn (eds.), *Handbuch* (fn. 14 above).

23 cf. Jürgen Kocka, *Unternehmensverwaltung und Angestelltenschaft am Beispiel Siemens 1847–1914* (Stuttgart, 1969); Heinrich August Winkler, *Mittelstand, Demokratie und Nationalsozialismus* (Cologne, 1972).

24 cf. Geoff Eley, *Reshaping the German Right: Radical Nationalism and Political*

Change after Bismarck (New Haven, 1980); Roger Chickering, *We Men who Feel Most German: A Cultural Study of the Pan-German League, 1886–1914* (Boston, 1984). Chickering lays particular emphasis on the role of the higher civil service in the formation of the Pan-German League.

25 David Blackbourn, *Class, Religion and Local Politics in Wilhelmine Germany: The Center Party in Württemberg before 1914* (Wiesbaden, 1980).

26 This contradicts the central thesis, in my view untenable, of F.K. Ringer, *The Decline of the German Mandarins: The German Academic Community, 1890–1933* (Cambridge, Mass., 1969).

27 This applies, not least, to the governing class in the Empire and in Prussia itself. From 1850 onwards the higher civil service had steadily increased its middle-class membership, and there were also extensive personal links between it and the educated middle class – this despite the fact that the civil service saw its task as the maintenance of the existing semi-constitutional system, even though that was to a certain extent contrary to the narrow-minded interests of the conservatives. See Wolfgang J. Mommsen, 'Preußisches Staatsbewußtsein und deutsche Reichsidee. Preußen und das Deutsche Reich in der jüngeren deutschen Geschichte' (translated in the present volume, pp. 41–56).

Culture and politics in the German Empire

1 *Wirtschaft und Gesellschaft* (Tübingen, 1922), p. 629.

2 *Unzeitgemäße Betrachtungen, Erstes Stück. David Friedrich Strauß, der Bekenner und Schriftsteller*, reprinted in Friedrich Nietzsche, *Werke in drei Bänden* (Darmstadt, 1958), vol. 2, p. 986.

3 On this, see Wolfgang J. Mommsen, 'Stadt und Kultur im deutschen Kaiserreich', in Thilo Schabert, *Die Welt der Stadt* (forthcoming).

4 At present there is no comprehensive study of this problem. See, however, Gordon A. Craig, *Germany 1866–1914* (Oxford, 1978), pp. 180–213; Eric J. Hobsbawm, The Age of Empire 1875–1514 (New York, 1987); Thomas Nipperdey, *Wie das Bürgertum die Moderne fand* (Munich, 1988); Nipperdey, *Religion im Umbruch* (Munich, 1988); Hermann Glaser, *Die Kultur der Wilhelminischen Zeit. Topographie einer Epoche* (Frankfurt, 1984). For the more specific question of the victory of modern art, see Peter Paret, *The Berlin Secession: Modernism and its Enemies in Imperial Germany* (Cambridge, Mass., 1980); also Birgit Kulhoff, *Bürgerliche Selbstbehauptung im Spiegel der Kunst. Untersuchungen zur Kulturpublizistik der Rundschauzeitschriften im Kaiserreich (1871–1914)* (Bochum, 1990). The study by Corona Hepp, *Avantgarde. Moderne Kunst, Kulturkritik und Reformbewegungen nach der Jahrhundertwende* (Munich, 1987), is too impressionistic and not very convincing. The publications by the Projektkreis of the Fritz-Thyssen-Stiftung on *Kunst, Kultur und Politik im Deutschen Kaiserreich* are of fundamental importance, especially Ekkehard Mai and Stephan Waetzoldt (eds.), *Kunstverwaltung, Bau- und Denkmal-Politik im Kaiserreich* (Berlin, 1981); Mai, Waetzoldt and Hans Pohl (eds.), *Kunstpolitik und Kunstförderung im Kaiserreich* (Berlin, 1982); and Mai, Jürgen Paul and Waetzoldt (eds.), *Das Rathaus im Kaiserreich. Kunstpolitische Aspekte einer Bauaufgabe im 19. Jahrhundert* (Berlin, 1982).

5 cf. Katharina Mommsen, *Gesellschaftskritik bei Theodor Fontane und Thomas Mann* (Heidelberg, 1973), pp. 19–29.

6 Quoted in Winfried Neudinger, 'Akademiebeschimpfung – Anti-Festrede zur 175-Jahr-Feier', in Thomas Zacharias (ed.), *Tradition und Widerspruch. 175 Jahre Kunstakademie München* (Munich, 1985), p. 50. See also Paul Böckmann, 'Der Zeitroman Fontanes', in Wolfgang Preisendanz (ed.), *Theodor Fontane* (Darmstadt, 1983), p. 92.

7 For an essential survey, see Jürgen Kocka (ed.), *Bürgertum im 19. Jahrhundert. Deutschland im europäischen Vergleich*, 3 vols. (Stuttgart, 1988/89); see also Ulrich Engelhard, *"Bildungsbürgertum«. Begriffs-und Dogmengeschichte eines Etiketts* (Stuttgart, 1986) and Jürgen Kocka (ed.), *Bildungsbürgertum im 19. Jahrhundert*, part I, *Bildungssystem und Professionalisierung in internationalen Vergleichen* (Stuttgart, 1985).

8 Lothar Gall, *Bürgertum in Deutschland* (Berlin, 1989), p. 379.

9 Dieter Langewiesche, 'Bildungsbürgertum und Liberalismus im 19. Jahrhundert', in Kocka (ed.), *Bildungsbürgertum*, part IV (Stuttgart, 1989), p. 101.

10 *op. cit.*, p. 83.

11 cf. Franz Mehring, *Aufsätze zur deutschen Literatur von Hebbel bis Schweichel*, ed. Hans Koch (Berlin, 1961), p. 221.

12 On this, see Peter Sprengel, *Gerhart Hauptmann. Epoche – Werk – Wirkung* (Munich, 1984), pp. 52f.

13 *op. cit.*, pp. 46f.

14 See Dominik Bartmann, *Anton von Werner. Zur Kunst und Kunstpolitik im Deutschen Kaiserreich* (Berlin, 1985), pp. 35ff.

15 See Wolfgang J. Mommsen, 'Stadt und Kultur', pp. 11ff. Numerous examples are given in Mai, Paul and Waetzoldt, *Das Rathaus im Kaiserreich*, passim.

16 Ekkehard Mai, *Die Düsseldorfer Malerschule und die Malerei des 19. Jahrhunderts*, catalogue of the exhibition *Die Düsseldorfer Malerschule* at the Kunstmuseum, Düsseldorf, 13 May to 8 July 1979 (Düsseldorf, 1979), p. 35.

17 cf. Richard Hamann and Jost Hermand, *Deutsche Kunst und Kultur von der Gründerzeit bis zum Expressionismus*, vol. 1 (Munich, 1971), p. 34.

18 Gall, *Bürgertum in Deutschland*, pp. 471f., 449.

19 Karl Gustav Fellerer, *Studien zur Musik des 19. Jahrhunderts*, vol. 1, *Musik und Musikleben im 19. Jahrhundert* (Regensburg, 1984), p. 241.

20 See the penetrating study by Hans Mayer, *Richard Wagner* (Hamburg, 1959), still unsurpassed.

21 See Ferdinand Tönnies, *Der Nietzsche-Kultus. Eine Kritik* (Lepizig, 1897), pp. 11ff.; also Walter Kaufmann, 'Prologue: The Nietzsche Legend', in *Nietzsche: Philosopher, Psychologist, Antichrist* (3rd edn., New York, 1968), pp. 3ff..

22 cf. Nietzsche's unquestionably bitter and exaggerated remark in his pamphlet *Der Fall Wagner* (ed. Dieter Borchmeyer, Frankfurt, 1983, p. 126): 'The Germans, procrastinators *par excellence*, are today the most backward cultured nation in Europe.'

23 cf. Hermann Lübbe, 'Fontane und die Gesellschaft', in Wolfgang Preisendanz (ed.), *Theodor Fontane*, p. 360.

24 Quoted in Katharina Mommsen, *Fontane*, p. 44.

25 Lübbe, *Fontane*, p. 366.

26 In a speech on 18 February 1901 Wilhelm II said, among other things: '[...] if culture is properly to fulfil its task, it must penetrate to the very lowest levels of society. It can do this only if it is uplifting, not by descending into the gutter.' (Quoted in Bartmann, *Anton von Werner*, p. 177.)

27 *Stenographische Berichte des preußischen Abgeordnetenhauses*, 1895, vol. 1, 25th session, 21 February 1895, col. 790. See also Manfred Brauneck,

Literatur und Öffentlichkeit im ausgehenden 19. Jahrhundert. Studien zur Rezeption des naturalistischen Theaters in Deutschland (Stuttgart, 1974) and Helmut Praschek (ed.), *Gerhart Hauptmanns Weber. Eine Dokumentation. Mit einer Einleitung von Peter Wruck* (Berlin/GDR, 1981).

28 cf. Max Weber, *Gesamtausgabe* I/4, *Landarbeiterfrage, Nationalstaat und Volkswirtschaftspolitik. Schriften und Reden 1892–1899*, ed. Wolfgang J. Mommsen in collaboration with Rita Aldenhoff-Hübinger (Tübingen, 1991), Anhang I, 'Erklärung zur Umsturzvorlage'.

29 On this, see Robin Lenman, 'Politics and Culture: The State and the Avant-Garde in Munich 1886–1914', in Richard Evans (ed.), *Society and Politics in Wilhelmine Germany* (London, 1978), pp. 90–111.

30 cf. Christopher B. With, *The Prussian Landeskunstkommission 1862–1911: A Study in State Subvention of the Arts* (Berlin, 1986).

31 Letter to Liebermann, 2 March 1909, in Alfred Lichtwark, *Briefe an Liebermann* (Hamburg, 1947), p. 205.

32 cf. Anton von Werner, *Erlebnisse und Eindrücke 1870–1890* (Berlin, 1913), a striking instance of Wilhelmine complacency.

33 cf. Werner Haftmann, *Malerei im 20. Jahrhundert* (Munich, 1954), pp. 74ff.

34 cf. Peter Paret, *The Berlin Secession*, pp. 38ff.; quotations in Werner Doede, *Die Berliner Secession. Berlin als Zentrum der deutschen Kunst von der Jahrhundertwende bis zum Ersten Weltkrieg* (Frankfurt am Main/Berlin/Vienna, 1977), pp. 10f.

35 Haftmann, *Malerei im 20. Jahrhundert*, p. 76.

36 Werner Doede, *Berlin. Kunst und Künstler seit 1870. Anfänge und Entwicklungen* (Recklinghausen, 1961), p. 82.

37 *Die Reden Kaiser Wilhelms II.*, ed. Johannes Penzler, vol. 3 (Leipzig, 1907), p. 61.

38 See Peter Paret, 'Art and the National Image: The Conflict over Germany's Participation in the St Louis Exhibition', *Central European History* XI (1978), pp. 173ff.; Paret, *The Berlin Secession*, pp. 113–155; Bartmann, *Anton von Werner*, pp. 194–211.

39 cf. Paret, *The Berlin Secession*, pp. 134ff.

40 Reichstag debate, 16 February 1904, *Stenographische Berichte über die Verhandlungen des Reichstages*, 11th legislative period, Ist session 1904–1905, vol. 198, p. 1001 A.

41 *op. cit.*, p. 1026. Singer thereupon corrected himself: 'I meant to say, with Anton von Werner at its head.'

42 For reaction in the leading journals of art criticism, cf. Kulhoff, *Bürgerliche Selbstbehauptung*, pp. 215ff.

43 On the Tschudi affair, see Bartmann, *Anton von Werner*, pp. 213–246.

44 See Gerhard Bott, *Jugendstil. Vom Beitrag Damstadts zur internationalen Kunstbewegung um 1900* (Darmstadt, 1969) and also the contemporary discussion by Alexander Koch and Victor Zobel, *Darmstadt. Eine Stätte moderner Kunst-Bestrebungen* (Darmstadt, 1905).

45 cf. Kurt Junghans, *Der Deutsche Werkbund. Sein erstes Jahrzehnt* (Berlin, 1982), pp. 21ff. and passim. The yearbook of the Deutscher Werkbund was headed with the slogan 'Die Durchgeistigung der deutschen Arbeit'.

46 *op. cit.*, p. 141.

47 For an essential discussion of these questions, see Robin Lenman, 'Painters, Patronage and the Art Market in Germany 1850–1914', *Past and Present* 125 (1989) and the recent study by Horst Ludwig, *Geld und Politik um 1900 in München. Formen und Ziele der Kunstfinanzierung und Kunstpolitik während der Prinzregentenära (1886–1912)* (Berlin, 1986).

48 cf. Hobsbawm, *op. cit.*, p. 232

49 Nietzsche, *Der Fall Wagner*, p. 126 (cf. fn. 22 above).
50 Nipperdey, *Wie das Bürgertum die Moderne fand*, p. 63.
51 Max Weber, *Gesammelte Aufsätze zur Wissenschaftslehre* (3rd edn., Tübingen, 1968), p. 180.
52 Hobsbawm, *op cit.*, p. 235.
53 Volkmar Hansen and Gert Heine (eds.), *Frage und Antwort. Interviews mit Thomas Mann 1909–1950* (Heidelberg, 1983), p. 51.
54 Thomas Mann, *Betrachtungen eines Unpolitischen* (Berlin, 1918), p. 84.
55 cf. Rainer Maria Rilke, 'Über den jungen Dichter', *Werke in sechs Bänden*, vol. II/2 (Frankfurt am Main, 1982), p. 561.
56 *Philosophie des Geldes*, ed. David B. Frisby and Klaus Christian Köhnke, *Gesamtausgabe*, vol. 6, pp. 627ff.
57 *op. cit.*, pp. 675f.
58 cf. Alfred Kelly, *The Descent of Darwin: The Popularization of Darwinism in Germany, 1860–1914* (University of North Carolina Press, 1981), pp. 101f., 106ff.
59 See Fritz Stern, *The Politics of Cultural Despair* (Berkeley, California, 1961), pp. 116ff.

The latest crisis of the Wilhelmine Empire

1 Theodor Schieder, 'Bismarck – gestern und heute', in Lothar Gall (ed.), *Das Bismarck-Problem in der Geschichtsschreibung nach 1945* (Cologne/Berlin, 1971), pp. 364f.; also Schieder, 'Das Reich unter der Führung Bismarcks', in Peter Rassow (ed.), *Deutsche Geschichte im Überblick. Ein Handbuch* (2nd edn., Stuttgart, 1962); Schieder, *Das Deutsche Kaiserreich von 1871 als Nationalstaat*, vol. 20 of *Wissenschaftliche Abhandlungen der Arbeitsgemeinschaft für Forschung des Landes Nordrhein-Westfalen* (Cologne, 1961), pp. 40f.
2 Schieder, *Kaiserreich*, pp. 86f.
3 See, especially, Wolfgang Sauer, 'Das Problem des Nationalstaats', in Helmut Böhme (ed.), *Probleme der Reichsgründungszeit 1848–1879* (Cologne/Berlin, 1968), pp. 468ff.
4 *op. cit.*; Michael Stürmer, 'Konservativismus und Revolution in Bismarcks Politik', in Stürmer (ed.), *Das kaiserliche Deutschland. Politik und Gesellschaft 1870–1918* (Düsseldorf, 1970), pp. 156f.; Dieter Groh, 'Die mißlungene "Innere Reichsgründung"', *Revue d'Allemagne* 4 (1972); and Groh, *Negative Integration und revolutionärer Attentismus. Die deutsche Sozialdemokratie am Vorabend des Ersten Weltkrieges* (Frankfurt am Main, 1973), pp. 27ff.
5 Hans-Ulrich Wehler, *Bismarck und der Imperialismus* (Cologne/Berlin, 1969); cf. also *Militärgeschichtliche Mitteilungen* 9 (1971), pp. 197ff.; Wehler, 'Bismarcks Imperialismus und späte Rußlandpolitik unter dem Primat der Innenpolitik', in Stürmer (ed.), *Das kaiserliche Deutschland*, pp. 237ff.
6 Wehler, *Bismarck*, p. 137.
7 Sauer, 'Problem des Nationalstaats', pp. 473ff.
8 Carl Schmitt, 'Staatsgefüge und Zusammenbruch des 2. Reiches', in Schmitt (ed.), *Der Deutsche Staat der Gegenwart*, vol. 6 (Hamburg, 1934), pp. 25ff.
9 Michael Stürmer, 'Staatsstreichgedanken im Bismarck-Reich', *Historische Zeitung* 209 (1969), pp. 566ff.

10 Eugene A. Anderson, *The Social and Political Conflict in Prussia 1858–1864* (Lincoln, Nebraska, 1954).

11 Helmut Böhme, *Deutschlands Weg zur Großmacht. Studien zum Verhältnis von Wirtschaft und Staat während der Reichsgründungszeit 1848–1881* (Cologne/Berlin, 1966); Böhme, 'Thesen zur Beurteilung der gesellschaftlichen, wirtschaftlichen und politischen Ursachen des deutschen Imperialismus', in *Der moderne Imperialismus*, ed. with an introduction by Wolfgang J. Mommsen (Stuttgart, 1971), p. 38. See also, especially, Helmut Böhme (ed.), *Probleme der Reichsgründungszeit*, p. 14, where the year 1879 is described as marking the 'close of the era of Imperial unification'.

12 This applies most clearly to Bülow's period of government: Bülow openly admitted that successes in foreign policy were of value as a means of stabilizing the domestic political situation. This has been impressively documented in the case of Alfred von Tirpitz's naval policy by Volker R. Berghahn, *Der Tirpitz-Plan. Genesis und Verfall einer innenpolitischen Krisenstrategie unter Wilhelm II.*, vol. 1, *Geschichtliche Studien zu Politik und Gesellschaft* (Düsseldorf, 1971); cf. the review in *Militärgeschichtliche Mitteilungen* 11 (1972), pp. 196ff.

13 Rainer Lepsius, 'Parteiensystem und Sozialstruktur. Zum Problem der Demokratisierung der deutschen Gesellschaft', in Wilhelm Abel (ed.), *Wirtschaft, Geschichte und Wirtschaftsgeschichte. Festschrift zum 65. Geburtstag von Friedrich Lütge* (Stuttgart, 1966), pp. 371ff.

14 Quoted in Hans Herzfeld, *Johannes v. Miquel. Sein Anteil am Ausbau des Deutschen Reiches bis zur Jahrhundertwende*, vol. 2 (Detmold, 1938), p. 183.

15 cf. Wolfgang J. Mommsen, introduction to Friedrich Naumann, *Schriften zur Verfassungspolitik*, ed. Theodor Schieder for the Friedrich-Naumann-Stiftung (Cologne/Opladen, 1964), vol. 2 of Friedrich Naumann, *Werke*.

16 Quoted in John C.G. Röhl, *Deutschland ohne Bismarck. Die Regierungskrise im Zweiten Kaiserreich 1890–1900* (Tübingen, 1969), p. 179 (cf. also the earlier English edition, *Germany without Bismarck: The Crisis of Government in the Second Reich, 1890–1900*, London, 1967). See the review of the German edition in *Militärgeschichtliche Mitteilungen* 10 (1971), pp. 217ff.

17 *op. cit.*

18 Naumann, *Verfassungspolitik*, p. 267.

19 Quoted in Röhl, p. 229.

20 In the Budget Committee of the Reichstag on 6 February 1913 Tirpitz associated himself with Churchill's proposal of a ratio of naval strength of 10:16. At the same time, however, the German government informed Sir Edward Grey that it was not interested in opening negotiations on the matter.

21 Report by Baroness Spitzenberg: cf. *Tagebuch der Baronin Spitzenberg, geb. Freiin von Varnbüler. Aufzeichnungen aus der Hofgesellschaft des Hohenzollernreiches*, ed. Rudolf Vierhaus (Göttingen, 1960), p. 509.

22 To Eisendecher, 4 June 1911, Eisendecher papers, 1/1–7, Politisches Archiv des Auwärtigen Amtes, Bonn.

23 Despite the recalcitrant nature of the material, this has been described in detail in a commendable study by Peter-Christian Witt, *Die Finanzpolitik des Deutschen Reiches von 1903 bis 1913. Eine Studie zur Innenpolitik des Wilhelminischen Deutschland*, 415, *Historische Studien* (Lübeck/Hamburg, 1970).

24 It is important to stress this distinction: contrast Dirk Stegmann's richly documented and otherwise highly instructive *Die Erben Bismarcks. Parteien und Verbände in der Spätphase des wilhelminischen Deutschland. Sammlungspolitik 1897–1918* (Berlin/Cologne, 1970). There was a qualitative difference between the two brands of 'Sammlungspolitik': the purpose of

Bethmann Hollweg's was to bind the bourgeois parties into the existing semi-constitutional system and induce them to make common cause against Social Democracy, whereas the advocates of the other – in particular, the Conservatives and the CVdI – toyed with plans for repressive legislation against the Social Democrats, a retreat from universal suffrage and moves towards towards corporatism, which inevitably brought them into conflict with the government itself.

25 *Stenographische Berichte über die Verhandlungen des Deutschen Reichstages*, vol. 283, p. 67 D.
26 *Verhandlungen des Deutschen Reichstages*, vol. 291, p. 6157 D.
27 Quoted in Hans-Günter Zmarzlik, *Bethmann Hollweg als Reichskanzler 1909–1914*, vol. 11, *Beiträge zur Geschichte des Parlamentarismus und der politischen Parteien* (Düsseldorf, 1957), p. 131.
28 See also Groh, *Negative Integration*, pp. 471ff.
29 Wilhelm II to the Crown Prince, 22 November 1913; reproduced in Hartmut Pogge von Strandmann, Anhang II, in Pogge von Strandmann and Imanuel Geiss, *Die Erforderlichkeit des Unmöglichen. Deutschland am Vorabend des Ersten Weltkrieges*, vol. 2, *Hamburger Studien zur neueren Geschichte*, ed. Fritz Fischer (Frankfurt am Main, 1965), p. 38.
30 Pius Dirr (ed.), *Bayerische Dokumente zum Kriegsausbruch und zum Versailler Schuldspruch* (4th edn., Munich, 1928), p. 111.
31 cf. Wolfgang J. Mommsen, 'Domestic Factors in German Foreign Policy before 1914', *Central European History* 6 (1973), pp. 37f. (re-translated in the present volume, pp. 163–188). Erwin Hölzle's recent dramatized account of the matter – the facts of which have been known for a long time – completely overlooks the point that the Anglo-Russian negotiations became significant, primarily, because of their domestic political consequences; their diplomatic effect was limited, since Bethmann Hollweg did not assume in the first place that Great Britain would remain neutral in the event of war. Hölzle's thesis that the failure of Ballin's *démarche* in Berlin substantially influenced the German government's decisions after 23 July 1914 is untenable and is not borne out by the evidence. See Erwin Hölzle, 'Landung in Pommern', *Frankfurter Allgemeine Zeitung*, no. 160, 13 July 1973, and Hölzle, *Geheimnisverrat und der Kriegsausbruch 1914* (Göttingen, 1973).
32 Diary entry by Kurt Riezler, 14 July 1914: Kurt Riezler, *Tagebücher, Aufsätze, Dokumente*, ed. with an introduction by Karl-Dietrich Erdmann, vol. 48, *Deutsche Geschichtsquellen des 19. und 20. Jahrhunderts* (Göttingen, 1972); cf. the review in *Militärgeschichtliche Mitteilungen* 14 (1973), pp. 236ff.
33 Walther Rathenau, *Ein preußischer Europäer. Briefe*, edited with an introduction by Margarete von Eynern (Berlin, 1955), p. 134.

Domestic factors in German foreign policy before 1914

1 Gordon A. Craig, 'Political and Diplomatic History', in Felix Gilbert and Stephen R. Graubard (eds.), *Historical Studies Today* (New York, 1972), pp. 356ff.
2 For a systematic treatment of this problem, see Hans Rothfels,

Gesellschaftsform und auswärtige Politik (Laupheim, 1956); also the essays in *Die anachronistische Souveränität. Zum Verhältnis von Innen- und Außenpolitik*, Sonderheft 1, ed. Ernst-Otto Czempiel, *Politische Vierteljahresschrift* (1969); and Karl Dietrich Bracher, 'Kritische Bemerkungen über den Primat der Außenpolitik, in *Faktoren der politischen Entscheidung. Festgabe für Ernst Fraenkel zum 65. Geburtstag* (Berlin, 1963), pp. 115ff.

3 Eckart Kehr, *Der Primat der Innenpolitik. Gesammelte Aufsätze*, ed. Hans-Ulrich Wehler (Berlin, 1965), p. 152.

4 *op. cit.*, p. 155.

5 For an example, cf. Willibald Gutsche and Annelies Laschitza, 'Forschungen zur deutschen Geschichte von der Jahrhundertwende bis 1917', in *Historische Forschungen in der DDR*, Sonderband, *Zeitschrift für Geschichte* (1970), p. 476.

6 cf. Vladimir Ilyich Lenin, *Selected Works* (Moscow, 1967), p. 770.

7 W. W. Rostow, *The Stages of Economic Growth* (Cambridge, 1968), pp. 106ff.

8 Collective headed by Fritz Klein, *Deutschland im Ersten Weltkrieg*, I, *Vorbereitung, Entfesselung und Verlauf des Krieges bis Ende 1914* (Berlin, 1968).

9 George William F. Hallgarten, *Imperialismus vor 1914*, 2 vols. (2nd edn., Munich, 1963); Hallgarten, *Das Schicksal des Imperialismus im 20. Jahrhundert* (Frankfurt am Main, 1969).

10 This approach is represented, notably, by Fritz Fischer and his school, in particular Imanuel Geiss and Klaus Wernecke. See Fritz Fischer, *Griff nach der Weltmacht. Die Kriegszielpolitik des kaiserlichen Deutschland 1914–1918* (3rd edn., Düsseldorf, 1968); Fischer, *Krieg der Illusionen. Die deutsche Politik von 1911–1914* (Düsseldorf, 1969); Fischer, *Weltmacht oder Niedergang. Deutschland im Ersten Weltkrieg* (Frankfurt am Main, 1965); Imanuel Geiss, 'The Outbreak of the First World War and German War Aims', *Journal of Contemporary History* 1 (1966), no. 3, pp. 75–91; Geiss, *Julikrise und Kriegsausbruch 1914. Eine Dokumentensammlung*, 2 vols. (Hanover, 1963–64); Hartmut Pogge von Strandmann and Imanuel Geiss, *Die Erforderlichkeit des Unmöglichen. Deutschland am Vorabend des Ersten Weltkrieges* (Frankfurt am Main, 1965); Klaus Wernecke, *Der Wille zur Weltgeltung. Außenpolitik und Öffentlichkeit im Kaiserreich am Vorabend des Ersten Weltkrieges* (Düsseldorf, 1970). See also Wolfgang J. Mommsen, 'The Debate on German War Aims', *Journal of Contemporary History*, 1 (1966), pp. 47ff.

11 This approach is to be found in many recent studies, though not all are equally stringent or radical. See, in particular, writings by Hans-Ulrich Wehler, Dirk Stegmann, Helmut Böhme and – with some qualifications – Volker Berghahn: Hans-Ulrich Wehler, *Bismarck und der Imperialismus* (Cologne, 1969); Wehler, *Krisenherde des Kaiserreiches 1871–1918* (Cologne, 1970); Wehler, 'Bismarcks Imperialismus und späte Rußlandpolitik unter dem Primat der Innenpolitik', in Michael Stürmer (ed.), *Das Kaiserliche Deutschland* (2nd edn., Darmstadt, 1976), pp. 235ff.; Dirk Stegmann, *Die Erben Bismarcks. Parteien und Verbände in der Spätphase des Wilhelminischen Deutschland. Sammlungspolitik 1897–1918* (Cologne, 1970); Helmut Böhme, 'Thesen zur Beurteilung der gesellschaftlichen, wirtschaftlichen und politischen Ursachen des deutschen Imperialismus', in Wolfgang J. Mommsen (ed.), *Der moderne Imperialismus* (Stuttgart, 1971), pp. 31ff.; Volker Berghahn, 'Zu den Zielen des deutschen Flottenbaus unter Wilhelm II.', *Historische Zeitschrift* 210 (1970), pp. 34ff.; Berghahn, *Der Tirpitzplan. Genesis und Verfall einer innenpolitischen Krisenstrategie unter Wilhelm II.* (Düsseldorf, 1971); Berghahn, 'Flottenrüstung und Machtgefüge', in Stürmer (ed.), *Das Kaiserliche*

Deutschland, pp. 378ff.

12 This approach, though it is not usually applied to questions of foreign policy, is represented by Gerhard A. Ritter, Hans-Günther Zmarzlik, John C.G. Röhl, Gustav Schmidt and Hans-Jürgen Puhle. See Gerhard A. Ritter, Georg Kotowski and Werner Pöls, *Das Wilhelminische Deutschland* (Frankfurt am Main, 1965); Hans-Günther Zmarzlik, *Bethmann Hollweg als Reichskanzler 1909–1914* (Bonn, 1957); John C.G. Röhl, *Deutschland ohne Bismarck. Die Regierungskrise im Zweiten Kaiserreich 1890–1900* (Tübingen, 1969) (cf. also the earlier English edition, *Germany without Bismarck: The Crisis of Government in the Second Reich, 1890–1900*, London, 1967); Röhl, *Zwei deutsche Fürsten zur Kriegsschuldfrage. Lichnowski, Eulenburg und der Ausbruch des Ersten Weltkrieges* (Düsseldorf, 1971). In his more recent work, however, Röhl has come closer to the Fischer camp. See also Hans-Jürgen Puhle, 'Parlament, Parteien und Interessenverbände 1890–1914', in Stürmer (ed.), *Das Kaiserliche Deutschland*, pp. 340ff. and Gustav Schmidt, 'Deutschland am Vorabend des Ersten Weltkrieges', in *op. cit.*, pp. 397ff.

13 *Das Schicksal des Imperialismus*, p. 140.

14 *op. cit.*, p. 34.

15 cf. fn. 10 above.

16 For a more detailed assessment of Fischer's views, see Mommsen, 'The Debate', pp. 47ff., and Mommsen, 'Die deutsche "Weltpolitik" und der Erste Weltkrieg', *Neue Politische Literatur* 16 (1971), pp. 482ff.

17 cf. Fischer, *Krieg der Illusionen*, pp. 231ff. John C.G. Röhl, in 'Admiral von Müller and the Approach of War 1911–1914', *Historical Journal* XII (1969), pp. 651ff., has shown that Walter Goetz, the editor of the diaries of Admiral von Müller (cf. *Der Kaiser. Aufzeichnungen des Chefs des Marinekabinetts Admiral Georg von Müller über die Ära Wilhlems II.*, Göttingen, 1965, pp. 124ff.), on which our knowledge of this conference almost entirely depends, omits vital sections of the text, notably the second half of the following passage (from the words 'but does not'). The passage clearly reveals Moltke as the advocate of a preventive war:

The Chief of the General Staff says: war, the sooner the better, but does not draw the logical inference, namely: Russia or France, or both, to be given an ultimatum, unleashing war with right on our side. [In the] Afternoon, wrote to the Chancellor about influencing the press.

It is difficult to avoid the conclusion that the conference was dominated by the assumption that war might break out at any moment – not a far-fetched notion, since Europe was in the midst of a serious Balkan crisis. One vital problem was the question how to persuade German public opinion that a European war on behalf of Austria's ambition to create a semi-independent Albania was justifiable. Hence the Emperor's suggestion, 'Now go to the press with a vengeance': cf. Bethmann Hollweg to Kiderlen-Wächter, 17 December 1912, in *Die Große Politik der europäischen Kabinette* (Berlin, 1922–27), vol. 39, no. 15,553 (hereafter *GP*).

18 As the document cited in fn. 17 (above) shows, the Chancellor had not heard about the 'war council' before 16 December. Admiral von Müller evidently made no reference to the conference when he wrote to the Chancellor in the afternoon of 8 December, indicating that something should be done at this critical juncture to get the press to prepare public opinion for the possibility of a European war on behalf of Austria-Hungary. This, however, would imply that von Müller was in fact of the view that the result of the conference had been

'nil'. It is unlikely, incidentally, that von Müller deliberately misled the Chancellor on the matter, as he usually acted as the latter's ally against Tirpitz.

19 Bethmann Hollweg managed to pacify the Emperor by pointing out that Grey's message was not, in the end, so disastrous, at any rate as long as Germany refrained from acting provocatively: cf. Bethmann Hollweg's memorandum, 18 December 1912, *GP*, vol. 39, no. 15,560, pp. 9f. He had already given Tirpitz and Heeringen to understand that an official propaganda campaign in favour of new armaments would not be desirable. The Chancellor's remarks on the matter make amusing reading (*op. cit.*, pp. 147f.):

I must, however, insist quite emphatically that they do not enter into arrangements behind my back, with regard to His Majesty among others, that nothing in the slightest by way of preliminary work that may have been carried out in their departments be made public, and that I should on no account tolerate any press agitation on behalf of these projects.

Neither gentleman seems to have been bold enough to invoke the arguments that the Emperor used at the 'war council' of 8 December 1912!

20 Fischer's thesis rests on the unspoken assumption that Germany had enjoyed a position of economic dominance in the Ottoman Empire and did not face competition from other industrial states until the years immediately before 1914. In fact, however, all German ventures in this region had been heavily dependent on the Caisse de la Dette Publique, which was dominated by the French, and had been closely associated with foreign, mainly French, banks, in particular the Banque Impériale Ottomane. The first sections of the Baghdad Railway could not have been built without substantial support from these institutions: cf. Donald C. Blaisdell, *European Financial Control in the Ottoman Empire* (New York, 1966), pp. 124ff. It should also be pointed out that the Germans succeeded in increasing their shareholding in the Dette Publique from an original 8 per cent to about 30 per cent in 1914. This significantly strengthened their influence, although the French remained the most powerful group of shareholders: cf. Raymond Poideven, *Les Relations économiques et financières entre la France et l'Allemagne de 1898 à 1914* (Paris, 1969), p. 697. The splitting-up of the economic activities of the western powers that took place in the Ottoman Empire after 1909 did not necessarily imply a worsening of Germany's position. The treaty agreed between a German and a French group on 15 February 1914 concerning respective spheres of influence and economic commitments in the region might, like the agreement reached in March 1914 between the d'Arcy Group and the Deutsche Bank on the joint exploitation of the Mesopotamian and Anatolian oil fields, have turned out more favourably for the German side, but the Deutsche Bank was fully satisfied. See, for example, *GP*, vol. 37/I, no. 14,888, p. 435. Fischer's account, in *Krieg der Illusionen*, pp. 424ff., is rather misleading.

21 cf. *Bismarck und der Imperialismus* (3rd edn., Cologne, 1972), pp. 17ff., where Wehler sets out the principles of his theory. See my review in *Central European History* 2 (1969), pp. 366ff. See also Wehler's introduction to *Imperialismus* (2nd edn., Cologne, 1972), pp. 11ff.

22 This point is also made by Böhme, 'Thesen', pp. 39ff.

23 Kehr, *Primat*, p. 150.

24 Böhme, 'Thesen', pp. 48f. For Böhme, German imperialism was an

attempt by the government, and the groups and interests from which the government drew its support, [...] to deal with the social changes that were taking place in a society being rapidly transformed by headlong industrialization, not – as in the 'socialist' blueprint – through radical reform in the shape of an upheaval in property relations, but through paralysis, diverting attention on to schemes to make Germany a great national and world power and preserving the domestic political status quo without the need for reform.

25 See Berghahn, 'Zu den Zielen des deutschen Flottenbaus', pp. 34ff.; Berghahn, *Der Tirpitzplan*, pp. 592ff. According to Berghahn, Tirpitz's strategy had failed by 1909 and should not be regarded as a decisive factor in German domestic politics from then onwards, even though Tirpitz continued to enjoy great prestige among parliamentary politicians.

26 This view partly coincides with that of Berghahn, who also suggests that a distinction should be drawn between the 'kleine Sammlung' favoured by the agricultural interest and heavy industry and the 'große Sammlung' pursued by Tirpitz and Bülow. It should be noted, however, that a difference in kind as well as in scale is involved here: the 'große Sammlung' was seen as including the majority of the middle classes and the Centre party. Stegmann consistently confuses the two types of 'Sammlungspolitik', to the detriment of his argument.

27 On Bülow's attempt to revitalize the Emperor's 'personal rule', cf. Röhl, *Deutschland ohne Bismarck*, pp. 123f., 147f., 251ff. As early as 1896, shortly before he was appointed Secretary of State at the Foreign Office, Bülow expressed the view that the problems of the constitution could be solved only by a form of 'royalism *sans phrase*' (*op. cit.*, p. 187). See also his remark of 1897 (*op. cit.*, p. 229): 'I am putting the main emphasis on foreign policy. Only a successful foreign policy can help to reconcile, pacify, rally, unite.' On the anti-parliamentary thrust of Tirpitz's naval policy, see Berghahn, 'Zu den Zielen des deutschen Flottenbaus', pp. 36ff., and Berghahn, *Der Tirpitzplan*, pp. 14ff.

28 Bülow to Tirpitz, 25 December 1908, in Otto Hammann, *Bilder aus der letzten Kaiserzeit* (Berlin, 1922, p. 148):

You refrain, however, from expressing an opinion whether, in view of the great superiority, which you yourself emphasize, of the English fleet over our own naval forces at the present time – a superiority, moreover, which the English people seems utterly determined to retain in future – it would be at all possible for our battleships to go decisively into action. If, however, there is a justifiable fear that our fleet, in its present strength, would be kept blockaded in our ports by the superior strength of the English naval forces – if we have to reckon on the likelihood that for the time being we should be forced on to the defensive in a naval war with England – then the question arises whether it would not be advisable to turn our attention to the improvement of our coastal defences, the enlargement of our stock of naval mines and the creation of a powerful submarine fleet, rather than concentrate exclusively on increasing the number of our battleships.

29 cf. Peter Christian Witt, *Die Finanzpolitik des Deutschen Reiches von 1903–1913. Eine Studie zur Innenpolitik des Wilhelminischen Deutschlands* (Lübeck, 1970), pp. 303f.

30 Imperialist concerns had previously played a somewhat secondary role in Conservative ideology. The Conservative party had mainly followed the official line and not joined in the pressure on the government. Although the Farmers' Alliance had come out in favour of a highly aggressive brand of nationalism, the Conservatives had no clearly defined conception of an imperialist policy. If anything, they opposed imperialist ventures whenever their own economic interests were affected. See Hans-Jürgen Puhle, *Agrarische Interessenpolitik*

und preußischer Konservativismus im Wilhelminischen Reich (1893-1914). Ein Beitrag zur Analyse des Nationalismus am Beispiel des Bundes der Landwirte und der Deutsch-Konservativen Partei (Hanover, 1966), pp. 86ff., 241f.

31 For a detailed if somewhat unoriginal account of these negotiations, see Alexander Kessler, *Das deutsch-englische Verhältnis vom Amtsantritt Bethmann Hollwegs bis zur Haldane-Mission* (Erlangen, 1938). See also Hans Joachim Henning, *Deutschlands Verhältnis zu England in Bethmann Hollwegs Außenpolitik 1909-1914* (doctoral thesis, Cologne, 1962).

32 cf. in particular Bethmann Hollweg's memorandum for Kiderlen-Wächter, 3 April 1911, *GP*, vol. 28, no. 10,347, p. 409.

33 cf. *GP*, vol. 29, pp. 107f., note, and Kiderlen-Wächter's telegram to Schoen, 30 June 1911, in which there is an allusion to his intention of 'finally eliminating the Moroccan problem as a source of friction in international relations', *op. cit.*, no. 10,578, p. 155. See also Bethmann Hollweg's statement in the Reichstag, 9 November 1911: 'Morocco was a constantly festering wound in our relations not only with France but with England . . . the settlement of the Moroccan matter [cleared] the decks, including in our relations with England' (*Stenographische Berichte über die Verhandlungen des Reichstages*, vol. 268, p. 7713, 3 A–B).

34 This is convincingly demonstrated in Alfred A. Vagts, 'M.M. Warburg & Co. Ein Bankhaus in der deutschen Weltpolitik 1905-1935', *Vierteljahresschrift für Sozial- und Wirtschaftsgeschichte* 45 (1958), pp. 253ff. See also the diaries of Regendanz, who acted as an agent for the German government, in F.W. Pick, *Searchlight on German Africa: The Diaries and Papers of Dr. Regendanz* (London, 1939), and Joanne St. Mortimer, 'Commercial Interests and German Diplomacy in the Agadir Crisis', *Historical Journal* 10 (1967), which, however, substantially overstates the importance of the business interests behind Regendanz.

35 Kiderlen-Wächter's ill-considered handling of the press was severely criticized in the Reichstag as early as 1912: see the debates in the Budget Committee as well as exchanges on the floor, 17 February 1912, *Verhandlungen des Reichstages*, vol. 283, pp. 96 Aff. For an account of Kiderlen-Wächter's press policies, see Wernecke, *Der Wille zur Weltgeltung*, pp. 26ff. Details of the Secretary of State's negotiations with Class are also in Dieter Fricke *et al.* (eds.), *Die bürgerlichen Parteien*, vol. I (Leipzig, 1970), pp. 11f.

36 cf. Kiderlen-Wächter's memorandum for Wilhelm II, 3 May, *GP*, vol. 29, no. 10,549, p. 108:

Our public opinion, with the sole exception of the Social Democratic party, would blame the Imperial government if events in [Morocco] were simply allowed to run their course. Conversely, it may be assumed with certainty that practical results would win round many dissatisfied voters and, perhaps, have a not insignificant effect on the outcome of the forthcoming Reichstag elections.

37 Helmuth von Moltke, *Erinnerungen, Briefe, Dokumente 1877-1916* (Darmstadt, 1922), p. 362.

38 cf. Bethmann Hollweg's speech in the Reichstag, 9 November 1911, *Verhandlungen des Reichstages*, vol. 268, p. 756 A and his letter to Eisendecher, 16 November 1911, Eisendecher papers, 1/1-7, Politisches Archiv des Auswärtigen Amtes, Bonn:

War for the Mannesmann brothers would have been a crime. But the German people toyed so irresponsibly with war this summer. This has put me in a very serious frame of mind; I had to oppose it. Even at the risk of heaping the nation's anger upon my head.

39 Rostow, *Stages of Economic Growth*, p. 116.
40 cf. Wolfgang J. Mommsen, *Max Weber und die deutsche Politik 1890–1914* (2nd edn., Tübingen, 1974), pp. 130f.
41 He appealed, for example, to Delbrück and Lamprecht to support the official scheme for an inheritance tax as a politically acceptable way of financing the Army Bill of 1913.
42 cf. Bethmann Hollweg to Eisendecher, Eisendecher papers, 1/1–7: 'The Emperor is again in a state of extreme nervousness. Every foolish resolution that the Reichstag committee has passed in the Army Bill – and there are certainly enough of them – irritates him intensely, and every day what he would really like to do is to dissolve, or to threaten dissolution . . . I am well aware that my way of practising politics is becoming more unacceptable to the Emperor with every day that passes.' See also Kurt Stenkewitz, *Gegen Bajonett und Dividende* (Berlin, 1960), pp. 117f. and Count Kuno Westarp, *Konservative Politik im letzten Jahrzehnt des Kaiserreichs* I (Berlin, 1935), p. 238.
43 This trend is reflected in Reichstag debates on a number of motions designed to establish a clearer definition of the 'Kommandogewalt': for example, on 23 January and 5 and 6 May 1914, *Verhandlungen des Reichstages*, vol. 2252, pp. 6730ff., and vol. 294, pp. 8480ff.

On 6 May 1914 the new War Minister, von Falkenhayn, spelled out the privileges of the Crown, justifying the quasi-independent position of the Imperial Military Cabinet and the War Ministry *vis-à-vis* the Reichstag (*op. cit.*, vol. 294, p. 8515 B). See also Zmarzlik, *Bethmann Hollweg als Reichskanzler*, pp. 135f:

The powers of the King of Prussia with regard to the armed forces of Prussia, and to those of the other states attached to them through conventions, are contained in the Constitution and extended in the Imperial Constitution; they have not been restricted in any respect. His Majesty the King and Emperor exerts these powers entirely independently within the law. No kind of associate right on the part of the Reichstag exists, although it is not, of course, disputed that the Reichstag is competent to express its wishes on military matters in the course of its legislative activity.

44 cf. Walther Rathenau, *Tagebücher 1907–1922*, ed. Hartmut Pogge von Strandmann (Düsseldorf, 1967), p. 182.
45 'J.J. Ruedorffer' (Kurt Riezler), *Grundzüge der Weltpolitik* (Berlin, 1913), p. 229.
46 cf. Bethmann Hollweg's speech in presenting the Army Bill on 22 April 1912, *Verhandlungen des Reichstages*, vol. 284, pp. 1300ff.
47 This strategy is perhaps spelled out most clearly in a letter of Jagow to Eisendecher, 24 July 1913, Eisendecher papers.
48 As yet there is no satisfactory discussion of these questions. For the present, see the studies by Vagts (fn. 34 above) and Poidevin (fn. 20) and the survey by Wolfgang Zorn, 'Wirtschaft und Politik im deutschen Imperialismus', in *Wirtschaft, Geschichte, Wirtschaftsgeschichte. Festschrift zum 65. Geburtstag von Friedrich Lütge* (Stuttgart, 1966), pp. 340ff.
49 cf. Böhme, 'Thesen', pp. 42f.
50 Walther Rathenau, 'Deutsche Gefahren und neue Ziele', in *Gesammelte Schriften. Zur Kritik der Zeit, Mahnung und Warning* (Berlin, 1925), pp. 272, 276; cf. also Rathenau, *Tagebücher*, pp. 168f., which contains notes on conversations with Bethmann Hollweg on this matter.

51 Fischer claims that Bethmann Hollweg came round to the idea of a German-led central European economic association as early as 1912. It is doubtful, however, whether Rathenau's note 'Bethmann in general agreement' indicates anything more than vague sympathy with the notion. There is no evidence at all for the view that the German government's decisions were influenced by such thinking. In his essay 'Weltpolitik, Weltmachtstreben und deutsche Kriegsziele', *Historische Zeitschrift* 199 (1964), pp. 324ff. and in *Krieg der Illusionen*, pp. 368ff. Fischer suggests that the '*Mitteleuropa* plans' and the plans for a German Central Africa were merely two sides of the same coin. In my own view, Egmont Zechlin's objections, in 'Deutschland zwischen Kabinetts- und Wirtschaftskrieg', *Historische Zeitschrift* 199 (1964), pp. 398ff., are largely correct. Fischer's reply, in *Krieg der Illusionen*, pp. 529ff., is not entirely convincing. Even in September 1914 the Imperial Home Office regarded these schemes as unrealistic and argued for a continuation of the existing system of bilateral trade treaties.

52 See, for example, Zimmermann to Lichnowsky, 23 January 1913, *GP*, vol. 34/I, no. 12,718, p. 237.

53 cf. Bethmann Hollweg to Lerchenfeld, 6 June 1914' (in *Bayerische Dokumente zum Kriegsausbruch*, ed. Pius Dirr, 3rd edn., Munich/Berlin, 1925, p. 113):

... the Emperor had never waged a preventive war, nor would he do so. There were some in the Empire, however, who believed that a war would have a healthy effect on domestic conditions in Germany, and would help the conservative cause. He, the Imperial Chancellor, on the other hand, believed that a war, with its quite unforeseeable consequences, might enormously increase the strength of Social Democracy, which preached peace, and might topple a number of thrones.

54 *Griff nach der Weltmacht*, pp. 59ff.; *Krieg der Illusionen*, pp. 85ff., 182 and passim.

55 Bethmann Hollweg's own position is apparent from his memorandum for Kiderlen-Wächter, 5 April 1911, *GP*, vol. 28, no. 10,441, pp. 408f.

56 See pp. 163–71 and fnn. 17–19 above.

57 cf. Conrad von Hötzendorf, *Aus meiner Dienstzeit 1906–1918* (Vienna, 1921–1923), vol. III, p. 670.

58 For a detailed account, see Wernecke, *Der Wille zur Weltgeltung*, pp. 244ff. There is no evidence, however, for the claim by Wernecke and Fischer that this 'press war' was deliberately staged in order that the German public could be prepared for war; cf. *Krieg der Illusionen*, pp. 542ff.

59 For the conservative opposition, see Westarp, *Konservative Politik* I, pp. 182ff. The repeated attempts by the Conservatives in the Reichstag from 1913 onwards to blame the government for its excessively weak behaviour towards the Social Democrats were mainly designed to undermine Bethmann Hollweg's prestige within the establishment. On the Gebsattel affair, see Pogge von Strandmann, *Die Erforderlichkeit des Unmöglichen*, pp. 16–31.

60 cf. Moltke's discussion with Jagow in May or June 1914, published in Egmont Zechlin, 'Motive und Taktik der Reichsleitung 1914', *Der Monat* XVIII, no. 209 (February 1966), pp. 92 and 93.

61 Vagts, 'M.M. Warburg', p. 353.

62 cf. Kurt Riezler, *Tagebücher, Aufsätze, Dokumente*, ed. with an introduction by Karl Dietrich Erdmann (Göttingen, 1972), entry for 27 July 1914, pp. 192f. The comment by Heydebrand to which Bethmann Hollweg referred in July 1914 must have been made earlier, since Heydebrand was not in Berlin at that moment and was politically inactive for the time being.

63 *op. cit.*
64 cf. statement to Lerchenfeld, quoted in fn. 53 above.
65 This is apparent from a remark of Moltke's to Conrad, in which he tried to explain the German government's aversion to the idea of a preventive war: 'On our side, unfortunately, we are constantly looking for a declaration by England that she will not join in. England will never make this declaration.' (Quoted in Conrad von Hötzendorf, *Aus meiner Dienstzeit* III, p. 670).
66 *GP*, vol. 39, no. 18,883, pp. 628ff.
67 Contrary to the arguments of Albertini and Fischer, the German government did not base its political strategy on the assumption that Britain would remain neutral in the event of a European war, though it did everything it could to secure British neutrality at the moment of crisis. See Dieter Groh, 'Die geheimen Sitzungen der Reichshaushaltskommission am 24. und 25. April 1913', *Internationale Wissenschaftliche Korrespondenz zur Geschichte der deutschen Arbeiterbewegung*, nos. 11/12 (1971), pp. 29ff. On 5 June Bethmann Hollweg told Bassermann: '... if there is war with France, every last Englishman will march against us'; cf. Bassermann's letter to Schiffer, 5 June 1914, Schiffer papers 6, Hauptarchiv Berlin. This is confirmed by a report by Lerchenfeld on 4 June 1914:

As far as England is concerned, his [Bethmann Hollweg's] remarks were roughly as follows: At all times, British power had stood against the strongest power on the continent. First against Spain, then against France, later against Russia and now against Germany. England did not want war. He – the Imperial Chancellor – knew for certain that the English government had repeatedly declared in Paris that it would have no part in a policy of provocation or in an unprovoked war against Germany. That did not prevent the fact that if it came to war, we should not find England on our side.

See *Bayerische Dokumente zum Kriegsausbruch*, no. 1, p. 112. As a letter from Bethmann Hollweg to Eisendecher of 18 December 1912 shows, the Chancellor had previously voiced a similar view. See also the memorandum for Wilhelm II, 18 December 1912, *GP*, vol. 39, no. 15,560, pp. 9f.

68 What was crucial about the Anglo-Russian naval discussions, therefore, was not their impact on international relations *per se* – as Zechlin, 'Deutschland zwischen Kabinetts-und Wirtschaftskrieg', pp. 348ff. argues – but their effect on the domestic political situation.
69 cf. report by Koester, 20 July 1914, *Deutsche Gesandtschaftsberichte zum Kriegsausbruch 1914. Berichte und Telegramme der badischen, sächsischen und württembergischen Gesandten aus dem Juli and August 1914*, ed. August Bach for the Auswärtiges Amt (Berlin, 1937), no. 5.
70 cf. also Fischer, *Krieg der Illusionen*, pp. 688f.
71 cf. report by Hauptmann, 24 February 1918, quoted in Wolfgang Steglich, *Die Friedenspolitik der Mittelmächte 1917–18*, vol. I, (Wiesbaden, 1964), p. 418.
72 It is not possible in the present essay to give an exhaustive account of the German government's political calculations during the July crisis. I hope to be able to do so in a forthcoming study, 'Die Politik des Reichskanzlers Bethmann Hollweg als Problem der politischen Führung'. In the meantime, see Wolfgang J. Mommsen, *Das Zeitalter des Imperialismus* (Frankfurt am Main, 1969), pp. 272ff. and Mommsen, 'Die latente Krise des Deutschen Reiches 1909–1914', in Leo Just *et al.* (eds.), *Handbuch der deutschen Geschichte*, vol. IV, 2 (Frankfurt am Main, 1972). On Germany's aim of using the Serbian question as a touchstone of Russia's warlike intentions, see Hoyos's notes on his interview with

Viktor Naumann, *Österreich-Ungarns Außenpolitik*, ed. L. Bittner (Vienna/Leipzig, 1930), VIII, no. 9966 and Alfred von Tirpitz, *Erinnerungen* (Leipzig, 1919), p. 227.
73 Riezler, *Tagebucher*, 23 July 1914, p. 188.
74 Fritz Fischer and Imanuel Geiss, especially, have steadfastly maintained that the plan to isolate the Serbian war was not only a gross illusion but also a convenient pretext. The members of Bethmann Hollweg's immediate entourage, however, actually believed that the crisis could be resolved without what the Chancellor called, on more than one occasion, a European 'conflagration'. That the intentions on which this belief rested were at least subjectively honest is borne out by the fact that there were even calculations in government circles about the possibility of concluding an alliance with Russia, at Austria-Hungary's expense, in the event that the crisis passed without a European war. See Riezler, *Tagebücher*, 23 July 1914, p. 189 and Bethmann Hollweg's statement to Theodor Wolff, 5 February 1915, which confirms Riezler's notes (see Theodor Wolff, *Der Marsch durch zwei Jahrzehnte* (Berlin, 1936), p. 442):

I then told Sazonov during the crisis – this is strictly between ourselves – that he could let the Austrians have their punitive expedition: the moment would arrive when we should come to an agreement. Not on the back of the Austrians, naturally, but on their shoulders, so to speak.

75 Riezler, *Tagebücher*, 14 July 1914, p. 185.
76 In a sense, this did not apply to the Social Democrats, since the government approached Haase and, a few days later, the party's executive committee, although only Südekum was available. The literature on the government's negotiations with the Social Democrats is controversial. See Dieter Groh, *Negative Integration und revolutionärer Attentismus. Die deutsche Sozialdemokratie am Vorabend des Ersten Weltkrieges 1909–1914* (Berlin, 1917) and Groh, 'The Unpatriotic Socialists and the State', *Journal of Contemporary History* 1 (1966), pp. 151ff. Little is known about contacts between the government and the leaders of the bourgeois parties. Westarp records that he paid a number of visits to the Wilhelmstraße during the crisis, but he evidently learned little: cf. Westarp, *Konservative Politik* I, p. 407. Heydebrand, the leader of the Prussian Conservatives, was still completely in the dark about diplomatic developments as late as 3 August: cf. his letter to Westarp of 3 August, Heydebrand-Westarp correspondence. (I am grateful to Baron Hiller von Gärtringen for this information.)
77 We still have to rely largely on guesswork in assessing the attitudes of the parties towards Bethmann Hollweg's policies during July 1914. The Conservatives were solidly in favour of a 'forward policy', but did not begin to press for war until fairly late in the day. The leading conservative newspaper, the *Post*, seems to have been very reluctant to join the chorus of pro-Austrian voices during the first weeks of July: cf. Jonathan French Scott, *Five Weeks: The Surge of Public Opinion at the Eve of the Great War* (New York, 1938), pp. 191ff. The National Liberals would probably have preferred Tirpitz as Chancellor: cf. Bassermann to Schiffer, 5 June 1914 (see fn. 67 above). They would certainly have welcomed a policy based on what they regarded as the highly successful strategy that had been followed during the Bosnian crisis of 1908. The Centre party had been committed since 1912 to a policy of firm support for Austria-Hungary: cf. E. Malcolm Carroll, *Germany and the Great Powers, 1866–1914: A Study in Public Opinion and Foreign Policy* (New York, 1938; reprinted 1975), pp. 747ff.

Public opion and foreign policy in Wilhelmine Germany

1 See, in particular, Eberhard Naujocks, *Bismarcks auswärtige Pressepolitik und die Reichsgründung (1865–1871)* (Wiesbaden, 1976).

2 Studies of the relations between state press policies and foreign policy are uneven in quality, even in empirical terms. The pioneering accounts by E. Malcolm Carroll, *Germany and the Great Powers, 1866–1914: A Study in Public Opinion and Foreign Policy* (New York, 1938; reprinted 1975) and Oron James Hale, *Publicity and Diplomacy* (London, 1940) are remarkably wide in their range, but do not establsh any close links between official information policy and public opinion. Günter Heidorn, *Monopole – Presse – Krieg. Die Rolle der Presse bei der Vorbereitung des Ersten Weltkrieges* (Berlin, 1960) is a somewhat ideological treatment. Klaus Wernecke, *Der Wille zur Weltgeltung. Außenpolitik und Öffentlichkeit im Kaiserreich am Vorabend des Ersten Weltkrieges* (Düsseldorf, 1970) uses a large array of press cuttings to present a large-scale picture of Germany's drive for world power, but does not provide any insights into the structural connections between public opinion and political decision-making. Walter Vogel, *Die Organisation der amtlichen Presse- und Propagandapolitik des Deutschen Reiches* (Berlin, 1941) confines itself to providing an account of the institutional structures of state press policies before 1914. Only for the Bülow era do we have any thorough-going analysis of official press policies and their influence on government policy in general. See especially Peter Winzen, *Bülows Weltmacht-Konzept. Untersuchungen zur Frühphase seiner Außenpolitik, 1897–1901* (Boppard, 1977) and – with interesting material – Paul Kennedy, *The Rise of the Anglo-German Antagonism 1860–1914* (London, 1980), esp. pp. 362ff. Paul Elzbacher, *Die Presse als Werkzeug der auswärtigen Politik* (Jena, 1918) is totally useless. Isolde Rieger, *Die Wilhelminische Presse im Überblick* (Munich, 1957) is a good general survey but tells us little about the interrelations between government policy and public opinion.

3 This has been convincingly shown, by and large, by Geoff Eley, *Reshaping the German Right: Radical Nationalism and Political Change after Bismarck* (New Haven, 1980). See also Konrad Schilling, *Beiträge zu einer Geschichte des radikalen Nationalismus in der wilhelminischen Ära, 1890–1909* (doctoral thesis, Cologne, 1967).

4 Monts to Bülow, 20 June 1895, quoted in Kennedy, *Antagonism*, p. 227.

5 Holstein to Kiderlen-Wächter, 30 April 1897, *op. cit.*

6 Max Weber, *Gesammelte Politische Schriften* (Tübingen, 1913), p. 23.

7 cf. John C.G. Röhl, *Deutschland ohne Bismarck. Die Regierungskrise im Zweiten Kaisrreich 1890–1900* (Tübingen, 1969), p. 179 (cf. also the earlier English edition, *Germany without Bismarck: The Crisis of Government in the Second Reich, 1890–1900*, London, 1967): 'I should regard myself as an executive instrument of His Majesty, to a certain extent as his political chief of staff. With me, personal rule would begin, in a good but real sense.'

8 Friedrich Naumann, *Demokratie und Kaisertum*, first published in 1900, may in some ways be regarded as a blueprint for this new Caesarist style of Imperial rule as practised under Bülow.

9 Quoted in Winzen, *Bülows Weltmacht-Konzept*, p. 67.

10 cf. Prince Bernhard von Bülow, *Deutsche Politik* (Berlin, 1916), p. 227.

11 On this, see Katherine Anne Lerman, *Bernhard von Bülow and the Governance*

of Germany, 1900–1909 (doctoral thesis, Sussex, 1984), pp. 175ff.

12 cf. Risto Ropponen, *Die russische Gefahr. Das Verhältnis der öffentlichen Meinung Deutschlands und Österreich-Ungarns gegenüber der Außenpolitik Rußlands in der Zeit zwischen dem Frieden von Portsmouth und dem Ausbruch des Ersten Weltkrieges* (Helsinki, 1976), pp. 165ff.

13 Bülow in the Reichstag, 10 December 1901, *Stenographische Berichte über die Verhandlungen des Reichstages*, vol. 179, pp. 413ff. See also Prince Bernhard von Bülow, *Denkwürdigkeiten*, vol. 1 (Berlin, 1930), pp. 475f.

14 For a good piece of evidence, see Holstein's report to Count Hatzfeld, 26 October 1899, in Gerhard Ebel and Michael Behnen (eds.), *Botschafter Graf von Hatzfeld. Nachgelassene Papiere 1838–1901*, part 2 (Boppard, 1976), pp. 1280ff., with some representative press cuttings.

15 See also Frederic L. von Holthoon, 'Public Opinion in Europe during the Boer War', in *Opinion publique et politique extérieure*, vol. 1, 1870–1950, University of Milan and École Française of Rome (Rome, 1981), p. 399:

The British, who always overestimated the power of the government over the press, bitterly complained to the Wilhelmstraße about the anti-British sentiment expressed in the leading German newspapers. They saw this as a deliberate campaign by the government. They drew the embarrassing response that the German Foreign Office [and] the Reichskanzler could do nothing about this, however much they tried.

16 The most recent account of Kiderlen-Wächter's Moroccan policy of 1911 is Geoffrey Barraclough, *From Agadir to Armageddon: Anatomy of a Crisis* (London, 1982). This book does not, however, discuss Kiderlen-Wächter's devious attempts to manipulate German 'public opinion' in the interests of his Machiavellian strategy. See, however, Emily Oncken, *Panthersprung nach Agadir. Die deutsche Politik während der 2. Marokkokrise* (Düsseldorf, 1981).

17 The full details of Kiderlen-Wächter's dealings with the press came to light in closed sessions of the Budget Committee. See *Protokolle des Hauptausschusses des Deutschen Reichstags*, 17 November 1911, 111th session, p. 12, Zentralarchiv der DDR, Potsdam. Kiderlen-Wächter said (*op. cit.*, p. 14):

One of the main reasons why the idea of gaining a firm foothold in Morocco had spread was Dr Class's pamphlet. He had become familiar with this pamphlet before it had been published. That did not mean, however, that he had agreed with it. Rather, he had 'expressly advised against publication' when the gentleman had shown him the draft. The pamphlet, incidentally, would have been judged differently if it had been published in full, since it also said, for example, that we should peacefully acquire not only Morocco but also the Rhône department.

18 *op. cit.*, p. 12.

19 cf. *Verhandlungen des Reichstages*, vol. 263, p. 7808 B; also Kiderlen-Wächter's statement, 17 February 1912, *op. cit.*, vol. 283, pp. 102 D, 103 A–C.

20 *op. cit.*, p. 103 D; cf. also his statement in the Budget Committee of the Reichstag, 111th session, p. 14.

21 *Verhandlungen des Reichstages*, vol. 268, pp. 7716 C, 7718 D.

22 For details, see Vogel, *Organisation*, pp. 19ff.

23 2 December 1912, *Verhandlungen des Reichstages*, vol. 286, pp. 2494 A–B.

24 cf. Erich Matthias and Eberhard Pikart (eds.), *Die Reichstagsfraktion der deutschen Sozialdemokratie 1898–1918*, first part (Düsseldorf, 1966), pp. 280f.

25 The continuing controversy over the role of the 'war council' of 8 December

1912 cannot be discussed at length here. See John C.G. Röhl, 'An der Schwelle zum Weltkrieg: Eine Dokumentierung über den "Kriegsrat" vom 8.Dezember 1912', *Militärgeschichtliche Mitteilungen* 21 (1977), pp. 77–134 and Röhl, '"Die Generalprobe". Zur Geschichte und Bedeutung des "Kriegsrates" vom 8. Dezember 1912', in Dirk Stegmann, Bernd-Jürgen Wendt and Peter-Christian Witt (eds.), *Industrielle Gesellschaft und politisches System* (Bonn, 1978), pp. 366ff. For a critique of these interpretations, see Wolfgang J. Mommsen, 'The Topos of Inevitable War in Germany in the Decade before 1914', in Volker R. Berghahn and Martin Kitchen (eds.), *Germany in the Age of Total War* (London, 1981), pp. 43f., fnn. 26 and 27 (for the German version, see *Der autoritäre Nationalstaat. Verfassung, Gesellschaft und Kultur im deutschen Kaiserreich*, Frankfurt am Main, 1990, pp. 393f.); see also Bernd F. Schulte, 'Zu der Krisenkonferenz am 8. Dezember 1912 in Berlin', *Historisches Jahrbuch* 102 (1982), pp. 183ff., with new material from the Hopman papers. Schulte's fierce polemics, however, are inapposite, since the new material presented by him and Röhl basically bears out the interpretation given above.

26 cf. Röhl, 'An der Schwelle', p. 100.
27 Kiderlen-Wächter's reply and the article 'Um Durazzo' are reproduced in *op. cit.*, pp. 102ff.
28 Since the publication of my essay 'Domestic Factors in German Foreign Policy before 1914', *Central European History* 6 (1973) (re-translated in the present volume, pp. 163–188), a considerable amount of new evidence has come to light, without, however, entailing any substantial modification of the account given there (cf. p. 169f. above). Although Bethman Hollweg and Kiderlen-Wächter could not afford completely to ignore the Emperor's demand that the public be prepared for war, in practice they suppressed all direct government propaganda to that effect; and that policy did not change after the Army Bill had been passed. In reality, the government was following in the wake of public opinion, not leading it.
29 *Verhandlungen des Reichstages*, vol. 289, pp. 4513 A–B.
30 For details, see Mommsen, 'Der Topos vom unvermeidlichen Krieg,' pp. 33ff. (in *Der autoritäre Nationalstaat*, pp. 396ff.).
31 14 May 1914, *Verhandlungen des Reichstages*, vol. 295, p. 8834.
32 cf. Manfred Rauh, *Die Parlamentarisierung des Deutschen Reiches* (Düsseldorf, 1977). Rauh overstates, however, the extent of such changes before 1914.
33 The rather delicate, and highly Machiavellian, attempts by the Bethmann Hollweg government to win support for its policies during the July crisis by manipulating the press are beyond the scope of this essay. Despite the work of Fritz Fischer, Egmont Zechlin and Klaus Wernecke, they have not yet been exhaustively investigated. See also Ropponen, *Die russische Gefahr* and J.F. Scott, *Five Weeks: The Surge of Public Opinion on the Eve of the Great War* (New York, 1973). Broadly speaking, the government sought to play down the crisis and dampen nationalist hysteria, even after the ultimatum to Serbia of 27 July 1914, because it hoped to be able to confine the conflict and, failing that, to convince the German public that the conditions under which a European war would have to be waged would be favourable. It was vital that the odium of having started the war should be incurred by the Russians. On this score, Bethmann Hollweg's overtures to the Social Democrats have rightly been the object of special attention. The government was particularly anxious for the press to back its line that support for Austria-Hungary was justified from the start – a view that was in fact opposed only by the *Rheinisch-Westfälische Zeitung*. Otherwise, the government refrained from attempting to influence the press directly; but then it scarcely needed to.

The spirit of 1914 and the ideology of a
German 'Sonderweg'

1 *Mars und Venus. Erinnerungen 1914–1916* (Stuttgart, 1954), pp. 18f.
2 *op. cit.*, p. 144.
3 On the role of university teachers in the formulation of the 'ideas of 1914', see Klaus Schwabe, *Wissenschaft und Kriegsmoral. Die deutschen Hochschullehrer und die politischen Grundlagen des Ersten Weltkrieges* (Göttingen, 1969), pp. 19–45. For a masterly analysis of the role of philosophers, see Hermann Lübbe, *Politische Philosophie in Deutschland. Studien zu ihrer Geschichte* (Stuttgart, 1963), pp. 173–238. For the role of sociologists, see Hans Jonas, 'Die Klassiker der Soziologie und der Erste Weltkrieg', inaugural lecture, Erlangen (manuscript).
4 cf. Schwabe, *Wissenschaft*, pp. 22f.
5 First war issue, *Süddeutsche Monatshefte*, 'Nationale Kundgebung der deutschen und österreichischen Historiker' (1914), p. 800.
6 *Deutsche Reden in schwerer Zeit* (Berlin, 1914), pp. 206f.
7 Max Weber, *Gesamtausgabe* (hereafter *MWG*) I/15, p. 462.
8 *op. cit.*, pp. 777f.
9 'Deutschlands innere Wandlung', speech delivered on 7 November 1914 (Straßburg, 1914), pp. 9, 11 and passim.
10 cf. an article in the *Frankfurter Zeitung* on the 'ideas of 1914', 24 December 1914; reprinted in Johann Plenge, *1789 und 1914. Die symbolischen Jahre in der Geschichte des politischen Geistes* (Berlin, 1916), pp. 171–175.
11 *op. cit.*, p. 15.
12 Werner Sombart, *Händler und Helden. Patriotische Besinnungen* (Munich/Leipzig, 1915), p. 92.
13 *op. cit.*, p. 142.
14 *op. cit.*, p. 143.
15 Ernst Troeltsch, *Die deutsche Freiheit* (Berlin, 1915), p. 28.
16 Friedrich Naumann, 'Die Freiheit in Deutschland', manuscript (1917), in *Werke*, ed. Theodor Schieder (Opladen, 1963ff.), vol. 2, pp. 455, 460.
17 Plenge, *1789 und 1914*, p. 15.
18 *MWG* I/15, p. 660 (report in *Fränkischer Kurier*).
19 I am grateful for this information to Jeffrey Verhey, who is currently preparing a thesis at the University of California, Berkeley on '"The Spirit of 1914": Public Opinion and Integral Nationalism in Germany during World War I'.

The social consequences of World War I:
the case of Germany

1 Figures from Marc Ferro, The Great War 1914–1918 (London, 1973) and, for Germany, Gerhard Bry, Wages in Germany 1871–1945 (Princeton, 1960).
2 Gerd Hardach, *Der Erste Weltkrieg 1914–1918* (Munich, 1973), p. 173.
3 cf. Gerhard Bry, *Wages*, p. 209; contemporary indices vary slightly. Calver gives 229 *per cent*, Quente 257 per cent and the Statistisches Reichsamt 313 per cent. See *ibid.*

4   Jürgen Kocka, *Facing Total War: German Society 1914–1918* (Leamington
    Spa, 1984), pp. 35f.
5   *op. cit.*, p. 33. In the German edition (*Klassengesellschaft im Krieg. Deutsche
    Sozialgeschichte 1914–1918*, 2nd edn., Göttingen, 1978), p. 27, class divisions
    are somewhat more strongly emphasized; likewise, the title alludes directly to
    the fact that class conflict was a central political question during the war.
6   Dietmar Petzina, Werner Abelshauser and Anselm Faust, *Sozialgeschichtliches
    Arbeitsbuch III. Materialien zur Statistik des Deutschen Reiches 1914–1945*
    (Munich, 1987), p. 83.
7   *op. cit.*, p. 208.
8   Bry, *Wages*, p. 310, Table 75.
9   cf. Bentley B. Gilbert, *British Social Policy, 1914–1935* (Ithaca, New York,
    1970), p. 12.
10 See the figures given in Kocka, *Klassengesellschaft*, p. 74.
11 Petzina *et al.*, *Sozialgeschichtliches Arbeitsbuch*, p. 82.
12 Knut   Borchardt,   *Wachstum,   Krisen,   Handlungsspielräume   der
    Wirtschaftspolitik. Studien zur Wirtschaftsgeschichte des 19. and 20.
    Jahrhunderts* (Göttingen, 1982), p. 154.
13 See *Geschichte und Gesellschaft*, Jg. 8, 1982, pp. 415sq., *Geschichte und
    Gesellschaft*, jg. 9, 1983, pp. 124sq.
14 Borchardt, *Wachstum*, p. 154: .'Der Staat von Weimar beruhte auf der
    Koalition von Unternehmern und Gewerkschaften, die sich unmittelbar bei
    Kriegsende zu einer Art Burgfireden verabredet hatten, um eine befürchtete
    radikale Revolution zu verhindern'.
15 Roessler, Konrad, *Die Finanzpolitik des Deutschen Reiches im 1. Weltkrieg*,
    Schriften des Instituts für das Spar-, Giro- und Kreditwesen an der Universität
    Bonn, Bd. 37 (Berlin, 1967), p. 177.
16 Petzina et. al., *Sozialgeschichtliches Arbeitsbuch*, p. 57.

The German revolution, 1918–1920

1   For detailed references, see the excellent survey of the recent literature by
    Hartmut Pogge von Strandmann, 'Die deutsche Revolution von 1918', in
    Deutschlandstudien, vol 2, ed. Robert Picht (Bonn, 1975), pp. 49–74; also the
    recent comprehensive bibliography by Georg P. Meyer, *Bibliographie zur
    deutschen Revolution 1918–19* (Göttingen, 1977).
2   Arthur Rosenberg, *Entstehung der Weimarer Republik* (Berlin, 1928; reprinted
    Frankfurt, 1969 etc.).
3   Walter Tormin, *Zwischen Rätediktatur und sozialer Demokratie. Die
    Geschichte der Rätebewegung in der deutschen Revolution 1918–19*
    (Düsseldorf, 1954); Eberhard Kolb, *Die Arbeiterräte in der deutschen
    Innenpolitik 1918–19* (Düsseldorf, 1962); Peter von Oertzen, 'Die großen
    Streiks der Ruhrbergarbeiterschaft im Frühjahr 1919. Ein Beitrag zur
    Diskussion über die revolutionäre Entstehungsphase der Weimarer Republik',
    Vierteljahreshefte für Zeitgeschichte 6 (1958), now also in Kolb (ed.), *Vom
    Kaiserreich zur Weimarer Republik* (Cologne, 1972), pp. 185–217; von
    Oertzen, *Betriebsräte in der Novemberrevolution. Eine politikwissenschaftliche
    Untersuchung über Ideengehalt und Struktur der betrieblichen und
    wirtschaftlichen Arbeiterräte in der deutschen Revolution 1918–19*
    (Düsseldorf, 1963). This general approach has been complemented by the pub-
    lication of comprehensive collections of documents, notably of the proceedings

of the Central Council of Workers' and Soldiers' Councils, *Der Zentralrat der deutschen sozialistischen Republik 19.12.1918 bis 8.4.1919. Vom ersten zum zweiten Rätekongreß*, vol. 1, ed. Eberhard Kolb and Reinhard Rürup (Leiden, 1968). See also the synoptic account by Eberhard Kolb in his essay 'Rätewirklichkeit und Räteideologie in der deutschen Revolution von 1918–19', originally published in Helmut Neubauer (ed.), *Deutschland und die russische Revolution* (Stuttgart, 1968), pp. 94–110 and now included in Kolb's collection cited above.

4 cf. Hans Dähn, 'Die lokale und regionale Revolutions- und Rätebewegung 1918–19 in der DDR-Geschichtsschreibung', *Archiv für Sozialgeschichte* 15 (1975), pp. 452–470; also Lutz Winckler, 'Die Novemberrevolution in der Geschichtsschreibung der DDR', *Geschichte in Wissenschaft und Unterricht* 21 (1970), pp. 216–234; A. Decker, 'Die Novemberrevolution und die Geschichtswissenschaft der DDR', *Internationale Wissenschaftliche Korrespondenz zur Geschichte der Arbeiterbewegung* 10 (1974), pp. 269–299. A typical example of the schizoid approach to the councils that is found in GDR historiography, leaving aside the matter of a strictly prescribed Marxist–Leninist explanatory framework, is the volume of the *Zeitschrift für Geschichtswissenschaft* devoted to the question (vol. 17, 1969). In his article 'Die Bedeutung der Novemberrevolution' (*op. cit.*, pp. 209–212) Klaus Mammach argues that the *Räte* were essentially a tool of counter-revolution, whereas Diehl ('Die Bedeutung der Novemberrevolution 1918', *op. cit.*, pp. 14–32) accepts that the councils offered an opportunity for democratic change. See also the brief survey by H.-J. Fieber and Heinz Wohlgemuth, 'Forschungen zur Novemberrevolution und zur Gründung der KPD', in *Historische Forschungen in der DDR 1960–1970*, Sonderheft, *Zeitschrift für Geschichtswissenschaft* 18 (1970), pp. 508–514.

5 Bruno Gebhardt, *Handbuch der deutschen Geschichte* (Stuttgart, 1959), vol. 4, *Die Zeit der Weltkriege*, p. 88. In later editions, however, Erdmann modifies this claim. In the early 1950s Hans Herzfeld maintained – admittedly, without the benefit of the work of Tormin and von Oertzen – that the Majority Social Democrats 'prevented the introduction of the Russian soviet system and the establishment of a dictatorship of the proletariat': cf. *Die moderne Welt 1789–1945*, part 2, *Weltmächte und Weltkriege. Die Geschichte unserer Epoche 1789–1945* (Braunschweig, 1952), p. 240.

6 cf. fn. 3 above.

7 Oskar Anweiler, *Die Rätebewegung in Rußland 1905–1921* (Leiden, 1958); Anweiler, 'Der revolutionsgeschichtliche Zusammenhang des Rätesystems, *Politische Vierteljahresschrift*, Sonderheft 2 (1970).

8 See especially Peter Lösche, *Der Bolschewismus im Urteil der deutschen Sozialdemokratie 1903–1920* (Berlin, 1967).

9 The most forceful expressions of this thesis are in Kolb, 'Rätewirklichkeit und Räteideologie', pp. 180ff. and Rürup, introduction to *Arbeiter- und Soldatenräte im rheinisch-westfälischen Industriegebiet. Studien zur Geschichte der Revolution 1918–19* (Wuppertal, 1975), pp. 8f.

10 cf. von Oertzen, *Betriebsräte in der Novemberrevolution*, which also contains a coded claim that a return to a councils system as a form of political authority would be feasible.

11 Reinhard Rürup, *Probleme der Revolution in Deutschland 1918/19* (Wiesbaden, 1968), p. 50.

12 Ulrich Kluge, *Soldatenräte und Revolution. Studien zur Militärpolitik in Deutschland 1918–19* (Göttingen, 1975); Kluge, 'Militärrevolte und Staatsumsturz. Ausbreitung und Konsolidierung der Räteorganisationen im rheinisch-westfälischen Industriegebiet'; Kluge, 'Der Generalsoldatenrat in

Münster und das Problem der bewaffneten Macht im rheinisch-westfälischen Industriegebiet', both in Rürup (ed.), *Arbeiter- und Soldatenräte*, pp. 39–82 and 315–392.

13 Heinrich Mut, 'Bauernräte und Landarbeiterräte 1918', *Vierteljahreshefte für Zeitgeschichte* 21 (1973), pp. 1–38.

14 *Probleme der Revolution*, p. 20.

15 For a thorough and impressive analysis of this question, see Erich Matthias's introduction to Susanne Miller and Heinrich Potthoff, *Die Regierung der Volksbeauftragten 1918–19. Quellen zur Geschichte des Parlamentarismus und der politischen Parteien*, first series, *Von der konstitutionellen Monarchie zur Parlamentarischen Republik*, vol. 6/I (Düsseldorf, 1969). The introduction has also been published separately under the title *Zwischen Räten und Geheimräten. Die deutsche Revolutionsregierung 1918–19* (Düsseldorf, 1970). See especially pp. 69f.

16 Quoted in Heinz Hürten, 'Soldatenräte in der Novemberrevolution 1918', *Historisches Jahrbuch* 90 (1970), p. 306.

17 Kolb's examples of such declarations of intention on the part of the workers' and soldiers' councils date almost entirely from the spring of 1919 onwards – in other words, from a time when the councils had already gone on to the defensive and their legitimacy was at issue – rather than the opening phase of the revolution. See Kolb, *Die Arbeiterräte*, pp. 328ff. and, more recently, Eberhard Kolb and Klaus Schönhoven, *Regionale und lokale Räteorganisationen in Württemberg 1918–19* (Düsseldorf, 1976), pp. LXV and 278f. The resolution of the Second Assembly of the Württemberg Workers' and Soldiers' Councils of 1–3 March 1919 that Kolb reproduces here was clearly linked to attempts to assign the councils a well-defined permanent role within the political system at that stage. As far as the early phase of the revolution is concerned, Kolb himself stresses the fact that the old administrative apparatus continued to function undisturbed (p. 93).

18 The only exception, it would appear, was the strike by officials in Mülheim an der Ruhr between 5 and 9 February 1919, which the workers' and soldiers' council succeeded in circumventing. But even here it was agreed to rescind dismissals of unpopular officials and elect a new workers' and soldier's council. See Irmgard Steinisch, 'Linksradikalismus und Rätebewegung im westlichen Ruhrgebiet. Die revolutionären Auseinandersetzungen in Mülheim an der Ruhr', in Rürup (ed.), *Arbeiter- und Soldatenräte*, pp. 203f.

19 Udo Bermbach, 'Das Scheitern des Rätesystems und der Demokratisierung der Bürokratie', *Politische Vierteljahresschrift* 8 (1967), pp. 445–460, esp. p. 456.

20 cf. Hans Mommsen, 'Die Bergarbeiterbewegung an der Ruhr 1918–1933', in Jürgen Reulecke (ed.), *Arbeiterbewegung an Rhein und Ruhr* (Wuppertal, 1974), pp. 275–314; also Erhard Lucas's pioneering studies, revealing much information about these events, 'Ursachen und Verlauf der Bergarbeiterbewegung in Hamborn und im westlichen Ruhrgebiet. Zum Syndikalismus in der Novemberrevolution', *Duisburger Forschungen* 15 (1971), pp. 1–119 and Lucas, *Zwei Formen von Radikalismus in der deutschen Arbeiterbewegung* (Frankfurt am Main, 1976). Lucas's view, however, that the form of working-class radicalism exemplified by the 'Hamborn worker' offered a constructive alternative to the political standpoints represented by the different working-class parties is not easy to sustain. On the history of syndicalism and syndicalist organizations in the German labour movement, see the revealing study by Hans M. Bock, *Syndikalismus und Linkskommunismus von 1918–1923. Zur Geschichte und Soziologie der Freien Arbeiter-Union Deutschlands (Syndikalisten), der Allgemeinen Arbeiter-Union Deutschlands und der Kommunistischen Arbeiter-Partei Deutschlands* (Meisenheim, 1969).

Gerald D. Feldman *et al.*, 'Die Massenbewegungen der Arbeiterschaft in Deutschland am Ende des Ersten Weltkrieges (1917–1920)', *Politische Vierteljahresschrift* 13 (1972), pp. 84–105 also deals usefully with the whole problem, though it does not make the distinction between revolutionary movements of a primarily political character and syndicalist movements of social protest. In the author's view, Feldman *et al.* still link the mass movements too closely to the party-political groupings within the working class and understate their spontaneous character and anti-party thrust. It was precisely at this stage that the call for working-class unity resumed an important role.

21 Text reproduced in Gerhard A. Ritter and Susanne Miller (eds.), *Die deutsche Revolution 1918–19. Dokumente* (2nd edn., Hamburg, 1975), p. 242.

22 See Francis L. Carsten, *Revolution in Central Europe 1918–1919* (London, 1972), pp. 78ff. and the interesting study by H. Hartmann, presenting new material, 'Rätedemokratie in Österreich 1918–1924', *Österreichische Zeitschrift für Politikwissenschaft* 1 (1972), pp. 73–87; also Hartmann, *Die verlorene Räterepublik. Am Beispiel der Kommunistischen Partei Deutschösterreichs* (Vienna, 1971). See in addition the essay by Carsten in the *Festschrift* for Fritz Fischer, 'Revolutionäre Situationen in Europa 1917–1920', which also points out, however, that in Austria there was fierce opposition outside the Social Democratic party to the councils movement.

23 For a discussion of efforts *ex post facto* to integrate the decentralizing 'socialization' sought by the masses into Marxist theory, cf. von Oertzen, *Betriebsräte in der Novemberrevolution*, pp. 99ff.; special mention should be made of Karl Korsch in this connection. As far as the KPD was concerned, events temporarily delivered power within the party to the utopian wing, for whom forward movement was all-important and concrete policies in aid of long-term goals were of no interest.

24 Mommsen, 'Bergarbeiterbewegung', p. 292.

25 For the Essen socialization movement, see von Oertzen, 'Die großen Streiks' (fn. 3 above); Jürgen Tampke, 'The Rise and Fall of the Essen Model, January–February 1919', *Internationale wissenschaftliche Korrespondenz zur Geschichte der Arbeiterbewegung* 13 (1977), pp. 160–172; also, for the military aspect, Ulrich Kluge, 'Essener Sozialisierungsbewegung und Volksbewegung im rheinisch-westfälischen Industriegebiet', *Internationale wissenschaftliche Korrespondenz zur Geschichte der Arbeiterbewegung* 8 (1972), pp. 56ff. I am grateful for additional important suggestions to Gunhild Wittenborn, *Bergarbeiterbewegung im Ruhrgebiet im Frühjahr 1919* (state examination dissertation, Düsseldorf, 1977).

26 Reprinted in Ritter and Miller (eds.), *Die deutsche Revolution*, pp. 267–269.

27 Ordinance of Council of People's Representatives, 18 January 1919, reprinted in abridged form in Ritter and Miller (eds.), *Die deutsche Revolution*, p. 270. See also Hans Spethmann, *12 Jahre Ruhrbergbau*, vol. 1 (Essen, 1928), pp. 149ff., which describes events from the employers' point of view and – with characteristic bias – mainly sees the Spartacists' hand at work in them.

28 *Die Neue Zeit* 37 (1919), no. 15 (10 January 1919).

29 Paul Lensch, 'Revolutionsprobleme', *Die Glocke* 4 (1919), vo. 1, no. 4 (1 February 1919).

30 See the record of Barth's speech in *Allgemeiner Kongreß der Arbeiter- und Soldatenräte Deutschlands vom 16. bis 21. Dezember 1918 im Abgeordnetenhause zu Berlin* (Berlin, n.d.), pp. 164f. See also David W. Morgan, *The Socialist Left and the German Revolution: A History of the German Independent Social Democratic Party, 1917–1922* (London, 1975), pp. 190f. and Hartfrid Krause, *USPD. Zur Geschichte der Unabhängigen Sozialdemokratischen Partei Deutschlands* (Frankfurt, 1975).

31 Tampke's claim, contrary to earlier assumptions, that the Spartacists played a role in initiating the Essen socialization movement is not particularly convincing. The Spartacists jumped on to a bandwagon that was already in motion. They may have done so earlier than the USPD, but they were not able to affect the movement's direction in any significant way, let alone suppress its syndicalist character. Tampke's source material, incidentally, consists of statements made by Communists after the event and its evidentiary value is limited. The attempts to direct the protest movement primarily against the officials of the mine companies reflect the mood of the miners rather than the doctrinal principles of Communist strategy.

32 This objection applies to von Oertzen's thesis in 'Die großen Streiks', in Kolb (ed.), *Vom Kaiserreich zur Weimarer Republik*, pp. 196f. In the form proposed by the miners – and not only by them – the socialization programme was, rather, an immediate expression of protest. It was not practicable, however, under modern industrial conditions – not, at any rate, through the socialization of heavy industry by state decree.

33 For a good example of the sort of demands that workers associated with the notion of 'socialization' (although the vital differences are not clearly recognized), see I. Marßolek, 'Sozialdemokratie und Revolution im östlichen Ruhrgebiet. Dortmund unter der Herrschaft des Arbeiter- und Soldatenrates', in Rürup (ed.), *Arbeiter- und Soldatenräte*, p. 290, dealing with Lünen. Among the 'very concrete' (*sic!*) ideas that these workers associated with 'socialization' were: '(1) Democratization of the workplace (with the ultimate aim of collective management by workers); (2) control of, and information concerning, the entire conduct of business of the enterprise; (3) reduction and eventual abolition of private profits.' This programme is hard to square with the classical conception of socialization professed by the various socialist parties. It shows, however, that workers were interested first and foremost in an immediate improvement in their working conditions and social welfare and were not looking for a fundamental transformation of the social order, with all that that would entail.

34 Koenen himself was a revolutionary shop steward: in other words, he actually had a syndicalist background. See Morgan, *The Socialist Left*, pp. 229f.

35 This also applies, for example, to the Leipzig strikes of 27 February to 10 March 1919, in which the spontaneous demand for powerful works councils played a central role. See *op cit.*, pp. 221f.

36 Morgan's statement (*op. cit.*, p. 225) that 'the socialization movement in the Ruhr was a genuine multi-party, even supra-party, movement' is misleading in its emphasis. It was *because* the movement was extra-parliamentary in origin and had 'direct action' as its main aim that the rejection of the key ideological and doctrinal differences between the socialist parties seemed logical.

37 cf. Cairns, *Generalstreik und Noske-Blutbad in Berlin* (Berlin 1919), p. 9. In Berlin there had been bitter disputes from the start among the socialist parties on the question of the masses' demand for joint involvement in the general strike. Although the KPD at first succeeded in seizing the initiative, it was also the first eventually to withdraw from active participation in the strike committee, and in the light of what has been said it becomes easier to understand why so much importance was attached to the question of the handling of the press in this connection. The KPD justified its withdrawal from the strike committee on the grounds that if the committee was to be an expression of the revolutionary will of the masses, then it would have to eliminate the counter-revolutionary press – including *Vorwärts*, which was fighting tooth and nail against the strike – and, equally, ought not only to countenance the revolutionary press but to support it by increasing its supplies of newsprint. By taking the opposing

view, it maintained, the strike committee was allowing itself to be made a a tool of the counter-revolution.

38 In some cases there was even open conflict between the mass of striking workers, with their 'syndicalist' aspirations, and Communist-controlled executive councils. In Düsseldorf in mid-February 1919, for example, the workers at Rheinmetall abruptly removed the executive council (for reasons that are not entirely clear) and installed a new one that had its confidence. This latter body, however, was extremely short-lived: a day later the members of the ousted council succeeded in restoring the *status quo ante*, with the help of the 'revolutionary security force'.

39 See also fn. 17 above.

40 Unlike the MSPD, the Austrian Social Democratic party had established a political partnership with the councils movement from the start, thereby significantly strengthening its own position *vis-à-vis* both the middle class and the far left during the months that saw the the collapse of the Austrian Empire and the creation of the Austrian Republic. Early attempts to monopolize the councils movement completely and to exclude the extreme-left groupings soon had to be abandoned. In contrast with what happened in Germany, the ruling Austrian Social Democratic party gave a completely free hand to the councils movement in Austrian cities until the movement petered out naturally, from early 1920 onwards. The Austrian socialists, admittedly, were no less at the mercy of the Europe-wide revolutionary surge of the spring of 1919 than were their German colleagues. By adopting a highly flexible policy towards both the councils and the far left, however, they largely avoided the polarization within the working-class camp that was so significant in the German case. That said, the Austrian example shows that it is a mistake to argue that the outcome of the German revolution might have been quite different if the MSPD had taken an essentially favourable line towards the *Räte*. Hartmann rightly concludes, with regard to Austria, that the power of the councils, even when their influence was at its height, was 'primarily defensive in nature' ('Rätedemokratie in Österreich', p. 86) – a verdict that tallies with the thesis argued here.

41 2nd Congress of Workers', Peasants' and Soldiers' Councils of Germany, Herrenhaus, Berlin, 8–14 April 1919, stenographic record (Berlin, n.d.), pp. 803ff.

42 Text of the programme in Wilhelm Mommsen (ed.), *Deutsche Parteiprogramme* (Munich, 1960), pp. 445–447.

43 On this, see the studies by E. Lucas, *Märzrevolution im Ruhrgebiet 1920* (2nd edn., Frankfurt, 1974) and, especially, George Eliasberg, *Der Ruhrkrieg von 1920* (Bonn-Bad Godesberg, 1974), which argues a convincing case for the 'spontaneous character of the mass movement' in the *Ruhrkampf* (cf. esp. p. 261); also R. Luke, 'Beiträge zum Kapp-Putsch und Ruhrkampf', *Archiv für Sozialgeschichte* 12 (1972), pp. 545–551.

44 The Majority Social Democrats' share of the vote fell from 37.9 per cent in 1919 to 21.6 per cent, while the USPD increased its share from 7.6 per cent to 18 per cent. What was most notable, however, was that the KPD did unusually badly, with a mere 2 per cent. This shows that the mass movements of 1919, culminating in the call to 'socialize' workplaces for the benefit of their workers, should not be lumped together with the coups and attempted coups carried out by the far left and had little in common with socialism in the generally accepted Marxist sense.

Index

Abel, Wilhelm 104, 272
administration *see* civil service and
  bureaucracy
Africa: society and state in Europe in
  age of liberalism 71; imperialism 75,
  79–80, 82, 86, 88, 90–3; foreign
  policy and domestic factors 168, 175,
  176, 182, 278; foreign policy and
  public opinion 192, 195, 196–7, 202
agriculture: system of skirted decisions,
  Empire as 9, 10, 259; Prussian
  conception of state 48, 55; society
  and state in Europe in age of
  liberalism 68–9, 74; imperialism 98;
  economy, society and state 104,
  112–14; state and society, latent crisis
  of 146, 148, 149, 155, 157; foreign
  policy 172, 177, 277; First World
  War, social consequences of 225–7,
  232; *see also* Farmers' Alliance
Albertini, Luigi 161, 281
Alldeutscher Verband *see* Pan-German
  League
Allgemeiner Deutscher Arbeiterverein
  see General German Workers' Union
Alsace and Alsace–Lorraine 49; Zabern
  affair 97, 156, 203
Anderson, Eugene N. 143–4, 258, 271
Angola 82, 90, 92, 93, 195, 202
Anweiler, Oskar 235, 288
architecture 125–6

aristocracy and propertied classes:
  system of skirted decisions, Empire as
  11, 16, 18; constitution of 1871 24,
  26, 35–6; Prussian conception of
  state 43, 45–6, 48–51, 53, 55;
  imperialism 76–8, 96; economy,
  society and state 104, 113–14, 116,
  118; culture and politics 120; state
  and society, latent crisis of 145, 148,
  158; foreign policy and domestic
  factors 164, 167, 169, 171–2, 174,
  180–1, 183; foreign policy and public
  opinion 189, 190, 196; First World
  War 205, 207, 208, 217, 221–2, 232
armaments and rearmament 43, 89,
  159, 168, 181, 184, 199
armed forces (*especially* army) and
  militarism 36, 78; system of skirted
  decisions, Empire as 14, 18; Prussian
  conception of state 42, 43, 44, 50–1,
  53–4; state and society, latent crisis
  of 143, 157, 158–9; foreign policy
  and domestic factors 165, 170, 177,
  180, 181, 183–5, 279; foreign policy
  and public opinion 201, 202–3;
  revolution against 236, 237, 238–40,
  241, 243, 253
Army League 43, 78, 95, 98, 157, 179,
  191, 201
arts *see* culture; literature; music; visual
  arts